Extreme Programming
Examined

The XP Series

Kent Beck, Series Advisor

Extreme Programming, familiarly known as XP, is a discipline of business and software development that focuses both parties on common, reachable goals. XP teams produce quality software at a sustainable pace. The practices that make up "book" XP are chosen for their dependence on human creativity and acceptance of human frailty.

Although XP is often presented as a list of practices, XP is not a finish line. You don't get better and better grades at doing XP until you finally receive the coveted gold star. XP is a starting line. It asks the question, "How little can we do and still build great software?"

The beginning of the answer is that, if we want to leave software development uncluttered, we must be prepared to completely embrace the few practices we adopt. Half measures leave problems unsolved to be addressed by further half measures. Eventually you are surrounded by so many half measures that you can no longer see that the heart of the value programmers create comes from programming.

I say, "The beginning of the answer …" because there is no final answer. The authors in the XP Series have been that and done there, and returned to tell their story. The books in this series are the signposts they have planted along the way: "Here lie dragons," "Scenic drive next 15 km," "Slippery when wet."

Excuse me, I gotta go program.

Titles in the Series

Extreme Programming Explained: Embrace Change, Kent Beck
Extreme Programming Installed, Ron Jeffries, Ann Anderson, and Chet Hendrickson
Planning Extreme Programming, Kent Beck and Martin Fowler

Extreme Programming
Examined

Giancarlo Succi
Michele Marchesi

ADDISON–WESLEY

Boston • San Francisco • New York • Toronto • Montreal
London • Munich • Paris • Madrid
Capetown • Sydney • Tokyo • Singapore • Mexico City

Many of the designations used by manufacturers and sellers to distinguish their products are claimed as trademarks. Where those designations appear in this book, and we were aware of a trademark claim, the designations have been printed in initial capital letters or in all capitals.

The authors and publisher have taken care in the preparation of this book, but make no expressed or implied warranty of any kind and assume no responsibility for errors or omissions. No liability is assumed for incidental or consequential damages in connection with or arising out of the use of the information or programs contained herein.

The publisher offers discounts on this book when ordered in quantity for special sales. For more information, please contact:

Pearson Education Corporate Sales Division
One Lake Street
Upper Saddle River, NJ 07458
(800) 382-3419
corpsales@pearsontechgroup.com

Visit us on the Web at www.awl.com/cseng/

Library of Congress Cataloging-in-Publication Data

Succi, Giancarlo, 1964–
    Extreme programming examined / Giancarlo Succi, Michele Marchesi.
        p. cm.—(XP series)
    Includes bibliogaphical references and index.
    ISBN 0-201-71040-4 (alk. paper)
    1. Computer software—Development.   2. Extreme programming.
I. Marchesi, Michele.   II. Title.   III. Series.
QA76.76.D47 S83 2001
005.1'1—dc21

                                                        2001022392

ISBN 0-201-71040-4
Text printed on recycled paper.
1 2 3 4 5 6 7 8 9 10—EB—0504030201
First printing, May 2001

Thanks to Michela,
for these wonderful twenty years with her.
—Michele

Thanks to Francesca,
for her love, her affection, and her patience.
—Giancarlo

Contents

Introduction

—Michele Marchesi and Giancarlo Succi

Only geniuses can make difficult things simple, while any idiot can make a simple task difficult! Albert Einstein used to say something like that, and we think that it applies quite well to Extreme Programming. Extreme Programming—aka XP—(and other flexible methodologies) are an extreme attempt to dramatically simplify the process of developing software systems, focusing on what delivers value: the requirements for the system and the code that implements the system. There isn't much else!

In Extreme Programming everything starts with the requirements, in the form of user stories. The customers deliver and prioritize the user stories. The developers analyze such stories and write tests for them . . . and everything ends with code. The code is developed by pairs of developers to increase quality. The code is refactored to make it simpler. The code is tested against requirements, constantly . . . and there is nothing in between!

Both requirements and code are subject to careful scrutiny: as mentioned, the code does exactly what the user stories tell and nothing more and is always maintained to its highest possible form.

This collection contains experiences in Extreme Programming and other flexible methodologies. It discusses what is in Extreme Programming—requirements and code—and how we can improve it.

The flow of the topics in this book is top-down. We start with the foundations, then we move to process, practices, tool support, and experiences, and end with possible new avenues for exploration.

This book starts with a discussion of the essence of XP and other flexible methodologies. Martin Fowler argues about the role of design. Peter Merel synthesizes the principles of XP.

The second part focuses on methodologies and processes. After a discussion of the value systems of XP and other methodologies by Dirk Riehle a comprehensive analysis of frameworks and other large software development practices take place through the contributions of Lars-Göran Andersson, Mark Collins-Cope, Carsten Jacobi, Even-André Karlsson, Martin Lippert, Hubert Matthews, Stefan Roock, Bernhard Rumpe, Henning Wolf, and Heinz Züllighoven.

In the third part, several authors attempt to combine what other people consider incompatible: flexible methodologies and UML. Jutta Eckstein and Rolf Katzenberger compare the Unified Software Development Process (USDP) with XP; Giuliano Armano and Michele Marchesi present experience in the field inside newly created companies. Marko Boger, Toby Baier, Frank Wienberg, and Winfried Lamersdorf detail an interesting approach to fast modeling software systems. Sergio Focardi and the two of us explain why XP is a genetically different way of developing software using the formalism of stochastic graphs. Joshua Kerievsky conciliates design patterns with XP.

The fourth part contains experiences and consideration of three key practices of XP: pair programming (Alistair Cockburn and Laurie Williams), testing (Philip Craig, Steve Freeman, Peter Gassmann, Tim Mackinnon, and Kevin Rutherford), and refactoring (Neelam Soundarajan).

The fifth part reviews existing tools for supporting pair programming with a focus on refactoring (Ralph Johnson); XP-specific team support (Jim des Rivières, Erich Gamma, Ivan Moore, Kai-Uwe Mätzel, Jan Schümmer, Till Schümmer, André Weinand, and John Wiegand); and testing (Renato Cerqueira and Roberto Ierusalimschy).

Karl Boutin, Michael Kircher, Manfred Lange, David Levine, Peter Sommerlad, and Don Wells present their experiences in XP in Part 6.

Champagne at the end! Sparkling ideas on how to address some terrifying aspects of XP are presented at the end of the book! Christian Wege and Frank Gerhardt outline their approach to teaching XP. Arie van Deursen, Tobias Kuipers, and Leon Moonen address the issue of legacy code. Andrei Alexandrescu explains how flexible methodologies can be implemented in C++. Paolo Predonzani, Giancarlo Succi, and Tullio Vernazza discuss how to handle the management of variants in an extreme environment. The inherent extreme flexibility of software agents is discussed by Luigi Benedicenti, Raman Paranjape, and Kevin Smith. Jason Yip, Giancarlo Succi, and Eric Liu explain how several products developed using XP can be organized in a line of production, without becoming heavyweight.

About the Authors

Michele Marchesi is a professor at the Dipartimento di Ingegneria Elettrica e Elettronica, Università di Cagliari. Giancarlo Succi is a professor at the Department of Electrical and Computer Engineering, University of Alberta.

Part 1

Foundations of XP
and Flexible Techniques

Chapter 1

Is Design Dead?

—Martin Fowler

For many that come briefly into contact with Extreme Programming, it seems that XP calls for the death of software design. Not just is much design activity ridiculed as "Big Up-Front Design," but such design techniques as the UML, flexible frameworks, and even patterns are de-emphasized or downright ignored. In fact XP involves a lot of design, but does it in a different way from established software processes. XP has rejuvenated the notion of evolutionary design with practices that allow evolution to become a viable design strategy. It also provides new challenges and skills as designers need to learn how to do a simple design, how to use refactoring to keep a design clean, and how to use patterns in an evolutionary style.

Extreme Programming (XP) challenges many of the common assumptions about software development. Of these, one of the most controversial is its rejection of significant effort in up-front design, in favor of a more evolutionary approach. To its detractors this is a return to "code and fix" development—usually derided as hacking. To its fans it is often seen as a rejection of design techniques (such as the UML), principles, and patterns. Don't worry about design: If you listen to your code a good design will appear.

I find myself at the center of this argument. Much of my career has involved graphical design languages—the Unified Modeling Language (UML) and its forerunners—and patterns. Indeed, I've written books on both the UML and patterns. Does my embrace of XP mean I recant all of what I've written on these subjects, cleansing my mind of all such counterrevolutionary notions?

Well I'm not going to expect that I can leave you dangling on the hook of dramatic tension. The short answer is no. The long answer is the rest of this chapter.

Planned and Evolutionary Design

For this chapter I'm going to describe two styles in which design is done in software development. Perhaps the most common is evolutionary design. Essentially, evolutionary design means that the design of the system grows as the system is implemented. Design is part of the programming process, and as the program evolves the design changes.

In its common usage, evolutionary design is a disaster. The design ends up being the aggregation of a bunch of ad hoc tactical decisions, each of which makes the code harder to alter. In many ways you might argue this is no design; certainly it usually leads to a poor design. As Kent puts it, design is there to enable you to keep changing the software easily in the long term. As design deteriorates, so does your ability to make changes effectively. You have the state of software entropy; over time the design gets worse and worse. Not only does this make the software harder to change, it also makes bugs both easier to breed and harder to find and safely kill. This is the "code and fix" nightmare, where the bugs become exponentially more expensive to fix as the project goes on.

Planned design is counter to this and contains a notion born of other branches of engineering. If you want to build a doghouse, you can just get some wood together and get a rough shape. However if you want to build a skyscraper, you can't work that way—it'll just collapse before you even get halfway up. So you begin with engineering drawings, done in an engineering office like the one my wife works at in downtown Boston. As she does the design she figures out all the issues, partly by mathematical analysis, but mostly by using building codes. Building codes are rules about how you design structures based on experience of what works (and some underlying math). Once the design is done, then her engineering company can hand the design off to another company that builds the skyscraper.

Planned design in software should work the same way. Designers think out the big issues in advance. They don't need to write code because they aren't building the software but designing it. So they can use a design technique like the UML that gets away from some of the details of programming and allows the designers to work at a more abstract level. Once the design is done they can hand it off to a separate group (or even a separate company) to build. Since the designers are thinking on a larger scale, they can avoid the series of tactical decisions that lead to software entropy. The programmers can follow the direction of the design and, provided they follow the design, have a well-built system.

Now the planned design approach has been around since the 70s, and lots of people have used it. It is better in many ways than "code and fix" evolutionary design. But it has some faults. The first fault is that it's impossible to think through all the issues that you need to deal with when you are programming. So it's inevitable that, when programming, you will find things that question the design. However, if the designers are done, moved onto another project, what happens? The programmers start coding around the design and entropy sets in. Even if the designer isn't gone, it takes time to sort out the design issues, change the drawings, and then alter the code. There's usually a quicker fix and time pressure. Hence entropy (again).

Furthermore there's often a cultural problem. Designers are made designers due to skill and experience, but they are so busy working on designs they don't get much time to code anymore. However, the tools and materials of software development change at a rapid rate. When you no longer code, not just can you miss out on changes that occur with this technological flux, you also lose the respect of those who do code.

This tension between builders and designers happens in building too, but it's more intense in software. It's intense because there is a key difference. In building there is a clearer division in skills between those who design and those who build, but in software that's less the case. Any programmer working in high design environments needs to be very skilled. Skilled enough to question the designer's designs, especially when the designer is less knowledgeable about the day-to-day realities of the development platform.

Now these issues could be fixed. Maybe we can deal with the human tension. Maybe we can get designers skillful enough to deal with most issues and have a process disciplined enough to change the drawings. There's still another problem: changing requirements. Changing requirements are the number one big issue that causes headaches in software projects that I run into.

One way to deal with changing requirements is to build flexibility into the design so that you can easily change it as the requirements change. However, this requires insight into what kind of changes you expect. A design can be planned to deal with areas of volatility, but while that will help for foreseen requirements changes, it won't help (and can hurt) for unforeseen changes. So you have to understand the requirements well enough to separate the volatile areas, and my observation is that this is very hard.

Now some of these requirements problems are due to not understanding requirements clearly enough. So a lot of people focus on requirements engineering processes to get better requirements in the hope that this will prevent the need to change the design later on. But even this direction is one that may not lead to a cure. Many unforeseen requirements changes occur due to changes in the business. Those can't be prevented, however careful your requirements engineering process.

So all this makes planned design sound impossible. Certainly they are big challenges. But I'm not inclined to claim that planned design is worse than evolutionary design as it is most commonly practiced in a "code and fix" manner. Indeed, I prefer planned design to "code and fix." However, I'm aware of the problems of planned design and am seeking a new direction.

The Enabling Practices of XP

XP is controversial for many reasons, but one of the key red flags in XP is that it advocates evolutionary design rather than planned design. As we know, evolutionary design can't possibly work due to ad hoc design decisions and software entropy.

At the core of understanding this argument is the software change curve. The change curve says that as the project runs, it becomes exponentially more expensive to make changes. The change curve is usually expressed in terms of phases: A change made in analysis for one dollar would cost thousands to fix in production. This is ironic, as most projects still work in an ad hoc process that doesn't have an analysis phase, but the exponentiation is still there. The exponential change curve means that evolutionary design cannot possibly work. It also conveys why planned design must be done carefully, because any mistakes in planned design face the same exponentiation.

The fundamental assumption underlying XP is that it is possible to flatten the change curve enough to make evolutionary design work. This flattening is both enabled by XP and exploited by XP. This is part of the coupling of the XP practices: Specifically, you can't do those parts of XP that exploit the flattened curve without doing those things that enable the flattening. This is a common source of the controversy over XP. Many people criticize the exploitation without understanding the enabling. Often the criticisms stem from critics' own experience in which they didn't do the enabling practices that allow the exploiting practices to work. As a result they got burned, and when they see XP they remember the fire.

There are many parts to the enabling practices. At the core are the practices of testing and continuous integration. Without the safety provided by testing, the rest of XP would be impossible. Continuous integration is necessary to keep the team in sync, so that you can make a change and not be worried about integrating it with other people. Together these practices can have a big effect on the change curve. I was reminded of this again here at ThoughtWorks. Introducing testing and continuous integration had a marked improvement on the development effort. Certainly enough to seriously question the XP assertion that you need all the practices to get a big improvement.

Refactoring has a similar effect. People who refactor their code in the disciplined manner suggested by XP find a significant difference in their effectiveness compared with doing looser, more ad hoc restructuring. That was certainly my experience once Kent had taught me to refactor properly. After all, only such a strong change would have motivated me to write a whole book about it.

Jim Highsmith, in his excellent summary of XP, uses the analogy of a set of scales. In one tray is planned design, in the other is refactoring. In more traditional approaches planned design dominates because the assumption is that you can't change your mind later. As the cost of change lowers, you can do more of your design later as refactoring. Planned design does not go away completely, but there is now a balance of two design approaches to work with. For me it feels like that before refactoring I was doing all my design one-handed.

These enabling practices of continuous integration, testing, and refactoring provide a new environment that makes evolutionary design plausible. However, one thing we haven't yet figured out is where the balance point is. I'm sure that, despite the outside impression, XP isn't just test, code, and refactor. There is room for designing before coding. Some of this is before there is any coding; most of it occurs in the iterations before coding for a particular task. But there is a new balance between up-front design and refactoring.

The Value of Simplicity

Two of the greatest rallying cries in XP are the slogans "Do the Simplest Thing That Could Possibly Work" and "You Aren't Going to Need It" (known as YAGNI). Both are manifestations of the XP practice of Simple Design.

The way YAGNI is usually described, it says that you shouldn't add any code that will only be used by a feature that is needed tomorrow. On the face of it this sounds simple. The issue comes up with such things as frameworks, reusable components, and flexible design. Such things are complicated to build. You pay an extra up-front cost to build them, in the expectation that you will gain back that cost later. This idea of building flexibility up-front is seen as a key part of effective software design.

However, XP's advice is that you not build flexible components and frameworks for the first case that needs that functionality. Let these structures grow as they are needed. If I want a Money class today that handles addition but not multiplication, then I build only addition into the Money class. Even if I'm sure I'll need multiplication in the next iteration, and understand how to do it easily, and think it'll be really quick to do, I'll still leave it till that next iteration.

One reason for this is economic. If I have to do any work that's only used for a feature that's needed tomorrow, that means I lose effort on features that need to be done for this iteration. The release plan says what needs to be worked on now. Working on other things for the future is contrary to the developers' agreement with the customer. There is a risk that this iteration's stories might not get done. Even if this iteration's stories are not at risk, it's up to the customer to decide what extra work should be done—and that might still not involve multiplication.

This economic disincentive is compounded by the chance that we may not get it right. However certain we may be about how this function works, we can still get it wrong—especially since we don't have detailed requirements yet. Working on the wrong solution early is even more wasteful than working on the right solution early. And the XPerts generally believe that we are much more likely to be wrong than right (and I agree with that sentiment).

The second reason for simple design is that it is contrary to the principle of traveling light. A complex design is more difficult to understand than a simple design. Therefore, any modification of the system is made harder by added complexity. This adds a cost during the period between when the more complicated design was added and when it was needed.

Now this advice strikes a lot of people as nonsense, and they are right to think that. Right, provided that you imagine the usual development world where the enabling practices of XP aren't in place. However, when the balance between planned and evolutionary design alters, then YAGNI becomes good practice (and only then).

So to summarize. You don't want to spend effort adding new capability that won't be needed until a future iteration. And even if the cost is zero, you still don't want to do it because it increases the cost of modification even if it costs nothing to put in. However, you can only sensibly behave this way when you are using XP or a similar technique that lowers the cost of change.

What on Earth Is Simplicity Anyway

So we want our code to be as simple as possible. That doesn't sound like that's too hard to argue for. After all, who wants to be complicated? But of course this begs the question "what is simple?"

In Extreme Programming Explained (XPE), Kent gives four criteria for a simple system [Beck2000]. In order, with the most important first, they are:

- ✧ Runs all the tests
- ✧ Reveals all the intention
- ✧ Has no duplication
- ✧ Uses fewest classes or methods

Running all the tests is a pretty simple criterion. No duplication is also pretty straightforward, although a lot of developers need guidance on how to achieve it. The tricky one has to do with revealing the intention. What exactly does that mean?

The basic value here is clarity of code. XP places a high value on code that is easily read. In XP "clever code" is a term of abuse. But some people's intention revealing code is another's cleverness.

In Chapter 13 of this book, Josh Kerievsky points out a good example of this. He looks at possibly the most public XP code of all—JUnit. JUnit uses decorators to add optional functionality to test cases, such things as concurrency synchronization and batch set-up code. By separating out this code into decorators it allows the general code to be clearer than it otherwise would be [Gamma+1995].

But you have to ask yourself if the resulting code is really simple. For me it is, but then I'm familiar with the decorator pattern. But for many that aren't it's quite complicated. Similarly, JUnit uses pluggable methods, which I've noticed most people initially find anything but clear. So might we conclude that JUnit's design is simpler for experienced designers but more complicated for less experienced people?

I think that the focus on eliminating duplication, both with XP's "Once and Only Once" and the Pragmatic Programmer's DRY (Don't Repeat Yourself), is one of those obvious and wonderfully powerful pieces of good advice. Just following that alone can take you a long way. But it isn't everything, and simplicity is still a complicated thing to find.

Recently I was involved in doing something that may well be overdesigned. It got refactored and some of the flexibility was removed. But as one of the developers said, "it's easier to refactor overdesign than it is to refactor no design." It's best to be a little simpler than you need to be, but it isn't a disaster to be a little more complex.

The best advice I heard on all this came from Uncle Bob (Robert Martin). His advice was not to get too hung up about what the simplest design is. After all you can, should, and will refactor it later. In the end the willingness to refactor is much more important than knowing what the simplest thing is right away.

Does Refactoring Violate YAGNI?

This topic came up on the XP mailing list recently, and it's worth bringing out as we look at the role of design in XP.

Basically, the question starts with the point that refactoring takes time but does not add function. Since the point of YAGNI is that you are supposed to design for the present not for the future, is this a violation?

The point of YAGNI is that you don't add complexity that isn't needed for the current stories. This is part of the practice of simple design. Refactoring is needed to keep the design as simple as you can, so you should refactor whenever you realize you can make things simpler.

Simple design both exploits XP practices and is also an enabling practice. Only if you have testing, continuous integration, and refactoring can you practice simple design effectively. But at the same time keeping the design simple is essential to keeping the change curve flat. Any unneeded complexity makes a system harder to change in all directions except the one you anticipate with the complex flexibility you put in. However, people aren't good at anticipating, so it's best to strive for simplicity. However, people won't get the simplest thing first time, so you need to refactor in order get closer to the goal.

Patterns and XP

The JUnit example leads me inevitably into bringing up patterns. The relationship between patterns and XP is interesting, and it's a common question. Joshua Kerievsky argues that patterns are underemphasized in XP and he makes the argument eloquently, so I don't want to repeat that. But it's worth bearing in mind that for many people patterns seem in conflict with XP.

The essence of this argument is that patterns are often overused. The world is full of the legendary programmer, fresh off his or her first reading of *Design Patterns,* who includes 16 patterns in 32 lines of code [Gamma+1995]. I remember one evening, fueled by a very nice single malt, running through with Kent a paper to be called "Not Design Patterns: 23 Cheap Tricks." We were thinking of such things as use an if statement rather than a strategy. The joke had a point, that patterns are often overused, but that doesn't make them a bad idea. The question is how you use them.

One theory of this is that the forces of simple design will lead you into the patterns. Many refactorings do this explicitly, but even without them, by following the rules of simple design, you will come up with the patterns even if you don't know them already. This may be true, but is it really the best way of doing it? Surely it's better if you know roughly where you're going and have a book that can help you through the issues instead of having to invent it all yourself. I certainly still reach for GOF whenever I feel a pattern coming on. For me effective design argues that we need to know the price of a pattern is worth paying—that's its own skill. Similarly, as Joshua suggests, we need to be more familiar with how to ease into a pattern gradually. In this regard XP treats the way we use patterns differently from the way some people use them, but certainly doesn't remove their value.

But reading some of the mailing lists, I get the distinct sense that many people see XP as discouraging patterns, despite the irony that most of the proponents of XP were leaders of the patterns movement too. Is this because they have seen beyond patterns, or because patterns are so embedded in their thinking that they no longer realize it? I don't know the answers for others, but for me patterns are still vitally important. XP may be a process for development, but patterns are a backbone of design knowledge, knowledge that is valuable whatever your process may be. Different processes may use patterns in different ways. XP emphasizes both not using a pattern until it's needed and evolving your way into a pattern via a simple implementation. But patterns are still a key piece of knowledge to acquire.

My advice to XPers using patterns would be:

✧ Invest time in learning about patterns.
✧ Concentrate on when to apply the pattern (not too early).
✧ Concentrate on how to implement the pattern in its simplest form first, then add complexity later.
✧ If you put a pattern in, and later realize that it isn't pulling its weight, don't be afraid to take it out again.

I think XP should emphasize learning about patterns more. I'm not sure how I would fit that into XP's practices, but I'm sure Kent can come up with a way.

UML and XP

Of all the questions I get about my involvement with XP, one of the biggest revolves around my association with the UML. Aren't the two incompatible?

There are a number of points of incompatibility. Certainly XP de-emphasizes diagrams to a great extent. Although the official position is along the lines of "use them if they are useful," there is a strong subtext of "real XPers don't do diagrams." This is reinforced by the fact that people like Kent aren't at all comfortable with diagrams. Indeed, I've never seen Kent voluntarily draw a software diagram in any fixed notation.

I think the issue comes from two separate causes. One is the fact that some people find software diagrams helpful and some people don't. The danger is that those who do think that those who don't should, and vice versa. Instead we should just accept that some people will use diagrams and some won't.

The other issue is that software diagrams tend to get associated with a heavyweight process. Such processes spend a lot of time drawing diagrams that don't help and can actually cause harm. So I think that people should be advised how to use diagrams well and avoid the traps, rather than hear the "only if you must (wimp)" message that usually comes out of the XPerts.

So here's my advice for using diagrams well.

First keep in mind what you're drawing the diagrams for. The primary value is communication. Effective communication means selecting important things and neglecting the less important. This selectivity is the key to using the UML well. Don't draw every class—only the important ones. For each class, don't show every attribute and operation—only the important ones. Don't draw sequence diagrams for all use cases and scenarios—only . . . you get the picture. A common problem with the common use of diagrams is that people try to make them comprehensive. The code is the best source of comprehensive information, since the code is the easiest thing to keep in sync with the code. For diagrams comprehensiveness is the enemy of comprehensibility.

A common use of diagrams is to explore a design before you start coding it. Often you get the impression that such activity is illegal in XP, but that's not true. Many people say that when you have a sticky task it's worth getting together to have a quick design session first. However, when you do such sessions:

✧ Keep them short.
✧ Don't try to address all the details (just the important ones).
✧ Treat the resulting design as a sketch, not as a final design.

The last point is worth expanding. When you do some up-front design, you'll inevitably find that some aspects of the design are wrong, and you only discover this when coding. That's not a problem, provided that you then change the design. The trouble comes when people think the design is done, and then don't take the knowledge they gained through the coding and run it back into the design.

Changing the design doesn't necessarily mean changing the diagrams. It's perfectly reasonable to draw diagrams that help you understand the design and then throw the diagrams away. Drawing them helped, and that is enough to make them worthwhile. They don't have to become permanent artifacts. The best UML diagrams are not artifacts.

A lot of XPers use CRC cards. That's not in conflict with UML. I use a mix of CRC and UML all the time, using whichever technique is most useful for the job at hand.

Another use of UML diagrams is ongoing documentation. In its usual form this is a model residing on a case tool. The idea is that keeping this documentation helps people work on the system. In practice it often doesn't help at all.

- ✧ It takes too long to keep the diagrams up to date, so they fall out of sync with the code.
- ✧ They are hidden in a CASE tool or a thick binder, so nobody looks at them.

So the advice for ongoing documentation comes from these observed problems.

- ✧ Only use diagrams that you can keep up to date without noticeable pain.
- ✧ Put the diagrams where everyone can easily see them. I like to post them on a wall. Encourage people to edit the wall copy with a pen for simple changes.
- ✧ Pay attention to whether people are using them. If not, throw them away.

The last aspect of using UML is for documentation in a handover situation, such as when one group hands over to another. Here the XP point is that producing documentation is a story like any other, and thus its business value is determined by the customer. Again the UML is useful here, provided the diagrams are selective in order to help communication. Remember that the code is the repository of detailed information; the diagrams act to summarize and highlight important issues.

On Metaphor

Okay I might as well say it publicly: I still haven't got the hang of this metaphor thing. I saw it work, and work well, on the C3 project, but it doesn't mean I have any idea how to do it, let alone how to explain how to do it.

The XP practice of metaphor is built on Ward Cunningham's approach of a system of names [Cunningham1995]. The point is that you come up with a well-known set of names that acts as a vocabulary to talk about the domain. This system of names plays into the way you name the classes and methods in the system.

I've build a system of names by building a conceptual model of the domain. I've done this with the domain experts using UML or its predecessors. I've found you have to be careful doing this. You need to keep to a minimal simple set of notation, and you have to guard against letting any technical issues creep into the model. But if you do this I've found that you can use this to build a vocabulary of the domain that the domain experts can understand and use to communicate with developers. The model doesn't match the class designs perfectly, but it's enough to give a common vocabulary to the whole domain.

Now I don't see any reason that this vocabulary can't be a metaphorical one, such as the C3 metaphor that turned payroll into a factory assembly line. But I also don't see why basing your system of names on the vocabulary of the domain is such a bad idea either. Nor am I inclined to abandon a technique that works well for me in getting the system of names.

Often people criticize XP on the basis that you do need at least some outline design of a system. XPers often respond with the answer "that's the metaphor." But I still don't think I've seen metaphor explained in a convincing manner. This is a real gap in XP, and one that the XPers need to sort out.

So Is Design Dead?

Not by any means, but the nature of design has changed. XP design looks for the following skills.

- A constant desire to keep code as clear and simple as possible
- Refactoring skills so you can confidently make improvements whenever you see the need
- A good knowledge of patterns: not just the solutions but also appreciating when to use them and how to evolve into them
- Knowing how to communicate the design to the people who need to understand it, using code, diagrams, and above all: conversation

That's a fearsome selection of skills, but then being a good designer has always been tough. XP doesn't really make it any easier, at least not for me. But I think XP does give us a new way to think about effective design because it has made evolutionary design a plausible strategy again. And I'm a big fan of evolution—otherwise who knows what I might be?

References

[Beck2000] K. Beck. *Extreme Programming Explained*. Addison-Wesley, 2000.

[Cunningham1995] W. Cunningham. "EPISODES: A Pattern Language of Competitive Development." In *Pattern Languages of Program Design 2*. Vlissides, Coplien, Kerth, eds. Addison-Wesley, 1995.

[Gamma+1995] E. Gamma, R. Helm, R. Johnson, J. Vlissides. *Design Patterns: Elements of Reusable Object-Oriented Software*. Addison-Wesley, 1995.

Acknowledgments

Over the last couple of years I've picked up and stolen many good ideas from many good people. Most of these are lost in the dimness of my memory. But I do remember pinching good ideas from Joshua Kerievsky.

I also remember many helpful comments from Fred George and Ron Jeffries. I also cannot forget how many good ideas keep coming from Ward and Kent.

I'm always grateful for those that ask questions and spot typos.

About the Author

Martin Fowler is the Chief Scientist at ThoughtWorks, Inc. in Chicago, Illinois. You can find additional contact information and writings at www.martinfowler.com.

Chapter 2

The Tao of
Extreme Programming

—Peter Merel

A mature XP process is distinguished by reference to historical precedents. Guidelines for coaching are drawn from the resulting context.

Dragons of Mist and Wind

Around 500 B.C., according to the Han dynasty Grand Historian, the eunuch Ssu-Ma Chi'en [Chi'en1961], in the then Chinese imperial capital of Chou, the scholar and orator, Confucius sought out the sage Lao Tse.

Confucius had achieved fame promoting an ideal of social perfection via obedience and learning. He identified fixed social roles and catalogued symmetrical relationships between them. He defined a competitive etiquette depending on the moral order of the universe, as revealed by the mandate of heaven, as interpreted by the learned masters, as encoded in their tests, calendars, rituals, and plans. For thousands of years the vast Chinese civil service employed this method. A hundred derivatives—Mencians, Legalists, Neo-Confucians—sprang up to dispute the finer points, yet all agreed that chaos derives from neglect of the proper ritual, or from leaders performing rituals incorrectly.

Traditional software methodology resembles a Confucian doctrine. It pursues perfection of process through the communication of stylized documents between technical specialists arranged in fixed roles. It emphasizes the completion and filiation of consistent forms at predetermined times. Proponents of traditional methodology likewise explain failures and slippages as lapses in process, or as management applying process incorrectly.

For his part, Lao Tse probably did not exist, and certainly was not the author of the work attributed to him [Mair1990]. Even the name is invented, meaning only "old philosopher" or "old philosophy." In a story likely originating with the rogue Chuang Tse, a Twain-esque vagabond who promoted anti-Confucian ideas through satire and riddles, Lao was a Chou dynasty imperial librarian who exiled himself from a decaying empire. On a high pass smothered in snow, a border guard, Yin Hsi, demanded that before quitting China Lao Tse record his learning for posterity. In response, the sage jotted the poem called *Tao Te Ching*, which loosely translates as *Concerning Flow and Harmony*. Lao then departed for parts unknown, disappearing even from myth.

There are striking similarities between Extreme Programming (XP) and Lao's verse. Although Kent Beck has not yet departed for parts unknown, his method, like *Tao Te Ching*, is concerned with direct feedback, iterative process, and disposable artifacts. Beck deposes static documents from their Confucian place of honor, treating them as lightweight conveniences rather than idols of consistency and completeness. In the place of symmetrical artifacts perfected in phases, XP pursues a kind of *Tai Chi* of development, a martial art of interlocking, rhythmic practices intended to maintain open communication, opportunistic scheduling, and close partnership between customers and developers.

The meeting of Confucius and Lao was invented long ago. Their respective philosophies have been revised, jumbled, combined with Buddhism, and iteratively glossed to justify a vast canon of magic, politics, morality, armed conflict, yoga, chicanery, and assorted hype. The story of their meeting in 500 B.C. perfectly illustrates the tension of their relationship.

According to Ssu-Ma Chi'en, Confucius found Lao busy in the offices of the imperial library at Chou. Confucius came armed with a panoply of probing questions concerning the timing and conduct of propitious ritual, and the revered words of the ancient masters. Lao replied that ritual is empty, that men benefit only by seizing opportunity, that anyone calling himself master is foolish, and that he had nothing to tell Confucius but to forget scholarship and study nature.

Confucius returned to his disciples who were eager to learn the outcome of the confrontation. "I can catch fish, shoot birds, and trap rabbits," said Confucius, "but what am I to do with dragons of mist and wind?"

The Flow of Development

The experience of flow is surface;
The world of things is drama.
The world represents all that exists and might exist;
Flow manifests all that happens and may happen. [Lao2000]

Traditional methods document the artifacts of schedule, budget, requirements, and design in order to control development. These static artifacts capture the intention of a project, yet they fail to account for its *tao*, its flow. The flow of development erodes old intentions and creates new ones, forcing an ever widening gap between artifact and perception. The effort needed to complete, correct, and maintain consistency between artifacts increases exponentially with the scope of a project, yet even small developments may swiftly overrun their banks.

Implications spread from requirements like melting ice. Code swells to accommodate them. Fast fixes and redundancies spread like weeds until source bears no resemblance to design. Schedules inflate like balloons, and budgets stretch or snap. The widening produces stress, heroics, low morale, staff churn, and management intervention. Politics kicks in and software quality disappears beneath stopgaps and recriminations.

According to the Standish Group [Standish1995], almost a third of all traditional software projects are cancelled before delivery. Another half double their initial budget and time frame. The ritual of diagrams, charts, spreadsheets, and specs is grasped ever tighter by management, yet each document begins and ends with open speculation on the quality and timeliness of a deliverable.

The key insight in XP is that development must be regulated by dynamic discipline. Architecture is validated by small, throwaway prototypes. Requirements are detailed by regular consultation between developers and customers. Schedule is specified by cyclic negotiation. Budget is obtained by iterative feedback. Code is delivered in concrete features of restricted granularity but testable effect. Quality evolves through merciless automated testing of features and the units that comprise them. Each feature undergoes continuous integration with an evolving whole, and a regimen of whole-system refactoring keeps the project in balance, prepared to respond swiftly to change.

These disciplines are not captured by any traditional development artifact. XP doesn't dispense with artifacts, but instead reduces them to disposable chunks that decay and evolve as business needs are reappraised. XP artifacts track, but do not pretend to control, and so they can be maintained in harmony with the flow of development.

The Stories of San Michele

A certain knowledge of system requirements is traditionally expected to spring fully formed from the mind of the customer, rather than to evolve with their growing understanding of a solution. These requirements are stored like grain, as if once documented they become more enduring than the need that evokes them. Yet it is only natural that requirements swiftly rot, along with the analyses that derive from them.

> *[This is] the tide of nature,*
> *An eternal decay and renewal* [Lao2000]

Requirements are forever reinterpreted within unintended contexts. Layers of translation like Chinese Whispers combine to tangle the project. Each requirement has a range of misunderstanding, and their combination stretches almost to a Cartesian product of these ranges. When requirements are combined with nonfunctional qualities, the situation may be made only worse, as these qualities provide no means to assess associated costs and make tradeoffs.

Requirements are also vulnerable to flights of fancy. Even commonplace fantasies entail considerable expense for little real benefit to a customer. When such expenses are eventually experienced, large swaths of the requirements are arbitrarily discarded, and development becomes mired in half-solutions. New projects spring from the dregs of the old to entice an interminably dissatisfied customer.

To nail down every requirement in sufficient detail that its meaning is unmistakable may require more time than the provision of a working solution. The more precise the specification, the sooner change obsoletes it, and the most detailed requirements leave developers little freedom to apply their skills to improve a solution.

So it seems the greater a business's investment in documenting its requirements, the deeper its dissatisfaction with the deliverable that results.

The XP user story cuts cleanly through this Gordian knot. A user story does not define a requirement in a traditional sense, but an underlying business need. The system requirement for a front door, for example, might read

> *There shall be a panel placed symmetrically such that the user, upon turning and pulling a knob opposite three or more hinges, shall cause the panel to swivel on its vertical axis so that a human of standard dimensions may operate said knob with either hand, but first requiring the unfastening of a lock, the lock being a latch only reset by the insertion of a key conforming to the national standard for keys, the said panel being of no less than two inches in thickness and made of a wood or some other material conforming at least to the durability and stiffness of . . .*

A Front Door use case diagram may be no less complex. Such descriptions seem pedantic and unlikely, yet the author has been presented with similar requirements for less commonplace mechanisms that roll on to fill hundreds of pages.

A corresponding user story would simply say

> The owners and their friends, but no one else, need an easy way to enter the house from the street.

This distinction is sufficient that skilled artisans can suggest solutions and give estimates of time and cost for consideration by the customer. And no more.

At first working with such stories may seem sloppy and incomplete, but the key to their effective use is iterative feedback. Perhaps the most beautiful house on Earth, the Villa San Michele on the isle of Capri in the bay of Naples, was constructed in just this way. Its creator and first resident, the Swedish physician Axel Munthe, described his process.

> *Nobody knew so far what it was going to look like, nor did I. All we had to go by was a rough sort of sketch drawn by myself with a piece of*

charcoal on the white garden-wall. I cannot draw anything, it looked as if drawn by the hand of a child. [. . .]

This is the loggia, [I said,] with its strong arches, we will decide by and by how many arches there will be. Here comes a pergola leading up to the chapel, never mind the public road running straight across my pergola now, it will have to go. Here looking out on Castello Barbarossa comes another loggia, I do not quite see what it looks like for the present, I am sure it will spring out of my head at the right moment. [. . .] Here comes a large terrace where all you girls will dance the tarantella on summer evenings. [. . .] This is an avenue of cypresses leading up to the chapel which we will of course rebuild [. . .] and here looking out over the bay of Naples we are going to hoist an enormous Egyptian sphinx of red granite, older than Tiberius himself. It is the very place for a sphinx. I do not see for the present where I shall get it from but I am sure it will turn up in time. [. . .]

The whole garden was full of thousands and thousands of polished slabs of coloured marble, africano, pavonazetto, giallo antico, verde antico, cipollino, alabastro, all now forming the pavement of the big loggia, the chapel, and some of the terraces. [. . .] What had once been Maestro Vincenzo's house and his carpenter's workshop was gradually transformed and enlarged into what was to become my future home. [. . .] I knew absolutely nothing about architecture, nor did any of my fellow-workers, nobody who could read or write ever had anything to do with the work, no architect was ever consulted, no proper drawing or plan was ever made, no exact measurements were ever taken. It was all done all' occhio *as Maestro Nicola called it.* [Munthe1929]

Just as Munthe described, XP user stories are kept to a fine granularity so that the misunderstandable range of their solution is small, so that estimates can become firm, and so stories can be changed, reprioritized, or discarded as customer perceptions of need change. Because only a vision and few specific details are described, XP developers must consult customers directly and regularly to transform a story into concrete engineering tasks. XP's interlocking disciplines nevertheless ensure the customer's vision is realized to the extent permitted by its budget. The customer is able to direct the work in easily manageable chunks. Developers are never asked to solve irrelevant or artificial problems. The user stories become foci for development, not abstractions for debate.

The Three Treasures of the Coach

Frank Lloyd Wright's masterpiece, *Falling Water*, transports its audience as an object of the highest art, a tribute to the ingenuity of its great architect. But it leaks. It is damp and spawns mildew, and it is so focused in its symmetry that an inhabitant can find no space to adorn with expressions of their own life [Hildebrand1991]. *Falling Water* dwells among the world's most triumphant art, yet San Michele is unmistakably the more desirable dwelling.

Wright specialized in houses, and *Falling Water* is his finest. How did Munthe, an untutored medical doctor, beat the twentieth century's greatest architect at his own game?

It's clear Munthe had a strong grasp of the antiquities of Europe, along with the cultural and technical fluency needed to communicate with his Anacapresi artisans. His autobiography, *The Story of San Michele*, further reveals a deep compassion, reserve, and common touch refined by decades of intimate medical practice at all levels of Parisian society. These are just the "three treasures" lauded by Lao Tse in *Tao Te Ching*.

> *By compassion one finds courage.*
> *By reserve, strength.*
> *By commonality, influence.* [Lao2000]

It was Munthe's compassion that afforded the doctor the support and understanding of the Anacapresi. In Lao Tse, compassion isn't mere kindness, but a willingness to enter into long-term relationships, to accept and nurture the viewpoints of developers, managers, and customers, with any of whom you may disagree, to help them find ways to accept each other and build their community. Where Wright dominated his workmen and blinded his disciples with his prolific genius, Munthe was the faithful partner of his peasant craftsmen. While employing them he also served as their scribe and physician for decades.

To cultivate compassion, a Coach must pay careful attention to the needs of each member of their team. Follow carefully instead of competing with them. Draw them out instead of shouting them down. Learn their views and take them into account before speaking. Especially when they seem naive or stubborn, don't ridicule or dismiss them, but find a way for them to retain their dignity and self-respect. Isn't this obvious? Perhaps so, but it's easy to forget when needed most.

> *Compassion is the finest weapon and best defence.*
> *If you would establish harmony,*
> *Compassion must surround you like a fortress.* [Lao2000]

Compassion alone is not enough to make a Coach. The champions of opposing viewpoints need an impartial and trustworthy reception. Tact is essential. Reserving opinions and judgments makes consensus much easier to build. Easy consensus forms harmonious relationships throughout the team. There is a feedback effect here; harmonious relationships reduce the likelihood of friction and politics occurring in the first place.

> *[Be] firm but not cutting, pointed but not piercing,*
> *Straight but not rigid, bright but not blinding.* [Lao2000]

To cultivate reserve, you must let other team members speak their minds before you speak. Ask questions instead of taking positions. Encourage a novice to spike a bad solution, rather than forbidding it. Don't side with developers, managers, or customers, but guard your opinions concerning a dispute. Rather than staking a position, help the disputants understand each other's way of thinking.

> *The enlightened use weapons only when there is no choice,*
> *And then calmly, and with tact.* [Lao2000]

When gentility becomes impossible, a Coach must apply the "rolled-up newspaper" swiftly, with conviction and vigor. This must be dictated by necessity, not by feelings of frustration, and in private, with a swift return to open, friendly relations. The Coach must be trustworthy, especially with those members of the team who are not. Yet even here reserve is required: Boasting about the application of the newspaper returns as animosity and mistrust. The necessity of such violence must be treated as you would sad news.

> *Thorns and weeds grow wherever an army goes,*
> *And lean years follow a great war.* [Lao2000]

Finally, the Coach must not lose the common touch with their teams. If they act aloof, coaches lose the ability to affect the team. Distance builds resistance. So, among developers, the Coach must provide vision and perspective, but must always encourage other members of the team to express it. The Coach may have the title and act the role of manager, architect, or customer, but they must still relate to developers as a developer.

In the company of managers and customers, the Coach must become the preferred lever to use to move the developers. No matter what company they find, the Coach should be "one of us," not "one of them." In a meeting involving developers, management, and customers, the Coach's compassion and reserve are truly tested. To be effective, a Coach must accept, but not own, responsibility for the whole development. If they're successful, the team should claim the achievement as their own.

> *The river carves out the valley by flowing beneath it.*
> *Thereby the river is master of the valley.*
> *In order to master people one must speak as their servant;*
> *In order to lead people one must follow them.* [Lao2000]

The Coach is a demanding role that allows few opportunities to enjoy slack or take things lightly. The Coach is like the pilot of a ship. Taking things lightly makes things hard. Enjoying slack may lead the whole team into difficulties. The Coach must avoid hasty decisions and fickleness, for the flow of development is easily diverted and swiftly dissipated.

Becoming Extreme

Neither a fine Coach nor skilled artisans are sufficient to move a development from the muddy shallows into smooth water. To do this requires the development of harmony in the project as a whole.

It is difficult for many people to accept that heroics, long hours, and high stress are not the most effective ways to improve the quality and timeliness of a project. It's counterintuitive to think that less difficulty and more fun can produce more enduring, more successful, and more prolific work.

Most developers are used to heroics, regarding them as professional diligence. Most managers are used to stress, regarding it as cure rather than symptom of slippage. And most customers are used to ignorance of process, regarding it as a domain of haggard savants and inscrutable science. When a corporate culture has bought in to these habits, challenges will be treated with considerable suspicion.

Indeed, when an XP group outcompetes old development styles, a hostile reaction can easily occur. Though the successful introduction of XP might promote harmony, attempting to introduce it can become a highly charged political struggle. How can XP be employed by an established development group without running this risk?

Changing group culture should always be thought of as seduction. Rather than declaring war on a culture by heated debate and displays of erudition, suggest small changes, and these only to individuals. Introduce simple disciplines and let their benefits speak for themselves. Don't preach XP; solve small problems and let the solutions grow.

Empty their minds,
Fill their bellies,
Weaken their ambitions,
And strengthen their bones. [Lao2000]

Eventually these individual practices begin to cover the process. Some developer's unit test reproducibly. Perhaps others develop a fondness for pairing. Customers see some user stories estimated, scheduled, and delivered. The Coach has conducted stand-up meetings, demonstrated a few refactorings, and conducted a CRC or two. When team members have accepted such practices in isolation, the team will naturally begin to think about how they could connect.

Some of the team will have nosed around and found out where you're coming from. Eventually you will find a champion among them. Let him or her talk. Then you need only follow diligently and fix little problems, work gently to help the practices interlock, and help the process flow.

When there is general developer commitment but the rest of the organization hasn't yet bought in, conduct an Extreme Hour [Merel+2000] involving customers and Quality Assurance (QA). Encourage skepticism, but let developers answer questions where possible. Make sure upper management expresses explicit support for the team's ability to define its own process. When your organization comes up with viable alternatives, try them out and share them with the XP community. It costs nothing to communicate process, and the feedback will be invaluable.

When XP really starts to hum, the old habits will occasionally still reassert themselves. People truly seem to seek out drama. When schedules must be defended, budgets reined in, and long hours worked, when architecture is neglected in favor of quick fixes, when corporate culture is forced onto developers, when rivalry over pay and equity, responsibility and title breaks out, the project begins to rob its customers. These are times when the rhetoric of excellence, professionalism, and team spirit is heard loudest.

> *When harmonious relationships dissolve*
> *Then respect and devotion appear;*
> *When a nation falls to chaos*
> *Then loyalty and patriotism are born.* [Lao2000]

When team members return to their old ways, an XP project will lose flow *fast*. Because XP provides few artifacts to fall back on, this kind of stall can seem disastrous. But because XP provides few artifacts to get in the way, it's easy to pull out of the stall. A review of process, a review of schedule, a review of standards, a rotation of engineering tasks, or, with tact, the application of the rolled newspaper, and off you go again.

The prerequisite without which XP must fail is commitment from upper management. You can't sneak XP past people who expect big design up front or cowboy coding. You can't fake a paper-heavy process with analysts, or low-discipline process with programmers. An XP proponent in a Confucian-style business may be able to take advantage of some practices in isolation, pairing and unit-testing especially, but they shouldn't expect high flow from more than a few developers or for more than a few days. If they confront Confucian forces without upper management support, they will lose touch with the team. Losing touch with the team, their effort will be wasted.

Development in Harmony

When XP practices work in harmony with one another, flow ramps up. Load factor dives. Developers and customers describe a sensation of speed, and the business is challenged to keep up with the project. These experiences will subside again, but as iterations continue, architecture and standards evolve, and rhythm sets in, the frequency of occasions of high flow steadily increases.

A team that flows consistently is in a kind of harmony. This isn't a fleeting moment of balance, but a dynamic equilibrium that accommodates rapid change. Harmony occurs when the elements of the team's practice interlock, anticipate, and reinforce one another.

Harmony doesn't come from knowing everything about XP. In fact, it comes when the team no longer pays any attention to XP, but uses it without thinking. Likewise, treating the experience of harmony as an ideal cannot deliver it. You can't go fast by demanding speed, competing to increase project velocity, aspiring to deliver more user stories faster, or *wanting* to flow. Harmony occurs with a self-reinforcing "pop" [Cockburn+1999].

When XP pops, team members may begin to feel stressed by the speed of development. In pairing especially, there is little opportunity to spend time surfing, listening to private music, or talking with loved ones on the phone. "Goof-off time" disappears. Work at this pace is exciting but draining, so the Coach must be careful to watch for and alleviate signs of fatigue. This is why working a 40-hour week is an XP practice.

At the same time, development itself becomes tremendous fun. Developers in a harmonious team laugh a lot. They connect in their personal lives. They play games. They learn to anticipate and buoy each other up. Their egos diminish, and their joy in working together swells. They act like this naturally, not by decree. The cyclic nature of XP provides a rhythmic certainty in their work. This is not the homogeny of an army, but the daily routine of a farm.

When a nation ignores flow,
Horses bear soldiers through its streets;
When a nation follows flow,
Horses bear manure through its fields. [Lao2000]

References

[Chi'en1961] S. Chi'en. *Records of the Grand Historian of China.* Trans. B. Watson. Columbia University Press, 1961.

[Cockburn+1999] A. Cockburn, et al. *Nonlinearity of XP.* On-line at http://www.c2.com/cgi/wiki?NonlinearityOfXp. 1999.

[Hildebrand1991] G. Hildebrand. *The Wright Space: Pattern & Meaning in Frank Lloyd Wright's Houses.* University of Washington Press, 1991.

[Lao2000] T. Lao. *GNL's Not Lao*. Trans. P. Merel. On-line at http://home.san.rr.com/merel/gnl.html. 2000.

[Mair1990] V. H. Mair. *Tao Te Ching*. Bantam Books, 1990.

[Merel+2000] P. Merel, et al. *Extreme Hour*. On-line at http://www.c2.com/cgi/wiki?ExtremeHour. 2000.

[Munthe1929] A. Munthe. *The Story of San Michele*. E.P. Dutton & Co., Inc., 1929.

[Standish1995] The Standish Group. *CHAOS*. Standish Group International, Inc., 1995.

Acknowledgments

Kudos to the crews at Websense and GMAC for their patience with a novice coach. Thanks to Kent, Ward, and Ron for their courage. Many thanks to my wife, Lori for letting me waste sunny weekends tinkering with this chapter.

About the Author

Peter Merel is the chief architect and core engineering coach for Omnigon International. Peter has two decades of experience as a programmer. He has also worked as coach, mentor, and leader on major projects for HP, GMAC, AC Nielsen, Foxboro, Fujitsu, Telstra, and Plessey. He is best known on-line for his regular contributions to the c2 wiki-web, and his aggressive defense of on-line civil liberties in Australia in the early 90s. Peter lives in Coronado, California, and can be e-mailed at peter@san.rr.com.

Part 2

Methodology and Process

Chapter 3

A Comparison of the Value Systems of Adaptive Software Development and Extreme Programming: How Methodologies May Learn from Each Other

—Dirk Riehle

Today, we see an increasing interest in new software development methodologies that put humans at the center of the development process. Adaptive Software Development (ASD), Extreme Programming (XP), and others are exemplars of this new breed of development methodologies. They are all based on the assumption that for coping with high speed and high change, traditional management techniques are inadequate. Effectively, the new methodologies are based on a different value system than the old ones. A value system is a system of beliefs about what constitutes the fundamental aspects of software development: Developers, customers, markets, products, requirements, and so on. This chapter presents a simple model of value systems and compares the value systems of two exemplary new development methodologies, ASD and XP. The purpose of this comparison is to determine more easily whether techniques of one methodology can be adapted and used by another methodology, thereby helping authors of methodologies to learn better from other methodologies.

Introduction

Traditional management practice of software development sees the development process as something that must be planned and controlled in order to reliably achieve the planned result. The underlying assumption is that the process can in fact be controlled and that this is beneficial to the outcome of the process. In its extreme form, this belief has been formulated by Osterweil in his famous ICSE 9 keynote speech on software development processes: Software processes are software too [Osterweil1987]. His keynote suggests that developers execute processes much like computers execute software applications. This approach has given rise to research in software process modeling and enactment that is still going on today. The underlying assumption that humans execute processes much like machines has found its way into current terminology and thinking. As a recent example, Pohl et al. write of developers as being guided by tools and as performing processes [Pohl+1999].

The underlying assumptions of equating humans with computers and that processes can be planned on a fine-grain level are not shared by all. Osterweil's assurance has been rejected immediately by Lehman in his response to Osterweil's presentation [Lehman1987]. Evolutionary prototyping, for example, views software development as a shared learning experience of both customers and developers [Floyd+1992; Budde+1992]. Naur views computing as a fundamentally human activity [Naur1992]. Catering for human needs in software development processes is in stark contrast with viewing developers as resources that can be utilized at will.

This distinction has its consequences: What is called traditional management above uses different techniques for carrying out development than does evolutionary prototyping. For example, traditional approaches use formal textual requirement specifications to determine and communicate requirements to developers, whereas evolutionary prototyping prefers using prototypes to discuss requirements and ensure timely feedback from customers. This difference between the traditional approach and evolutionary prototyping is just one difference (albeit one of key importance). Other differences are how a development methodology views customers, how it fosters creativity and innovation, how it views changes in the market and in requirements, and so on.

The overall set of assumptions underlying a development methodology is its value system, a system of beliefs about the world in general and software development in particular. The value system is reflected in the techniques the methodology provides to its users. A technique makes sense in the context of a development methodology only if it is compatible with the methodology's value system.

A technique is like a conceptual tool: It has been designed to do certain tasks well and hence can be used effectively to carry out these tasks. Beyond this context of application, the technique breaks down much like a tool breaks down. Though human ingenuity in the use of a technique allows for some adaptation, a technique cannot be used effectively if it is at odds with the value system of the underlying methodology in the context of which it is being applied.

Similarly, users of the methodology must share the value system to make effective use of the methodology and its techniques. Only if these three pieces (a coherent value system, techniques that are compatible with the value system of a methodology, and users that share the values) come together harmoniously, can a methodology be effective.

Currently, we see the emergence of several new development methodologies with similar underlying value systems, for ASD [Highsmith2000], XP [Beck2000], SCRUM [Beedle+2000], Crystal [Cockburn2001], and others. They view themselves as lightweight methodologies, that is, as methodologies that come without much overhead so that they can be applied easily. In my reading, "lightweight" means that these methodologies do away with much of the administrative overhead of traditional methods (like extensive paper-based documentation or elaborate process handbooks).

This understanding of being "lightweight" has its consequences: The new methodologies tend not to be dogmatic about when and how to apply the techniques they provide. The metaphor of a technique as a "conceptual tool" captures this spirit well: A technique is used when it seems appropriate, and it is dropped when it does not seem to help anymore in a specific situation. The methodology becomes a meta-framework that determines what is considered important about software development and how techniques have their place in it, but it does not specify when and how to use a specific technique.[1] Again, in contrast to this, traditional methodologies tend to be more prescriptive about when and how to use a technique.

---

1. Extreme Programming, one of the two methodologies discussed in this article, considers it important that all of its techniques be used together (to make up for each other's weaknesses). Hence it appears to be closed toward adopting new techniques and changing existing ones. I believe that XP will evolve further and that this aversion is only a temporary state of a development methodology it its early stages.

For survival in the market and for providing continuing value to users, it is essential that the new methodologies be continually refined and possibly extended with new and enhanced techniques.

One possible way for a methodology to achieve this is to learn from other methodologies and to adapt from them what works for itself. How precisely can we define whether a certain technique from another methodology works for the methodology we are currently using? Obviously we could just try, but this may turn out to be too expensive. A better way is to analyze the technique in question for its compatibility with the methodology's own value system and the existing techniques. The result of this analysis may not provide the final answer, but the analysis may save time and money if it rules out incompatible techniques up-front.

This chapter carries out a comparison of two recent and promising new development methodologies (ASD and XP) with respect to their value systems (see the sections, *Review of ASD and XP, Value Systems,* and *Compatibility of ASD and XP*). The comparison is based on a model of value systems for development methodologies (see the section, *Value Systems*). Based on the comparison, conclusions are drawn about compatibility and potential learning of techniques from the respective other methodology. The chapter closes with a discussion of where the approach of value system analysis may take us (see the *Conclusion*).

Review of ASD and XP

Adaptive Software Development is a new software development methodology that addresses "the Internet economy," that is, an economy of high speed and high change [Highsmith2000]. Highsmith uses Complex Adaptive Systems theory [Holland1995] to explain the fundamental assumptions he makes about software development and its markets.

Extreme Programming is another new development methodology that was specifically conceived to work in the face of vague and changing requirements, so it targets a similar environment as ASD [Beck2000]. Beck, currently the only author of a book on XP, is explicit in what he views as the underlying values of XP (Communication, Simplicity, Feedback, and Courage).

This section reviews both methodologies (with a strong focus on what each views as its underlying value system). The next section presents a model of value systems that lets us reinterpret the value systems of both ASD and XP to better support their comparison.

Review of Adaptive Software Development

ASD addresses the economy of increasing returns [Arthur1996]. High speed and high change characterize this economy, which underlies the Internet and the market of today's dot-com companies. High speed and high change induce a complexity that cannot be handled by traditional approaches. High speed and high change make a market unpredictable and the development process unable to be planned in the traditional sense of controlling the process.

Arthur and then Highsmith use Complex Adaptive Systems (CAS) theory [Holland1995] to describe the complexity of this market. Both conclude that in the economy of increasing returns, being able to adapt is a significantly more important success factor than being able to optimize.

CAS theory provides three main concepts to explain the world: agents, environments, and emergence. Agents compete and cooperate to get work done, but the final result is not the outcome of the work of any particular agent or process. Effectively, the result emerges from the overall competition and cooperation of the agents. System behavior cannot be predicted from the individual behavior of agents, because simple cause-and-effect reasoning has broken down.

Highsmith transfers the CAS model to software development, viewing the development organization as the environment, its members as agents, and the product as the emergent result of competition and cooperation. This has profound consequences. Accepting and living with unpredictability and uncertainty asks for a new approach to software development.

The first goal of any development organization is to be able to respond quickly to changes, that is, to be adaptive. Adaptiveness can not be commanded; it must be nurtured. This nurturing is realized through a management model that Highsmith calls the Adaptive Leadership-Collaboration model. It leads to an environment in which adaptation and collaboration thrive so that local order can emerge. Local order scales over several levels, from the individual, to work groups, and to the whole development organization. By nurturing adaptive behavior in every cell, the overall system becomes adaptive.

Highsmith recommends two key strategies for creating an adaptive and collaborative environment. The first strategy asks managers to focus less on process than on products, that is, the results of collaboration. Managers must apply rigor to the results of the process rather than prescribing the process. The second strategy asks managers to provide tools and techniques for fostering self-organization across virtual teams. Virtual teams are teams that are distributed around the world. This second strategy is needed only if ASD is applied to large-scale software development. The early rapid application development (RAD) approaches have often been criticized as not scaling up. It is an explicit goal of Highsmith to overcome this criticism with ASD.

The focus on products asks for an iterative approach, because the result of each iteration becomes the main input to steering the process. Each iteration consists of three phases: speculation, collaboration, and learning. Speculation on the product means the discussion and subsequent definition of what is to be achieved in an iteration. Highsmith calls this activity speculation to make explicit that what others may call planning is truly speculation about the future. It follows a collaboration phase in which team members collaborate toward a product that incorporates the features as suggested from the speculation phase and from the ongoing external input. In the final learning phase of an iteration, the result is reviewed in light of the speculation, and the next iteration is being prepared.

Each iteration, called adaptive cycle, has the following properties.

⋄ It is mission driven, based on the project vision.
⋄ It is component rather than task based (result driven).
⋄ It is limited in time.
⋄ Each time-box is only one iteration in a larger set of iterations.
⋄ It is risk driven.
⋄ It is change tolerant.

Change is viewed as the opportunity to learn and to gain a competitive advantage rather than as a detriment to the process and its results.

Different techniques support executing the speculation/collaboration/ learning activity in each cycle. Highsmith presents a host of such techniques that support the development process.

It is important to note which role Highsmith assigns to techniques as part of the overall process. No single activity is important and has to be applied, not even specific combinations are a must. Highsmith expects no activity to be a silver bullet for anything, even though he expects specific learning and collaboration techniques to be used in most ASD projects. The main reason for this is that every technique has a certain context of applicability. Beyond its context, a technique starts to work unreliably or even breaks down. Because Highsmith has a wide variety of projects in mind for ASD, he does not enforce specific techniques, as there will certainly be situations in which they break down.

Review of XP

Beck's description of Extreme Programming separates it into several parts:

- ◆ *Values:* A value in the XP sense is a description of "how software development should feel." (This is the best definition I have found in [Beck2000]). XP is based on the following four values: Communication, Simplicity, Feedback, and Courage.
- ◆ *Principles:* A principle in XP is something that we use to determine whether a practice (see below) is something that can be used successfully in an XP context. Beck presents the following five principles, as derived from the values: Rapid Feedback, Assume Simplicity, Incremental Change, Embrace Change, and Quality Work.
- ◆ *Activities:* In a separate dimension, Beck views the following four activities as the cornerstones of software development, and hence to be supported by matching practices: Coding, Testing, Listening, and Designing.
- ◆ *Practices:* A practice in XP is a technique that project members use to successfully carry out any of the aforementioned activities. In [Beck2000], Beck presents 12 practices, ranging from The Planning Game as a technique to carry out schedule and feature negotiation to 40-Hour Week, a warning not to do overtime over extended periods of time.
- ◆ *Strategies:* Finally, to successfully execute practices in the real world, Beck presents several strategies that describe experiences and heuristics of how to achieve this.

Of primary interest here are the values and principles and how they interact with the so-called practices, because the practices are the techniques that can possibly be transferred to other methodologies.

The value of communication represents the XP belief that communication between project members is key to a successful project (and hence needs to be supported by practices). It is not stated why communication is so important, but it is safe to assume that communication is viewed as the main enabler of coordination and collaboration on a project. It is important to note that in [Beck2000] communication always means verbal communication.

The value of simplicity represents the XP belief that you should not invest in the future but only in your immediate needs. If future needs materialize as immediate needs at some point in the future, the proper application of XP practices will have put developers into a situation that lets them successfully cope with the new need. Underlying this value is the assumption that the future cannot be reliably predicted and that taking care of it today is economically unwise.

The value of feedback represents the XP belief that it is important to have a running system at any time that gives developers reliable information about its functioning. (Here feedback is not feedback between humans but rather feedback about the development state.) Effectively, the system and its code base serve as the incorruptible oracle to report about the progress and state of development. Feedback serves as a means for orientation and deciding where to go.

The value of courage represents the XP belief that humans are the single most significant aspect of software development. It is human courage that resolves problematic situations and lets a team leave local optima behind to reach greater goals. The value of courage represents XP's fundamental trust in humans to make a project succeed.

The values are elaborated and made more precise through the aforementioned principles, which are basically an explanation of the values.

The 12 XP practices presented in [Beck2000] are closely knit. They tie in with each other well. As Beck explains, this was an explicit goal, because each of the practices is not only an old and well-known practice, but also a practice that has been shown *not* to work in many circumstances. Only by integrating them are the weaknesses of any of the practices rendered irrelevant, because the other practices make up for them.

The XP practices are in flux. On the Web, we can find a more elaborate (and evolving) description of the XP practices [Wiki2000; XPorg2000].

These Web pages, as well as the discussions on the Extreme Programming mailing list [XPmlist2000] suggest that XP is open to adopting new techniques.

Value Systems

From the outset, both ASD and XP appear to be very similar. Both address software development processes that face uncertainty and continuous change. A closer look, however, shows the following differences:

- *Motivation:* ASD is motivated by the inappropriateness of traditional management in the new economy of increasing returns. Making software development a humane experience again is a key motivation of XP.
- *Attitude toward techniques:* ASD believes that techniques are important but no silver bullets. Developers use techniques judiciously to solve problems at hand. XP strongly relies on a specific combination of predefined techniques.
- *Levels of scale:* ASD addresses small, medium, and large development teams that are potentially distributed. XP addresses only small teams (up to ten developers) that must be co-located.

Still, ASD and XP seem to have a common core of themes and beliefs, which we identify as a value system. If we want any of the methodologies to learn from the others, we must provide a basis for comparing value systems to determine compatibility of techniques. No such basis exists to my knowledge.[2]

---

2. It is interesting to note that the Capability Maturity Model (CMM) plays this role for traditional software development methodologies. The CMM is a set of metrics for evaluating instances of development methodologies as they are practiced by a specific organization [Paulk1995]. Though this may not have been its original intent, the CMM represents quite a clean description of the value system underlying traditional development methodologies. Every methodologist who submits his or her methodology to the CMM acknowledges the value system of the CMM to be the value system of his methodology. This is helpful, because most methodologies have no explicit value system.

A Model of Value Systems

We need to step back from the specific descriptions of ASD and XP given earlier. As I mentioned, my review of these two methodologies uses the structure of the main books on this subject. This structure may not necessarily represent the weight each of the methodologists assigns to an aspect of his methodology. It may simply be a teaching device to better communicate certain ideas while deferring the discussion of further issues to later expositions.

This section presents a simple model of value systems for software development methodologies. This model is not exhaustive; I view it more as a beginning of further research into value systems for development methodologies. However, the concept of value system has grown out of earlier research into development methodologies carried out by Floyd et al. [Floyd+1992] and Züllighoven et al. [Budde+1992]. In their critiques of the dominant management paradigm, they were very much aware of the fundamental differences in assumptions about software development.

The model has the following fundamental dimensions.

- *Role of humans in software development:* What are the role and contribution of humans in software development? These include the roles and responsibilities of customers, developers, and managers, as well as their recognition as being humans beyond playing roles.
- *Relationship between humans in software development:* What is the role and importance of human relationships in software development? How important is communication, collaboration, and competition? Should it be hindered or fostered, structured or free-floating?
- *Relationship between humans and technology:* What is the role of technology (techniques, tools, and media) in software development? Does technology dominate humans or do humans control technology? How is it applied? How do humans work with technology?
- *Purpose of software development:* Why do we carry out a specific software development process (next to satisfying customers)? To "rush and cash" by delivering a good enough product as fast as possible, to do satisfying work, or to advance humanity?[3]

---

3. I think it is not naive to list human advancement here. For example, the IEEE code of ethics confirms that every IEEE member agrees on fostering human advancement through better understanding and use of technology. Similarly, most academic projects have this goal.

Each dimension needs elaboration, and each aspect of a dimension needs to be weighted against the other aspects. Quantitative weighting is possible but difficult. I use dimension-specific weighting. For example, I qualify each aspect of the Purpose of Development dimension as being either key, support, or unimportant (not applicable is also possible, which is to say that the aspect is not mentioned in the methodology description).

Comparison of ASD and XP

Table 3.1 compares ASD with XP using the model of value systems just described.

TABLE 3.1 High-Level Comparison of the Value Systems of ASD and XP

	ASD	XP
Role of humans	Central undisputed agents.	Central undisputed agents.
Role of developers	Steer product, adapt it to changing requirements.	Steer process/product, use predefined techniques to do so.
Role of managers	Steer process/product, adapt it to changing requirements.	Steer process/product, use predefined techniques to do so.
Role of customers	Provide input to steer process; are involved.	Provide input to steer process; are involved.
Role of human relationships	Main enabler of innovation, ability to adapt.	Main enabler of innovation, work satisfaction.
Role of communication	Is key for emergence.	Is key for working toward results.
Role of cooperation	Is key for emergence.	Is key for working toward results.
Role of competition	Is key for emergence.	N/A
Relationship between humans and technology	Humans control technology; technology is a tool.	Humans control technology; technology is a tool.
Application of technology	Humans utilize technology at will.	Humans utilize technology within predefined framework.

Continued on next page

TABLE 3.1 High-Level Comparison of the Value Systems of ASD and XP (*continued*)

	ASD	XP
Type of technology	Lightweight technology is preferred.	Lightweight technology is preferred.
Purpose of development	Survival and thriving of organization.	Product delivery while doing satisfying work.
Product delivery	Is key.	Is key ("playing to win").
Do satisfying work	Is support.	Is key ("playing to win").
Advance humanity	N/A	N/A

The comparison of Table 3.1 is rather coarse-grained. However, it provides a framework to zoom in on more fine-grained issues.

Compatibility of ASD and XP

ASD and XP are similar in many aspects (which should not come as a surprise by now). Of more interest are the differences between the value systems of these two methodologies. From Table 3.1, we gather the following differences.

- In ASD, people use technology as they see proper. In XP, they use technology only insofar as it fits the framework of predefined techniques.
- In ASD, human relationships are a key enabler of emergent results. In XP, communication and cooperation are important to work toward a result; competition is not.
- In ASD, doing satisfying work supports the main goal of product delivery but is not of key importance. In XP, doing satisfying work is equally important as delivering a product.

A more fine-grained analysis shows further differences. It is not carried out here, though. For the purposes of this chapter, these three key differences and their consequences are sufficient material for discussion.

Use of Techniques/Practices

ASD has a laissez-faire approach toward specific techniques. If they are useful and solve a problem at hand, project members use them, otherwise they ignore them. From this perspective, every technique may be put to use, in particular if we keep in mind that adaptive behavior of agents is key in ASD. Therefore, techniques need not be compatible with each other, but adaptation through humans will in the end make them compatible.

XP has strong feelings about its techniques. They must be practiced, and they must be practiced together, otherwise a developer would not be doing XP. As mentioned earlier, XP's set of techniques is not fixed. However, it will be slow to adapt new techniques if the requirement of closely-knit integration is maintained.

As a consequence, ASD will be fast to adopt new techniques, whereas XP will be slower to do so. As another consequence, XP's techniques will continue to be more effective than ASD's techniques (even if these are the same techniques), because of XP's strong focus on keeping the techniques closely integrated.

On the other hand, XP is tied to its techniques, whereas ASD can easily let go of techniques that appear inadequate for a specific project situation. Hence, XP's applicability is strongly constrained to a context in which its predefined techniques work, whereas ASD is open to any new situation. In some sense, ASD has a stronger and better defined meta-framework than XP.

Competition Among Project Members

ASD's belief in emergent results is one of the strongest differences from other methodologies, including XP. This is in line with ASD's departure from a traditional management approach. As a consequence, ASD techniques are unlikely to fully block competition among project members but rather to try to set appropriate goals in the form of project results.

XP does not mention the issue of competition among project members. Being unclear in this respect, XP managers are left to their own devices when facing a situation of competition. This may lead to problematic decisions. An XP manager should not adopt an ASD technique that fosters competition if he or she does not also believe in positive and constructive competition among project members.

It is clearly advisable for XP to review its position toward competition to avoid potential clashes if it wants to adopt techniques from ASD.

Good Enough Work versus Quality Work

ASD's focus on adaptation rather than optimization supports the concept of "good enough" work and results. Highsmith takes the derogative connotation out of "good enough" by calling it the total best solution in a given situation.

XP on the one hand strives for simplicity and not investing in the future unless immediately needed. On the other hand, the importance of doing satisfying work and equating it with quality work suggests that the quality, and hence the investment in the product, may go beyond what is actually needed. Obviously, this strongly depends on the individual developer and what he or she views as quality work that will satisfy him or her.

Therefore, some of the ASD techniques that strongly focus on developing good enough software do not work for XP. For example, for ASD, redundant source code is not a problem; it may even be a necessary byproduct of a competitive environment. XP insists on stating everything "once and only once" and thereby tries to fully eliminate redundant code.

Conclusion

In the world of software development methodologies, no specific methodology stands out as the one dominant player. Also, as of today, no clear winner is on the horizon. To survive, thrive, and grow, a methodology must be able to learn from other methodologies and successfully adapt to changing market requirements.

Learning and adaptation can be a painful experience, in particular if the underlying value systems of two methodologies are incompatible. But even with compatible value systems, learning may still be difficult. This chapter compares two new development methodologies, Adaptive Software Development and Extreme Programming. Both have compatible value systems so that one might expect that they could easily exchange techniques and learn from each other. However, an analysis of the value systems of both methodologies shows that despite all similarities, several incompatibilities remain that hinder immediate adoption of techniques by one methodology from the other.

On a more general level, the model of value system presented in this chapter can serve as a basis for comparing further methodologies with ASD and XP and with each other. The model needs to be extended and refined, but it already serves a useful purpose, as this chapter shows. As the emergence of the new breed of methodologies shows, there is a clear need for distinguishing and comparing them. I expect models of value systems to be at the heart of methods for comparing these new software development methodologies.

References

[Arthur1996] W. B. Arthur. "Increasing Returns and the New World of Business." *Harvard Business Review.* Volume 74, Number 4, 1996.

[Beck2000] K. Beck. *Extreme Programming Explained.* Addison-Wesley, 2000.

[Beedle+2000] M. Beedle, M. Devos, Y. Sharon, K. Schwaber, J. Sutherland. "SCRUM: A Pattern Language for Hyperproductive Software Development." In *Pattern Languages of Program Design 4.* N. Harrison, B. Foote, H. Rohnert, eds. Addison-Wesley, 2000.

[Budde+1992] R. Budde, K. Kautz, K. Kuhlenkamp, H. Züllighoven. *Prototyping.* Springer-Verlag, 1992.

[Cockburn2001] A. Cockburn, *Crystal "Clear": A Human-Powered Software Development Methodology for Small Teams.* On-line draft at http://members.aol.com/humansandt/crystal/clear. 2001.

[Floyd+1992] C. Floyd, H. Züllighoven, R. Budde, R. Keil-Slawik. *Software Development and Reality Construction.* Springer-Verlag, 1992.

[Highsmith2000] J. A. Highsmith III. *Adaptive Software Development.* Dorset House, 2000.

[Holland1995] J. H. Holland. *Hidden Order: How Adaptation Builds Complexity.* Addison-Wesley, 1995.

[Lehman1987] M. M. Lehmann. "Process Models, Process Programs, Programming Support." In *ICSE 9 Conference Proceedings.* IEEE Press, 1987.

[Lichter+1997] H. Lichter, M. Schneider-Hufschmidt, H. Züllighoven. "Prototyping in Industrial Software Projects: Bridging the Gap Between Theory and Practice." In *Software Project Management: Readings and Cases.* Irwin-Verlag, 1997.

[Naur1992] P. Naur. *Computing: A Human Activity.* Addison-Wesley, 1992.

[Osterweil1987] L. J. Osterweil. "Software Processes Are Software Too." In *ICSE 9 Conference Proceedings.* IEEE Press, 1987.

[Paulk1995] M. C. Paulk. "How ISO 9001 Compares with the CMM." *IEEE Software.* Volume 12, Number 1, 1995.

[Pohl+1999] K. Pohl, K. Weidenhaupt, R. Domges, P. Haumer, M. Jarke, R. Klamma. "PRIME—Toward Process-Integrated Modeling Environments." *ACM TOSEM.* Volume 8, Number 4, 1999.

[Wiki2000] Various authors. *Extreme Programming.* On-line at http://c2.com/cgi/wiki?ExtremeProgramming. 2000.

[XPorg2000] D. Wells. *Extreme Programming: A Gentle Introduction.* On-line at http://www.extremeprogramming.org. 2000.

[XPmlist2000] Various authors. Discussion of Extreme Programming practices and principles. On-line at http://www.egroups.com/group/extremeprogramming. 2000.

Acknowledgments

I would like to thank Jim Highsmith, Hans Wegener, and Heinz Züllighoven, as well as John Arrizza, Malte Kröger, Dave Thomas, and the anonymous reviewers for their helpful feedback on this article.

About the Author

Dirk Riehle is a software developer and resident metamodeler at SKYVA International in Boston, Massachusetts (www.skyva.com, www.skyva.de). In his work, he focuses on the architecture and implementation of metamodels for model-driven business systems. Dirk holds a Ph.D. from ETH Zürich and is a frequent author on the subjects of object orientation, patterns and frameworks, and software architecture. He welcomes feedback at dirk@riehle.org or through www.riehle.org.

Chapter 4

Let's Get Layered: A Proposed Reference Architecture for Refactoring in XP

—Mark Collins-Cope and Hubert Matthews

Extreme Programming (XP) is a highly incremental development process with a strong focus on incremental design by refactoring. This has presented two major problems, the first an image problem with respect to the quality of XP-based designs; the second a technical problem in that compiled languages such as C++ may become resistant to refactoring, as poor source code structure may lead to increasingly long compile/link cycles.

This chapter presents a simple visual metaphor in the form of an architectural layering model that we believe should be included in the body of knowledge one would expect of an Extreme Programmer.

The model presented is intended to assist in countering the poor design argument, to assist in the structuring of C++ (and other) source code, to give additional motivation for following the Once and Only Once principle, and, in general, to provide a framework for decision making during refactoring.

The model presented contains five layers, which are as follows: the interface layer, the application layer, the domain layer, the infrastructure layer, and the platform layer. It should be noted that the model is presented as a reference framework and does not imply that all applications should contain all layers.

Introduction

Architectural layering is a visual metaphor whereby the software that makes up a system is divided into bands (layers) in an architectural diagram. Many such diagrams have been used, and by way of introduction we show two of these.

Szyperski [Szyperski1998] presents a view of a strictly layered architecture, as can be seen in Figure 4.1. Note that this model has the device drivers below the operating system (O/S)—a topic we will return to discuss later in this chapter.

Figure 4.2 shows a type of ad hoc architecture diagram [Carlson1999] that is not uncommon in modern technical documentation. The example shown describes the architecture of the IBM San Francisco product.

Some common themes run through these diagrams:

⋄ That it is possible to identify a number of layers in the construction of pieces of software

⋄ That some layers sit on top of others (although there may be some question as to what one layer being above another actually means—see *Layering Semantics*)

⋄ That one may broadly categorize layers as being either horizontal (applicable across many, if not all, business domains) or vertical (applicable across a subset or only one domain)

Turning to Unified Modeling Language (UML) class diagrams (a younger notation), we notice that common convention usually places

| Apps |
| LIBS |
| O/S |
| Device Drivers |
| Hardware |

FIGURE 4.1 Layered architecture (example from Szyperski)

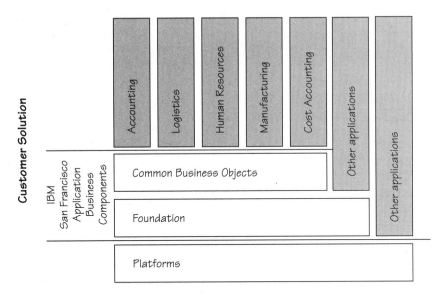

FIGURE 4.2 Typical ad hoc architectural layering diagram

subclasses, which are more specialized, below their parents, which are more general-purpose. This convention is the exact opposite of the architectural convention *highest is most specific*, and the cause of an undoubtedly confusing visual metaphor mismatch (see Figure 4.3), which we discuss further in our article *The Topsy Turvy World of UML* [Matthews+2000].

This chapter takes a revised look at application layering, with a particular focus on clarifying the unstated assumptions in such diagrams,

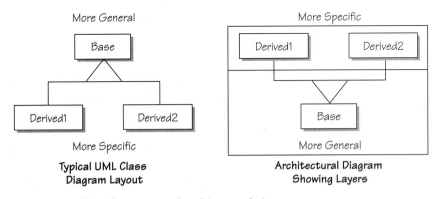

FIGURE 4.3 Class diagrams and architectural views

and proposes a five-layer architectural reference model for component-based object-oriented (OO) applications that can be used to assist in decision making during refactoring.

Proposed Model

Motivation

The objectives behind the architectural reference model presented in this chapter are:

- To provide a framework for decision making during refactoring
- To support and reinforce the appropriate application of good OO design principles, in particular those concerned with stability and dependency management, which are important in ensuring the fast compile/link cycles necessary to refactor effectively in C++
- To give additional support and an underlying motivation to the Once and Only Once rule, and
- To provide clarification of the meaning of layering in a component context

Reference Model

Architectural layering is a visual metaphor whereby the software that makes up a system is divided into bands (layers) in an architectural diagram. In most layering schemes, low-level system software is placed at the bottom of such diagrams, and application-specific software is placed at the top (see Figure 4.4).

We define the architecture of a system as the structural relationship between the individual components that together create an application as a whole. We define a component as an (object-oriented) software development deliverable implementing a well-defined interface that is released at the binary (or equivalent) level, which may have a number of well-defined extension points to enable it to be customized.

I'd like to emphasize three points here.

1. *Framework* is a term for a software deliverable that is generally assumed to 'drive' an application, leaving hooks for customization. As can be seen in Figure 4.5—in which certain components 'drive' higher layers, while also being 'driven' by them, we do not see a clear distinction between components and frameworks, but rather

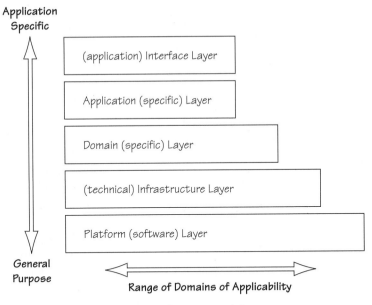

FIGURE 4.4 Layered architecture reference model

view them as a continuum. We use the term *component* generically across this continuum.

2. For the purposes of this chapter, we discuss components as an extension of object technology, but note that we accept that components can be written in non-OO languages.

3. The definition of a component is presented here and does not preclude source parameterized components: In this case, one would generate the binary file having instantiated the parameters in order to fit it into the framework described.

Examples of components conforming to this definition might include .o or .a files on a UNIX system, and .obj, .dll or .ocx files on a Windows-based system.[1] Note, however, that in most of the following discussion we consider the *design view* of components, which we represent as packages in UML notation.

---

1. We see technologies such as CORBA, COM and Java Beans as *component interoperability support technologies*, which may or may not be present in a component-based system. In Figure 4.5, they are not present.

- -

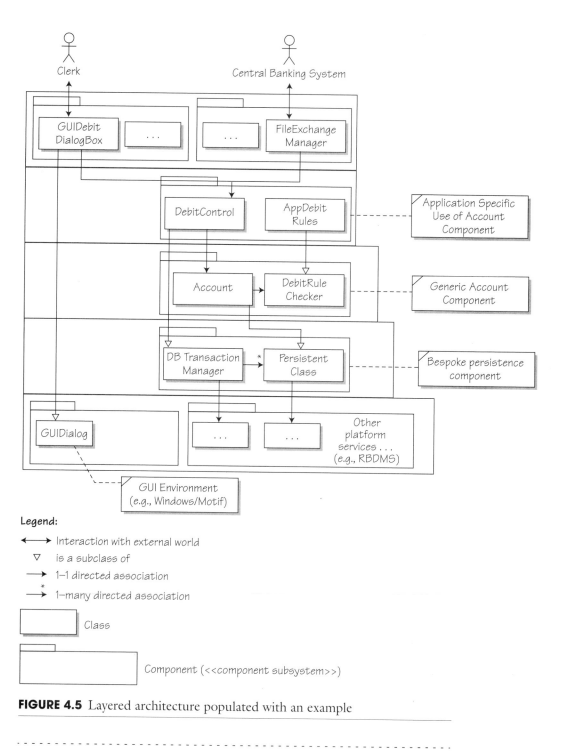

Legend:

◄──────► Interaction with external world

▽   is a subclass of

───► 1–1 directed association

──*─► 1–many directed association

▭   Class

▭   Component (<<component subsystem>>)

FIGURE 4.5 Layered architecture populated with an example

Figure 4.4 shows our proposed reference model. Figure 4.5 shows the same model populated with a number of classes, components, and relationships between them, taken from an example banking application. Two external *actors* [Jacobson+1992] interact with the system: A bank clerk (using a debit dialog box), and an external banking system (using an intermediate file format).

The layers presented in this model may be summarized as follows:

✧ Highest (and most specific) in the layering is the application *interface* layer.[2] This layer is responsible for managing the interaction between the outside world and the lower layers within the application. It typically consists of components providing graphical user interface (GUI) functionality—managing the interface to human users, and/or components providing external system interfaces—managing the interface to external systems. This layer often contains what Jacobson et al. call 'boundary' classes [Jacobson+1992].

In the example application shown in Figure 4.5, we can see two classes packaged within this layer. The GUIDebitDialogBox class implements an application specific dialog (to enter a debit). The FileExchangeManager class reads an external file format. Both classes use the application specific DebitControl class to process the information they receive from the outside world.

✧ Below this is the *application* specific layer. This layer comprises objects and components that encapsulate the major business processes and associated business rules automated within an application. Typically it will contain many objects akin to Jacobson's (use case) 'control' objects [Jacobson+1992]; and often also acts as the 'knowledge' layer in Fowler's operational/knowledge split [Fowler1997] (another description of this is separating policy from mechanism). It may also contain specialized subclasses implementing interfaces left 'open' (as in open-closed principle [Meyer1997; Martin1996]) by the more general purpose components in the layer below, and typically does not contain persistent business classes. Most importantly, this layer contains the "glue" to tie together components within the domain layer below.

In the example application shown in Figure 4.5, we can see two classes packaged within an application-specific debit component.

---

2. We chose the term interface rather than presentation, as some application interfaces are to external systems, and the term presentation tends to imply a user interface.

The DebitControl class takes over application control when asked to do so by one of the higher level interface classes. It then drives the domain level Account class to implement its functionality (which may involve several method calls on Account). Note that the DebitControl class is derived from a database transaction management class defined in the bespoke persistence component in the infrastructure layer.[3] The other class—AppDebitRules—implements the debit-rule checker interface (derived from the lower level Account component) to customize the debit checking rules as required by this application.

✧ Next is the business *domain* specific layer. This layer comprises components that encapsulate the interface to one or more business classes, which are specific to the domain (area of business) of the application and are generally used from multiple places within the application. They might also be used by a family of related applications—a software product line. This layer typically contains the 'entity' classes discussed by Jacobson et al. in [Jacobson+1992].

The example application shown in Figure 4.5 shows an Account component in this layer. The Account class is driven by higher level components to undertake account related activities such as debiting and crediting of money. As part of this, it uses a DebitRuleChecker interface (abstract class) to enable individual applications to customize the particular debit checking rules that may be applied (for example, can go overdrawn, can't go overdrawn, and so on). This is an example of the open-closed principle [Meyer1997; Martin1996] being used to implement an operational/knowledge split [Fowler1997]. Note also that, being persistent, the Account class is derived from the Persistent class in the infrastructure layer.

✧ Then comes the technical *infrastructure* layer. This layer is made up of *bespoke* components that are potentially reusable across any domain, providing general purpose 'technical' services such as persistence infrastructure and general programming infrastructure (for example, lists, collections).

The example application shown in Figure 4.5 shows a general purpose persistence component present in this layer. In this component, a DBTransactionManager class keeps tabs on a number of

---

3. This will implement database transaction begin and end commands, and manage the rollback of database changes, if necessary.

PersistentClasses,[4] which provide the hook by which higher-level domain classes may be made persistent.

✧ Finally, most reusable of all, is the *platform* software layer. This comprises standard or commonplace pieces of software that are *brought in* to underpin the application (for example, operating systems, distribution infrastructure (CORBA\COM), and so on). The example application shown in Figure 4.5 shows a relational database and a GUI class library being used to build the application.

Associated Rules

Some simple rules are associated with this model.

✧ There should be a clear and simple mapping between component structure and source code structure (the simplest being a one-to-one mapping).

✧ The level of a component is the highest level of any of its constituent classes.

✧ Components should not (and by the above definition, cannot) cross layers.[5]

✧ The compile time dependencies between components within any particular layer should be to components in either the same or a lower layer.

✧ The application and domain layers should be technology free.[6]

Layering Semantics

Most layering diagrams omit discussing the meaning of one layer appearing on top of another, or any description of the axis of the diagram. Earlier reviews of this chapter and the example shown in Figure 4.1 have led us

---

4. Transactions encapsulate a group of related operations, which business logic dictates must be either completed in their entirety, or not executed at all. The DBTransactionManager class is used to encapsulate this type of transaction. If the transaction succeeds, it can then automatically write all modified objects back to an underlying database—hence the need for tabs to be kept on all objects that may be modified.

5. Here we ignore issues of 'convenience' packaging for customers (for example, an account component that provides a GUI interface and some business logic may be packaged as a single component on release, following the RREP [Martin1996]).

6. However, they may contain abstract classes that are implemented in the interface layer and will contain technology.

to believe some further discussion of these aspects of the layering model presented here is desirable.

- ✧ *Vertical axis semantics:* The vertical axis of Figure 4.4 indicates the *specificity* (how specific it is to a particular application/environment) of a component in the application. The higher it appears in the layering of the reference model, the more specific it is. The lower it appears, the more general purpose it is. This has led us to coin the phrase *the center of gravity of the application*—essentially a way of classifying the overall architectural feel of a system as being either 'high' (very application specific, difficult to extend without substantial refactoring), or 'low' (good layering applied, likely to have hooks for extension with minimal refactoring).
- ✧ *Layer ordering (highest to lowest) is based on component compile time dependencies:* In Figure 4.1, Szyperski shows a layering model in which the device driver layer is shown below the O/S layer. While this seems appropriate at first glance, a deeper examination reveals the ordering in Szyperski's example is not based on the same criteria as the layering presented in our model. In our model, layer ordering is based on the dependencies between the components that reside within the layer. In the terms presented in this chapter, the device driver interface of an operating system is an *extension point* to enable customization of the operating system "component" to a particular piece of hardware. The operating system is *more* generic (general purpose) than the device drivers it uses (which are tied to particular hardware). The device drivers are also dependent on the operating system for their definition—their interface must conform to the calling interface used by the operating system (they will use the function prototypes defined in an operating system header file)—not the other way around. For this reason, we would present the middle three layers of Figure 4.1 as shown in Figure 4.6 (with additional detail to show interface definitions and instantiation of interface).[7]

---

7. Note, however, that using our classification scheme, the bottom two layers of Figure 4.6 would both reside at the platform layer—see *Conclusion* for further discussion of this. Note also, in a non-OO operating system, pointers to functions would be used instead of abstract interface instantiation. The dependency implications of this are, however, identical.

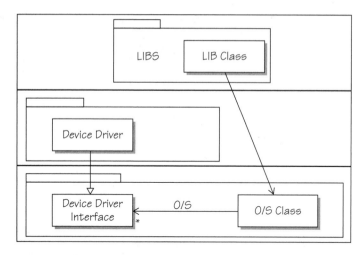

FIGURE 4.6 Szyperski's example using our layering rules

Summarizing, the layering semantics presented here tie together the concept of the specificity of a component (how much detail is filled in, how specific it is) with the notion of compile time dependencies. The higher a component in the model, the more specific it is likely to be, and the more dependent it is likely to be on other components, and vice versa.

Further Notes

A number of additional points are worthy of brief discussion.

- ✧ *A component oriented approach:* We have defined our view of architecture as one being based on the structural interrelationships between the binary components that are used to make up a system. We adopt this focus because at the end of the software development process we would like to have a number of well-defined and well-structured, loosely coupled, internally cohesive binary components that we may, without modification, use again in extending the current application (or possibly another application).

- ✧ *GUI components:* Not all GUI components reside at the interface level. The interface level may contain application-specific refinements of general purpose GUI components (for example, an application-specific dialog box); however, the *general purpose* elements themselves (for example, the generic dialog box from which the application-specific dialog box is derived) live at the platform level. The same is true for any general purpose GUI component without application-specific customization (for example, a graph drawing widget).

✧ *Substitutability:* Many discussions of architectural layering focus on being able to replace one *whole layer* with another—they are effectively treating the whole layer as a single component. This is *not* the purpose of the model presented here, which is intended as a guide to determining the contents of a particular component by deciding on the appropriate layer within which it should reside. Substitution would take place at the individual component level, not on a per layer basis.

How the Model Supports XP

A Simple Visual Metaphor for System Structure During Refactoring

XP focuses on the system metaphor to "push the system into a sense of cohesion" [Beck2000]. We believe a simple reference architecture, such as that proposed, will assist in visualizing the structural aspects of architecture and design during refactoring.

Consider the following examples from Fowler's *Refactoring* book [Fowler+1999], amended to make the UML conform to the highest-is-most-specific rule, and with the addition of layer divisions and component packaging to emphasize the points we are making.

In Figure 4.7, Fowler replaces a single employee class using a type code with an (extensible) hierarchy. Our architectural overlays add context to this process, demonstrating that Replace Type Code with Sub-classes may be viewed as moving the Employee class and its containing component from the application-specific layer to the more general purpose domain layer. Note that the derived classes (Engineer and Sales-person) now appear as application specific customization to the lower level Employee component, and that the refactoring visibly lowers the center of gravity of the application by finding the commonality and factoring out the difference.

In Figure 4.8, Fowler shows us how to split a GUI dialog class containing business logic into two. Our architectural overlays add context to

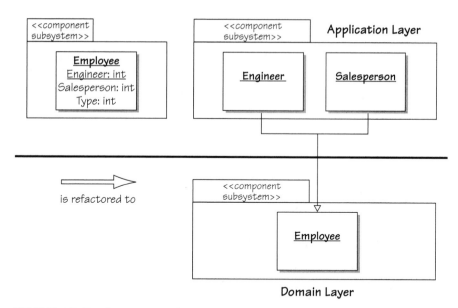

FIGURE 4.7 Replace type code with subclasses refactoring

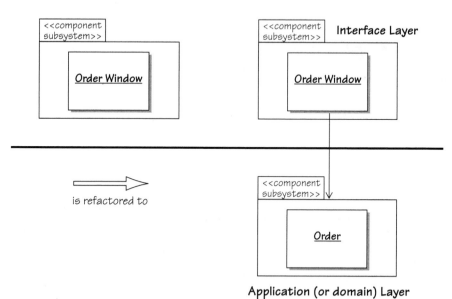

FIGURE 4.8 Separate domain from presentation

this, showing that, in doing so, what was previously an interface layer component has now been split into two components: one still in the interface layer, and one in the application specific (or possibly domain) layer. Again, the refactoring visibly lowers the center of gravity of the application.

In Figure 4.9, Fowler shows us an inheritance hierarchy with an inappropriately placed method, which is effectively polluting[8] its containing component by forcing it up to an inappropriate level. The refactored version shows the component split into two (over two levels), the method being to have getQuota moved out of the Employee class and into the Salesperson class. This enables the Employee component to reside at a more general level in the hierarchy, and again visibly lowers the center of gravity of the application.

Deciding Which Requirements Need to Be Done First

XP has the maxim: *Most difficult first*—but what is most difficult? Certainly one aspect of difficulty can be described with reference to the model: How many layers does the requirement cross?

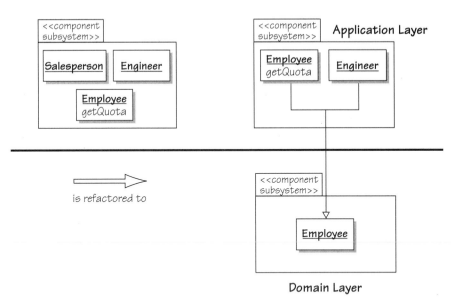

FIGURE 4.9 Push down method (reworked by us as pull up method!)

---

8. Pollution causes code smells. :-)

All requirements are not equal. Some requirements (or changes to requirements) obviously have a far greater impact than others. Consider a number of potential changes.

✧ A GUI dialog needs redesign (it was difficult to use). This probably affects only the interface layer.

✧ A GUI dialog needs additional criteria added (for example, customer spending last year) to enable a selection criterion it presents to be refined. This affects not only the interface layer, but also the application layer, as a new service [Collins-Cope1999] (select customer by sales) is required. Arguably, this change could also impact the domain layer.

✧ A persistence mechanism needs to be added. This is a big one, and may permeate right across the model!

This discussion gives us a slightly different perspective on the model, in that we can see that the layering also gives us an additional handle on the stable dependency principle [Martin1997]. Within the model, the higher layers are intended to be less stable than the lower layers.

Maintaining a High-Quality Set of Source Code Free of Unnecessary Dependencies

XP has a strong focus on source code quality. The rules associated with the reference model are intended to encourage the construction of applications from a number of well-defined binary components. The source code associated with these components should reflect this structure. Accordingly, we believe the reference architecture will ensure source code remains well-structured as systems grow in size and their design is refactored to accommodate new requirements. As we have already mentioned, source code structure is particularly important in languages like C++, which may become resistant to refactoring if dependency management is not a focus of attention.

The layering presented also supports a number of OO design principles.

✧ The open-closed principle [Meyer1997; Martin1996]—the idea being that lower layer components are closed against modification, and higher layer components extend the open aspects of them

- The stable dependencies principle [Martin1997]—the layers are organized based on expected stability of their contents, the lower layer components being more stable
- The acyclic dependency principle—the depend downward rule is effectively a specialization of this

A Brief Philosophical Aside

Many classification systems are blurred around the edges, and our layer classification is no exception. In his excellent book, *Darwin's Dangerous Idea* [Dennet1996], Dennet describes how examining the characteristics of a particular species of gull, starting in Britain and moving west to east around the globe, yields a set of gradually evolving changes until, as the loop closes and the examiner returns to Britain, a *different* species of gull is finally found next to the original! Species clearly have blurred edges, so we're in good company!

Compromises

The model presented here is not perfect, but a compromise between simplicity and meeting the stated set of objectives. Some potential shortcomings of the model are as follows.

- It would have been superficially pleasing to have a rule that said: You can only depend on the layer below you. However, upon deeper consideration we believe that the reason for this is an emphasis in previous discussions of layered architectures on complete substitutability of layers. As previously discussed in the *Further Notes* section (*Substitutability* bullet point), this is not the motivation behind the model presented here.
- There are clearly times when there will be sublayerings within the layers presented, and we could have made these explicit. However, we feel the price would have been too high in terms of additional complexity. Instead, we prefer to allow the option of discussing the "lower application" layer to resolve such issues.
- We have chosen to separate the infrastructure and platform layers based on a buy versus build criterion. Architectural purists may object to this—why should the layer in which a particular component resides be dependent on whether you buy or build it? Our

motivation is simple: We wanted to put the focus clearly on the aspects of the application being developed. For similar reasons, we have been unconcerned with sublayerings within the platform layer.

Conclusion

Summarizing, we have proposed a simple five-layered reference model and a number of associated rules to assist the Extreme Programmer. We have noted that, by convention, *UML class diagrams are upside down*, at least when considered in parallel with architectural layering conventions, and that this is a block to visualizing one aspect of what happens during refactoring. We have shown that once this is addressed, UML and the architectural model complement and reinforce each other.

We have identified examples from Fowler's *Refactoring* book that show that refactoring a polluted component assists in *lowering the center of gravity* of an application, bringing it more into line with the architectural model described, by *finding the commonality* (putting it into a lower layer) and *factoring out the differences* (providing appropriate hooks in the lower layer to enable higher layers to extend them in more application-specific ways). We have, therefore, demonstrated that the reference model provides an underlying rationale to some refactorings, at least.

We have discussed how the model supports good OO design principles, in particular those concerned with ensuring stable dependency management, and have emphasized and clarified the rules on which our layering model is based (specificity/generality and compile time dependency).

Coming back to the objectives detailed in the *Motivation* section, we believe the architectural reference model presented here:

⋄ *Provides a framework for decision making during refactoring* by providing a number of layers within which the developer can position components,

⋄ *Supports and reinforces the appropriate application of good OO design principles,* in particular those concerned with stability and dependency management, by enforcing a downward only dependency rule within the layers presented,

* *Gives additional support and an underlying motivation to the Once and Only Once rule* by encouraging components to be "moved down a layer" when refactored, and

* *Provides clarification of the meaning of layering in a component context* by stating clearly that the position of a layer should be based on the degree of specificity/generality of the components within it, and by tying this concept closely to that of compile time dependency management.

References

[Beck2000] K. Beck, *Extreme Programming Explained*. Addison-Wesley, 2000.

[Collins-Cope1999] M. Collins-Cope. "The RSI Approach to Use Case Analysis." In *Proceedings of TOOLS 29*, IEEE Computer Society. Nancy, France, June 7–10. On-line at http://www.ratio.co.uk/techlibrary.html.

[Carlson1999] B. Carlson. "Design Patterns for Business Applications: The IBM San Francisco Approach." *ObjectiveView*, Issue 3. On-line at http://www.ratio.co.uk/objectiveview.html. 1999.

[Dennet1996] D. C. Dennet. *Darwin's Dangerous Idea: Evolution and the Meanings of Life*. Touchstone Books, 1996.

[Fowler+1999] M. Fowler, K. Beck, J. Brant, W. Opdyke, D. Roberts. *Refactoring: Improving the Design of Existing Code*. Addison-Wesley, 1999.

[Fowler1997] M. Fowler. *Analysis Patterns: Reusable Object Models*. Addison-Wesley, 1997.

[Gamma+1995] E. Gamma, R. Helm, R. Johnson, J. Vlissides. *Design Patterns: Elements of Reusable Object-Oriented Software*. Addison-Wesley, 1995.

[Jacobson+1992] I. Jacobson, M. Christerson, P. Jonsson, G. Övergaard. *Object-Oriented Software Engineering: A Use Case Driven Approach*. Addison-Wesley, 1992.

[Martin1996] R. C. Martin, "The Open-Closed Principle." *C++ Report*, 1996.

[Martin1997] R. C. Martin. "Stability." *C++ Report*, 1997.

[Matthews+2000] H. Matthews, M. Collins-Cope "The Topsy Turvy World of UML." *ObjectiveView*, Issue 4. On-line at http://www.ratio.co.uk/objectiveview.html. 2000.

[Meyer1997] B. Meyer. *Object-Oriented Software Construction*, Second edition. Prentice Hall Professional Technical Reference, 1997.

[Szyperski1998] C. Szyperski. *Component Software: Beyond Object-Oriented Programming*. Addison-Wesley, 1998.

Acknowledgments

Particular thanks are due to Andy Vautier, Nigel Barnes, Faris Garib, Keith Haviland, and Andris Nestors of Accenture, upon whose 1 million+ line C++ project many of the underlying concepts presented in this chapter were formulated. Further detailed technical discussion this project can be found at http://www.ratio.co.uk/techlibrary.html.

About the Authors

Mark Collins-Cope can be reached at markcc@ratio.co.uk and Hubert Matthews can be reached at hubert@ratio.co.uk.

Chapter 5

Extreme Frameworking: How to Aim Applications at Evolving Frameworks

—*Stefan Roock*

Extreme Programming (XP) is a modern and powerful approach to the development of critical and highly innovative application software. Framework development is always critical and innovative, so XP should be suitable for framework development too.

The XP techniques frequently generate new versions of the software under development, which means that if XP is used for framework development, numerous new versions of the framework will be generated—and the framework interfaces will sometimes be changed. Since application code depends on the framework, the migration process of the application code to the new framework version becomes crucial.

This chapter discusses the versioning of frameworks and the migration of applications to new framework versions. Tentative solutions to the problem are presented as input for further discussion.

Motivation and Overview

"You'll never get it right the first time"—this is one of the key insights of XP [Beck2000; Cunningham1995]. Pair programming [Beck2000], refactoring [Opdyke1992; Fowler+1999], and aggressive unit testing [Jeffries1999; Fowler+1999] are all suitable techniques for achieving dramatic improvements in code and design quality. These are not the only XP techniques, but they are the ones that most affect the versioning of frameworks and the migration of application programs.

We have been developing and enhancing the JWAM framework [JWAM1999] with XP techniques since the beginning of 1999, and during this period we have observed remarkable improvements in quality (understandability, simplicity, correctness, robustness, and so on) since then. We call the use of XP techniques for framework development and application "Extreme Frameworking" (XF). This chapter deals with framework development using XP techniques in the area of interactive application software.

Although XP improved the quality of the JWAM framework, we observed major problems with the versioning of the framework and the migration of existing applications. In the following sections, first the importance of quality for framework development is emphasized. These quality requirements call for use of the XP techniques. Then, the technical source of the versioning and migration problem—the open-closed principle—is described. The next section looks at the question of who may be affected by framework versioning and in what way. The discussion of possible solutions for the versioning and migration problem requires a sound conceptual basis, which is given by the section, *Dimensions of Versioning and Migration*. On this basis, a possible migration process with supporting tools is sketched. Since work on the versioning and migration problem is still in progress, the presented "solutions" are meant as input for further discussion.

The contribution of this chapter is defining a starting point for discussion of the versioning and migration problem.

The following discussion does not only apply to XP; it is valid for framework development in general. The problems described are, however, more likely to occur in the context of XP.

Quality in Framework Development

Quality is crucial to frameworks. The users of frameworks are application developers who have to understand the architecture of the framework. The documentation of classes and the relationships between them is neccessary but sometimes not enough. The source code may be the last resort for application developers if the documentation is inaccurate [Meyer1995]. It is, therefore, often useful for application developers to have the source code of the framework at hand.

Software quality is often divided up into internal and external quality factors [Meyer1997]. External quality factors concern the users of the software system; internal ones are relevant only for the developers. This division does not apply to frameworks. As stated earlier, the users of the framework—the application developers—need to know the framework architecture (the internal structure), and they should have access to the framework source code. There is nothing, then, that might be called "internal quality factors."

Since XP deals not only with external quality factors but also with internal ones, it improves framework quality. Refactoring is done not just for the sake of framework developers; application developers also benefit from the refactoring of the framework.

But refactoring causes problems, too!

Framework development is worth the effort only if the resulting framework is used in numerous application projects. Modifications made to the framework may may lead to problems in the application projects, because the application programs have to be modified to work with the new framework versions. Application projects, then, put pressure on framework developers to maintain a degree of stability. This is why techniques are being sought that allow continuous refactoring of the framework without adversely affecting application development.

The Source of the Versioning Problem

As indicated, an important aspect of framework development is framework versioning. As frameworks are used for a large number of software projects in different developer organizations, it is not always possible to synchronize production of the framework with production of the applications. Frameworks must therefore evolve largely independently of the applications. However, when a new framework version is released, existing applications have to be synchronized with the new framework version.

The source of the versioning problem is the otherwise extremely useful open-closed principle introduced by Meyer [Meyer1997]. The open-closed principle means that the interface of a class can be fixed (that is, closed) for reuse by other clients; at the same time, the interface can be evolved (that is, open) through subclassing for further development. This well-established principle must be revisited for framework development.

Applications using frameworks usually have to subclass several classes of the (so-called white-box) framework. If the framework evolves, the superclasses of the application classes may change, thus invalidating the application program. This problem is also known as the "fragile base class problem" [Szyperski1998].

Dimensions of Versioning and Migration

The versioning of frameworks and the migration of applications to new framework versions can be discussed by referring to the dimensions shown in Figures 5.1 and 5.2.

The three dimensions relevant for framework versioning are "Migration support," "Compatibility," and "Product support." The framework developers may choose to support migration to new framework versions. This can be done in several ways: a history file describing what is new and different is provided, a guide to the new framework features is attached to the framework, a tool supporting migration is available, manpower is offered for the migration process, and so on. The demands with respect to migration support vary with the compatibility: Is the new framework version incompatible with the previous one, or is

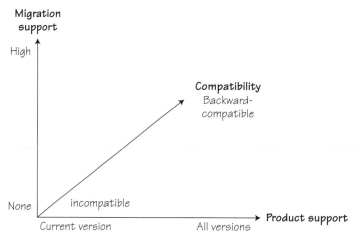

FIGURE 5.1 Dimensions relevant for framework versioning

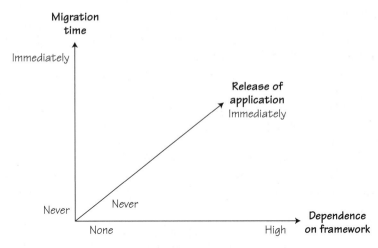

FIGURE 5.2 Dimensions relevant for application migration

it backward-compatible? Both dimensions influence product support: If migration to the new framework version is trivial, the framework developers may choose to support only the current version of the framework. If they do not expect the application developers to migrate immediately, they may choose to support more than one version, or even all previous versions, of the framework.

The dimensions relevant for application migration are "Migration time," "Release of application," and "Dependence on framework." The application developers may choose to migrate immediately or later to new framework versions. They may even choose never to migrate to the new framework version. Dependence on the framework may influence the choice of the time for the migration. If this dependence is low, it is easier to migrate immediately to a new framework version than if it is high. To lower migration effort, application developers may therefore choose to reduce dependencies on the framework. Both dimensions influence the release of the application. If the application developers migrate immediately to the new framework version, they may want to delay the release of the next application version until they have carried out some tests with the migrated application.

The following sections describe some topics of special interest with respect to the discussed dimensions.

Freeze Version

A very simple strategy is to freeze versions. That means that, on a conceptual level, no modifications are made to an existing framework version. To support this strategy, version information is part of the framework name. An example of such a strategy is Microsoft's COM [Szyperski1998]. Another example is the "Java product versioning specification" [Java1998]. If a new framework version is released, all classes of the framework have different names from the previous ones. For this reason, the new version does not replace the old one but exists parallel to it. The application may depend on the old framework version for a long time, and migration to the new framework version must be an explicit step.

An interesting aspect are error patches, which are useful on a theoretical level. On a practical level, they may cause problems. Clients of the components may have included workarounds for the errors in the framework. Installation of an error patch may result in errors in the application code. Error patches are therefore not allowed after release in the "Java product versioning specification."

This strategy would initially appear to solve the error patch problem. On the other hand, it is obvious that the framework must evolve (with error corrections and functional extensions). The "Freeze version" strategy ensures that running applications are not affected if a new framework version is installed. This is suitable for end users: If a system is installed together with a new framework version, the already installed applications are not affected.

But application developers also want to use error patches. The "Freeze version" strategy does not provide suitable support here.

Backward Compatibility

Backward compatibility is often employed for artifacts that are used by a very large number of clients. Prominent examples here are chip design (Intel 8086 up to 80486) and operating systems (MS-Windows operating systems 3.1/95/98).

Using this strategy, it is possible to extend the functionality of a framework without the existing interfaces and functionalities being modified. Backward compatibility enables old and new applications to be used with the same framework version.

This approach does, however, have some drawbacks, too. With every new framework version, more overhead is added to the framework.

New applications do not need the ballast resulting from backward compatibility. Moreover, a framework with a lot of overhead is hard to maintain and extend, and it is very hard to *ensure* backward compatibility for frameworks, given the possible side effects of extensions.

Deprecated Tags

In some programming languages (Java [Arnold+1998], Eiffel [Meyer1997]), it is possible to tag interfaces, classes, and operations as deprecated (in Java with the deprecated meta tag; in Eiffel, with the obsolete keyword). If a class uses a deprecated interface, class, or operation, compilation and execution of the program is possible, but the compiler issues warnings. This way, the application developers may use the warnings to migrate to the new framework version in small steps.

If an operation in the framework becomes superfluous, it may be marked as deprecated and removed in a later version. If an operation is renamed, a new operation with the new name may be introduced and the old one may be marked as deprecated.

This mechanism is powerful and easy to use, but it has its problems, too. The first problem concerns the question of how long a deprecated entity should remain in the framework. On a theoretical level, this question may be easy to answer: "one version." On a practical level, it isn't that easy. Very large applications may need more than one version cycle to migrate to the new framework version. If we look at the Java Development Kit (JDK), we find a lot of operations that have been deprecated since Version 1.1 (Version 1.3 had just been released when this chapter was written).

The second problem is caused by moving classes between packages or renaming packages. In this case, all classes within the package become deprecated. Since these deprecated classes have no inheritance relationship with the new classes, typing problems occur.

The third problem is that deprecated tags do not cover all possible refactorings. Renaming of classes or modifications of the pre- and postconditions of an operation cannot be easily covered with the deprecation mechanism.

Parallel Versions

The parallel version strategy provides three versions of a framework in each case: the outdated, the current, and the future version [Roock+1998].

This strategy introduces a framework life cycle. This life cycle means that a framework version goes through three stages over time.

1. The current version
2. The outdated version
3. The future version

At each point in time, a framework version is in one of the three stages. The current version is the version that should be used by "active" application projects. It is supported and maintained, and its interfaces do not change. Any application shipped to a customer must be based on the current version of the framework.

Operational applications may use the outdated version of the framework. The outdated version is still supported but no longer enhanced. Developers maintaining an application based on the outdated framework version know that they must migrate to the current version in the future.

The future version is the next scheduled framework version. It has a well-defined interface and functionality that are fixed when this version is released. Software projects may use the future version as a specification from the project start in order to access the interfaces or functionality of the new framework version. The condition here is that they do not ship their application until after the future version has become the current one. The version life cycle of application programs and frameworks is shown in Figure 5.3. In the example, Version 3 of the frame-

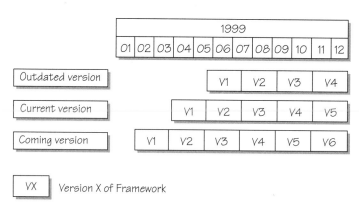

FIGURE 5.3 Example versions of a framework

work is due in July 1999, Version 2 is the current version, and Version 1 is outdated.

The parallel version strategy has two main drawbacks.

✧ Maintaining parallel versions requires more development effort than a single version concept.
✧ The parallel version concept shares an important problem with deprecated tags: One version may not be enough to migrate all application programs.

Discussion of Versioning and Migration Dimensions

None of the described dimensions can be discussed in isolation from the others because the questions they address are not fully independent of each other. From the XP viewpoint, a combination of "deprecated tag" and "parallel versions" would appear to be reasonable. As discussed earlier, this may still require considerable migration effort on the part of the application developers, especially if a lot of applications rely on the framework. Additional migration support is therefore required. In the next two sections, support for the migration process is outlined.

The Migration Process

I have analyzed several techniques for handling the versioning and migration problem, and based on this analysis, some tentative ideas for a versioning and migration process are presented in this section.

Whenever a new framework version is released, the following steps are necessary to upgrade the application software.

1. Detect the modifications made to the framework since the last version.
2. Figure out which modifications must be made to the application code.
3. Modify the application code.
4. Ensure that the behavior of the application has not be changed.

The modifications to the application code are crucial to the migration process, but they are not sufficient.

Application developers develop a certain way of using the framework. Part of this routine may be invalidated with the introduction of the new framework version: operations may have been deleted, new abstract operations have to be redefined during subclassing, classes may have been renamed, and so on. The application developers must therefore "migrate" to the new framework version, as well.

This means that an additional step is necessary in the migration process:

5. Adapt the routines of the application developers.

Test classes are useful for Steps 1, 2, and especially, 4. In addition to test classes, documentation of the modifications is crucial in order to succeed with Steps 1, 2, and 5. Step 3 is somewhat special. In principle, it is clear what to do if Steps 1 and 2 are successful. Nevertheless, the work required for Step 3 may be awesome, error-prone, and costly, given the amount of source code that has to be modified in large projects. Tool support for Step 3 would therefore be appropriate. Possible tool support is sketched in the next section.

Tool Support

We have seen that adaptation of the application code to a new framework version should be supported by tools. One key tool here is the Modification-Detector. The Modification-Detector is able to detect design deltas between versions of source code. These design deltas contain the common refactorings (see [Fowler+1999]) but are not restricted to them. The Modification-Detector can detect some types of refactorings automatically (like removal of classes). For other refactorings, the framework developers have to provide additional information.

On the basis of the detected design deltas, a computer-readable history is created by the Modification-Detector. The History-Browser reads the generated history and provides different views of the history. The History-Browser is also able to to create a human-readable history.

The Migrator tool supports migration of the application software. It reads the history and the application code and creates a new version of the latter as output. These modifications to the application software can be done automatically for some framework refactorings (like renaming framework classes and operations). Other modifications (like adding new abstract operations) must be done manually by application developers. These manual modifications are supported by the Migrator tool, which points to the places in the application code that may have to be changed.

Unlike the Smalltalk Refactoring Browser, the described tools work off-line: Modification of the framework is done at a different time and place from modification of the application code.

Discussion and Future Work

The general aspects of versioning frameworks and migrating application projects have been discussed. It has been shown that not only the application software has to be migrated, but the application developers as well.

An important issue is tool support for modifying the application software. A small toolbox for this task has been outlined. Initial versions of the described tools covering a subset of the possible modifications are available; the Migrator tool is currently under construction. Completion of the tools will be a major part of the future work, as will the development of design patterns supporting versioning and migration. Combining these design patterns with the described migration process and support tools would appear to be particulary promising.

References

[Arnold+1998] K. Arnold, J. Gosling. *The Java Programming Language*, Second edition. Addison-Wesley, 1998.

[Beck2000] K. Beck. *Extreme Programming Explained*. Addison-Wesley, 2000.

[Cunningham1995] W. Cunningham. "EPISODES: A Pattern Language of Competitive Development." In *Pattern Languages of Program Design 2*. Vlissides, Coplien, Kerth, eds. Addison-Wesley, 1995.

[Fowler+1999] M. Fowler, K. Beck, J. Brant, W. Opdyke, D. Roberts. *Refactoring: Improving the Design of Existing Code*. Addison-Wesley, 1999.

[Java1998]. *Java Product Versioning Specification*. On-line at http://www.javasoft.com. 1998.

[Jeffries1999] R. E. Jeffries. "Extreme Testing." In *Software Testing & Quality Engineering*. 1999. On-line at http://www.stqemagazine.com/. 1999.

[JUnit1999] K. Beck, E. Gamma. *JUnit*. On-line at http://www.junit.org. 1999.

[JWAM1999] *The JWAM Framework*. On-line at http://www.jwam.de. 1999.

[Meyer1995] B. Meyer. *Object Success*. Prentice Hall, 1995.

[Meyer1997] B. Meyer. *Object-Oriented Software Construction*, Second edition. Prentice Hall, 1997.

[Opdyke1992] W. F. Opdyke. "Refactoring Object-Oriented Frameworks." Ph.D. diss. University of Illinois at Urbana-Champaign, 1992.

[Roock+1998] S. Roock, H. Wolf, H. Züllighoven. "Frameworking." In *IRIS 21* "Information Systems Research in Collaboration with Industry," In *Proceedings of the Twenty-first Information Systems Research Seminar in Scandinavia*. N. J. Buch, J. Damsgaard, L. B. Eriksen, J. H. Iversen, P. A. Nielsen, eds. 1998.

[Szyperski1998] C. Szyperski. *Component Software*. Addison-Wesley, 1998.

Acknowledgments

I wish to thank the following colleagues at the University of Hamburg for supporting my work, namely: Heinz Züllighoven, Guido Gryczan, Henning Wolf, and Martin Lippert.

About the Author

Stefan Roock is at the University of Hamburg (Vogt-Kölln-Str. 30, 22527 Hamburg) and APCON Workplace Solutions GmbH (Friedrich-Ebert-Damm 143, Friedrich-Ebert-Damm 143, 22047 Hamburg). He can be reached at roock@jwam.de or through http://swt-www.informatik.uni-hamburg.de.

Chapter 6

Hierarchical XP: Improving XP for Large-Scale Projects in Analogy to Reorganization Processes

—*Carsten Jacobi and Bernhard Rumpe*

Extreme Programming (XP) is a lightweight methodology particularly suited for small-sized teams that develop software that has only vague or rapidly changing requirements. The discipline of systems engineering knows it as "approach of incremental system change" or also as "muddling through." In this chapter, we introduce three well-known methods of reorganizing companies, namely, the holistic approach, *the* incremental approach, *and the* hierarchical approach. *We show similarities between software engineering methods and company reorganization processes. In this context, we discuss the XP approach and how the elements of the hierarchical approach can improve XP. We provide hints on how to scale up XP to larger projects, for example, those common in the telecommunication industry.*

Introduction

XP [Beck2000] is a lightweight methodology for small-sized teams developing software with vague or rapidly changing requirements. XP can be regarded as an explicit reaction to the complexity of today's modeling techniques like the Unified Process [Jacobson+1999], the V-model [KBSt1997], Catalysis [D'Souza+1999], or the Open Modeling Language [Firesmith+1997]. XP focuses especially on a small number of best practices, disregarding many others advocated by the other methodologies. Being a relatively new, promising approach, XP still has to be proven in various projects regarding its superiority and usefulness when compared with other approaches. Measuring the quality of a software development in quantitative numbers is a complex issue, so we will mainly have a common-sense understanding of the advantages of XP over other methods. XP will evolve, reducing its weaknesses and increasing its strengths. This article is not a criticism of XP, but suggests an improvement in one of its obvious weaknesses.

A weakness of XP is that it is designed for a single small team of fewer than a dozen team members; therefore, it has its problems scaling up for larger projects. Fortunately, applying the XP approach in projects seems to considerably downsize the number of necessary participants, but there is still a number of areas where hundreds of developers work on producing one single software product. For example, the telecommunication industry is under enormous pressure to add to and improve functionality of its products. The time-to-market span in the mobile phone business needs a fast and flexible process for large projects. Switching systems need to be adapted for each customer and for each country: XP could play its role here too.

The main obstacles against scaling up of XP are lack of documentation (therefore, the exponential increase of necessary communication between developers) and lack of stable interfaces and stable requirements. Consequently, scaling up of XP will probably be indispensable in order to adopt methodical practices from other methodologies.

In industry, a big reengineering wave started in the 80s, in which companies tried to be more efficient regarding their competitors. From the discipline of systems engineering, we are acquainted with three approaches suited for managing a reorganization project. In the Total Systems approach [Picot+1979], the desired properties of a new system are defined first, and then the whole system is introduced into the new organization like a big-bang invention. In the Incremental Systems approach, also known as "Muddling Through," a set of small changes leads incrementally to local optimization. Through small changes of the company structure and organization and its supporting software system, a series of small localized improvements lead to a suboptimal organization form.

Since both approaches have several drawbacks, system engineering provides a third approach called "Hierarchical Structuring" of system development, or "Mixed Scanning." This approach combines the advantages of both other approaches, usually leading to better reorganization projects and, therefore, to an overall optimization.

Some similarities exist between the Extreme Programming approach and the Incremental Systems developing approach, as well as between the total system development and the classic object-oriented (OO) methods approach. It is, therefore, an interesting issue to transfer the combination of these two approaches from systems engineering to the software engineering discipline. There are two basic advantages.

⬦ The combination leads to a scaleup of the Extreme Programming approach to larger projects by hierarchically structuring the teams.
⬦ It features a successful methodology—named Genesis—for organizing a hierarchical approach, which can be transferred to the software engineering discipline.

Both of these points have interesting aspects. Of course, scaling XP up to a larger project allows you to apply the XP approach even if the system becomes more complex, needing more people to be involved. Another advantage is that there is a proven methodology to get a hierarchical reorganization process organized; this can be easily adopted to the software engineering discipline.

In the following section, we briefly repeat the aspects of XP that are of interest in this context. We also discuss some of the advantages of XP over traditional OO methods to get a basis for the following discussion. In the third section, we introduce three different approaches to reorganize parts of the company and discuss their advantages and drawbacks. This will show the analogy to software process models and will point out some possible improvements for XP. In the fourth section, we discuss what XP can learn from company reorganization approaches and how a successful methodology (Genesis) can be used to incorporate XP.

XP: Brief Introduction and Discussion

The fourth section discusses adaptations of XP to a hierarchical variant. This is based on the principles of XP that we briefly introduce in this section. We suggest that readers familiar with the basics of XP skip this section.

According to [Beck2000], the lightweight methodology XP basically consists of:

⬦ *Four values:* Communication between the programmers and between programmers and customers, simplicity of design, the early feedback through small changes in the releases, and the courage of programmers to do whatever is necessary,

◈ A number of *software engineering principles*, discussed below,

◈ *Four basic activities:* Coding, testing, listening, and designing, and

◈ A number of *practices* that help structure the basic activities in order to achieve the basic principles

Out of the four basic values, a number of principles have been derived; this is again partially quoted from [Beck2000]. Here are some fundamental ones.

◈ *Rapid feedback:* XP advocates very early a rapid (if possible, daily) feedback that allows programmers to focus on the most important software features.

◈ *Assumed simplicity:* XP tries to focus on the simplest possible implementation that works. Therefore, it focuses only on today's problem and does not plan future extensions of software. In particular, it does not plan for reuse at all.[1]

◈ *Incremental change:* A big change will never work at the first try. XP advocates small changes to enhance the system incrementally with desired functionality. This idea is based on the concept of refactoring, first introduced in [Opdyke+1993].

◈ *Embracing change:* "The best strategy is the one that preserves the most options while actually solving your most pressing problem." [Beck2000].

◈ *Quality work:* Quality is what finally matters. It emerges as a dependent variable of the three already mentioned variables. The XP approach tries to ensure excellent quality by focusing on basic principles that have proved useful and trying to keep the motivation of programmers up to its highest level.

For more on the software engineering principles, please refer to [Beck2000].

There are four basic activities in the XP approach: *Coding, testing, listening,* and *designing.* As a lightweight methodology, XP explicitly aban-

---

1. Disregarding reuse issues comes simply from the observation that approaches that explicitly try to reuse software have not been very successful in this task. Furthermore, software seems to be most reusable if simple. So disregarding reuse may, in fact, lead to a higher reuse rate.

dons any explicit activity of documenting and analyzing the system. Analysis remains a rather implicit, but continuous, activity that happens in everyday communication with the customer. Documentation is explicitly discouraged. Therefore, it is not surprising that coding is one of the most important activities in the XP approach. The second important activity is the testing of written code. In order to ensure that the written code actually works, the XP approach advocates writing a high number of tests to check whether the code is correct. The test suite can be seen as a specification: Some of the tests are written by programmers themselves to ensure that programs they wrote actually work; in addition, customers or explicit testers write functional tests to ensure the system meets the desired functionality. The third basic activity for XP programmers is listening. This means XP programmers listen to customers' needs and intentions, as well as to those of other programmers, by means of their everyday communication. Finally, even in the XP approach, it is sometimes necessary to step back from everyday coding and do some general design. This is of particular interest if changes to systems become more complicated.

Even minor changes have an impact on large parts of the system. A little bit of design is part of the daily business for all programmers in XP. Even though good design is difficult to evaluate, a number of hints exist. For example, the good design puts functionality that operates on data near to that data. It also tries to concentrate pieces of functionality within one place in the system, not distributed among numerous units. In order to establish all the goals XP advocates, good design also gives us several practices that should be followed.

- *The planning game:* Based on business priorities and technical estimates, the scope of the next release should be determined. Please note that releases depend slightly on one or more of their incremental developments.
- *Small releases:* One release should be done almost every day or couple of days.
- *Simple design:* Systems should be designed to be as simple as possible. This means, in particular, that unused functionality that further complicates the system should be removed.
- *Testing:* Unit tests are written by programmers; functional tests are written by customers to demonstrate that a feature actually works.

- *Refactoring:* The techniques of refactoring deal with structural changes to a system that don't affect its behavior. They simplify the system, remove unused code, add flexibility, or improve communication between the parts. This can be done, for example, by splitting or joining classes or moving methods or attributes from one class to another [Opdyke+1993].

- *Pair programming:* Two programmers sit at one machine. What one programmer writes is immediately reviewed by the other. They continually communicate with each other to ensure directly the high quality of their code.

- *Collective ownership:* Every programmer may change each part of the program at any time. There is no single owner of the code.

- *Continuous integration:* The idea is to integrate the new code and build the system many times a day, whenever a task is completed. Of course, each time the new version of the system is checked against the set of all tests.

- *On-site customer:* In order to ensure continuous communication, not only among programmers but also with at least one customer, it is important to have one customer in the team all the time. He can immediately answer all the questions that programmers have.

- *Coding standards:* This is self-explanatory.

For a more complete list and detailed list of these practices, please refer to [Beck2000].

Today, the XP approach is mainly used for small projects (from one to ten team members). It has been successful within small-scale projects but has not really been applied to larger projects. Due to its basic values and principles, we may assume that XP in its current form does not easily scale up to larger projects. However, if we compare the XP approach with classically oriented methods like the already mentioned Catalysis, the Unified Process, or the methodology framework provided by OPEN, we discover several advantages of XP. Compared with classical analysis design implementation or with more modern Inception-Elaboration-Construction-Transition life cycle, XP is more flexible and includes more explicitly the needs and intentions of all project participants. As in XP, the stages of analysis, design, and implementation are no longer separated; the analyst and the implementer are basically united in a single person. This, on one hand, allows us to forget about a thorough analysis documentation. On the other hand, the implementer is directly in touch with the customer, and therefore knows his intentions thoroughly when mediated by the analyst. Such considerable increase in motivation is paired with the appropriate decrease in misunderstandings on the communication path from the customer to the implementer.

All in all, XP is a promising approach with a number of strengths and a few weaknesses that can be improved. This chapter presents an approach to tackling the specific problem of scaling XP up to larger projects. The characteristic advantages and disadvantages of XP are similar to those experienced by companies that are reorganizing, such as those in the automobile industry in the 80s and 90s. For this reason, the next section will show the improvements made when reorganizing companies. This gives us more hints for improving XP.

Three Approaches to Company Reorganization

Many more or less successful approaches were developed to reorganize companies in the past. A systemization of these approaches divides them into three different types [Veitinger1995].

- ✧ The *holistic approach*, also called *Total Systems approach*
- ✧ The *incremental approach*, also called *Muddling Through*
- ✧ The *hierarchical approach*, also called *Mixed Scanning* or *Piecemeal Scanning*

We briefly introduce each of these in its own right, and then compare them with each other.

The Holistic Approach

The holistic approach tries to manage the whole complexity of a planning process in one comprehensive step and does not divide the problem into any smaller parts. With this approach, it is necessary to understand the whole problem in detail before working out a solution. This needs a broad information basis and a detailed as-is analysis. To initialize a reorganization process, one also has to tag one's targets exactly. Only then can various alternatives be generated and the best-fitting alternative be chosen.

For a detailed as-is analysis of an existing system in a complex environment, it is sometimes useful to structure it into subsystems. Each subsystem, with its functionality described through visible input and output, will then be analyzed separately. After the as-is analysis, we can again regard those subsystems as a black-box description of a system. This is basically the same approach as if a new system were being built by starting with rough planning on a high level, treating all subsystems of a lower level as black boxes. The holistic approach is typically used in operation research, statistical decision theory, and systems analysis. When trying to reorganize more complex systems, certain difficulties occur.

- The capacity of solution solvers is inadequate for a detailed analysis of all possible solutions and their consequences.
- The derived description, that is, information-flow, does not fulfill the requirements.
- The process is time consuming and costly (partly because of the detailed analysis phase).
- Provided the system is open to future change, all economic influences must be precisely estimated.

A significant disadvantage remains the enormous need for high-level competence and detailed holistic knowledge to work out a solution. Numerous reorganization projects of complex systems failed only because the solution was not reached in time.

The Incremental Approach

The incremental approach develops the system step-by-step. The primary target is not a perfect solution for a problem but a continuous progress. Consequently, the real targets of reorganization exist only on a very high level. Whether the activities are still effective and meet the targets must, therefore, be checked periodically. A typical example of an incremental approach is the continuous improvement process KAIZEN, originated in Japan. It is based on the assumption that all steering and control mechanisms can be changed independently. Six principles characterize the incremental approach.

- *Step-by-step comparison and analysis:* The reorganization process starts with the actual system and tries to improve it in small steps. The problem solver focuses on the well-known elements.

- *Restricting the number of alternative solutions:* Possible solutions are restricted since the modifiable elements stand for only a small part of the whole system.
- *Restricting regarded consequences:* As we can modify only a small part of the system, the consequences of a problem solution may regard only these few elements; otherwise, the changes are not acquainted with context.
- *Simplification:* Make a complex problem easy by dividing it into several smaller ones, and solve them first (but independently) before going further to a final solution.
- *Repeating analysis and evaluation:* A certain situation may always be improved by finding a better solution than the existing one.
- *Healing negative symptoms:* Quickly remove weak points of a big complex system, without trying to develop overall solutions. This approach is also called inductive.

The incremental approach is easy to use and of great help when quick improvements for small elements are needed. This is achieved by involving only the employees who best know their processes. The disadvantages of this approach are the lack of innovative solutions and the lack of one common target.

The Hierarchical Approach

Both the holistic and the incremental approach are combined here. Starting with an overall view of a reorganization project, the whole system is divided into modular, very detailed elements. When we work on such elements, we are always able to give feedback on a higher conceptual level in order to check targets and singular planning. Several requirements should be fulfilled to make this approach successful.

- The problem should be clearly defined by an input/output relationship and, furthermore, divided into elements. Possible criteria for the division are processes, products, or functions.
- Clearly defined targets for each element are needed.
- The target should be approached step-by-step through improvements on each particular step.
- A special form of project management is necessary to handle the communication and coordination of the modular elements appropriately.

Experience shows that the coordination task, especially, is a great success factor when it comes to practical solutions that fulfill the targets adequately.

The analysis of each of the three approaches shows various ways to undertake a reorganization process. All have been used in practice. The holistic approach is normally implemented when changing bigger organization structures if personal interests are involved. A solution in such a case cannot be reached by involving the employees, since it takes incredible planning time, and personal objections are then bad driving forces. With personal objections involved, there is a high risk of not reaching the goals at all. The incremental approach, on the other hand, is chosen in case of highly complex structures without an overall detailed reorganization concept. There are only high-level targets, which do not allow explicit suggestions on the operational level. Last, but not least, the hierarchical approach has become a common choice for reorganizing companies. It allows them to combine the power and knowledge of employees on the detailed level while solving problems with innovative concepts. Targets are well-defined, and a special coordination function is established in the project management. To satisfy all principles of a hierarchical approach, one basic method, named Genesis, has been brought to light, with great success [Wildemann1997]. This method helps, by means of coordination, to reorganize all elements in a system with defined targets.

Genesis: Managing the Change

Genesis is a management concept that consists of a combination of proper tools and techniques to improve the objectives of a business process and that also includes some management elements to guarantee the success. It is used to simplify work, taking advantage of a very efficient cross-functional team concept without many levels of authorities, and to operationalize a strategy for managing a change. Genesis is a way to reach and quickly implement solutions in a defined process with inputs and outputs. The Genesis approach:

- ✧ Supports readiness to change things,
- ✧ Encourages every subordinate to check one's personal field of action or obstacles and to use this evaluation,
- ✧ Makes a big impact through implementing a lot of individual steps,

- ✧ Solves problems that can be handled by the subordinates themselves,
- ✧ Helps realize partial solutions with small efficiency,
- ✧ Activates creativity, the idea pool, and the performance of all subordinates, and
- ✧ Encourages each employee's responsibility for his own task area.

The Genesis hierarchical approach can be organized through a series of workshops with a clearly defined program for the reorganization object. It starts with a preparation phase, where the project organization, the high-level targets, and the objectives of this reorganization are defined. Usually, all team members that work in this project are taught the same problem-solving methods in order to have one common language. After setting up the rough structure and the project team, a first planning workshop starts. Participants in this planning workshop usually come from management. Management defines the basics of the new, innovative concept and then divides the system up into its elements. To add to it, all targets for the elements and their process input and output are defined in the first workshop. For each element, a new workshop is defined. To coordinate all these workshops, there is a core team in the project organization with special tasks, meeting regularly. In these meetings, problems are discussed, for example, whether a solution for one element affects another. Such problems are first checked by members of the project organization group. Ideally, discussions concerning possible effects on other elements should not arise at all; this would be an indication that the whole system was divided into wrong elements.

Numerous case studies show that the hierarchical approach has proved to be the most successful for reorganizing companies whenever very detailed information is necessary with respect to the processes but, at the same time, implementation of new innovative concepts is desired. The holistic approach did not yield acceptable solutions, as an entire, undivided system was too complex to handle. The incremental approach also did not achieve the targets set, because each solution for an element can be perfect in its own right but not always perfect for the whole system. The key method for reorganizing companies with the hierarchical approach was the Genesis method. The success of this method was shown in more than 500 workshops with an average savings of about $250,000 [Wildemann1997]. The success factors of the Genesis method are:

- Involvement of all employees, also top management and management
- Defined communication steps, for example, a top management presentation after four days to put pressure on finding solutions
- Defined communication concept and coordination of multiple teams
- Supporting a clearly defined target through all workshops and team activities

The description of the different approaches show that the hierarchical approach combines the advantages of the holistic and incremental approaches, thus eliminating their disadvantages. The major success factor of the hierarchical approach is a management process that is described by Genesis. In the following section, we will try to use this hierarchical approach to improve XP in a new way.

Combining XP and the Hierarchical Approach

In the previous sections, we witnessed a characterization of the XP approach as a lightweight software methodology and three variants for company reorganization. Today, to achieve success in a competitive market, it is imperative that companies supply their business with extensive software support. A company reorganization always goes together with the adaptation of existing and the introduction of new software. Therefore, it is a natural consequence to combine suitable approaches that come from technical and management disciplines, particularly if both approaches possess structures with similar characteristics. Therefore, the first step toward such a combination can be a comparison of the discussed approaches. Despite existing differences, a comparison also reveals some similarities between the following approaches to software development and company reorganization (see Table 6.1).

The holistic approach has several characteristics in common with the classical software engineering approaches, starting with the Waterfall model but also newer object-oriented approaches, like the Unified Process [Jacobson+1999]. They, for example, share a centralized approach, providing a small coordination team with great power, but lack adequate customer/employee participation. Their major advantages are:

TABLE 6.1 Comparison of Software Deveopment and Company Reorganization Approaches

Software Development	Company Reorganization
Classical software engineering (Waterfall and heavyweight OO)	Holistic approach
Extreme Programming	Incremental approach
Hierarchical Extreme Programming	Hierarchical approach

- ✧ A common, clearly identified target, and
- ✧ A structured process that leads the team through the software development phases

They share major disadvantages.

- ✧ A lack of involvement of employees in charge of the holistic approach, whereas in the object-oriented approaches, the respective customers play a minor role. We miss, in particular, the early feedback of the end users.
- ✧ Missing customer/employee participation, leading to reduced acceptance of the solution. It is far easier to convince people of new ideas when they actively help to shape them.

The incremental approach is comparable to XP. Both are rather decentralized, and both have a minor focus on local improvements of existing structures/systems. Such improvements can be released early and get a fast feedback. Their major advantages are:

- ✧ High involvement of employees/customers and, as a result,
- ✧ High acceptance of the solution

XP and the incremental approach also have some disadvantages in common.

- ✧ Applying this approach to several local problems usually does not lead to a shared improvement with multiple teams. Instead, local improvements may contradict each other.
- ✧ The approach is unstructured and can therefore not be used for working out an overall concept by a complex problem in which the involvement of several persons is necessary.

One interesting question is whether the hierarchical approach, as a combination of the holistic and incremental approaches, can be carried over to the software development discipline. Currently, newer object-oriented approaches, such as the Unified Process, incorporate some of the elements of the hierarchical approach. However, these approaches are too heavyweight to fully support the advantages of the hierarchical approach. Therefore, we decided to start with the Extreme Programming approach and build a hierarchical structure on it. The advantages of this approach have partly been discussed before: While retaining a lightweight methodology, it becomes feasible to structure larger projects into a bunch of smaller XP projects that still have a common target to achieve. The approach taken also fits nicely into the Genesis program, which basically consists of two important elements.

✧ On the top level we set up a goal-oriented project management that organizes the problem as a high-level structure by working out a rough concept.
✧ Each of the now localized problem parts is solved through an Extreme Programming approach by defining its own XP team.

Figure 6.1 demonstrates this advantage of the hierarchical approach compared with the other two approaches. Each circle is a team member; tight connections of circles form a team.

The XP teams function primarily on an independent basis; nevertheless, they are coupled in a slack manner by a top-level management

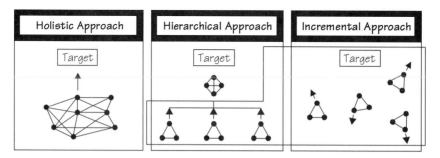

FIGURE 6.1 Comparing the three approaches of company reorganization

team, called a "steering committee," that keeps track of the overall goal and measures local improvements. Even though the XP teams dealing with local problems are to be formed as principally independent units, some cross-dependencies usually arise. It is important to keep these cross-dependencies as lean as possible. However, dealing with the complexity of today's information systems, this is a difficult issue. Today, software engineering techniques still do not sufficiently provide mechanisms to define crisp and small interfaces between software parts (and their development projects). If the actual initial problem structure and its software solution turn out to be inadequate, an appropriate refactoring of this structure is encouraged. This goes along with dynamic restructuring of the XP teams, which is useful anyway to dynamically react to varying workloads. Refactoring at this level is surely more expensive, as it crosses team boundaries. Therefore, it is imperative to have the top-level project management on hand to handle these kinds of restructurings.

By organizing the software development process in a hierarchical manner, we always focus on one common target and use a structured process to reach this goal. The involvement of the employees will lead to a high acceptance of the solution, starting from middle up to highly complex project settings. Ideally, XP project teams are defined in a way similar to how company departments are. The XP project team structure therefore is organized similar to the company structure, and each XP team recruits its customer(s) from its associated department(s).

A certain part of the software infrastructure of a company is not localized in one (or a few) departments, but its usage is spread over a number of departments. Of course, its development or enhancement is still a matter of one XP project, but if several of these software subsystems are to be restructured or enhanced, then the setup of the XP project structures in analogy to department structures is not appropriate anymore. This can partly be solved by identifying pilot departments with pilot customers that are able to cover the needs and desires of other departments' users as well.

These considerations show that the hierarchical Extreme Programming approach needs a good, yet lean, project organization. This is supported by the Genesis program and can be carried over to software project structures. Five major principles can be identified that characterize the hierarchical approach (see Figure 6.2).

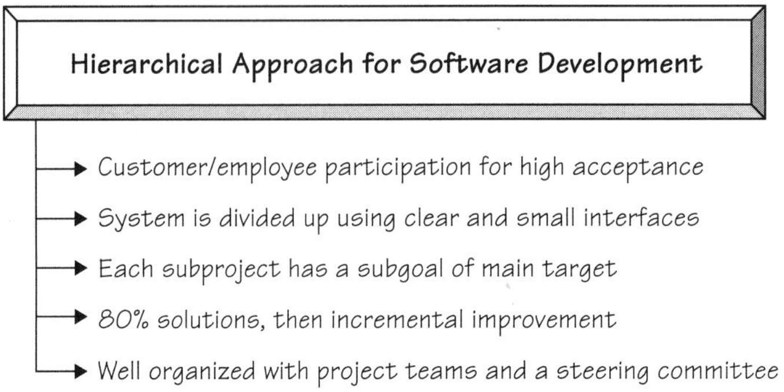

```
┌────────────────────────────────────────────────┐
│   Hierarchical Approach for Software Development │
└────────────────────────────────────────────────┘
      ├──→ Customer/employee participation for high acceptance
      ├──→ System is divided up using clear and small interfaces
      ├──→ Each subproject has a subgoal of main target
      ├──→ 80% solutions, then incremental improvement
      └──→ Well organized with project teams and a steering committee
```

FIGURE 6.2 The five major principles of the hierarchical approach

These principles are a combination and adaptation of corresponding XP principles and principles from the hierarchical reorganization approach.

✧ To reach high acceptance, the solution is worked out with customer/employee participation. This is particularly important in order for the customers to accept the resulting new software system/company structure.

✧ The whole system is divided up into subsystems with a lean and crisp interface. The inputs and outputs—namely the data structures and the information flow between the subsystems—need to be clearly defined. Subsystems are respectively evolved through XP teams and implemented.

✧ Each XP team has as a target its associated subsystem, thus contributing to the main target, namely the development of the whole system.

✧ The worked-out software solutions will be improved in an incremental process in order to be successful very quickly. In a number of releases, the team explores and extends the desired system functionality.

✧ The hierarchical approach needs to be well organized, with a project team and a steering committee following a Genesis program. The steering committee is an ideal place to develop and maintain the common system metaphor. This cannot be decentralized in several XP teams but needs central coordination.

Most of the additional principles and practices of XP that were introduced in the second section carry over to the hierarchical approach without major changes. However, some of these principles need slight enhancement. The test suite becomes even more important when the XP teams have interfaces to each other. Tests that check the correctness of the cross-project functionality and, therefore, the correctness of the interfaces need to be conducted automatically.

Case Study: Bidding Software

As a first case study (in non-hierarchical XP) in a management circle on "Electronic Sourcing" held at the Technical University of Munich, we decided to develop a software able to support different parts of the purchasing process. This management circle was joined by purchase managers of BMW, Dresdner Bank, DaimlerChrysler, Philipps, and so on. To find out what features should be developed, we started with a planning workshop with mainly customer and consultant participation. In order to systemize purchasing processes, we started by identifying existing needs and continued with controlling the purchasing activities. Different concepts like on-line broker, purchasing card, and on-line shopping malls were evaluated, and on-line biddings were identified as the most valuable technique to reduce costs. This workshop was dominated by the participants of the management circle and members of the business and economics institute. In a second workshop, where information technology people were also involved, we defined the core features of the business-to-business (B2B) real-time on-line bidding software. In a first (non-hierarchical) XP project, the on-line bidding software was developed. All elements of the software were developed using an incremental approach with short feedback loops to the customer (intensive meetings two to three times a week, weekly releases). In this way, we were able to develop a bidding software in a very short time with a high acceptance by the customers, namely, the consultants using the software for actual B2B on-line biddings. The software started productive use after only eight weeks of development but is still evolving through adding flexibility and new functionality. This evolution is necessary to ensure meeting the needs of consultants and their customers that cannot be foreseen in this highly innovative field of e-commerce. With this software, we realized an impressive number of auctions with a volume of millions of euros in two months, with an average savings of approximately 20 percent.

In a second and larger effort, extension subprojects, which also use the XP process for their development, have been defined. An overall steering committee is ensuring that all subprojects stay on track.

A second case study dealing with hierarchical XP is currently under investigation. The results will surely take time, as a hierarchical approach to XP cannot be implemented in the field as fast as XP can.

Conclusion

In the context of the FORSOFT project and its industrial partners, we had a close look at the basic question of software engineering. FORSOFT focuses on both theoretical and practical issues of software development and management issues, in particular, on their combination. This chapter focuses on the particular question of how to optimize and reorganize companies that make heavy use of software products.

If a company is reorganized, this usually means restructuring its software products, databases, and network infrastructure, because a company reorganization usually concentrates on optimization of its business cases. In this chapter, we have introduced and discussed different software development processes, as well as different company reorganization approaches. In particular, we have discussed similarities and differences between these approaches and concluded that an extension of the Extreme Programming approach by elements of the hierarchical reorganization process leads to a considerable scaleup of the XP approach. Furthermore, the XP approach, extended this way, can be integrated nicely with the hierarchical reorganization process, allowing the use of both at the same time.

Another interesting issue that should be discussed further is that the hierarchical approach cannot singularly be carried over to software development discipline. Usually both disciplines—reorganizing a company and restructuring the software—go hand in hand. Therefore, it turns out to be extremely useful to combine the hierarchical management approach with the software development approach in a hierarchical software and company restructuring setup. Thanks to integrated project structure, we can usually expect far better results than if we use the centralized approach, which does not involve employees/clients enough, or a decentralized or unstructured approach that does not focus sufficiently on the global target.

References

[Beck2000] K. Beck. *Extreme Programming Explained*. Addison-Wesley, 2000.

[D'Souza+1999] D. D'Souza, A. C. Wills. *Objects, Components, and Frameworks with UML: The Catalysis Approach*. Addison-Wesley, 1999.

[Firesmith+1997] D. Firesmith, B. Henderson-Sellers, I. Graham. *OPEN Modeling Language (OML) Reference Manual*. SIGS Books, 1997.

[Jacobson+1999] I. Jacobson, G. Booch, J. Rumbaugh. *The Unified Software Development Process*. Addison-Wesley, 1999.

[KBSt1997] Koordinierungs- und Beratungsstelle der Bundesregierung für Informationstechnik. "V-Modell." *Allgemeiner Umdruck Nr. 250. Vorgehensmodell*. Bundesdruckerei Bonn, 1997.

[Opdyke+1993] W. Opdyke, R. Johnson. "Creating Abstract Superclasses by Refactoring." *Technical Report*. Dept. of Computer Science, University of Illinois and AT&T Bell Laboratories, 1993.

[Picot+1979] A. Picot, B. Lange. "Synoptische versus inkrementale Gestaltung des strategischen Planungsprozesses: Theoretische Grundlagen und Ergebnisse einer Laborstudie." *ZfbF* 31, 1979.

[Veitinger1995] M. Veitinger. *Controlling von Reorganisationsprozessen in der Logistik: Eine empirische Untersuchung*. Universitätsverlag München, 1995.

[Wildemann1997] H. Wildemann. *Produktivitätsmanagement: Handbuch zur Einführung eines kurzfristigen Produktivitätssteigerungsprogramms mit GENESIS*. TCW Verlag München, 1997.

Acknowledgments

This work was partially supported by Siemens AG Munich, the Bayerische Forschungsstiftung under the FORSOFT II research consortium, and the Bayerisches Staatsministerium für Wissenschaft, Forschung und Kunst under the Habilitation-Förderpreisprogramm.

About the Authors

Carsten Jacobi can be reached at Lehrstuhl für Betriebswirtschaftslehre, Munich University of Technology, Germany (http://www.bwl.wiso.tu-muenchen.de). Bernhard Rumpe can be reached at Software & Systems Engineering, Department of Computer Science, Munich University of Technology, Germany (http://www.rumpe.de/).

Chapter 7

JWAM and XP: Using XP for Framework Development

*—Martin Lippert, Stefan Roock,
Henning Wolf, and Heinz Züllighoven*

*We started using the Extreme Programming (XP) techniques
for designing and implementing the JWAM[1] framework in the
beginning of 1999. With the help of these techniques, we succeeded in evolving the JWAM framework from a "student's
project" into a real-life professional application framework that
is used in several commercial applications today.*

*In this chapter we report on our experiences with XP in gen-
eral and with XP for framework development in particular for
more than one year. The following sections describe how we use
the XP techniques and how we have adapted them to our specific
programming domain—the development of application frameworks for large-scale application software. This chapter also discusses some of the problems encountered during XP and their
potential solutions.*

History of JWAM

JWAM is a Java framework supporting the development of large-scale
interactive software systems according to the tools and materials
approach. The foundation of the JWAM framework was laid in 1997 by
research assistants and students of the Software Engineering Group at

---

1. WAM is the German acronym for Java tools, automatons, and materials. More information about WAM can be found in [Riehle+1995]. JWAM is the corresponding
   Java framework and can be downloaded from [JWAM].

the University of Hamburg, and it was a pure university project. We used it as a sandbox for gaining some experience with new concepts and with framework development in general. We also used it for teaching purposes.

In 1998 we felt that JWAM had the potential for professional software development. We thought it to be a solid technical base for large-scale software development, giving support to developers with a proven design. Important steps in commercializing the framework were a redesign of parts of the framework and the explicit definition of a framework development process and its management. Early in 1999 we began to use XP techniques in a team of seven framework developers and redesigned parts of the framework. First, we used refactoring [Opdyke1992; Fowler+1999], pair programming [Beck1999], and test classes [Firesmith1996; Junit1999]. Then we added the planning game and continuous integration [Beck1999].

The redesign of the framework had one major goal: simplifying the framework. With this goal in mind, we refactored the framework and introduced a separation of the framework core from framework components based on this core. Before we began refactoring, there was one framework compound with more than 600 classes. After refactoring we had a framework kernel with about 100 classes plus test classes. The rest of the original classes were divided into separate framework components or had become useless during the refactoring process.

In March 2001, more than 10 professional projects in different application domains use JWAM.

We use all of the XP techniques, and we were quite successful in introducing them to our team. Of course, we had to adapt some of the techniques to our situation. Currently, we further develop the JWAM framework in pairs only, and nearly every framework class has a test class. If you want to know more about the JWAM framework take a look at [JWAM].

The Setting

The JWAM framework is both rooted in the university and has its commercial context. Within the university we use JWAM for teaching and as a sandbox for trying out new concepts. Within the commercial context we have founded the Apcon Workplace Solutions Ltd. The company uses JWAM for professional application development. This combination of academic and industrial settings gives us the chance to use leading-edge concepts in commercial projects very fast. On the other hand, the requirements of the industrial projects trigger the research activities at the university.

Figure 7.1 shows the business use case for the development and usage of the JWAM framework. Note that the different actors may map to the same persons.

Framework developers may also develop applications, teach framework design, or coach software teams. Application developers do nothing but application development, but may evolve over time into framework developers. Our students will develop both the framework and applications, but they don't teach or coach.

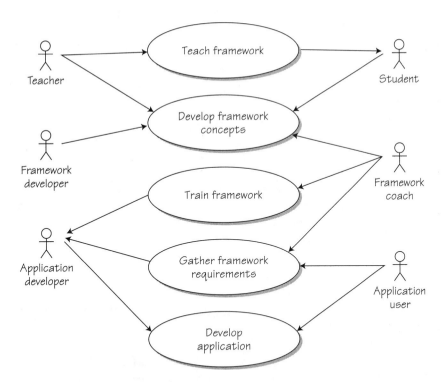

FIGURE 7.1 Business use case for JWAM development and usage

Lessons Learned

All of the XP techniques proved to be suitable for framework development. Of course, we had to adapt some of the techniques, and we learned that we were using others in a suboptimal way at first. The following sections are structured like the book by Kent Beck [Beck2000] and explain our experiences using the XP techniques.

Planning Game

We use story cards for the planning game. Every framework developer may write story cards about new ideas he or she has or document requirements of the framework users (that is, the application developers). In addition, we the framework developers, prioritize the story cards. We, and not the users, decide which one should be realized first. This usage of the story cards differs from what is described in [Beck2000], where the users, in our case the application developers using the framework, should rank the story cards. We've adapted the planning game to our needs in this way because we don't produce an individual piece of software. The framework is the technical base for many application developers spread over many companies and over different business domains. Therefore, our users cannot coordinate themselves about the ranking of the story cards—we have to do it in line with our plans for the future of the framework.

Another adaptation of the planning game is the slightly different content of the story cards we write. In most cases these "in-house" story cards don't contain pure requirements like the original story cards described in [Beck2000]. We also use story cards to write down solutions to open problems and open requirements. The reason for this usage is the slightly different role of the story card writers. Many of the cards are written by a framework developer as a result of a discussion inside the team, with his or her pair (see the *Pair Programming* section), or with an application developer using the framework. The rest of the story cards are written by application developers while coding.

Since the JWAM framework isn't a pure in-house framework, it is not that easy to integrate application developers into the framework development team. Nevertheless we feel that this is necessary. We try to solve the problem the other way around: Framework developers work as application developers part time. They pair with application developers and thus gain insight into their way of using the framework. In addition, expertise about the framework is spread into the application projects fast.

We have discovered that the stories are useful for planning but—in our case—they are not sufficient. We needed additional techniques to get a view of the overall picture, especially the interconnections between the story cards. If one story cannot be developed in the estimated period of time, it may be necessary to reschedule dependent stories. In addition, we needed to divide the bulk of the story cards into handy portions and make our planning more transparent to our framework customers. Therefore, we have enhanced the planning game by document types of the WAM approach [Züllighoven1998]: baselines and project stages.

We use project stages and baselines for scheduling. A project stage defines which consistent and comprehensive components of the system should be available at what time. The project stages are an important document type for communicating with application developers. We use them to make the development progress more transparent to our customers. The project stages are the basis for discussing the development plan and rescheduling it, depending on users' needs. Often they are scheduled by the management of the software development team. Figure 7.2 shows an example of three project stages of our framework development process. We write down at what time we want to reach what goal and what we have to do to realize the aspired goal. Typically the project stages are scheduled backward from the end to the beginning since most important external events (vacations, training programs, fixed dates for exhibitions, fixed dates for customer

Subgoal	Realization	When
JWAM 1.5 delivered	Sample application is running, all tests are fine	3/31/2000
New tool construction subframework designed	Review and refactor existing component, implement additional requirements requested by application developers	5/16/2000
Task oriented documentation ready for review by application developers	Improve task documentation for framework core, rewrite documentation for new tool construction	8/30/2000

FIGURE 7.2 Example project stages

meetings and project meetings) and deadlines are fixed when projects are established.

Baselines are used to detail planning within one project stage. They do not focus on dates but define what has to be done, who does it, and who controls it in what way. In contrast to the project stages, baselines are scheduled from the beginning of the period to the end.

Within the baselines table (see Figure 7.3), we write down who is responsible for what baseline and what it is for. The last column contains a remark about how to check the result of the baseline. The baselines table helps us identify dependencies between different steps inside the framework development (see "What For" column). The last three columns are the most important ones for us. The first column is not that important because everybody is able to do everything (like with story cards). But it is important for us to know how to check the results in order to get a good impression of the project's progress. It is an indicator for possible rescheduling between the baselines. It also helps us sort the story cards, which are on a finer-grained level.

Who	Does What With Whom/What	What For	How to Check
Paul Bahr	Implementation of new tool construction	Preparation of tool construction review	E-mail to team and new tool construction available to team
Paul Bahr, Richard Simon, Daniela Mohn	Review of new tool construction	Refactoring of new tool construction	Review documentation available to team
Daniela Mohn, Paul Bahr	Refactoring of new tool construction	Modification of existing tools based on old tool construction	E-mail to team and refactored tool construction package available to team
Andrea Kuhl, Richard Simon	Refactoring and adaption of existing tools based on old tool construction	Test of complete framework and all existing examples	All existing tools are running with new tool construction

FIGURE 7.3 Example of baselines

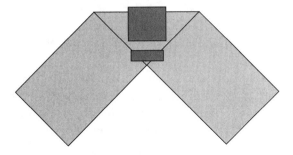

FIGURE 7.4 Conventional environment

Pair Programming

Pair programming has improved the quality (ease of use, simplicity, correctness) of the framework and has helped spread the knowledge about the JWAM framework over the team.

The physical environment is crucial. We started with a conventional setting consisting of desks with fixed cabinets at their sides (see Figure 7.4).

It was possible to program in pairs, but the switching of roles was very uncomfortable: We had to get up and change places. Therefore, we switched roles only a few times per day. After a while, we rearranged the furniture and arrived at an environment that facilitates the switching of roles (see Figure 7.5).

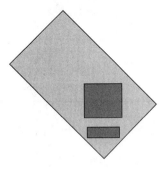

FIGURE 7.5 Rearranged environment for better role switching

With the new environment it is much easier to switch roles, and we do it frequently. But we think that a table with a circle at one end would be a further improvement (see Figure 7.6). We will test it in the near future.

Typing speed is important when programming in pairs. Whenever you have to wait for your buddy, due to his poor typing skills, you tend to become impatient. Then you will simply take over the keyboard, and you don't want to switch again. This is a general lesson: If there are two developers with similar skills, pair programming is rather smooth. If one developer is much faster and has to explain a lot of things to the other one, he or she has to be a patient person. Nevertheless, pair programming is efficient for "training on the job." After all, we can say that patience is worth it.

We have noticed that the role switching doesn't happen as often as it should according to [Beck2000]. This is no problem, and we think we know the reason behind this: Every story card is discussed by the framework team before it is realized by a pair. The discussion is not detailed enough to write the exact code for a card, but it clarifies the design of the potential solution. Therefore, both buddies have a clear vision of the solution, and each one is able to write it down. As a consequence, each buddy can write large sections of code without being interrupted or corrected by the partner. Keyboard switching in a pair occurs at natural breaks during programming. The term "natural" means interruptions intended by the buddy holding the keyboard.

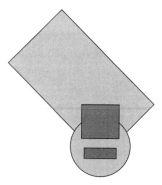

FIGURE 7.6 "Circle table" for pair programming

Test Cases

With pair programming we have improved framework quality; with test cases we maintain it. Without the test cases a lot of the refactoring we did in the past would have been less smooth.

Another side effect of test cases is simplicity. Since it is much easier to test a simple interface, nobody will program a class with a complex interface if it isn't necessary. Therefore, new framework interfaces and classes are quite simple.

We were used to designing by contracts (with pre- and postconditions [Meyer1997]) from the beginning of the JWAM development. We have found that test cases and contracts are complementary. Since the contracts are tested on executing an operation, we need not test primitive operations in detail. Often it is sufficient simply to call an operation. On the other hand, the contract model has its weakness: A contract is based on the concept of abstract data types (ADTs). ADTs not only have pre- and postconditions but also axioms. But only a very small number of the axioms can be expressed by invariants or postconditions because it is often necessary to call operations with side effects for realizing axioms. Since calling such operations in pre- and postconditions or invariants is not allowed, it is impossible to express them. But test cases can easily be used to express axioms. The way from an ADT definition via an interface declaration to a test case implementation is shown in the following code.

```
ADT Stack [T] -- Stack for items of type T
Types
  Stack, T
Operations
  New → Stack
  Pop (Stack) → Stack
  Top (Stack) → T
  Push (Stack, T) → Stack
  Empty (Stack) → Boolean
  Full (Stack) → Boolean
Preconditions
  Pop(Stack): not Empty(Stack)
  Top(Stack): not Empty(Stack)
  Push (Stack, T): not Full(Stack)
Axioms
  Empty(New)
  Pop(Push(s, t)) = s
  Top(Push(s, t)) = t
  Not Full(Pop(s))
```

```
interface Stack
{
  public Stack ();
    // ensure empty()
  public void pop ();
    // require !empty()
    // ensure !full()
  public Object top ();
    // require !empty()
    // ensure result != null
  public void push (Object o);
    // require o != null && !full()
    // ensure !empty()
  public boolean empty ();
  public boolean full ();
}


public class Stack_Test
{
  public void testNew ()
  {
    assert(_stack.empty());
  }
  public void testPushPop ()
  {
    Stack oldStack = _stack.clone();
    _stack.push(new AClass());
    _stack.pop();
    assertEquals(_stack, oldStack);
  }
  public void testPushTop ()
  {
    Object obj = new AClass();
    _stack.push(obj);
    assert(_stack.top() == obj);
  }
  public void testPush ()
  {
    _stack.push(new AClass ());
    assert(!_stack.empty());
  }
  public void testPop ()
  {
    _stack.push(new AClass ());
    _stack.pop();
    assert(!_stack.full());
  }
```

```
protected void setUp ()
{
  _stack = new StackImpl(); // StackImpl implements Stack
}
}
```

At first we reflected the inheritance hierarchy of the framework in the inheritance hierarchy of the test cases. Thus, we could easily reuse test cases and avoid semantic shifts in subclasses. That has proved to be very useful for framework-based application development. The programmer lets his application inherit from a framework class and programs a test case that inherits from the framework test case. Then, the test case will ensure that the axioms of the framework class still hold for the application class. But the approach has its drawbacks for Java interfaces. A Java class extends exactly one class but can implement a number of interfaces. Since interfaces lead to interface test classes, we would need multiple inheritance for the test classes. Since Java only supports single inheritance, we now use delegation between test classes to reflect inheritance and interface implementation. An example is shown in Figure 7.7.

We don't write negative tests for pre- and postconditions. Otherwise, we couldn't reuse our tests for subclasses. Since subclasses are allowed to weaken preconditions and restrict postconditions, our test cases probably wouldn't run for subclasses.

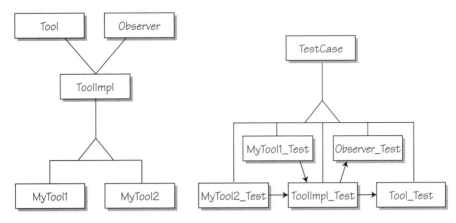

FIGURE 7.7 Use delegation between test classes to reflect inheritence between the operational classes

We currently use JUnit [JUnit1999] for testing, but we have modified it in a way that now all test methods of a test case are run, not just the declared ones. This improvement enables the usage of template test methods inside superclasses. We can define a test class for the superclass inside the framework, and we would like the subclass to be tested against this predefined test case, which may be filled by template methods. A second improvement allows us to reflect multiple interface implementation by delegation between the test classes.

We ship the test cases together with the framework to application developers for two reasons: First, the test cases will serve as a documentation of the intended use of the framework. Second, the test cases can be used by the application developers to locate errors. During framework-based application development, it is often difficult to find out whether a problem is located in the framework or in the application code. With the test cases at hand, the application developer can extend and modify them. If he detects an error in the framework, he simply can send the extended test case, which we will use to correct the framework class. A general rule is: If an error is detected in the framework, we first extend the test case so that the test signals the error. Then we correct the framework class.

Project Culture

We feel that the success of XP is highly dependent on project culture. We had two main proponents of XP on the framework team. They urged the team to be "extreme" all the time and not to fall back to their former behavior. This was not an easy task, but we think that we now (after a year) have an XP project culture that will stay without continuous intervention.

Continuous Integration

We use an integration computer that keeps the last integrated version and the last version released of the framework. The developers have work copies of the framework on their development machines. If the framework needs to be modified, the local working version is modified. Then the modified classes are copied to the integration computer. Integration is done on the integration computer, and the new version is announced to all framework developers. An integration is valid only if all test cases run through. If a new release has to be finished, the integrated version is copied to become the release version. We run the same tests for the release version as for the integration version, plus some additional ones.

We profit from the benefits explained in [Beck2000], but we also recognize that the integration process needs more and more time. The reason for this unacceptable effort is the size of the project. The framework consists of more than 850 classes, and we need to compile the whole framework for the integration to ensure the right compilation state of all classes. In addition, we need to test all examples of the framework. They cannot be tested automatically because of their interactive structure. But the only way to ensure the correctness of the integrated code and the whole framework after the integration is to test all examples. Our experience is that a normal integration needs approximately one hour. If you want short development cycles with continuous integration, this amount of time is too much. We have no concrete solution for this problem, but we try to shorten the time spent on each integration. One step toward this would be the automation of interactive tests, especially for the framework examples.

Application Migration

We are very aggressive with refactoring. This results in quite large modifications of the framework from one version to the next. Applications based on the framework have to migrate to the new framework version. This may result in rather high efforts for the application development team. As the number of framework users grows, this is not acceptable. Therefore, we currently work on a tool set to support the migration of application code. But in this chapter we do not focus on these topics. Take a look at Chaper 5 for a detailed discussion.

Conclusion

The XP techniques are useful for framework development. This is not an obvious result, because some people argue that framework development itself stands in contrast to Extreme Programming. They argue that the very idea of frameworks contradicts the simple design guideline of XP. We don't think that this is true. We use the framework as a reification of our experience. It gives us the possibility of training people by using the framework. Therefore, we do not insist on the design of the framework being the right one forever, and we try to keep the framework as simple as possible. We've described why and how we adapted XP techniques for our framework development. In using XP we have observed the following advantages:

✧ Higher quality of design and code of the framework
✧ Fewer errors in the framework
✧ Simpler design of the framework and therefore an improved understanding of the framework
✧ Reduced size of the framework (from 400 to 100 operational classes/interfaces)

But some open issues remain.

✧ How can we do continuous refactoring of the framework without disturbing our customers too much?
✧ It proved to be a good practice to introduce new concepts or technologies in applications first, before adding them to the framework (don't develop in stock). On the other hand, the framework needs to provide leading-edge concepts to remain competitive. Therefore, we sometimes need to introduce concepts that were tested only in prototypes. It is not clear what is best to do in these cases.

References

[Beck2000] K. Beck. *Extreme Programming Explained*. Addison-Wesley, 2000.

[Firesmith1996] D. G. Firesmith. "Object-Oriented Regression Testing." In *Wisdom of the Gurus*. C. F. Bowman, ed. SIGS, 1996.

[Fowler+1999] M. Fowler, K. Beck, J. Brant, W. Opdyke, D. Roberts. *Refactoring: Improving the Design of Existing Code*. Addison-Wesley, 1999.

[JUnit1999] K. Beck, E. Gamma. *JUnit*. On-line at http://www.junit.org. 1999.

[JWAM] *The JWAM Framework*. On-line at http://www.jwam.de.

[Meyer1997] B. Meyer. *Object-Oriented Software Construction*, Second edition. Prentice Hall, 1997.

[Opdyke1992] W. F. Opdyke. "Refactoring Object-Oriented Frameworks." Ph.D. diss. University of Illinois at Urbana-Champaign, 1992.

[Riehle+1995] D. Riehle, H. Züllighoven. "A Pattern Language for Tool Construction and Integration Based on the Tools and Materials Metaphor." In *Pattern Languages of Program Design*. J. O. Coplien, D. C. Schmidt, eds. Addison-Wesley, 1995.

[Züllighoven1998] H. Züllighoven. *Das objektorientierte Konstruktionshandbuch nach dem Werkzeug- und Materialansatz*. dpunkt-Verlag, 1998. German.

About the Authors

The authors are at the University of Hamburg, Computer Science Department, Software Engineering Group and APCON Workplace Solutions Company. They can be reached at {lippert, roock, wolf, zuelligh}@jwam.de.

Chapter 8

XP and Large Distributed Software Projects

—Even-André Karlsson and Lars-Göran Andersson

XP ideas have mainly been used in small colocated projects. Within Ericsson's GSM division, however, projects are both large and distributed. In this chapter we discuss some experience that we have had on applying ideas related to XP—such as daily builds, frequent iterations, planning increments based on customer value, and automatic testing—to this type of project. We discuss how our approach relates to the original XP ideas. Furthermore we suggest some additional practices that we have found useful in this context. We also discuss how the aspects of XP that we have not tried could be used, and what effect they would have.

Introduction

Extreme Programming (XP) was conceived and developed to address the specific needs of software development conducted in small teams in the face of vague and changing requirements [Beck2000]. It is a lightweight methodology challenging many conventional assumptions.

Ericsson's GSM division is the market leader within the GSM infrastructure market. Telecom systems are some of the largest and most complex software systems that are built today. It is not uncommon to have projects of up to 1 million person hours. Ericsson's development is also very distributed, with several design centers involved in developing different parts of the same product. Traditionally Ericsson's development process is very document focused; coding is usually not more than 10 percent to 15 percent of the overall effort.

However, the telecom market is changing rapidly with deregulation and the merging of the telecom, datacom, and mobile device (mobile phones, laptops, palm pilots, etc.) markets. In this context there is a need to shorten project lead times and better handle changing requirements. Ericsson's GSM division has conducted an improvement program, World Class Provisioning, over the last two years to secure and further strengthen Ericsson's market position. The work reported in this chapter is done within this program.

The rest of the chapter is organized as follows:

✧ An overview of the starting point for this improvement initiative, that is, daily build and incremental development

✧ The challenges of implementing daily build and automatic testing in this environment

✧ The necessary changes in the organization of design to take advantage of this infrastructure for large distributed projects

✧ The advantages and risks of these changes on the development organization

✧ The relationship between this work and the original XP ideas, specifically our experience in large and distributed projects and how the ideas in XP that we have not adapted could impact our development

This chapter mainly discusses the challenges faced in a large distributed environment when the development changes focus from components to features with daily build. These changes are, in our view, a prerequisite for scaling up the ideas of XP beyond one colocated team.

For commercial reasons, we do not disclose any facts or measurements from real projects, but all information discussed in this chapter has been implemented in several large multisite projects over the last two years. One example of experience from concluded projects is that the hit rate for test cases—test cases finding faults—has increased from 5 percent and 7 percent to 31 percent with feature-based testing. At the same time the fault density in product line test following feature test has decreased to 33 percent of the previous level. This shows that the feature teams are testing much more efficiently than traditional testing.

Daily Build and Incremental Development

Daily build is a software development paradigm that originated in the PC industry to get control of the development process, while still allowing the focus on end user requirements and code. A prime example of this is Microsoft [Cusumano1998], where a buddy pair of designer and tester is responsible for implementing a customer feature. The designer will check out and update all modules that are needed for the feature in parallel with other designers responsible for other features. The daily build is used to allow designers to fast-check the updated modules into the main code line to avoid large merge conflicts from parallel checkouts. The designer checking in changes first is the lucky one, as it is up to the designer checking in later to take care of any merge conflicts.

The PC industry has used daily build to avoid chaos in increasingly larger applications in an environment without a strong development process. Ericsson Radio Systems has chosen to implement daily build to increase the focus on end-user requirements and code, but from a different starting point with a traditionally strong development process. In this process the control of the code has been through detailed design documents, and code work has been focused on designers implementing one module each. One module could be impacted by several features, and one feature could impact several modules. Thus the code control mechanism in this process has been the thorough detailed design. Daily build is an orthogonal control mechanism, which to some extent is in conflict with designers responsible for separate modules. In this chapter we discuss our experiences with daily build in this environment.

The guiding principle also includes incremental development. It is therefore important to clearly define what we mean as the difference between these two concepts. Incremental development is the delivery of the total functionality in stages with a well-defined subset of the functionality in each stage. These subsets are planned on the project level. The frequency of increments can be rather different, down to one week for smaller projects.

Daily build is the team- or individual-controlled delivery of code to a main code line, which is built and tested daily. The functionality of the delivered code is completely controlled and used by the team or individual. The daily test only covers the functionality that existed in the system at the last stable baseline.

As we see from this, the main differences between daily build and incremental development are:

✦ Who controls and defines the deliveries
✦ The frequency

Daily build can be divided into three main components:

✦ Build
✦ Test
✦ Impacts on design

Build and Test

One of the components of daily build is the ability to build the system on a daily basis. This means that:

1. Designers must know where to put their code.
2. The code must be consistent; that is, interfaces (signal descriptions) must match bodies (blocks), and so on.
3. We must be able to compile the code in less than 24 hours.
4. The code and all other software needed must be loaded into the hardware.

We will discuss the impact of the second and fourth requirements on the system (the other two are self-evident), but first we discuss what we mean by the system and hardware in this context.

Ericsson is developing all components of a GSM network out to the mobile phone: the switch (either traditional circuit-switched AXE 10 or packet-switched GPRS/UMTS), base station controllers, and base stations, as well as the Management System. We could regard the system to be built as a complete GSM system, loaded into a GSM network. The system could also be each node in the GSM network, such as a base station controller. These nodes have standardized interfaces and are usually developed by separate product units. There are usually standardized products for testing the protocols between the nodes. The node is the level of system where we have currently focused the daily build activity, but ideally we should envision a daily build on a complete GSM network. We could also go into each of the nodes and look at separate subsystems as the system to be built. In this case the hardware has to be a simulator able to simulate the interfaces to the other subsystems. Doing a daily build on a lower level than system means that we lose many of the advantages, such as that the consistency check will be local.

Consistent code means that all impacts for a specific part of an end user functionality need to be in place at the same time. That is, if two modules interact to do something, the implementations of this interaction must be checked in at the same time. Take as an example a functionality that needs a new parameter in a function (signal). Both the caller and the called module have to implement the additional parameter at the same time. To achieve this efficiently both impacts should be implemented by the same individual or team; otherwise the amount of communications between teams to coordinate what to check in and when will be too high.

Loading the software into the hardware is not a trivial task in a telecom system for several reasons. First there exists a lot of data in the system—subscriber data, cell layout, and so on—which also needs to be loaded. There are two alternatives for this loading: either a complete reload with code and data, or a so-called function change where only the changed modules are loaded together with data-change information (DCI) providing a mapping from the old data structures to the new. The function change can be done in two ways, either complete from the previous version or increment, or a partial from the last build. A partial is faster but puts an extra burden on the designers, because they have to provide intermediate DCIs, as well as the final one, which the customer needs to upgrade the software during operation. The full DCI is slower because more modules must be loaded, but it is better from a end-user test perspective, because we test the final DCI all the time.

The second problem with loading is the amount of sourced software in particular in the Management System, which makes the loading of a system a rather complex task needing a lot of manual intervention. This must now be automated, but this is also for the better for the real installation, because it makes that task easier.

- -

Generally, on the build part we have encountered several technical barriers, none of which has been impossible to overcome, and we are able to build most systems in well under 24 hours, even if some still need up to a couple of days for a complete build from scratch. Being able to build the system quickly and efficiently is also an advantage for the development, independent of how often the build is performed.

Automatic testing is the second part of daily build, because it is of little use to be able to build a system on a daily basis if we can't ensure that it has a certain level of quality. The idea of the daily test is to ensure that nothing of the existing functionality in the system is broken, such as a regression test. This test has to be automatic because the amount of effort needed to do the tests manually every day is prohibitive. The test can include:

✧ The functionality level of the last increment
✧ The functionality level of the last successful build

The latter alternative makes it possible for teams to include test cases to safeguard their functionality in the test. Thus as soon as they have done their own test of the last build to ensure that it has the required functionality, passed test cases can be included in the automatic test. These test cases ensure that any future changes destroying their added functionality will be detected.

As discussed for build, the tests have to be on the level of the build: network, node, or subsystem. If the build fails, either during build or test, we are quite sure that it can be traced back to the last check-in, and those who have contributed to this check-in should be the ones to fix the problem. For further testing when the problems are fixed we still have the previous successful build. The teams will get the tested software back and can check to see whether their newly implemented functionality is working.

Since breaking the build is a rather serious matter, teams should be able to do part of the build and test steps in a private environment before submitting it to the main code line and a system build. Whether this private activity is cost effective has to be judged for each system, because it is not reasonable to do the same things twice. We recommend that each team do a code review, compile, and some form of module test before submitting the code. All regression testing of old functionality is done centrally. If we overemphasize the seriousness of breaking the build, we will get a lot of double work in testing; if we underemphasize, it will not get enough successful builds.

Usually function/system test activity of the previous increment is going on in parallel with the daily build activity of the current increment. We have two alternatives here:

- ✧ We can freeze the code line at the delivery of the increment, letting the function/system test proceed in a stable environment.
- ✧ We can let the function/system test use the same code line as the daily build.

The disadvantage of using a frozen code line is that we must maintain two branches: serious errors must be corrected both for the frozen code line and for the daily build code line. Using the same code line means that the function/system test will execute in a less stable environment, and we can never be sure whether a fault comes from something delivered in the last increment or last build. Similarly, test cases that passed earlier may now fail because of new, erroneous code in the latest build that was not detected by the automatic test. However, if we can include all passed test cases in the automatic test run daily, we can ensure some quality here. Even if the function/system test is executed in a more unstable environment, faults will be detected earlier.

If the number of test cases becomes too big to be run every day, we can alternate test cases so that all test cases are run at least once a week. If we have several hardware platforms, we can run the test cases alternatively on different platforms to get a full coverage. This scheme is used by Sybase to test its database software on all possible platforms.

Previously there has been rather limited incentive for automatic testing, as most test cases are run only once and the amount of regression test has been limited. In a daily build environment this is changing radically and automatic testing is a prerequisite. As for implementing a fast enough build support, the implementation of sufficient level of automatic testing is to a large degree a technical problem; that is, getting the right tool environment. However, for telecom systems, most of the software, such as protocol testers and emulators are in place to perform automated test cases. The challenge is to start writing tests so they can be automatically executed. Automatic testing is also an improvement that can be of use even with less frequent builds.

Design Impact of Daily Build

Up to now we have discussed the technical requirements of a daily build: fast build and automatic testing. To have any use of daily build design has to deliver code with some frequency—otherwise there is nothing to build. This code also has to be consistent so that it can be built. Note that there is no requirement on any functional content, because the new code is not executed by the automatic tests but for the team to use.

There are two main connected impacts on design of daily build: the organization of responsibility and the development process.

Organization of Design

Generally there are two ways of organizing design: based on end-user functionality, where one team is responsible for a customer feature, and based on system modules, where a team or individual is responsible for one or several modules and implements impacts from all features in these modules. With customer feature responsibility the team will implement changes in all modules necessary to get the end-user feature to work, possibly in parallel with other teams implementing impacts from other features in some of the same modules. These two ways of organizing design are not mutually exclusive—for example, we can have an organization with predominantly customer feature responsibility, but where some central modules are the responsibility of a separate team. In this case each module team has to coordinate when to implement the changes with all feature teams that need that module.

Daily build can only be fully implemented in an organization with predominantly customer feature design responsibility. Note that this responsibility has to extend to the system level at which we want to implement daily build, such as network, node, or subsystem. The reasons why feature responsibility is a prerequisite for taking advantage of daily build is the amount of coordination and planning needed between those responsible for delivering consistent parts of each module that can be built. That is, every module designer has, potentially, several features impacting his or her module, and each feature in turn impacts many other modules. In a feature team this coordination is handled within the team. However when concurrent updates of the module by different teams present a conflict, frequent build and automatic testing is a prerequisite for implementing feature teams, to ensure that what is checked in has the appropriate quality—that it has been appropriately merged with what was previously checked in.

The feature team can take either of two approaches to handling multiple impacts on the same module, either opportunistic or planned. Opportunistic handling means that anyone can check out a module and work on it in parallel with anyone else. The first to check in a change does not have to do any merging; all changes later have to merge with all who have worked in parallel and checked in before. This aspect of opportunistic handling is a big incentive for making small changes to the modules and checking them in frequently, thus serving as the engine of daily build. Planned handling means that each feature team has an allocated time window when they can work alone with the module. This window can be planned centrally or decentralized by the involved feature teams.

Note that even having several feature teams doing work in the same modules does not mean that we need to give up the idea of module responsibility. On the contrary this role becomes even more important in a feature team organization. The role changes from someone who does all the work in a module, to someone who is guiding, checking, and approving solutions and implementations proposed by each feature team. Of course the module responsibility should rest with the feature team that has the biggest or most complex impact on the module.

Development Process

The development process is also impacted by daily build. When we use a traditional waterfall development model, there is no code to be built until very late in the project, which means we lose most of the advantages of daily build. To get full advantage of daily build we have to split the development into smaller iterations, where each iteration is taken to executable code. This means that we must adapt the amount of design documentation to the iterative way of developing software.

One interesting aspect of design documentation is that it has two purposes: to support maintenance and enhancements of the system, and to serve as input to the next stage of the development process. For maintenance we usually need less documentation than for development, because for maintenance the design information need only be on an overview level—additional details appear in the code. For development, we need detailed design information as input to later stages, so the additional details must appear in the high-level design documentation to support the later stages. This need for detailed design documents is increased and enforced by the long time to coding in a waterfall project as well as the use of module responsibility, meaning that someone else will do the coding. The module designer is going to implement the impacts in the modules only from the design and has limited time to understand each individual feature or communicate with different feature designers. Working in feature teams using smaller iterations will allow us to put the information directly where it belongs. It is thus natural that the development process is adapted if we use feature teams and daily build, with a higher focus on code. We can start the coding of parts that don't need thorough design early, interleaved with design and possibly analysis of more complex parts. Information is put directly into the level of documentation where it belongs, based on maintenance needs. This iterative approach should not be driven too far. The team should plan how the feature should be developed in different increments; but this plan should be local to each team, maybe coordinated with other teams for access to common modules. Note that the daily build will enforce that there is such a feature plan; otherwise the code developed will be inconsistent and break the build.

In some approaches to daily build a feature team has a private branch of the code during the complete development of a feature and only checks in at the end. This is not recommended because it usually leads to major merging problems when several features are checked in toward the end. This could be solved with a detailed planning of the impacts of different module, avoiding the merge. This is rather difficult because planning must be on a central level, putting stress on the planner when there are changes in requirements or how long things take.

Another aspect of parallel design is the need to be able to merge different work products easily. This is usually supported at the syntactic level of ASCII files (e.g., code), but is less well supported for higher-level documentation, such as word processors (Word or FrameMaker) and design tools (e.g., Rational Rose). Some of these have merge facilities, but nothing that supports parallel work well.

Testing is also impacted by daily build in that, traditionally, there are several different test phases, such as basic, simulated, function, and system. The practice has been to include as much as possible in the earlier test phases, because it is more expensive to discover an error in a later test phase and the feedback takes longer. The disadvantage of using these test phases is a lot of overlap—that is, the same functionality is tested several times—and a long lead time. With daily build and automatic testing this assumption is not necessarily valid any more, because we can do any sort of test after the daily build. Thus a feature team should test the functionality where it is most efficient, and only once.

The Impacts of Daily Build, Iterative Development, Automatic Testing, and Feature-Oriented Development

We divide these impacts into two groups, one concerning the advantages of frequent build and automatic testing of the system, the other on organizing design in features teams to deliver frequently. We also discuss some pitfalls of reorganizing design to take advantage of daily build.

Frequent Builds and Automatic Testing

The major advantages of being able to build and test the system daily are as follows.

✧ We always have an executable system; even if the current build fails we can go back to the last stable one.

✧ Teams can always integrate their code into a running system and test it on a system level.

✧ We see progress very clearly, not only document status but real executable code. If a team has not delivered any code for a long time, we know we should investigate.

✧ We can get early and continuous quality feedback. Thus if a team is delivering substandard code this will be immediately discovered and can be fixed before the damage is too great.

✧ Faults are detected soon after they are introduced. This pertains not only to local faults but also to global system faults and interference with old functionality. Without daily build these types of faults are usually discovered later.

✧ It is easy to isolate errors, because in most cases they come from the new code in the current build, and the teams delivering this code should be able to fix the errors.

- System test can proceed in parallel with development, thus reducing the time needed for system testing at the end.
- When only one main branch is used for development and system testing, the need for parallel code updates disappears.

Feature Teams

The major advantages of using feature teams are as follows:

- The feature team has a focus on end-user functionality and code. They have full responsibility for implementing the feature and use the existing modules as means to achieve this functionality.
- Changes can be absorbed more easily by the feature team. That is, both external requirements changes and changes in the design can be handled within the team, without impacting other teams. Because most changes pertain to a specific feature, this is one of the major advantages of feature teams. With module responsibility a feature change has to be analyzed on a central level and distributed to each affected module. If there are changes in the design of one module for a feature and this impacts the work load for the module responsible other features may need to be rescheduled leading to more module responsibles being impacted. This is one of the effects we see when projects are doing frequent (down to weekly) centrally planned increments with module responsibility—the plans get very sensitive to both external and internal changes, and the work load on the architects and planners is very high.
- Associated projects are coordinated. Usually an associated system is required because of a feature. If the interaction to the associated system is through a module that is impacted by many features, the module responsible will not be able to fully understand the reason for each requirement and cannot efficiently communicate with the associated system. This leads to inefficient coordination if we don't use feature teams, which are responsible for both the feature and the impacts in the interface module and can make efficient tradeoffs with the associated system.
- Interface is coordinated. Usually changes in interfaces between modules are due to new features that need extended interaction.

When we use feature teams the interfaces are handled within the team; when we use module responsibility the interfaces have to be settled before each module is implemented to allow parallel work. This is usually an impossible task, leading to time-consuming coordination, rework, and integration problems.

There are also disadvantages to using feature teams. The major disadvantages are the potential degeneration of each module and interface. This is a real problem, which we propose to solve with a module coordinator who approves and checks what each feature team implements in the module.

The focus on early code can lead to a badly structured feature design requiring that later increments redo coding. To avoid this we need a certain level of analysis and planning for the development of the feature in increments by the feature team. Another constraint is distributed development organization when different sites are cooperating on a project. This means that either we have to have people from different sites on the same team or we must move modules between different sites. In either case this involves travel and computer-supported cooperative work tools, such as efficient configuration management and teleconferencing equipment.

Relation to XP Practices

In this section we discuss our work in relation to the original XP practices [Beck2000]

Planning is well covered already in our XP practices. Currently we do the planning on two levels. First we assign features to different increments of a release. There is constant communication between product management (business) and project management (technical and resources) on what can be included at which feature level. Then each team is assigned responsibility for the planning and development of each feature. Thus requirements are handled on two levels: Product management and the project management decide which features are in, and the feature team together with the product management representative decides the content of each feature. The detailed content is defined in requirement specifications. The nature of these systems, which are governed by international standards, means that the requirements are not that unstable; it is more a question of which features are the most profitable and the ambition level within each feature.

Our experience with other XP practices has been as follows:

◇ The small releases practice is not simple, as the rollout of new telecom software into a network is a rather complex process, but we are reducing the period between customer deliveries from 12 months to 3 to 4 months.

◇ The metaphor is a less-established practice, because we still have a lot of very detailed high-level documentation, and actually sometimes lack the 10,000-foot view.

◇ The simple design practice is not done well. We still tend to use far too much time up front to develop the full design on paper. However, we believe that as we get more experienced this will start to change.

◇ Automatic testing is starting up. We are discussing the need for basic tests to cover all functionality, such as whether an automatic system-level test that covers several basic test cases in different modules could eliminate the need for basic test cases. With the feature teams we also solve the problem, mentioned by Beck [Beck2000], of how to synchronize the function tests with design, because the feature team takes care of both development and testing. The concept of writing (basic) test cases first is not practiced to any large extent yet. However, user test cases are written before the code, and we are also discussing letting the test cases take over more of the functional specifications.

◇ Refactoring is also a practice that we have not used in the XP way. We do restructurings of our system, but these are usually large and traumatic experiences.

◇ We do not use pair programming as described in XP. This will be one of the practices that we need to put in place when we want to reduce the amount of high-level documentation and up-front design even further than what can be achieved with a feature team. Combining pair programming with module architects/ coordinators is interesting in that there should always be a module coordinator in the pair when complex things are done with a module. This would be a good way to ensure consistency and competence transferance in a large system.

- Feature teams introduce collective ownership because the feature team impacts all modules necessary for the feature.
- Continuous integration is implemented through daily build. Note that we have this mechanism on two levels, one for the feature team itself on a private branch and one for the complete system. The reason for keeping these two branches separate is to reduce the impact of any errors.
- The 40-hour week is not practiced as described in XP. However, because Ericsson is a European company, there is a higher adherence to normal working hours. That is, the normal Swedish working week is 40 hours, and overtime is paid for most technical staff or compensated for with paid time off.
- Having an on-site customer is not trivial, because Ericsson is developing products for the open market. We do, however, have a product management (internal customer) representative in each feature team.
- Coding standards are already quite well implemented in Ericsson. We have a thorough code review process, called desk check. The desk check could, with the introduction of pair programming, be reduced.

In summary we have started to apply some of the principles of XP. Our major contribution to the XP practices might be the focus on feature teams and the introduction of the module architect role to allow the other practices to scale up.

Our experiences so far have been largely positive, but it is definitely a challenge to introduce these types of changes to such a large, distributed organization. The cultural challenges have not been major, as the Ericsson culture, although international, is rather homogenous due to a standardized way of working on a large system. Sites have reacted to these changes differently, based on their technical position in the system. For instance, those who have had responsibility for a complex central part of the system have been more reluctant to allow others to code their parts than those who have been responsible for subsystems closer to the customer.

References

[Beck2000] K. Beck. *Extreme Programming Explained*. Addison-Wesley, 2000.

[Cusumano+1998] M. A. Cusumano and R. W. Selby. *Microsoft Secrets: How the World's Most Powerful Software Company Creates Technology, Shapes Markets, and Manages People*. Simon & Schuster, 1998.

About the Authors

Even-André Karlsson can be reached at Q-Labs, Ideon, S-22 370 Lund; Even-Andre.Karlsson@q-labs.se. Lars-Göran Andersson can be reached at Ericsson Radio Systems AB, S-164 80 Stockholm, Sweden; Lars-Goran.Andersson@era.ericsson.se.

Part 3

Flexible Techniques
and UML

Chapter 9

XP Inside the Trojan Horse: Refactoring the Unified Software Development Process

—*Jutta Eckstein and Rolf F. Katzenberger*

The standardization of UML and maybe soon of the Unified Software Development Process (USDP) leads to a high acceptance of approaches employing them both. Often a project would progress faster by using a more lightweight process like Extreme Programming (XP). But since XP is not widely enough accepted, people are looking for a way to introduce XP without mentioning the name of the process at the beginning. In fact, naming is just one concern. Another is how to make XP appear to be USDP without being trapped by the heavier process.

We want to show that, despite all differences, XP and the USDP have much more in common than is commonly assumed. We want to show a bridge between those processes. They provide several commonalities, mainly the following:

- *The people who live inside the process are dominant for the process, or the other way round: If the process is not accepted by the people it cannot be used for the project.*
- *USDP as well as XP regard the use cases (or user stories) of the system as the base unit. The realization of the use cases form the contents of a release. The use cases are used to verify that the goals of the system are met.*
- *Both processes employ incremental and iterative development, where both believe that it is important to keep the cycles really small.*

This chapter shows, that if a team is forced to follow the USDP, but would like to use a lighter process like XP, it can do so. The USDP provides a framework in which XP can live.

Introduction

The standardization of UML and maybe soon of the Unified Software Development Process (USDP) leads to a high acceptance of approaches employing them both. Some projects might progress faster by using a more lightweight process like Extreme Programming (XP). Unfortunately, since XP is not yet widely enough accepted, many people are looking for a way to benefit from XP without actually mentioning that name at the beginning. In fact, naming is just one concern. Another is how to make XP appear to be USDP without getting trapped in a heavier process. This chapter discusses whether XP could be considered an implementation of the USDP framework.

The Trojan Horse

Paris, the son of King Priam of Troy, took beautiful Helen to Troy. Unfortunately, at that time, Helen was the wife of Menelaus, the king of Sparta. To bring Helen back, Menelaus gathered an army of Greeks and launched an expedition against Troy.

For nearly 10 years, the Greeks were unable to capture Troy. In the end, they resorted to a trick: a mighty, hollow wooden horse was built. Inside, Greek soldiers were hiding. The Greek fleet sailed a short distance away from Troy. Sinon, himself a Greek, was left before the gates of Troy and managed to convince the Trojans that he had left the Greek army in anger. He said the horse was an offering to the goddess Athena; therefore taking the horse into the city would make Troy invulnerable. Despite urgent warnings, the Trojans broke down parts of the city wall and dragged the horse inside. Later that night, the Greek soldiers left the horse and overwhelmed the Trojans. Since that time, the term "Trojan Horse" has been a synonym for a gift that is not quite what it seems.

Motivation

One size does not fit all. The ongoing debate about software development processes sometimes seems to neglect this insight. But what can customers and developers do when they are trapped in what they perceive to be the wrong process for their purposes? We want to show that, despite all differences, XP and the USDP have much more in common than is commonly assumed. We want to show a bridge between those processes. Although we have only investigated how one can cross it from the banks of USDP to XP, it should be possible to cross in the opposite direction, too.

We are not interested in how any reconciliation of those two processes should be named. We are prepared to accept that following our suggestions might not result in XP. It might not result in USDP either. We hope it results in something that suits the needs of the people involved in the process they have tailored.

Before we start, here is one caveat: Although USDP is often used as a synonym for the Rational Unified Process (RUP) [Kruchten1998], they are not the same. The RUP is a commercial product that is much more specific than USDP, especially when it comes to configuration management and tool usage. There is considerable overlapping between USDP and RUP, but we have chosen USDP because it is a framework that is closer to the level of abstraction of XP than RUP is.

A Short Glance at the Horse

USDP is designed to be a *use case driven, architecture-centric* software development process that proceeds in iterations, incrementally producing results by exercising workflows.

Phases and Workflows

Figure 9.1 [Jacobson+1999] shows the four phases of the USDP, as well as its five core workflows.

Phases are defined as the *timespans between each two milestones of a development process.* As Jacobson writes:

> *The four phases constitute a development cycle and produce a software generation. A software product is created in an initial development cycle. Unless the life of the product stops at this point, an existing product will evolve into its next generation by a repetition of the same sequence of inception, elaboration, construction, and transition phases, but with a different emphasis on the various phases. Cycles can be triggered by various ways. In practice, cycles may overlap slightly: The inception and elaboration phase may begin during the final part of the transition phase of the previous cycle* [Jacobson+1999].

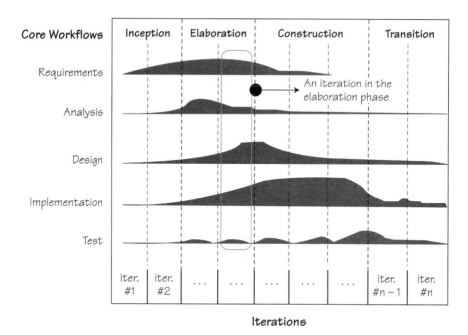

FIGURE 9.1 Phases and workflows of USDP

All phases of a development cycle consist of at least one iteration, and each iteration terminates successfully (we hope), at a milestone.

During the *inception* phase, a vision of the end product is developed, and the business case for the product is presented. The *elaboration* phase is devoted to specifying most of the use cases of the product and designing the system architecture. *Construction* means transforming the results produced during former phases into a product that can, in principle, be handed over to the user community. Since the architecture should be stable after elaboration, there are no large-scale changes expected during construction. Last but not least, the *transition* phase is devoted to moving the product into beta release, correcting minor deficiencies, and finishing by-products like training materials and on-line help content.

USDP defines *workflows* as *realizations of (a part of) a business use case.* In the end, this means that so-called *workers* participate in a workflow, exerting *activities* and thereby producing *artifacts*. A workflow itself is *a sequence of activities that produces a result of observable value.* As we saw in Figure 9.1 the workflow for collecting requirements spreads well over three phases of the development cycle.

Let us take a closer look at the terms just mentioned.

- ✧ *Workers* are defined as positions that can be assigned to a person or a team, requiring responsibilities. Workers are not only individuals, they are individuals at a specific position. The individual designated as a worker must provide a set of skills and qualifications necessary at the intended position. It is important to distinguish between workers and roles. Roles are not positions, but the qualifications that are needed for taking a specific position.
- ✧ *Activities* are defined as units of work that imply well-defined responsibilities for the workers involved, yield a well-defined result (set of artifacts) based on a well-defined input (another set of artifacts), and are delimited by a boundary by which they can be referred to when tasks are assigned to individuals. The granularity of an activity is generally a few hours to a few days. It usually involves one worker and affects one or only a small number of artifacts. Activities may be repeated several times on the same artifact, especially from one iteration to another as the system is refined and expanded. Repeated activities may be performed by the same worker but not necessarily by the same individual.
- ✧ *Artifacts* are defined as tangible pieces of information that are created, changed, and used by workers when performing activities. Artifacts can be changed only through well-defined activities. The artifacts are the things the project produces or uses while moving forward. Artifacts are most likely to be subject to version control and configuration management.

The Anatomy of the Horse

Having sorted out the more technical aspects of USDP, let us now investigate what XP can bring to USDP. Both processes share much more than is commonly assumed.

The Base: Values

XP and USDP both refer to similar *values* for justifying what they propose. XP is supposed to be based on four values:

1. Communication
2. Feedback
3. Simplicity
4. Courage

Actually, these are derived values. Kent Beck [Beck2000] points out that there is "a deeper value, one that lies below the surface of the other four—respect. If members of the team do not care about each other and what they are doing, XP is doomed." Compare this to what Ivar Jacobson says about people taking part in software development:

> *People are crucial. People are involved in the development of a software product throughout its entire life cycle. They finance the product, schedule it, develop it, manage it, test it, use it, and benefit from it. Therefore, the process that guides this development must be people oriented, that is, one that works well for the people using it* [Jacobson+1999].

Seen from this perspective, both USDP and XP are based on values that intend to make a software development process respect the needs of the people who are expected to use it.

The Key Aspects of USDP

USDP is designed to be a *use case driven, architecture-centric* software development process that proceeds in iterations, incrementally producing results. What does this mean, and how is XP related to it?

Use Case Driven Development

Use cases describe how users of a system can achieve a goal (something of value for them) by interacting with that system [Cockburn1998]. Although use cases are typically described by textually listing the interactions between the users and the system, there is no formal standard that covers such textual specifications. The Unified Modeling Language (UML) just offers use case diagrams, which contain little more than ellipses named after their corresponding use cases, interconnected by a limited set of relationships. In addition, neither XP nor USDP insist on using any given templates for documenting use cases.

Essentially, nothing in USDP forbids us to write down use cases on simple index cards, as is common practice in XP. It can be said, however, that user stories in XP are less formal than the lists of interactions that are usually captured during projects that have adopted USDP.

According to both XP and USDP, use cases are then prioritized considering two factors:

1. Risk
2. Functionality (scope)

That is, the decision that use cases are to be realized next, is based on assumptions about how much of the desired functionality can be gained and how much risk can be extinguished in the next iteration. But whereas USDP simply delegates the task of prioritizing to a developer, XP establishes a planning game for the same purpose: Businesspeople—that is, customers—come up with the functionality they want to see implemented after the next iteration, and technical people—that is, developers—give estimates of the resulting costs and risks. The customer then picks up the use cases he wants to be implemented next, maybe dropping some others that have become less important meanwhile.

Should some use case be too large to be implemented straightforward, XP offers iteration planning to handle this by splitting up the use case into several implementation tasks. Developers are then free to accept responsibility for any tasks they want, and they have the last word when it comes to estimating the efforts needed. USDP suggests splitting up use cases into manageable tasks too, but single tasks are then assigned to individual developers, who are held accountable for them.

We think that the differences between XP and USDP are far too small to prevent one from reconciling the two processes. Referring to the premise that people are crucial, we resolve the incongruities in favor of XP.

Architecture-Centric Development

With respect to the definition of software architecture, there is nothing to be added to what Ivar Jacobson has said:

*We need an architecture. Fine. But what do we really mean by
"architecture of software systems"? As one searches the literature on*

software architecture, one is reminded of the parable of the blind men and the elephant. An elephant is what each of the blind men happened to encounter—a big snake (the trunk), a piece of cord (the tail), or a small tree (the leg) [Jacobson+1999].

Since the term lacks a concise definition, we decide to focus only on its usage in XP and USDP.

Jacobson [Jacobson+1999] states that "a large and complex software system requires an architect [sic], so that the developers can progress toward a common vision." Unfortunately, that vision is not described any further, but we find it acceptable to equate it with what XP calls the overarching system metaphor. Kent Beck [Beck2000] seems to suggest just that: "The metaphor in XP replaces much of what other people call 'architecture.'" Among other things, according to USDP, the architecture is needed to understand the system and to organize the development.

It has been noted by Kent Beck [Beck2000], however, that architecture as "the big boxes and connections" does not necessarily "push the system into any sense of cohesion." The system metaphor is not the same as an "architecture baseline," the USDP term for a set of artifacts that are an agreed basis for further evolution and development of the architecture. An architecture baseline may employ "architectural patterns," which is the USDP term for patterns as described, for example, in the POSA book [Buschmann+1996]. Taking this into account, we find it acceptable to call the architecture baseline a realization of the system metaphor.

USDP defines the contents of the architecture baseline as architectural views on the use case model, the design model, and so on. Looking at, let us say, the examples that Jacobson, gives for an architectural view on the design model [Jacobson+1999], we notice that this view contains, for instance, high-level package and class diagrams that omit most of the details. XP, however, does not require that developers create and maintain such high-level diagrams, since in XP that kind of information is shared by oral communication rather than by diagrams. It would be too far fetched to equate the XP-style of oral communication with high-level diagrams in USDP, but essentially, they serve the same purpose.

Incremental/Iterative Development

Both XP and USDP promote the use of iterations, that is, of relatively short time spans that, hopefully, terminate successfully at a given milestone. However, USDP requires the workers to proceed in a kind of miniature waterfall model[1] within an iteration: first comes analysis, then design, then implementation, and so on. We think that this requirement is due to an unnecessarily strict interpretation of *traceability*. The UML defines a trace as a dependency that indicates a historical or process relationship between two elements that represent the same concept without specific rules for deriving one from the other. For instance, consider the trace dependency between the use case model and the design model in Figure 9.2, as suggested by USDP.

For the sake of simplicity, we define models as packages of artifacts here. Traceability between models then means that the analysis model contains artifacts, or classes, that are derived from artifacts within the use case model, or use cases.

We consider trace dependency to be an invariant that must hold at each milestone but not within an iteration. Actually, it is nearly impossible to guarantee full traceability within an iteration: There will always be moments in time when the trace dependencies between models are incorrect or even broken. This inconsistent state, however, must be over at the end of an iteration.

Commonly, trace dependencies are unnecessarily taken to be historical relationships, too. For instance, dependencies like the ones shown in Figure 9.2 could be interpreted as requiring historical relationships within an iteration. Consider Figure 9.3. Actually, this is neither correct nor practicable. It prevents direct feedback from design to analysis, because, at least de jure, we must wait until the next iteration to correct our analysis model. Similarly, we are not allowed to test some designs in advance to check whether our understanding of the problem domain is correct. Instead, any problems that occur within an iteration that

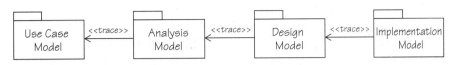

FIGURE 9.2 The meaning of <<trace>>

1. A *waterfall model* is the theory in which analysis, design, implementation, and test are phases in software development which form a sequence, such as a waterfall. Returning to earlier phases is not allowed after these phases have been terminated. The original waterfall model, however, wasn't as strict.

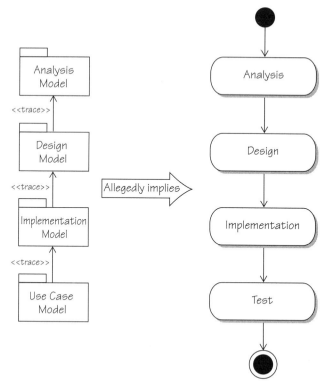

FIGURE 9.3 Does <<trace>> mean "waterfall model?"

require us to go back to an earlier activity make the developers miss the milestone, at least in theory. We dare say that it is common practice to correct minor mistakes of already terminated activities even later on in an iteration, which is effectively corrupting the miniature waterfall model within an iteration.

The theoretical sequence of activities should rather be different, too. We can think of the trace dependency as merely a stamp put on the models after the fact. Like any other stamp, such a dependency does not substantially change the items it connects. It is just a statement that a specific state of an artifacts is traceable to another state of another artifact now. To achieve this, during an iteration we may as well proceed as shown in Figure 9.4. That is, we gain the freedom to switch from analysis to design to any other activity within an iteration as often

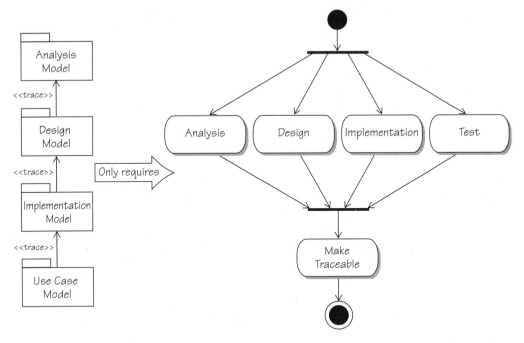

FIGURE 9.4 A reasonable interpretation of <<trace>>

as we like, and we establish traceability rather as refinement than as a trace dependency just at the end of an iteration. A similar attitude can even be found in a software development process that is formally stricter than USDP, namely in Catalysis, where it is described as a pattern: "Refinement is a relation, not a sequence" [D'Souza+1999].

But do we need to establish traceability at all? There is a certain incongruity between XP and USDP when it comes to traceability and documentation. XP has often been mistakenly believed to drop documentation and traceability altogether, which is not true. Instead, XP requires customers and developers to take the costs of traceability into consideration, too. That is, in XP establishing traceability is also a task to be considered during the planning game. If developers can manage to delegate this task to automated tools, there is nothing in XP that prevents them from keeping up traceability at virtually no cost, all of the time. This is where XP meets USDP, because USDP heavily relies on tool support for managing traceability—without tool support, there would be no way to ensure traceability. This is by no means different from the XP practice called *travel light*.

Refactoring the Horse

With the structure revisited as follows, USDP constitutes a process framework. Workers, artifacts, workflows, and activities are some of the elements that you can add, modify, or replace to evolve or adapt the process to the needs of your organization.

Flattening the Workers

A *role* is, per USDP definition, a set of relevant interfaces in a particular context. A worker is defined as a position, to be taken by a single person or by several people in a team who can play specific roles. Most of what XP calls roles are workers in USDP terms. The roles suggested by XP can be assigned to the corresponding USDP categories as shown in Table 9.1.

Workers in USDP are not simply roles. Instead, we might regard workers as formal parameters of a workflow. The types of those parameters are each defined by a set of required skills. USDP defines many different worker types, and it defines them quite loosely, in terms of their capabilities and what they are not expected to do. At runtime of a workflow, actual people become the actual parameters.

Though USDP explicitly distinguishes between people and workers, the distinction is sometimes blurred. For instance, as examples of people, USDP lists *architects, developers,* and *testers,* which are in fact all worker types.

In contrast, XP defines just a few USDP-like roles for people, and it says that if you have people who do not fit the roles, change the roles. One can subsume several USDP worker types under a single XP role by considering the skills implied by XP role to satisfy the definitions of several USDP worker types. This way, the USDP worker type hierarchy is flattened.

TABLE 9.1 Mapping XP Roles to USDP Roles and Workers

	XP Role
USDP Role	programmer, tester
USDP Worker	customer, tracker, coach, consultant, big boss

Dissolving the Activities

Workflows in USDP can be defined by UML activity diagrams, relating activities to single workers by separating them into one swim lane per worker. Each workflow typically comprises about five to seven activities performed by about three to five workers. Not a single workflow contains cycles.

Activities in USDP are mostly pseudo-defined by simply stating what the desired output is, in terms of artifacts that get created or transformed. There is rarely any concrete advice on how the desired transformations of the input artifacts into the output artifacts really work—USDP activities are not even black boxes. Activities are not stand-alone—they are always described in conjunction with the respective worker needed to do the job.

In contrast, XP defines just four basic activities: coding, testing, listening, and designing. Not a single one of these is well defined, but all of them are constrained by the four XP values (communication, simplicity, feedback, and courage). Many XP practices can be regarded as advanced activities. Usually XP practices are defined on a more generic level than are USDP activities. XP practices can therefore be regarded as realizations of USDP workflows, bypassing the pseudo-defined activities of USDP, as shown in Figure 9.5.

The overall architecture of USDP is structured along two dimensions. The vertical dimension represents the core process workflows. The horizontal dimension represents time and shows the life-cycle aspects of the process in terms of phases. Completing all the phases will

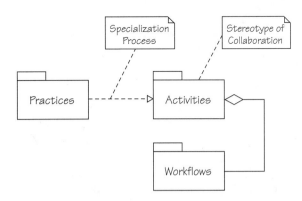

FIGURE 9.5 XP practices as realizations of USDP workflows

result in a release. In the same manner the XP practices are used for accomplishing a release. Therefore the XP practices could be regarded as a replacement for USDP activities, implementing the different workflows. Each of the practices is like a node in which a workflow and a phase meet. Table 9.2 shows how the XP practices map to the USDP activities in a specific workflow (here we show engineering workflows only). Table 9.2 refers to Figure 9.1, where we presented the interrelationships between the phases and the workflows in USDP.

Different time frames are associated with different phases depending on the release. For example, in the first release much more time will be spent on exerting practices in the inception phase. After several releases this phase will shrink. It may even happen that nothing is produced there at all. But sometimes at least the practices will be revived and perhaps new user stories will come up. The phases, workflows, and practices may sometimes overlap; for example, although the team's main activity is task planning, the user may write some new user stories. Seen from a workflow perspective, we can describe the typical distribution of practices among the phases as follows:

✧ *Requirements:* During inception, writing most of the user stories constitutes the main workload. This is normally done by the customer. In elaboration we formulate the commitment schedule by planning the small releases and, more importantly the contents of the next release. During construction the customer—maybe assisted

TABLE 9.2 Mapping XP Practices to USDP Activities

	Inception	**Elaboration**	**Construction**	**Transition**
Requirement	User stories	Small releases	Acceptance tests	Metrics
Analysis	CRC	Iteration planning	Task planning Pair programming	Accept change
Design	System metaphor	Unit tests	Refactoring	Continuous integration
Implementation	Coding standards	Simple design	Collective code ownership	Run all tests

by a developer—writes the acceptance tests, which will verify that the release is completed. Finally, in transition to releasing the system we collect and verify the metrics for calculating the project velocity, which is the base for future estimates.

- ✧ *Analysis:* At the beginning of a release, in inception, CRC card sessions prevail. Based on that we plan the next iteration, which is already the practice in elaboration. During construction we plan the tasks, for which pairs of developers accept responsibility. In transition, we are attentive to the feedback from the customer and accept the changes that he or she suggests.

- ✧ *Design:* Agreeing on and defining the system metaphor is mainly done in Inception. We implement the unit tests during elaboration, gaining a better understanding of the task. During construction we keep an eye on what needs to be refactored [Fowler+1999; Hunt+1999]. And because we don't want to have a system that fails to start, continuous integration is important for transition.

- ✧ *Implementation:* In preparation for a release we agree on a coding standard during inception. In elaboration, we always strive for simple design. The quality of the release will improve during construction because of collective code ownership. For transition, it is essential that all the tests run.

Sorting Out the Artifacts

As we stated earlier, the horizontal dimension of USDP architecture represents time and shows the life-cycle aspects of the process in terms of phases. XP does not force the team to develop in a sequence of phases. Instead, XP allows the team to address any tasks that are allegedly specific for a phase at any time, even in parallel. In other words, the horizontal dimension need not represent a linear time aspect in XP. For example, while developing, which USDP assigns to the construction phase, another user story may pop up that will have to be considered in the current release on demand of the customer. According to USDP, everything needed to fulfill this wish is restricted to an inception phase. Under USDP, the team would not be able to accept the new user story for the imminent release, because the construction phase has already started. In contrast, XP teams don't face any problem here, because even if the team is mainly concerned with construction, it can still do tasks that belong to a different phase.

XP defines most workflows dynamically. There are just two hard-coded workflows: the planning game and iteration planning. Dynamic definition of workflows is guided by XP values and principles. Thus, workflows become artifacts, too, and are thus subject to change.

Central artifacts in the USDP are six high-level models, described as UML packages: use case, analysis, design, deployment, implementation, and test [Fowler1997]. A model is defined as collected perspectives of the system, which can be rendered precise as abstractions of a system. Models are said to specify a system from a certain viewpoint and at a certain level of abstraction. Each of the models mentioned so far contains small artifacts, including many UML diagrams, related to each other by formal rules. Many artifacts are linked by traces across high-level models.

Following XP, only a few desired artifacts could be grouped into packages. All desired artifacts are chosen during the planning game. The two most important types of documents produced during or used in the planning game are user stories and commitment schedules. Traces in the form of acceptance tests are considered to be artifacts too; that is, their maintenance is not simply a by-product of a programmer's work. Without customer interaction, programmers act as intellectual nomads and travel light; that is, they drop everything that has lost its value for the project. On the other hand, documents can always be produced in the same manner as code is produced, which means that any demands for specific documents are captured as user stories. Such user stories are prioritized, estimated, and then implemented like any others. Of course the code, together with the unit tests, reflects the design and can therefore be regarded as a design artifact, too.

Conclusions

This chapter shows that if a team is forced to follow USDP, but would like to use a lighter process like XP, it can do so. USDP provides a framework in which XP can live. Both processes share several traits, mainly the following:

⬥ The people who live the process are paramount to the success of process. If the process is not adapted to and accepted by the individuals concerned, it cannot be used for the project.

⬥ USDP and XP regard the use cases (or user stories) of the system as the base means for capturing requirements. The realizations of use cases form the contents of a release. Also, use cases serve to verify that the goals of the system are met.

✧ Both processes employ incremental and iterative development. Both insist that it is important to keep the cycles really small.

Some points appear to be in different at first glance. Looking closer at them, as we did when refactoring the horse, it turns out that they do not contradict each other:

✧ *Phases:* USDP requires phases that follow one another sequentially, whereas XP is not constrained by any ordering of phases.

✧ *Artifacts:* USDP regards a lot of different artifacts as markers for the completion of a specific task. XP on the other hand concentrates on the code as the main artifact, although it is not limited to code documents only. Producing other artifacts is a task to be treated like any other task.

Unfortunately, there is still one major point left that may help the Trojans spot XP inside the USDP Trojan horse. It is the one we have to pay special attention to if we do not want to expose XP to the outside: the driving force. In USDP the technical people decide on the scope of a release in XP this decision is made by the businesspeople. The planning game may be an exciting experience for people following USDP, because all of a sudden the stakeholders are able to influence the development process.

We believe that USDP and XP have more in common than they have differences. For our camouflage to be effective, it is important that we know and hide those differences.

References

[Beck1999] K. Beck. "Embracing Change with Extreme Programming." *IEEE Computer.* Volume 32, Number 10, 1999.

[Beck2000] K. Beck. *Extreme Programming Explained.* Addison-Wesley, 2000.

[Buschmann+1996] F. Buschmann, R. Meunier, H. Rohnert, P. Sommerlad, M. Stal. *Pattern-Oriented Software Architecture: A System of Patterns.* John Wiley & Sons, Ltd., 1996.

[Cockburn1998] A. Cockburn. *Surviving Object-Oriented Projects: A Manager's Guide*. Addison-Wesley, 1998.

[D'Souza+1999] D. F. D'Souza, A. C. Wills. *Objects, Components, and Frameworks with UML: The Catalysis Approach*. Addison-Wesley, 1999.

[Fowler1997] M. Fowler. *UML Distilled: Applying the Standard Object Modelling Language*. Addison-Wesley, 1997.

[Fowler+1999] M. Fowler, K. Beck, J. Brant, W. Opdyke, D. Roberts. *Refactoring: Improving the Design of Existing Code*. Addison-Wesley, 1999.

[Hunt+1999] A. Hunt, D. Thomas. *The Pragmatic Programmer: From Journeyman to Master*. Addison-Wesley, 1999.

[Jacobson+1999] I. Jacobson, G. Booch, J. Rumbaugh. *The Unified Software Development Process*. Addison-Wesley, 1999.

[Kruchten1999] P. Kruchten. *The Rational Unified Process: An Introduction*. Addison-Wesley, 1999.

About the Authors

Jutta Eckstein can be reached at Objects in Action, Thierschstr. 20, 80538 Munich, Germany; jeckstein@acm.org. Rolf F. Katzenberger can be reached at Ludwig-Kirsner-Str. 4, 78166 Donaueschingen, Germany; rfk@acm.org.

Chapter 10

A Flexible Software Development Process for Emergent Organizations

—Giuliano Armano and Michele Marchesi

If one accepts that most changes in software development appear to arise from the need to control complexity, important events in the era of classical software development should be looked at anew. For instance, in our view the transition from "code and fix" to the waterfall process was an attempt to control the overall amount of within-team communication during system development, whereas the transition toward evolutionary processes was driven by the need to control changing or ambiguous requirements.

Nowadays, the Unified Software Development Process (USDP), built on top of the Unified Modeling Language (UML), is being adopted by an increasing number of software companies. Nevertheless, USDP has been criticized for not being sufficiently flexible in keeping pace with requirements change. This is mainly due to the overhead introduced by lengthy analysis and design, together with the need to keep them continuously synchronized with the corresponding source code.

Recently, Extreme Programming (XP) has been proposed as an alternative to USDP for its flexibility and for its capabilities of attaining a high level of quality through continuous testing and refactoring, while lightening analysis and design. In our opinion, we are perhaps witnessing yet another major change, aimed at improving the flexibility of software development, as required by modern organizations that have to cope with rapid changes in technology and global markets. After a brief comparison of USDP and XP, we discuss our experience in adopting a lightweight approach to software development that customizes USDP activities according to XP guidelines. The proposed approach, which could be considered an attempt to find a suitable trade-off between standardization and high flexibility, was adopted for developing a business-oriented Internet service for a company supported by the regional government of Sardinia.

Introduction

Prior to 1997 more than fifty methods were being used to support object-oriented software development, as the object-oriented paradigm appeared to be the most effective approach to conceptualization, analysis, design, and implementation within a common framework. This lack of standardization, which resulted in a serious fragmentation of the underlying market, was viewed by many large companies as a major obstacle to further development. The OMG standardization of the Unified Modeling Language [Booch+1999] was hailed as the solution to the problem, as the UML was sufficiently generalized to be adopted for building most applications. Further work led to the definition of the Unified Software Development Process [Jacobson+1999; Krutchen1998], a UML-compliant process based on use cases [Jacobson+1992], centered on the architecture, iterative and incremental.

This same period saw the emergence and explosion of the "new economy," intricately related with the Internet and with software technology. The new economy offers incredible money-making opportunities, and the related technological and business environment is changing at a speed unwitnessed before, the "Internet speed." Organizational changes that in the past took decades now happen in the space of years or even months, the time factor being crucial to their success. Organizations able to cope with changing environmental constraints are called *emergent* [Truex+1999].

In software development, this phenomenon led to the introduction of alternative approaches, with the object of reducing the overhead inherent in classical design-oriented approaches. Basically, these proposals are aimed at simplifying and speeding up software development processes by focusing on implementation, testing, and refactoring (e.g., SCRUM

[Schwaber1995], lightweight methodologies [Cockburn1998], XP [Beck2000], and adaptive software development [Highsmith2000]).

After discussing how flexibility in software development can be enhanced by reducing communication constraints, this chapter describes a process that enforces most of the XP guidelines by suitably customizing USDP. One significant difference between XP and the proposed process is that the latter incorporates refactoring in round-trip engineering activities.

Flexibility and Communication Constraints

It was the need to control increasing within-team communication that triggered the first major change in software engineering practices, that is, the transition from code-and-fix to the waterfall process [Royce1987]. In fact, as development teams became larger, the within-team communication flow increased more than linearly, lowering productivity.

The waterfall process addresses the problem of reducing the amount of necessary communication by defining a sequence of activities to be performed while developing a software system. Each activity involves only a limited number of developers bearing a specialized role, and communication concerning subsequent activities occurs in formal documents, which also facilitates future maintenance.

The classical waterfall process, however, was not sufficiently flexible to cope with the requirement changes likely to occur within software development projects. Thus, the need to keep pace with changing requirements resulted in the constraints imposed on communication being relaxed. In particular, control over communication was traded off for increased flexibility, thus giving rise to an evolutionary software process (see, for example, [Scacchi1987]). This kind of process is centered on iterations and increments, a single iteration step being typically a mini-waterfall process, usually devoted to improving the functionality of the system being developed, extending it in depth and/or in breadth. In these processes, team members are much more interactive, though role specialization is maintained. Formal analysis and design documentation are still very important, being produced and updated throughout the whole development process.

Evolutionary software processes are much more flexible than waterfall processes because they allow requirements to be modified during development and exhibit an adaptive behavior within a coarse-grained time slot. Nevertheless, the complete development cycle of a major system typically takes years, far too long for the new economy revolution. That is why we believe that another major change, aimed at enhancing flexibility, is in the making. In our view to achieve greater flexibility, software processes should further reduce their constraints on communication, thus improving their ability to adapt to any change in system requirements. In particular, greater flexibility could be obtained by forcing finer granularity on iterations; that is, by reducing the time slot allocated to their completion (thus giving rise to micro-waterfall iterations).

Over-simplifying the problem, requirements could be represented as a point in a multi-dimensional space of features (say $r \in R_n$) and their trajectory as a line parameterized with time (say $r(t)$). While in general $r(t)$ would become a curve, in cases where design requirements are not subject to change $r(t)$ would tend toward a straight horizontal line. To illustrate how the different kinds of process—waterfall, evolutionary, and flexible—follow the requirements trajectory, they will be considered taking into account a single feature (see Figure 10.1). As expected, a

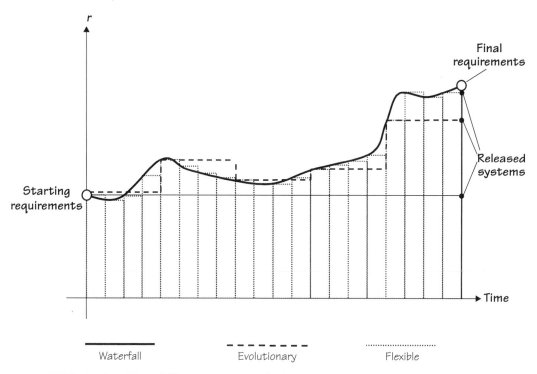

FIGURE 10.1 How different processes deal with changing requirements

waterfall approach has difficulties in coping with changes in requirements,[1] whereas evolutionary and flexible processes—with coarse and fine granularity respectively—are both able to keep track of the requirements trajectory.

XP and lightweight methodologies reduce communication constraints by focusing on small killer teams that, through simultaneous, high-discipline, precise development practices, are able to attain very high productivity without impairing quality. The reduction of written documentation other than code, the interchangeability of roles, continuous integration, testing, and refactoring are crucial to the success of these methodologies.

A Flexible Process for Rapidly Changing Environments

As already pointed out, there is an increasing need for standardizing software processes as well as for enhancing software development flexibility. To this end, we decided to customize USDP according to XP guidelines, thus obtaining a good trade-off between the needs for standardization and flexibility. Before going into further detail, let us first outline the characteristics of USDP and XP, the former being supported by several organizations as a de facto standard, the latter being the most popular lightweight process, focused on testing and refactoring.

The Unified Software Development Process

USDP is a customizable process [Jacobson+1999] defined on top of the UML [Booch+1999]. Following USDP guidelines, a software product created during an initial development cycle (first generation) will evolve through the repetition of a sequence of four phases: inception, elaboration, construction, and transition. Typically, several iterations occur within each phase. A single iteration encompasses core process workflows (i.e., requirements elicitation, analysis, design, implementation, testing, and deployment), the time spent on each workflow being dependent on the phase in which it occurs.

Table 10.1 shows how core process workflows are distributed within a single iteration, according to the phase in which the iteration occurs.

---

1. Changes on system requirements tend to be deferred to the maintenance phase.

TABLE 10.1 Life Cycle Phases Together with Core Process Workflows in the Unified Process

Core Process Workflows	Inception	Elaboration	Construction	Transition
Business Modeling	High	Decreasing	Almost none	None
Requirements	Low–increasing	High–medium	Decreasing–low	Low
Analysis and Design	Almost none	High	Decreasing–low	Almost none
Implementation	Almost none	Increasing	High	Low
Test	None	Low	High	Decreasing
Deployment	None	None	Increasing	High
Project Time Percentage	~10%	~30%	~50%	~10%

Note that elaboration and construction represent roughly 80 percent of the time required to deliver a software release, the elaboration versus construction ratio being about 60 percent.

Figure 10.2 summarizes some relevant features of USDP from different perspectives (process, underlying culture, and technology). In particular, let us point out that (1) analysis and design—as well as test cases—are based on anecdotal scenarios (i.e., use cases); (2) USDP encourages reviews at the various stages of software development; (3) the underlying culture is based on specific analysis and design activities, as well as on individual responsibilities; and (4) powerful tools or development suites are needed, or at least encouraged, to support the whole process, from requirements elicitation to configuration management and testing.

Extreme Programming

XP was proposed by Beck [Beck2000] in response to the need for finding better ways to develop software. First conceived for Smalltalk environments, XP is based on a system of four values: facilitate communication, seek simplicity, ensure continuous feedback, and proceed with courage. It has been tailored for small teams (up to 10 or 15 people), but it greatly enhances the productivity of these teams.

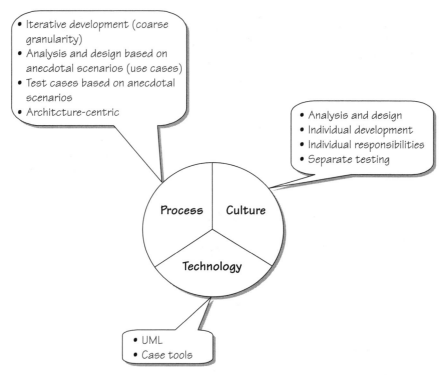

FIGURE 10.2 Process, culture, and technology of USDP

XP is inherently iterative and incremental. Increments can be derived from separate user stories, whereas iterations rely on refactoring. Its general rule is: "Build for change, not for the future." XP introduces metaphors to facilitate the communication (and elaboration) of the software architecture under development. The objective of software architectures is to give everyone—business and technical personnel alike—a coherent "story" within which to operate.

Figure 10.3 summarizes some relevant features of XP. In particular, let us point out that (1) XP encourages "fast" (i.e., fine-grained) iterations, thereby allowing a prompt response to changing requirements; (2) analysis and design as well as test cases are based on anecdotal scenarios (i.e., user stories); (3) the system under development is tested continuously and massively; (4) lengthy analysis and design are discouraged, whereas refactoring is encouraged; and (5) by adopting dynamic pair programming, XP entails team-oriented responsibilities.

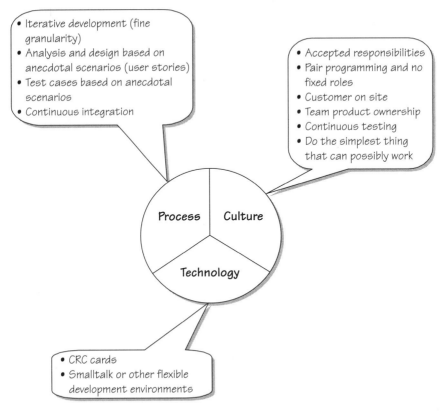

FIGURE 10.3 Process, culture, and technology of XP

UMLTalk, a Round-Trip Engineering Tool for Smalltalk

Before introducing our lightweight process for software development, let us briefly present UMLTalk, the tool that enables its implementation. UMLTalk is a research prototype developed in Visual Smalltalk. It operates on an object-oriented analysis model composed of UML class diagrams and performs various kinds of operations thereon. Let us note that to date UMLTalk cannot manage graphical information. In fact, it does not possess a graphical editor or viewer, having been designed to handle directly structural information on packages and classes, as well as their relationships, attributes, operations, and so on.

UMLTalk allows us to edit the OO model, that is, to add and delete the entities of UML class models and the various kinds of textual information associated with them. It also allows a model to be stored in and read from a file, using a proprietary format. However, its most used features are related to round-trip engineering activities. In fact, UMLTalk can be used to do the following:

1. Import a UML model compliant to the Rational Rose Petal file format (discarding its graphical information).
2. Import Smalltalk source files in "chunk" format. Currently, it supports Smalltalk Express, Visual Smalltalk, Visual Works 2.x and 3.x, and Squeak dialects.
3. Export a UML model according to the Rational Rose Petal file format.
4. Generate a Smalltalk source from a UML model, in one of the dialects in point 2.
5. Generate textual documentation on the model, in RTF or HTML format.
6. Merge two UML models, one of which could be generated by one of the import activities of points 1 and 2. If a conflict arises between the two models, it is resolved automatically or by asking the user which of the models is to be assigned higher priority.
7. Compute metrics on the UML model, and in particular C-K metrics [Chidamber+1994] and the metrics proposed in [Marchesi1998].

It is worth noting that, when a Smalltalk source is imported, the code of the methods is stored in a field of the model corresponding to the semantics field of Rose operations. In this way, the functional information contained in the Smalltalk source is not lost. Figure 10.4 shows the main window of UMLTalk.

Round-trip engineering is typically performed in the following way:

1. A first UML model is written using Rational Rose, and saved in its Petal file format. The round-trip is limited to UML class diagrams.
2. The model is imported into UMLTalk (saving it in its proprietary format). Then a first Smalltalk skeleton is generated, with classes, hierarchies, instance, and class variables and methods (limited to declaration and comment).
3. The developers write the methods bodies and possibly modify the Smalltalk model structure adding classes, variables, and methods, or modifying existing information.

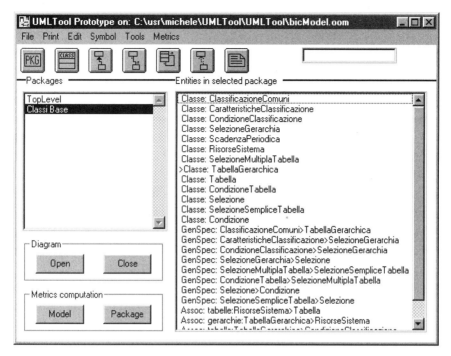

FIGURE 10.4 UMLTalk main window in action

4. The modified Smalltalk source is imported into UMLTalk and is merged with the model of Step 2. Method bodies are stored in the model. New entities that occur in the Smalltalk source but not in the UML model are added to it, any possible conflict being resolved with user intervention. This step can be performed several times, to keep the UML model aligned with Smalltalk code.

5. The UMLTalk model is exported into Petal format and imported in Rose class diagrams. Its graphic layout is given by the user. This activity is facilitated if the model is partitioned into several packages, each containing no more than 10 classes. The UML class diagrams can be edited and modified using Rational Rose, and then stored in a Petal file.

6. The modified Petal is imported into UMLTalk and is merged with the existing model, as in Step 4.

7. A Smalltalk source is generated from the UMLTalk model. This time, it includes the bodies of the methods already written and

imported from Smalltalk in previous steps. Only new methods need to be written.

8. Steps 3 to 7 may be iterated several times. Usually, the developers work on Smalltalk code and periodically import it to UMLTalk, merging it with the existing model. Exporting the model to Rose, as well as automatic generation of the textual documentation, is performed at any official release.

Figure 10.5 shows the data flows among Rational Rose, UMLTalk, and a Smalltalk IDE.

A Proposed Lightweight Process for Software Development

As stated before, USDP is an increasingly accepted standard, and XP is a software development process able to cope with requirements changing at Internet speed. Because USDP is a configured process, we approached the problem of software development by customizing USDP following most of the XP guidelines. It is worth noting, though, that our proposal differs from XP in the scope of the refactoring activities. Whereas XP encourages refactoring mainly at the implementation level, our approach extends it to design and architecture definition, taking advantage of round-trip engineering.

For the sake of simplicity, we refer to the four main phases defined by USDP—inception, elaboration, construction, and transition (see Table 10.2)—to describe how we distribute core process workflows in the process we have adopted. Note that now a substantial portion of construction phase has moved to transition, and elaboration has been lightened with respect to the sum of construction and transition, their ratio being less than 15 percent.

Rational Rose	UML Tool	Smalltalk IDE

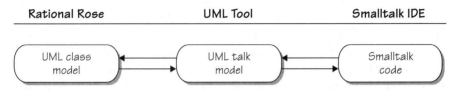

FIGURE 10.5 Using UMLTalk as a front end between Rose and Smalltalk to perform round-trip engineering

TABLE 10.2 Life-Cycle Phases Together with Core Processing Workflows in the Proposed Process

Core process workflows	Inception	Elaboration	Construction	Transition
Business Modeling	High	Decreasing	Almost none	None
Requirements	Increasing	High	Medium	Low
Analysis & Design	Almost none	High	Medium	Low
Implementation	None	Medium	High	Medium–low
Test	None	Medium	High	Decreasing
Deployment	None	Medium	Medium	High
Project Time Percentage	~10%	~10%	~40%	~40%

Inception

Inception is mainly concerned with business and domain modeling. In particular, according to XP guidelines, we depict requirements by means of user stories, created (and subsequently refined) during brainstorming sessions held with domain experts. User stories are first written on index cards, then stored as Microsoft Word documents. UML use case diagrams may be used to give an overall picture of user stories in graphical form. In our approach, inception does not entail any iteration or implementation activity.

Elaboration

Elaboration is the phase in which the problem to be solved is clearly understood, the basic architecture is established, and the greatest risks are eliminated. In our approach, this phase is centered on analysis and preliminary design (which we call *architectural design*), performed in turn by adopting Class Responsibility Collaboration (CRC) cards [Beck+1989; Wirfs-Brock+1990]. CRC cards are generated during brainstorming sessions and, once stabilized, are embodied into Rose as UML class diagrams. Figure 10.6 shows a CRC diagram expressed as a UML class diagram. As analysis and architectural design proceed, more implementation details are added to UML class diagrams, such as association relationships and attribute and operation definitions. Figure 10.7

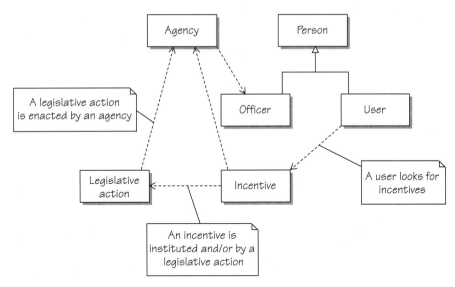

FIGURE 10.6 A CRC diagram drawn during a preliminary analysis of the system

shows the CRC diagram of Figure 10.6 transformed into a complete UML class diagram. Though it is less frequently done, state transition, activity, collaboration, and sequence diagrams can also be adopted, typically to represent the dynamic behavior of a class/method (state/activity diagrams) or important interactions among classes or subsystems (sequence/collaboration diagrams).

Although this phase is centered on analysis and architectural design, it entails iterations, with further gathering of user requirements and with implementation and testing of software modules. The development of these modules is focused on building the basic architecture of the system and on experimenting in areas where risk is higher. In this phase, we use round-trip engineering, generating code from UML class diagrams developed in the architectural design phase.

Construction

Construction is the iterative and incremental development of the system before its first release to the user. In our approach, it is centered on refactoring and makes extensive use of round-trip engineering.

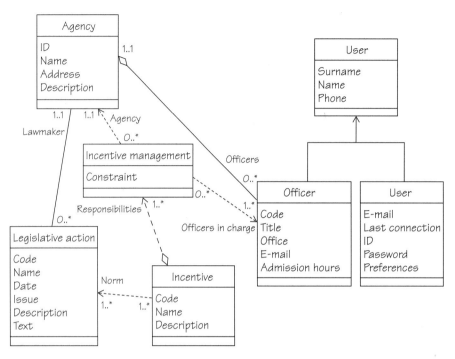

FIGURE 10.7 A class diagram that results from refining the preliminary analysis of the system

Iterations are done according to XP practices: User stories to be implemented are chosen in a planning game in which developers evaluate and accept their responsibilities. Pair programming is not, for the time being, extensively used. As for testing, it is strictly coupled with implementation activities. Typically, for each class that belongs to the system under development, a corresponding test class is defined and implemented. In this way, testing activities are uniformly distributed throughout the construction phase.

A single iteration may involve further requirement assessment and/or analysis. Its main focus, however, is on writing Smalltalk code and the corresponding tests. The system is kept as simple as possible, emphasizing the quality of the code and how well it fits into the system architecture. Developers change any code that does not meet these standards. Tests are aimed at ensuring that any problem introduced by a change is spotted.

UMLTalk is continuously used to keep the code aligned with UML class diagrams documenting it at a higher level. In particular, when new (or updated) Smalltalk methods must be incorporated into the corresponding model, UMLTalk is used to feedback Rose with the modified Smalltalk source. The problem of realigning model and code may also arise when changes are performed directly on UML class diagrams, although this happens very seldom. In this case, the UML model is used to update the Smalltalk code (still exploiting UMLTalk capabilities, this time in the opposite direction).

Transition

Transition consists of the development activities performed once the system has gone into production. In the process we propose, there is no substantial difference between construction and transition, and deployment is performed at the end of every iteration rather than deferred to the transition phase.

The Proposed Process at Work

We now illustrate the application whose development was the trigger for implementing the proposed process. It concerns the development of a system for business-oriented Internet services commissioned by BIC[2] Sardinia. The system is aimed at providing assistance to business-people or companies searching for available government grants, to be used to set up or improve their business. The system provides both an off- and on-line front end. Off-line front end consists of a local service used by domain experts for updating the database containing information about available grants. On-line front end consists of a Web service that assists in the search for government grants for businesses. First the user is prompted to provide information about his or her business plan. Then the system queries the database about available grants and selects the information that matches the user's profile. Finally, results are automatically reported to the user by means of dynamic Web pages.

A first attempt at capturing requirements revealed serious difficulties in eliciting the domain knowledge from experts. Considering the high likelihood of having to deal with ambiguous and/or shifting requirements, we decided to define a lightweight approach based on the UML

2. "BIC" stands for Business Innovation Centre, an European network aimed at supporting people and enterprises in setting up and improving their business activities.

and to adopt most of the XP guidelines. This is the process presented in the previous section. It is worth noting that the project started at the end of 1997, when XP practices were not yet refined. We believe that our project is one of the first attempts to put into practice a lightweight process implementing many (albeit not all) XP practices.

Requirements elicitation was done collecting user stories (in this case about 30 at the start of the project) considered relevant for illustrating the system's behavior. A conceptual analysis was performed with CRC cards suitably stored in Rose class diagrams. Figure 10.6 illustrates one sample diagram. Responsibilities (not shown in the figure) are stored in class descriptions. Twenty-two domain classes were identified during the elaboration phase, together with subsystems (i.e., packages), dependencies among classes, inheritance relationships, and responsibilities. To verify the feasibility and consistency of critical aspects, we implemented some classes at an early stage of development.

Domain classes were then refined, typically turning collaborations into associations and responsibilities into attributes and operations. Figure 10.7 shows a refined diagram (for the sake of simplicity, only a limited number of attributes are shown). The first implementation of the whole system resulted in 45 classes. Frequent reviews and, to some extent, pair programming were encouraged as means of disseminating among developers knowledge about the system to be implemented. Internal releases were delivered weekly.

The Smalltalk dialect used to develop the system was Smalltalk Express, a 16-bit free implementation for Microsoft Windows. Although dated, it proved suitable for our system.[3] Using UMLTalk, we were able to keep UML documentation up to date with the working system, meeting the standards adopted by the customer. A limited number of persons (five) was involved in the project, within a nonhierarchical team structure. System development up to the transition phase (i.e., the first deliverable release) required 15 person-months over a period of six months. The first delivered release was able to manage the grants database

---

3. In 1999 we tried to upgrade Smalltalk Express to its 32-bit successor Visual Smalltalk, but the producer informed us that this product line was no longer available. We estimate that converting the system to another commercial Smalltalk dialect, such as Visual Works or Visual Age Smalltalk, would not constitute a problem and could be done in a few weeks. We are also considering Squeak, an open-source Smalltalk implementation that could allow porting the system to a Linux operating system.

required for the system. BIC employees immediately started to use the system for populating the database.

Since then, the project has continued, improving the database management and adding the communications with the Internet. We experienced many delays caused by the development of the Internet-server module, implemented by another team that adopted a classical approach and used a commercial engine. At the beginning of 1999 the system was operational (it can be seen online, in Italian, at http://www.sentieroimpresa.it). In the meantime, it had grown to 65 classes and 20 more user stories were added.

Conclusion

The need to adapt to rapid changes in technology and global markets is impacting software engineering, as far as the flexibility of software development is concerned. In particular, small killer teams applying lightweight processes will very likely have a prominent role in software development.

This chapter briefly outlined a software process that follows XP guidelines by suitably customizing USDP activities and by extending refactoring (beyond the implementation phase) to design and architecture definition. As for the system depicted in the last section, refactoring was performed within a round-trip engineering cycle, obtained by using an in-house experimental tool, UMLTalk, as a bidirectional front end between Rational Rose and Smalltalk.

The proposed approach has proved to be effective in the BIC project, documenting how XP techniques and round-trip software engineering (supported by heterogeneous software tools) can be used to improve both flexibility and productivity.

References

[Beck+1989] K. Beck, W. Cunningham. "A Laboratory for Teaching Object-Oriented Thinking." *ACM Sigplan Notices.* Volume 24, Number 10, October 1989.

[Beck2000] K. Beck. *Extreme Programming Explained.* Addison-Wesley, 2000.

[Booch+1999] G. Booch, J. Rumbaugh, I. Jacobson. *The Unified Modeling Language User Guide*. Addison-Wesley, 1999.

[Chidamber+1994] S. R. Chidamber, C. F. Kemerer. "A Metrics Suite for Object-Oriented Design." *IEEE Transactions on Software Engineering*. Volume 20, Number 6, 1994.

[Cockburn1998] A. Cockburn. *Surviving Object-Oriented Projects: A Manager's Guide*. Addison-Wesley, 1998.

[Cockburn2001] A. Cockburn, *Crystal "Clear": A Human-Powered Software Development Methodology for Small Teams*. On-line draft at http://members.aol.com/humansandt/crystal/clear. 2001.

[Highsmith2000] J. A. Highsmith. *Adaptive Software Development: A Collaborative Approach to Managing Complex Systems*. Dorset House, 2000.

[Jacobson+1992] I. Jacobson, M. Christerson, P. Jonsson, G. Overgaard. *Object-Oriented Software Engineering: A Use-Case Driven Approach*. Addison-Wesley, 1992.

[Jacobson+1999] I. Jacobson, J. Rumbaugh, G. Booch. *The Unified Software Development Process*. Addison-Wesley, 1999.

[Krutchen1998] P. Krutchen. *The Rational Unified Process*. Addison-Wesley, 1998.

[Marchesi1998] M. Marchesi. "OOA Metrics for the Unified Modeling Language." In *Proceedings of 2nd Euromicro Conference on Software Maintenance and Reengineering*. Florence, Italy, March 8–11, 1998.

[Royce1987] W. W. Royce. "Managing the Development of Large Software Systems." In *Proceedings of the 9th International Conference on Software Engineering*, IEEE Computer Society, 1987.

[Scacchi1987]W. Scacchi. "Models of Software Evolution: Life Cycle and Process," *Technical Report, CMU Software Engineering Institute*. SEI-CM-10-1.0 ADA236120. October 1987.

[Schwaber1995] K. Schwaber. "The SCRUM Development Process." *OOPSLA 95*. Workshop on Business Object Design and Implementation, 1995.

[Truex+1999] D. P. Truex, R. Baskerville, H. Klein "Growing Systems in Emergent Organizations." *Communications of the ACM* Volume 42, Number 8, pp. 117–123. August 1999.

[Wirfs-Brock+1990] R. Wirfs-Brock, B. Wilkerson, L. Wiener. *Designing Object-Oriented Software*. Prentice Hall, 1990.

Acknowledgments

Our thanks to all persons involved in the project. A special thanks goes to Dr. A. Angius, former president of BIC Sardinia, for his vision and his help.

About the Authors

Giuliano Armano can be reached at DIEE—Università di Cagliari, piazza d'Armi, 09123 Cagliari, Italy; armano@diee.unica.it. Michele Marchesi can be reached at DIEE—Università di Cagliari, piazza d'Armi, 09123 Cagliari, Italy; michele@diee.unica.it.

Chapter 11

Extreme Modeling

—*Marko Boger, Toby Baier, Frank Wienberg,
and Winfried Lamersdorf*

*Extreme Programming (XP) has been widely appreciated as a
pragmatic software development process. But it has also been
criticized for being centred too much on coding, leaving behind
modeling and design. More traditional development processes
stress the importance of modeling. There appears to be a contradiction between these two different approaches.*

*In this chapter we discuss how the principles of XP can be
applied in the modeling phase. To achieve this it is necessary to be
able to execute models, as well as to test them. A solution providing this for the UML is presented. This allows a seamless integration of UML modeling into XP. We point out the value added to
both XP and UML modeling and propose Extreme Modeling.*

Introduction

In the area of object-oriented software engineering two of the most
important recent developments are the UML, on the one hand, and
Extreme Programming (XP) on the other. The UML has become the
lingua franca for designing and communicating the architecture of
object-oriented software systems. It is based on a long tradition of software engineering skills, and has emerged from different notations and

development processes now unified to one. The UML is widely applied, its roots and traditions accepted as best-of-practice. Unlike the UML, XP is a new development process, throwing overboard old traditions, saving only a few, composing them in a radical way, and applying them to their extreme. XP is centered around code. One of its most important cornerstones are tests, written before and during programming rather than after, and validated at all times.

It seems as though the appearance of XP has split the software development community in two factions. On one side are the traditionalists, convinced of the necessity of an intensive modeling phase to find appropriate architectures; on the other side are the radicals, disappointed by the failures of traditional ways and fascinated by the simplicity and the success of XP. There seems to be no in-between.

One of the things thrown overboard by XP that is most desired by the traditionalists is modeling, particularly with UML. In XP graphical notations like UML are only used rarely, such as for sketching and communicating some aspects of a system, mostly on the whiteboard. Even then XP graphical notation differs widely from traditional methods, where the design phase can take months before a single line of code is written.

This is the most controversial point between these two positions. The traditionalists argue that the system will lack overall architecture if coding starts right away. The radicals argue that the design rather than the problem will become the driver, and, as requirements change during development, the ability to react to flexibility will be lost, if the design and programming phases are divided.

Yet, where the traditionalists lack flexibility, the radicals lack a language with which to communicate and document their design. These disadvantages could be eliminated if the advantages could be unified synergetically. The obstacle is the division of the design phase from the programming phase. In this chapter we discuss the possibilities of uniting these two phases, of integrating UML into XP, and of applying the principles of XP to the modeling phase. This integrated approach is presented as Extreme Modeling (XM).

Meeting the Preliminaries

XP draws much of its strength from testing. This requires an executable form of the system under development, which is why XP is centered around code. In order to unite the modeling and implementation phase and to apply the principles of XP to modeling, two requirements have to be met: Models need to be executable and they must be testable. Though the traditional way only requires a good drawing tool and XP only requires a compiler and a simple test framework, Extreme Modeling requires intensive support by an integrated tool that is able to execute UML models and test models, support the transition from model to code, and keep code and model in sync. The following sections explain how execution of single UML diagrams and whole UML models have to be treated to support XM.

Executing UML Diagrams

A UML model is specified by different diagrams that are, as the name indicates, drawings. Each dynamic UML diagram shows a part of a model which has an operational semantics, so it should be executable, as has been shown for state diagrams [Harel1987; Harel1998] and message sequence charts [ITU1999].

Execution of the dynamic UML diagram types can be achieved by transforming the diagrams directly into executable code or by translating them into an intermediary format with precise operational semantics that can be interpreted by a machine. In our project we have chosen the latter: Each UML diagram is translated into a special kind of Petri net [Renew1999] by a newly developed compiler. The Petri nets engine, in turn, can be executed by a Petri nets. The results can be used to animate the original diagram so that the execution or simulation of it can be visualized. This translation procedure can be compared to the compilation of Java source to byte code, which can be interpreted by a Java Virtual Machine. The diagrams correspond to the Java code, whereas their Petri net representation corresponds to byte code. Accordingly we call this Petri net engine a UML Virtual Machine.

Unlike code, a model does not have to be completely specified to be executable. Under-specified parts (such as conditions of loops and branches) can be decided by the user at runtime or randomly. Our UML Virtual Machine also allows undeclared variables and assigns an according type at runtime; dynamic type checking is enforced. This gives the designers more flexibility at modeling time without sacrificing static typing for refined models and the final code.

During execution, our tool allows three modes: single-step, interactive-run, and automatic-run or simulation. A transition (arc) of the state-chart is translated into a sequence of substeps (in the UML this is called a run-to-completion step). In single-step mode, the user can trigger each substep interactively. The resulting changes can be watched in the diagram. In interactive-run mode, the execution proceeds automatically until an event from outside is expected. The user can then decide which events or method calls should be sent to the model. In automatic-run or simulation mode, one of the events or methods out of the set of now-accepted triggers is chosen randomly and the execution proceeds automatically.

We now briefly introduce all the dynamic UML diagrams and explain how they are executed. A state machine defines the states of an object, the events leading to state changes, and actions to be taken. During the execution of such a diagram, the actual state and its change can be visualized. The example of a state diagram in Figure 11.1 (adapted from *UML@work* [Hitz+1999]) can successfully be translated by our compiler, instantiated, and executed by the UML Virtual machine.

Activity diagrams express processes. In terms of execution, activity diagrams are very similar to state machines, the difference being that the focus is less on states and events and more on processes, branches, forks, and joins. During execution, the current activity is visualized and the transition to the next activity can be triggered. In the case of forks or conditions, either the user can choose an option or one is chosen randomly, depending on the execution mode.

Interaction diagrams are used to express example runs and come in two flavors, collaboration diagrams and sequence diagrams. These are interchangeable but stress different aspects. During execution, the modeler can see whether objects are active, waiting (suspended), or passive.

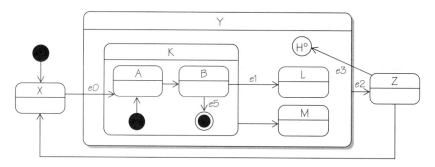

FIGURE 11.1 Example of a complex state diagram during execution

Figure 11.2 shows an example of a collaboration diagram, which was compiled and executed with our tool.

Interaction Between UML Diagrams

To be able to simulate and try out a single diagram is nice, but because each diagram in UML has a certain role in the modeling process they should be used collectively.

The class or static structure diagram provides architectural information gathered from the other diagrams. A class contributes to the system's behavior in the sense that it provides access methods for attributes and associations.

Together, state and activity diagrams specify the dynamic behavior of a system. We assume that a state machine models the state of a single object. It can be seen as a model of the life cycle of an object or as the protocol to use an object. Events are mapped to methods of the corresponding class.

Activity diagrams are used for modeling the fine-grained steps of a single method. Although they can be used on different levels of abstraction in the UML, we could argue that higher-level activity diagrams will eventually be implemented as a method of some controller or workflow object. Typical collaboration between objects can be shown with squence or collaboration diagrams.

Sequence diagrams specify interactions between sets of given objects. An interaction consists of messages that are sent from one object to another object of this set. Collaboration diagrams additionally contain information about which associations are used to find the other objects of the interaction. Also, a protocol of executing a UML model can either be visualized as a sequence or collaboration diagram.

All of these diagrams can be translated into the same underlying representation (Petri nets) by our compiler. To run the simulation, diagram

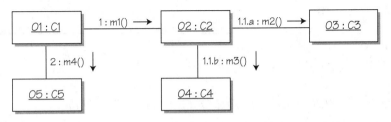

FIGURE 11.2 Example of a collaboration diagram during execution

instances and the corresponding Petri net instances are created. While running simultaneously, they interact through method calls and events. As inscription language we use Java, which is interpreted by the UML Virtual Machine. An example is shown later in this chapter.

Interaction Between UML Diagrams and Code

Because all annotations in the diagrams are in Java, messages can also be sent to real Java objects. The UML Virtual Machine contains a Java parser, so that the inscriptions can be checked for syntactical correctness. Method calls to Java objects are invoked using the reflection mechanism. A simple example is to call `System.out.println()` at the entry of a state. A more sophisticated example is the creation of a graphical user interface that can interact with the simulated system. Similarly, diagram instances are represented by Java wrapper objects that can be called from usual code.

The combination of these two mechanisms eliminates the difference between modelled and coded objects. An object can first be modelled graphically and later be implemented in Java. It can be used for execution in both cases. Thus a smooth transition from the design to implementation phase is made possible.

Keeping the Model and Code Consistent

Usually, modeling and coding are done in completely separate phases and different tools are used. This strongly hampers the consistency of model and code, and is often used as an argument why modeling should not be used in XP: Either the model becomes the driver and determines where the code is going, meaning that flexibility in the implementation phase is lost, or both model and code need to be changed, incurring high costs for change.

Code, just like the different UML diagrams, can be seen as one specific view on the model that is being constructed. If the meta model used to store this model is powerful enough to hold both diagrams and code in a consistent way, all diagrams as well as the code can be handled within one tool. If the model is changed from any one of these views, this is directly reflected in all other views.

The Principles of XP Applied to Modeling

In the previous section an approach for executing UML models was presented. While this can have a strong impact on the traditional, modeling-oriented process of software development, the focus in the following discussion will be on how executing models applies to XP. This will lead to a process we call Extreme Modeling. This discussion is guided by the basic principles and four values of XP, as stated by Kent Beck [Beck2000]. Good practices that are not touched by this, like pair programming, on-site customer, or listening, are left out. We start with the cornerstone of XP, testing.

Testing UML-Models

In XP, code is tested through other code. With Extreme Modeling there are additional possibilities:

- *Testing models through models.* Because diagrams can interact during execution, they can be used to express tests on other diagrams. Most typically, interactions (e.g., sequence diagrams) can test behavioral specifications (e.g., statechart diagrams).
- *Testing models through code.* Diagrams can be referenced and accessed from regular Java classes. This way usual tests, such as an XP test case written in Java relying on JUnit [Wells2000], can be used to test a (set of) state machine(s).
- *Testing code through models.* The interaction between code and model works in both directions, so that a class can be tested, for example, by a sequence diagram.

Not only can these test flavors be executed individually, they can be mixed at will. What is required is a test framework, similar to JUnit, that supports this way of testing. In fact, JUnit can be reused to a large extent as is. Some additional features are required though. It should be possible for tests to ask statechart diagram instances whether they are in a certain state. Then assertions in the style of JUnit assertions can check the expected state of the target object after a sequence of method invocations from a sequence diagram. This can be achieved in several ways; we propose to use a generated boolean method isInState(state).

Sequence diagrams are most typically used to express test cases. They can contain object instances deduced of the class junit.framework.Test. Such objects inherit methods for expressing assertions that can be called in the sequence diagram. To test code through diagrams, it is possible to use the JUnit framework directly, without further changes.

From these test cases a test suite can be generated. This can be done by instantiating and calling each such sequence diagram individually from a special test suite sequence diagram, or by adding each sequence diagram that contains an instance of `junit.framework.Test` automatically.

Two sequence diagrams are special: `setUp` and `tearDown`. These are used as in JUnit; the first is executed prior to any test sequence diagram, the latter after. This ensures that each test is executed in the same environment. With such extended testing abilities, all other XP basics can be reconsidered for modeling.

Rapid Feedback

Standard modeling processes do not provide feedback from the model, because the model cannot be executed or tested. The first feedback you get is when you actually start coding. With XM you can sketch out an idea of an architecture in the UML, run it interactively while it is still largely underspecified, and see what you get. Instantly, you get a feel for how your idea works. You can find problems and misunderstandings faster.

The programmers can always see whether the designed model is consistent, whether the behavior intended is actually modeled, or if the model is valid at all. This is feedback to the programmer that has not been possible before, and it is much more rapid. Therefore, Extreme Modeling improves the basic principle of rapid feedback.

Assume simplicity

Extreme Programmers always want to have the simplest possible design. While conservative UML modelers tend to design the whole system first, before starting to code, there is no need to do this anymore, because the cost of change is really low with a system in which model and code are always kept consistent. So you can start off with the simplest design that supplies the need. The advantage of having a graphical view on the system is that it enables us to find even simpler designs. So Extreme Modeling can enhance XP in this respect as well.

Incremental change

In XP, short development cycles are realized by the code passing all tests. Tests are the means to ensure that the system under development is consistent. Because with our approach, models can also be tested and validated, this notion is now applicable on the modeling level. As in XP, consistency results in a greater confidence in your work. This way you can embrace change during modeling.

Communication and feedback

With more and earlier feedback, communication between developers as well as with customers is greatly improved. It is a lot easier to communicate about a model than about code, and easier yet to communicate about a running and visualized model than about "dead drawings." Customers might not be able to comment on code. They might even have problems reading UML diagrams. But a running prototype appropriately visualized with the UML might do. Customers will be able to get and give feedback much earlier. Just like code tests, model tests improve documentation and communication of the system's features. Using graphical notations further enhances readability.

An Example

The construction of software systems is a practical matter. Thus an example demonstrating XM may help explain it. We have chosen an example that has already been used for the traditional process of modeling as well as for XP. The chosen problem can be found in *Designing Object-Oriented C++ Applications* [Martin1995] and is referred to as the Mark IV Coffee Machine problem. The development process for designing and implementing this example, once using traditional modeling with UML and Java and once using XP, can be found on-line [Weirich1999]

The problem at hand is the design of a coffee machine controlled by a Java chip. It should be able brew coffee and keep it hot on a heated plate. If the pot is removed, the brewing (if still running) must be interrupted and the heated plate turned off. It is not our intent to discuss the full development process from very early analysis to deployment. Instead, we start out after the problem has been well understood and a simple first model has been established. At this stage the traditional approach derives the class diagram shown in Figure 11.3.

Now let's continue in an XM fashion. Before we define any behavior, we write a test. For this we use a sequence diagram containing a test object and the controller object we want to test. The test object sends the message `brewButtonPushed()` to the controller, to which we add an empty method with this name. Next the test object checks

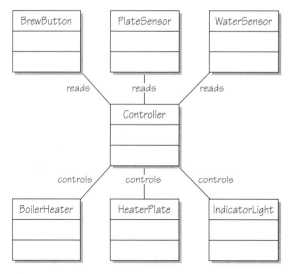

FIGURE 11.3 A first class diagram for a coffee machine

whether the controller object is in state "brewing." If we run the test now, it fails, because the controller's behavior is not modeled yet. We start with a very simple statechart diagram with only two states, off and on. A transition from off to on triggered by brewButtonPushed() is added, and our test succeeds.

When the water tank is empty, we want the controller to be in state off. We add a method tankDry() to our controller, which is called by the test object in the sequence diagram (see Figure 11.4). After that, we add a check to see whether the controller is in state off. Because the test fails now, we add the appropriate transition to the statechart diagram. We run the test again, and now it succeeds.

The next class to test is the boiler heater. It has to be turned on and off by the controller. We write another test, which checks the state of the boiler heater before and after brewButtonPushed() is sent to the controller. To get it running we add entry actions to the controller's states that turn the heater on and off. But wait, didn't the customer want the boiler to be turned off when someone removes the coffee pot? We need to refine the controller's statechart diagram, adding two sub-states to on (brewing and waiting), triggered by potRemoved() and

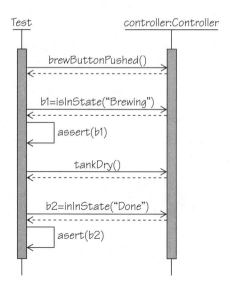

FIGURE 11.4 Sequence diagram for testing the boiler's behavior

potReturned(). Now we must change the boiler test so that we assert the boiler is in state off when the pot is removed. Now the test fails. We have to adjust the controller state machine to turn off the boiler when entering the waiting state and on again when entering the brewing state. The latter is done by moving the boiler.on() action from on to its substate brewing. Now the test passes again.

We continue with the plate heater. It behaves similarly to the boiler heater, but we do not want it to be turned off when brewing is finished—it should keep the coffee hot until it's removed. Hmm, seems like we need another state for the controller (we'll call it "done"), because now not everything is turned off at tankDry(). We create a new test to check that the boiler heater is still on after tankDry(), but off after potRemoved().

We change the controller's statechart diagram until all tests succeed. The result is shown in Figure 11.5.

After writing a few sequence diagrams that all run to our satisfaction we now write the code for the controller. To validate that the code fulfils its specification, we use the existing sequence diagrams as tests for this code. This can be done in both directions. So now we also transform the

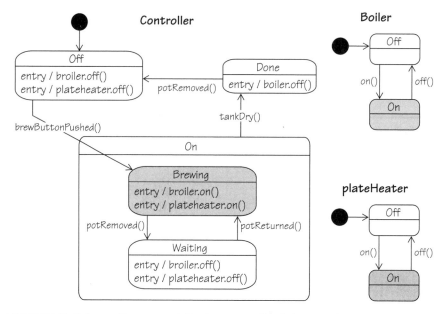

FIGURE 11.5 State diagrams while the controller is in state brewing

sequence diagrams to code. The code for the test shown in Figure 11.4 looks as follows.

```
public abstract class ControllerTest extends TestCase {
    Controller controller;
    }
    public void testControllerOnOff() {
            controller.brewButtonPushed();
            boolean b1 = controller.isInState("On");
            assert(b1);
            controller.tankDry();
            boolean b2 = boiler.isInState("Done");
            assert(b2);
    }
    public Test suite() {
            TestSuite suite = new TestSuite();
        suite.addTest(new Test ("testControllerOnOff"));
        return suite;
    }
}
```

To show that this code can be used to test both the model and the code, we build two subclasses of boiler test, one instantiating the statechart diagram and one instantiating the coded class:

```
public class BoilerModelTest extends BoilerTest {
    public void setUp() {
            controller = new ControllerModel();
    }
}


public class BoilerImplTest extends BoilerTest {
    public void setUp(){
        controller = new ControllerImpl();
    }
}
```

Both tests can be run successfully. The integration of diagrams and code also works on a greater scale; for example, the graphical user interface used in the solution of the Mark IV Coffee Machine [Weirich1999] can be used both for the graphical model and for the code implementation without changing the original code.

Current Status

The presented tool has been implemented, and a stable and usable prototype is available. The implementation is based on an open-source UML tool called ArgoUML [Robbins2000] and a Petri net tool developed at the University of Hamburg [Renew+1999]. We are currently able to execute state, activity, collaboration, and sequence diagrams. The translation of these to the corresponding Petri net representation works for almost all complex diagram elements, including forks and joins, complex states, history states, transition guards, and actions. In cases where the UML specification is vague about the exact semantics of a notation, we have chosen a particular. Details of the translation algorithm are beyond the scope of this chapter.

The developed tools and the development process of Extreme Modeling are currently evaluated in several practical applications. One of these is a technology study in cooperation with the software engineering company sd&m for a container logistic system for the new container harbor of Hamburg. The process of unloading containers from a ship, transporting them to the container storage system, and delivering them to a trolley is simulated. The system's behavior will be executed as a graphical model and as actual code. The graphical user interface will be used both for the executing model and for the running code. Results will be presented in a future publication.

The next planned steps are to investigate the possibilities of automatic code generation from sources other than class diagrams. For example, collaboration, activity, and statechart diagrams contain important information about possible method bodies.

We have only started to integrate a code editor that directly manipulates the underlying model into ArgoUML, but the current status is quite promising. The UML meta model 1.3 needs to be extended to hold such implementation details.

One of our current problems for larger models is that the handling of many diagram instances becomes difficult. To better support navigation, we plan to develop an improved browser.

Conclusion

So far extreme programmers have not integrated modeling languages into their process of development. We pointed out that the reason for this was that models as built with the UML were neither executable nor testable. We showed that translating UML models into a special kind of Petri net assigns them a formal operational semantics. This allows the execution and visualization of UML diagrams. Also, since these can interact, it is possible to use one diagram to test another. The executing engine presented allows bidirectional interaction of models and compiled code. A smooth transition from modeling phase to implementation is achieved. We showed how the appliance of the XP principles and values to modeling can bring benefit to both and lead to a new software development process, called Extreme Modeling [Bogert2000].

References

[Beck2000] K. Beck. *Extreme Programming Explained*. Addison-Wesley, 2000.

[Harel1987] D. Harel. "Statecharts: A Visual Formalism for Complex Systems." *Science Computer Programming*. Volume 8, 1987.

[Harel1998] D Harel. "On Modeling and Analyzing System Behavior: Myths, Facts, and Challenges." In *ECBS Conference and Workshop of Computer Based Systems, Maale Hachamisha*. IEEE CS Press, 1998.

[Hitz+1999] M. Hitz, G. Kappel. *UML@work*. dpunkt-Verlag, 1999.

[ITU1999] ITU. ITU-T Recommendation Z.120 (11/99)—message sequence chart (msc), 1999.

[Martin1995] R. C. Martin. *Designing Object-Oriented C++ Applications Using the Booch Methodology*. Prentice Hall, 1995.

[Renew+1999] O. Kummer, F. Wienberg. *Renew 1.1—User Guide*. 2000. On-line at http://www.renew.de/renew.pdf. 1999.

[Robbins2000] J. Robbins. *ArgoUML: The Cognitive CASE Tool*. On-line at http://argouml.tigris.org. 2000.

[Weirich1999] J. Weirich. *OOAD Design Problem: The Coffee Maker*. On-line at http//w3.one.net/~jweirich/java/coffee/Coffee-Maker.htm, 1999.

[Wells2000] D. Wells. *Extreme Programming: A Gentle Introduction*. On-line at http://www.extremeprogramming.org. 2000.

About the Authors

The authors can be reached at Hamburg University, Distributed Systems Group, Vogt-Kölln-Str. 30, 22527 Hamburg, Germany; {boger|baier|wienberg|lamersd}@informatik.uni-hamburg.de.

Chapter 12

A Stochastic Model of Software Maintenance and Its Implications on Extreme Programming Processes

—*Sergio Focardi, Michele Marchesi, and Giancarlo Succi*

Maintenance is an important phase of software development that usually consumes more than 50 percent of the overall development resources. A simple model based on random graphs can be used to describe the overall maintenance process and may provide evidence that programs developed using an XP approach are intrinsically "different."

Introduction

Maintenance is that phase of the software life cycle when existing software is modified to fix errors, restructure the system for greater efficiency, or ready it for future upgrades [Pressman1997]; it accounts for well over 50 percent of the total cost of software development. Despite their contribution to cost, software maintenance and evolution have been the subject of a surprisingly small number of empirical studies [Kemerer+1999]. Few models have been attempted and validated to describe the overall process and explain the effort required and the quality of the resulting system; more research might be necessary to attain a higher level of empirical validation [Ramil+1999].

Effective models for software maintenance and evolution would serve two purposes:

1. Guide the development process in an effort to minimize maintenance costs
2. Help predict the maintenance effort, thus supporting better scheduling and resource allocation

This chapter proposes a model of the effects of maintenance operations on software systems based on the theory of random graphs. Our model uses a random graph to represent a software system. The graph is populated by two types of nodes: strong nodes and weak nodes. Maintenance spreads through weak nodes as a contagion process that can be modeled as percolation on a Cayley tree. The model is used to give some insight on development processes based on refactoring, including Extreme Programming (XP) [Beck2000].

Modeling Software Maintenance: A Review of Earlier Approaches

The seminal work of Lehman [Lehman1980] to model the structure and effect of software maintenance and evolution has been followed by few studies. Two classes of models have been proposed in the literature: those focusing on the process of maintaining and evolving the system and those focusing on the effects of maintenance operations. On the basis of existing literature, Kemerer and Slaughter [Kemerer+1999] refer to the former as models for software evolution and the latter as models for software maintenance.

Models for describing the process of software development and maintenance focus on different techniques to describe the research methodology [Kellner1998]. Following Forrester [Forrester1971], system dynamics is the study of the dynamics of complex systems composed of interacting entities. The use of system dynamics to model software maintenance and evolution was proposed by Abdel-Hamid and Madnick [Abdel-Hamid+1991] and was later extended into a general project management framework by Rodrigues and Williams [Rodrigues+1996]. Petri nets [Bandinelli+1993] and generalized Petri nets [Kusumoto+1997] were proposed to describe process evolution either in general or with a focus on maintenance. Temporal logic was used to describe the effects of changes in software systems [Zhou+1999]. Succi [Succi+1995] proposed a morphogenetic approach using a set of evolution operators for the formal description of a program's evolution. Gamma analysis has also been applied to determine the different sequence of activities in the maintenance and evolution process [Kemerer+1999].

Models that focus on the code are often based on the analysis of code metrics. For example, Li and Henry [Li+1993] determine how object-oriented metrics, considered as a proxy of maintenance effort, are related to various versions of software systems. Succi and colleagues [Succi+2000] explore the effects of the presence of a domain library and of software reuse on the requests for maintenance from customers in two large software systems.

This chapter proposes a different approach. It focuses on the dynamics of the propagation of changes in a software system using the theory of random graphs. It attempts to model quantitatively, albeit in a stochastic sense, the dynamics of software maintenance costs.

The Representation of Software Systems with Random Graphs

In this chapter, we model the effects of changes on software systems using the theory of random graphs [Palmer1985; Bollobas1985]. Graphs have often been used to represent software systems. In particular, Briand and Colleagues [Briand+1996] provide a comprehensive representation of any software system as a collection of nodes and of various kinds of edges between nodes.

A node can be any software artifact, such as a design class, a piece of code (class, class definition, or member function), or a piece of documentation. An edge is any kind of link between two nodes, such as an inheritance relation between two classes, a definition-usage pair between two modules, a cross-reference between two pieces of documentation, or a trace between part of a model and requirements leading to its design.

Our approach assumes that different development methodologies entail different kinds of graphs, such that each methodology can be associated with one or more random graphs. The properties of the various methodologies can then be inferred by studying the associated random graphs.

A random graph G is a graph with N nodes and Q edges. We assume that edges are not directed. There are two fundamental probabilistic structures for representing random graphs which, following Palmer [Palmer1985], we refer to as model A and model B.

In model A, Q is a random variable. Let's assume that each pair of nodes i,j has the same probability p of being connected and that such probabilities are independent of each other. In a graph with N nodes, there are $N(N-1)/2$ possible edges. Therefore the random variable Q is distributed as a binomial random variable with mean $\langle Q \rangle = pN(N-1)/2$.

In model B, the number of edges Q is fixed. The number of graphs with N nodes and Q edges is:

$$\binom{N(N-1)/2}{Q} \tag{1}$$

and all graphs have the same probability:

$$\binom{N(N-1)/2}{Q}^{-1} \tag{2}$$

For large values of N, the two models are equivalent if $p = 2Q/N(N-1)$ [Palmer1985]; we will thus use the two models interchangeably. In both cases, the random graph G is fully represented by the number of nodes N and the probability p, that is, $G = G(Q,p)$.

If a graph is connected, the number of edges Q must be $N \le Q \le N(N-1)/2$. In model A, if N grows with constant probability p, the probability that a graph is connected tends to 1. In model B, when N grows holding constant the ratio $2Q/N(N-1)$, the probability that a graph is connected tends to 1. In other words, for large N, if the probability p or the ratio $2Q/N(N-1)$ remains constant, almost all graphs are connected.

The number r of edges that start from a node is called the degree of the node. The sum of all degrees is twice the number of edges:

$$\sum_{i=1}^{N} r_i = 2Q \tag{3}$$

A graph is called regular of degree r (or r-regular) if all nodes have the same degree r. In model A, for large values of N, the average degree is given by:

$$\langle r \rangle = p(N-1) \approx pN \tag{4}$$

When N tends to infinity, any random graph $G(N,p)$ tends to be regular if probability p is constant [Palmer1985]. This fact is reflected in model B if $p = 2Q/N(N-1)$ remains constant for growing N. Under this assumption, in model B, the average degree grows linearly with the number of nodes of the graph. In fact, for large N:

$$\langle r \rangle \approx \frac{\sum\limits_{i=1}^{N} r_i}{N} = \frac{2Q}{N} = \frac{pN(N-1)}{N} \propto N - 1 \approx N \tag{5}$$

If probability p is not constant, the degree r has a distribution that depends on how p grows with N.

We call the average degree of the graph that represents a software system the *degree* of the software system. The degree of such a system is a measure of complexity as it satisfies trivially the properties of complexity measures [Briand+1996]. In model B, the average degree is a constant; in model A, we approximate (in probabilistic sense) the average degree with:

$$\frac{\sum\limits_{i=1}^{N} r_i}{N} \tag{6}$$

Model B allows representing in a natural way the growth of the degree of a software system through its different development phases. It also allows modeling quantitatively—albeit in a probabilistic way—the growth of maintenance costs for different development phases.

One might object that software systems exhibit complex structures with regional localization of links different from the almost uniform and regular nature of large random graphs. There are several responses:

- ⬥ First, additional studies are required to ascertain the empirical distribution of links in software systems. Borrowing an expression from econometrics, the stylized facts of software systems (i.e., the statistical properties of their probabilistic representation) are not known in detail.
- ⬥ Second, although software systems might not be regular, it is however reasonable to approximate their random representation as if it were regionally regular. This signifies that the graph representing a

large software system can be decomposed into connected subgraphs, each approximately regular. This decomposition would raise the question of hierarchies in software representation and the existence of self-similarities of random representations.

◇ Third, and perhaps most important, the theory of random graphs is robust to changes in the graph topology. In fact, considering variable link probabilities or oriented graphs does not fundamentally change a random graph's basic properties, such as the scaling laws of their connected components.

We therefore suggest that representing large software systems as random graphs is a first approximation that allows establishing simple quantitative laws of the software maintenance process; successive empirical testing would be required. It should be noted that the theory of random graphs is general enough to provide ample room for calibration; findings from empirical testing might be represented within the basic framework of random graph theory.

The Propagation of Maintenance as a Contagion Process

To represent the effect of a change in a software system, we follow an approach similar to the one taken in epidemiology [Durrett1985; Liggett1999]. The spread of an infectious disease is modeled as an interacting particle system. A number of individuals occupy the sites of a (bi-dimensional) lattice. Each individual can be either healthy but susceptible to getting sick, or vaccinated/recovered and thus immune. Healthy but susceptible individuals randomly acquire the disease at a rate dependent on the number of sick individuals surrounding their sites. Sick individuals, in turn, recover at an independent rate and become immune. The disease spreads to healthy but susceptible individuals, reaches a peak, and then decays as a growing fraction of the population develops immunity.

To apply the same metaphor to software systems, we divide the nodes into two mutually exclusive classes: strong nodes and weak nodes. Strong nodes represent well-engineered modules, which are robust to changes, whereas weak nodes represent modules which, when affected by a maintenance change, require reworking. Strong nodes correspond to immune individuals, weak nodes to individuals that are healthy but susceptible to contagion. There is no way to tell a priori which nodes are strong or weak; weak nodes are revealed during the maintenance process following test procedures and/or the operational functioning of the system.

Because this work does not model the time to repair, we do not include a population of nodes under maintenance corresponding to sick individuals. We assume that only weak nodes are susceptible of maintenance. After maintenance, they are likely to become strong with a given probability. Maintenance is performed instantaneously but can spread to other connected weak nodes, which in turn may become strong.

The modification of the state of a node in a software system inevitably impacts connected nodes. If the node is well engineered, the impact is negligible; the maintenance might be limited to a change in a parameter. In this case, no neighbor node is affected and there is no further spreading of the process. In other cases, however, the node might require major reengineering. This reengineering process, in turn, is likely to affect neighboring weak nodes with a probability s, and so on. Software maintenance can therefore be represented as a process that starts from some weak node and propagates to other weak neighboring nodes. Figure 12.1 graphically shows an example of the maintenance process.

To formalize, let the system be composed of N nodes of which W are weak and S are strong. Let q be the ratio W/N. Given any node, the probability that another connected node is weak is q. Given any two connected weak nodes a and b, let s be the probability that a change in

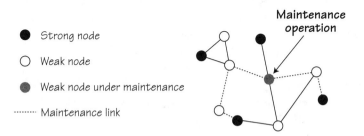

FIGURE 12.1 Modeling maintenance operation on a graph. Note that only a fraction of links are affected by maintenance

a will propagate to *b*. *q* and *s* are the statistical parameters that characterize different classes of software systems.

We assume that *q* and *s* are small and independent, and that the graph that represents the system under change is *r*-regular. As observed previously, most large graphs are approximately regular.

If a modification has to be performed on a strong node, the cost is small and the change does not propagate. If, however, modification is required on a weak node, it may result in a significant cost *C*. Let $F(x)$ be the probability distribution for *C*, that is, $F(x) = P(C \le x)$. The node under change is connected to *r* other nodes since the degree of the graph is *r*. Given that *q* is the probability that a connected node is weak and *s* the probability that a change propagates to connected weak nodes, the change propagates with probability *qs*. The overall cost of the change is a random sum of *S* terms, each with distribution *F*.

A key simplification is to assume that the effect of a modification to a weak node propagates along trees without forming loops. This assumption is reasonable. In fact, the theory of random graphs supplies the thresholds under which most components of a graph will be trees.

In a graph with *N* nodes, the probability threshold for the appearance of loops in connected components is $1/N$ [Palmer1985]. This means that in a large random graph, if the probability of connection of two nodes is less than $1/N$, most components are trees [Palmer1985]. Under these hypotheses, the probability that two nodes are connected by a change propagation is *pqs*. A reasonable stochastic model of graphs requires that $pqs \le 1/N$, as follows.

If changes propagate following trees, we can describe the process as propagation on a Cayley tree with *r* branches and with connection probability $t = qs$. In fact, after reaching a node, maintenance can propagate to one of *r* possible neighboring nodes with probability *qs* without ever forming a loop. Maintenance propagates following a tree selecting at each step among *r* possible nonintersecting paths.

A Cayley tree [Stauffer1994; Grimmett1989] is a graphical representation of a fixed-step branching process. Given a Cayley tree with *r* branches and probability of connection *t*, if *S* is the random variable that represents the number of nodes in the connected tree that includes the original node, the mean of *S* is

$$\langle S \rangle = \frac{1 + t}{1 - (r - 1)t} \tag{7}$$

The connected components of a Cayley tree are distributed according to an inverse power law of the type:

$$S^{-5/2} \exp(-cS), \ c \propto \left(t - \frac{1}{r-1}\right)^2 \tag{8}$$

In our case, $t = qs$.

Given the degree of a system, r, and given an estimate of maintenance propagation probabilities q and s, we have a complete characterization of the proceeding trees.

In this case, the cost of a change, CC, is given by the random sum:

$$\sum_{i=1}^{S} C_i$$

The average of the maintenance cost MC can be written as:

$$E(MC) = E\left(\sum_{i=1}^{S} C_i\right) = \sum_{s=0}^{\infty} p(s) E\left(\sum_{i=1}^{S} C_i\right) = \sum_{s=0}^{\infty} p(s) s E(C) = \langle S \rangle \langle C \rangle \tag{9}$$

The distribution F_{MC} of maintenance costs can be expressed as the sum of the S-fold convolutions of $F(x)$. In fact,

$$MC = \sum_{s=0}^{\infty} p(s)\left(\sum_{i=1}^{S} C_i\right)$$

and therefore

$$F_{MC} = \sum_{s=0}^{\infty} p(s) F^{*S}$$

We can now make use of the property that the Fourier transform of a convolution of two functions is the product of the respective Fourier transforms. If we know the characteristic function of F (i.e., its Fourier transform F^*), we can write:

$$F^*_{MC} = \sum_{s=0}^{\infty} p(s)(F^*)^S$$

This characterization only determines maintenance costs given a certain level of immunization. To determine the evolution of maintenance costs for different development processes, we have to take into account the probability that maintained nodes become strong. When maintenance is performed starting from a given node, we can, in fact, make different assumptions regarding the effects of maintenance.

In traditional approaches, when a bug is fixed or a change is made reflecting a modification of requirements, the focus is to change as little as possible, to keep the maintenance cost low, and to avoid possible side effects on the rest of the system. In this case, the nodes affected by maintenance do not become strong.

Under the preceding hypothesis, the cost of a maintenance operation is proportional to the size of the cluster of nodes affected; the proportion of weak and strong nodes does not change significantly over time. The maintenance cost can vary significantly for different operations, given that in percolation trees the distribution of cluster size follows the power law shown in Equation (8).

On the other hand, we could make the strict assumption that maintenance propagates following a tree of weak nodes and that every node of the tree becomes strong after maintenance. This could be the case in Extreme Programming, where maintenance produces a refactoring of the program such that each node becomes immune from further maintenance.[1] In this case, the average cost of maintaining a node will be much higher. We can thus represent the evolution of maintenance as the iteration of propagation on a Cayley tree. As more maintenance is performed, the number of weak nodes is reduced and maintenance costs decay.

We can estimate the decay of maintenance costs assuming that every time maintenance is performed the number of weak nodes is reduced by the average number of nodes maintained. The next maintenance step is thus performed on a reduced number of weak nodes, and so on. In this case, we can determine a recurrence relation for the evolution of maintenance costs. Suppose the i_{th} maintenance step was

---

1. In XP, refactoring is often performed simply to keep the code clean and concise, and not in response to and explicit need of maintenance. For the presented model, however, the cause of the intervention on the code is immaterial.

performed leaving W_i weak nodes; the successive step can be approximately expressed as:

$$q_{i+1} = \frac{W_i - S_i}{N} = q_i - \frac{1 + sq_i}{1 - (r-1)sq_i} \qquad (10)$$

$$S_{i+1} = \frac{1 + sq_{i+1}}{1 - (r-1)sq_{i+1}}$$

From this expression, an approximate dynamics of maintenance costs can be computed.

We can release the assumption of perfect maintenance by assuming that only a given fraction of weak nodes becomes strong; this strengthening of (only) a fraction of weak nodes might be due to partial maintenance or to erroneous maintenance that might add defects to be mended at a later time. Under this assumption, the immunization process is slackened. Maintenance decay can be estimated with the approach used for the refactoring case. At each maintenance step, the average number of nodes that become strong will be the average number of nodes repaired times a correcting factor that accounts for imperfect maintenance.

The dynamics of maintenance costs hinges on the behavior of the probability t. In this model, t is given by the probability of propagation from one weak node to another, times the probability of finding a weak node. The latter is determined by the characteristics of the software development process itself. We can make the reasonable assumption that Extreme Programming leaves a smaller number of weak nodes than traditional programming. From Equation (10), it is clear that reducing the number of weak nodes translates into significant savings in terms of maintenance costs.

Results and Conclusion

The maintenance propagation model presented in this chapter was simulated and recurrence equations computed. We considered two software systems, the first a small system with 2,000 nodes, the second a bigger one with 20,000 nodes. The average degree of both systems is estimated to be 40, as the average connectivity should be almost independent from the system size, at least for significant systems. The initial percentage of weak nodes is estimated to be 50 percent, and the probability, *s*, that a connected weak node has to be maintained is set to 0.1. These figures were determined by interviews with software engineers and takes into account all possible kinds of links among software modules. They should be substantiated with empirical studies; however, their specific values do not affect the qualitative behavior of the cost curves presented here.

For the two systems, we computed the maintenance costs versus time under two extreme hypotheses:

1. Maintenance is strictly aimed at fixing a bug or adding a feature, and leaves untouched what is already working. This is the classical engineering approach, under which the cost to maintain a node is low, but weak nodes remain weak after maintenance.
2. When a node must be modified, extensive refactoring is performed on it. This is the XP approach, yielding high maintenance cost, but under which weak nodes become strong after maintenance.

Figures 12.2 and 12.3 show the results for the two systems. The decreasing curves represent the average size of the cluster of nodes to be maintained under the hypothesis that all maintained nodes become strong after maintenance. These curves are proportional to the average maintenance costs as a consequence of Equation (9).

In the absence of refactoring, the average maintenance cost is approximately constant in time. For example, if the average cost is one fourth the cost of maintenance with refactoring, the constant line would approximately coincide with the line of five average-maintained, full-cost nodes. This line is the dotted line shown in Figures 12.2 and 12.3.

It is worth noting that, under this hypotheses, in the case of a 2,000-node system maintenance with refactoring is cost effective only after some 20 maintenance interventions (Figure 12.2); in a 20,000-node system, the proportion is similar, because economical advantage is realized only after about 200 maintenance interventions (Figure 12.3).

Note that the total maintenance cost is proportional to the integral of the curves. However, because in both the 2,000- and the 20,000-node systems the number of maintenance interventions necessary to establish an economic advantage for refactoring is *less* than that typically required in the real life cycle of a system, there would appear to be a benefit (at least in this preliminary trial) in adopting a refactoring approach.

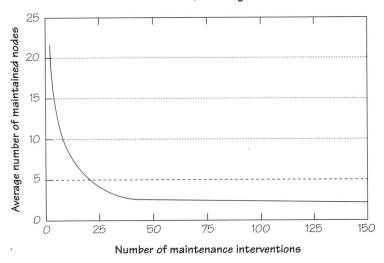

System with 2,000 nodes, 1,000 initial
weak nodes, and degree 40

FIGURE 12.2 The decreasing curve shows the decay of the average size of nodes involved in maintenance, which is proportional to the cost and function of the number of maintenance interventions for a system with 2,000 nodes of which half, or 1,000, are initially weak. See text for the meaning of the dotted line.

It should be noted that our results are dependent on the probability s. If s is high and the system is therefore close to the percolation threshold, the average size of initial clusters might be very big and the curves decrease quickly. On the other hand, if the system is not close to the percolation threshold, curves can be flatter and the economical advantage of refactoring less apparent. Empirical studies on real software systems must be performed to state the approximate value of parameter s and its variation over time.

The use of random graph theory in modeling the software maintenance process seems promising. It might prove to be advantageous even to model the whole development process, with additional assumptions to model the dynamic behavior of the graph representing the system under development.

We are presently working on more detailed models of software development and maintenance using the random graph approach; the goal is

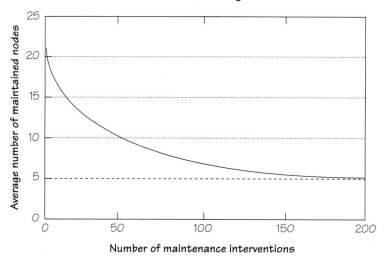

FIGURE 12.3 The curve shows the decay of the average size of nodes involved in maintenance for a system with 20,000 nodes, of which half, or 10,000 are initially weak. See text for the meaning of the dotted line.

to take into account the effect of other Extreme Programming development practices such as continuous testing and pair programming.

References

[Abdel-Hamid+1991] T. K. Abdel-Hamid, S. Madnick. *Software Project Dynamics: An Integrated Approach.* Prentice Hall, 1991.

[Bandinelli+1993] S. Bandinelli, A. Fuggetta, C. Ghezzi "Software Process Model Evolution in the SPADE Environment." *IEEE Transactions on Software Engineering.* Volume 19, Number 12, December 1993.

[Beck2000] K. Beck. *Extreme Programming Explained.* Addison-Wesley, 2000.

[Bollobas1985] B. Bollobas. *Random Graphs.* Academic Press, 1985.

[Briand+1996] L. Briand, S. Morasca, V. Basili. "Property-Based Software Engineering Measurement." *IEEE Transactions on Software Engineering.* Volume 22, Number 1, January 1996.

[Durrett11985] R. Durrett, ed. "Particle Systems, Random Media and Large Deviations." *American Mathematical Society,* June 1985.

[Forrester1971] J. W. Forrester. *World Dynamics.* Pegasus Communications, 1971.

[Grimmett1989] G. R. Grimmett. *Percolation.* Springer-Verlag, 1989.

[Kellner1998] M. I. Kellner. "Developing and Documenting Improved Software Maintenance Processes." *Tutorial at the 1998 International Conference on Software Maintenance.* Bethesda, Maryland, November 16–19, 1998.

[Kemerer+1999] C. F. Kemerer, S. Slaughter. "An Empirical Approach to the Study of Software Evolution." *IEEE Transactions on Software Engineering.* Volume 25, Number 4, 1999.

[Kusumoto+1997] S. Kusumoto, O. Mizuno, T. Kikuno, Y. Hirayama, Y. Takagi, K. Sakamoto. "A New Software Project Simulator Based on Generalized Stochastic Petri-net." In *Proceedings of the 1997 International Conference on Software Engineering,* Boston, May 1997.

[Lehman1980] M. M. Lehman. "Programs, Life Cycles, and Laws of Program Evolution." In *Proceedings of IEEE Special Issue on Software Engineering.* Volume 68, Number 9, l980.

[Li+1993] W. Li, S. Henry. "Object-Oriented Metrics that Predict Maintainability." *Journal of Systems and Software.* Volume 23, Number 2, 1993.

[Liggett1999] T. M. Liggett. *Stochastic Interacting Systems: Contact, Voter, and Exclusion Processes.* Springer-Verlag, November 1999.

[Palmer1985] E. M. Palmer. *Graphical Evolution: An Introduction to the Theory of Random Graphs.* John Wiley & Sons, 1985.

[Pressman1997] R. S. Pressman. *Software Engineering: A Practitioner's Approach,* Fourth edition. McGraw-Hill, 1997.

[Ramil1999] J. F. Ramil, M. M. Lehman. "Modeling Process Dynamics in Software Evolution Processes—Some Issues." In *Proceedings of the ICSE 1999 Workshop on Software Change and Evolution*, Los Angeles, May 1999.

[Rodrigues1996] A. G. Rodrigues, T. M. Williams. "System Dynamics in Software Project Management: Toward the Development of a Formal Integrated Framework." In *Proceedings of the 1996 International Conference on System Dynamics*, Boston, July 1996.

[Stauffer1994] D. Stauffer, A. Aharony. *Introduction to Percolation Theory*, Second edition. Taylor and Francis, 1994.

[Succi+1995] G. Succi, F. Baruchelli, G. Kovacs, M. Ronchetti. "Morphogenesis of a Program." *Studies in Informatics and Control*. Volume 4, Number 4, 1995.

[Succi+2000] G. Succi, L. Benedicenti, T. Vernazza. "Analysis of the Effects of Software Reuse on Customer Satisfaction in an RPG Environment." *UoC-ENEL-SERN-TR00198*, 2000.

[Zhou1999] S. Zhou, H. Zedan, A. Cau. "A Framework for Analysing the Effect of 'Change' in Legacy Code." In *Proceedings of the 1999 International Conference on Software Maintenance*, Oxford, England, August 30–September 3, 1999.

About the Authors

Sergio Focardi can be reached at The Intertek Group, 94 rue de Jevel, 75015 Paris, France; interteksf@aol.com. Michele Marchesi can be reached at DIEE—Università di Cagliari, piazza d'Armi, 09123 Cagliari, Italy; michele@diee.unica.it. Giancarlo Succi can be reached at the Department of Electrical and Computer Engineering, 238 Civil/Electrical Engineering Building, University of Alberta, Edmonton, Alberta, Canada T6G 2G7; Giancarlo.Succi@ee.ualberta.ca.

Chapter 13

Patterns and XP

—Joshua Kerievsky

Patterns and Extreme Programming (XP) both provide invaluable aid to those who design and develop software. But XP has thus far focused heavily on refactoring, while remaining all but silent about Patterns. In this chapter, I ask why, and ultimately show how Patterns are better when they are implemented the XP way, and how XP is better when it includes the use of Patterns.

Overengineering

We start our programming careers not knowing very much and producing software that reflects our inexperience: We create code that is bloated, buggy, and brittle, hard to maintain and hard to enhance. Over time, we become better software designers: We learn from authors, experts, and our own mistakes. Now we write highly flexible software that is generic and robust. When asked to write a new system, we know to inquire about current and future requirements, so that we can design software to handle current and future needs.

At this stage in our careers, Extreme Programming tells us that we often overengineer software. We've learned from our mistakes and don't want to repeat them, so we make great efforts to produce flexible and robust designs early in the life of a system. Unfortunately, we don't realize that all our work will be meaningless and wasteful if the system never needs such degrees of flexibility and robustness. We've overengineered.

I've overengineered. Honestly, it's kind of fun to sit in a room with other designers and think how to design software to accommodate many current and future requirements. We get to take all the lessons we've learned, especially the best practices, and apply them to the design. We often know that the list of requirements will change, but users or customers are always changing requirements. Nevertheless, we think we can be brilliant enough to design software so flexible that it won't really be a problem when the requirements change.

That is classic overengineering.

Today, Extreme Programming would expose this folly. It says that we must learn to let designs emerge and not anticipate what will be. XP says "do the simplest thing that could possibly work" because "you aren't gonna need it." And Kent Beck says:

> You need to choose the best way to work within a value system of communication, simplicity, feedback, and courage to keep you from overengineering out of fear [Beck2000].

Agreed. However, I must now quote my friend Norm Kerth. Norm has been around a while and has seen a lot. A year ago I asked him what he thought of XP. He said:

> I like everything that is in XP. What concerns me is what is not in XP [Kerth1999].

At the time, I just thought Norm was being conservative. But now I'm not sure. Noticeably absent from XP is the practice of using Patterns. Though some of XP's founders helped pioneer and build the Patterns community, no one has yet strongly articulated how Patterns fit into XP.

The Practice of Using Patterns

For a while, that simply didn't bother me. But now it does. It bothers me because my experiences with Patterns and XP lead me to believe that using Patterns is better in the context of XP practices, and XP practices are better when they include Patterns. This will take some explaining. I'll start by describing some of my experiences with Patterns and XP.

Starting in 1995, I began to immerse myself in Patterns. I was learning the Patterns literature, leading a weekly study group on Patterns, designing and developing software with Patterns, and organizing and running UP (an international conference about using Patterns). It would be an understatement to say that I was enthusiastic about Patterns.

At the time, like many who first learn Patterns, I was a bit overanxious to use them. That is not a good thing because it can make designs more complex than they need to be. But I wouldn't learn that until I started to learn about refactoring.

Around 1996, I was first exposed to refactoring. I started experimenting with it and quickly observed that refactoring was leading me away from certain principles I'd learned in my studies of Patterns. For instance, one of the mantras of the landmark book *Design Patterns: Elements of Reusable Object-Oriented Software* is "Program to an interface, not an implementation" [Gamma+1995].

The authors of *Design Patterns* do an excellent job of explaining why you'd want to follow this advice. In nearly every Pattern, there is a discussion of how your software becomes less flexible and less changeable when you program to a specific implementation. Interfaces nearly always come to the rescue.

But what if you don't need that flexibility or changeability? Why begin a design anticipating a need that may never arise? This was an awakening for me. So around that time I recorded the following Java idiom.

Don't Distinguish Between Classes and Interfaces

I used to place an "I" at the end of the names of my interfaces. But as I continue to learn more about the rhythm of refactoring, I'm starting to see the wisdom in making class and interface names look the same. Here's why: during development you know that you could use an interface to make something really flexible (vary the implementation) but there may be no real need to vary the implementation today. So instead of "over designing" by anticipating too much, you stay simple and make the thing a class. And somewhere you write a method signature that expects an object of that class type. Then, a few days, weeks, months later, there is a definite "need" for the interface. So you convert the original class into an interface, create an implementation class (that implements the new interface) and let your original signature (or signatures) remain unchanged [Kerievsky1996].

I continued to learn similar lessons as I studied refactoring, and gradually, the way I used Patterns began to change. I would no longer develop full-blown implementations of a Pattern up front. Now, I would be more judicious: If a Pattern could solve a design problem, if it could provide a way to implement a requirement, I would use it, but I would begin with the simplest implementation of the Pattern that I could code. Later, when enhancements or modifications were required, I would make the implementations more flexible or robust. This new way of working with Patterns was much better: It saved me time and made my designs simpler.

XP's Need for Patterns

As I continued to learn more about XP, I soon began to consider the fact that those who were articulating what XP is, and how it works, weren't saying anything about Patterns. The focus on the development side seemed to have shifted exclusively to refactoring. Build a little, test a little, refactor a little, and repeat.

Well, what happened to Patterns? The common answer I received was that Patterns encourage overengineering, while Refactoring keeps things simple and light. Now, I like refactoring about as well as anyone—I reviewed two early drafts of Martin Fowler's *Refactoring: Improving the Design of Existing Code* [Fowler+1999] and knew that it was destined to become a classic. But I also like Patterns and have found them to be invaluable in helping people learn how to design better software. So how could XP not include Patterns?

I wrote about my unease with respect to this issue in the *Portland Pattern Repository*. I asked whether the perfect XP team would consist of programmers and a coach who knew nothing about Patterns but who relied solely on refactoring to "let the code go where it needs to go." Ron Jeffries, who is arguably the world's most experienced XP practitioner, debated this subject answered:

> *A beginner can't listen to the code and hear what it says. He needs to learn Patterns (in the generic sense) of code quality. He needs to see good code (and, I suppose, bad) in order to learn to make good code.*
>
> *A question, and I mean it to be a question, is whether Patterns as presently constituted help with this. I think Beck's Smalltalk Best Practice Patterns do help, because they are very micro. I think Design Patterns are more iffy, as the Patterns and discussion get pretty big sometimes, and they may make big solutions seem desirable. Martin Fowler's excellent Analysis Patterns offer the same peril, the selection of a big solution when a small one would do* [Jeffries1999].

Are Patterns Dangerous?

A very interesting perspective on Patterns. While I've come to see that Patterns can be implemented and used judiciously, Ron seems to think that they are dangerous because they "make big solutions seem desirable." Elsewhere, Ron observes the common occurrence of how people who first learn Patterns are overanxious to use them.

I can't argue with the latter observation. As with anything new, even XP practices, people can be overanxious to use them. But do Patterns really encourage big solutions when small ones would do?

I think a lot depends on how you define and use Patterns. For instance, I have observed that many beginning Patterns users think that a Pattern is the same as its structure diagram (or class diagram). Yet when I point out to them that the Pattern can really be implemented in different ways, depending on needs, they begin to see that the diagram shows just one of many ways to implement the Pattern.

Simple and Sophisticated Pattern Implementations

There are simple implementations of a Pattern, and sophisticated implementations. The trick is to discover the problem that a Pattern addresses, match that problem to your current problem, and then match the simplest Pattern implementation (solution) to your problem. When you do that, you aren't using big solutions when small ones would do. You're leveraging best practices to solve your problems.

Difficulties can arise when people aren't well educated about Patterns. Ron mentioned the way that Patterns are "presently constituted"—that is to say, how they are communicated by authors today. I would agree that the Patterns literature has some flaws. The books on Patterns are dense, and it can take time to understand the problems that Patterns solve so that you can intelligently match a Pattern to your particular needs.

This matching is extremely important. If you get it wrong, you could be overengineering or just screwing up your design altogether. Experienced Patterns users do make mistakes and then often see the problems that result. But these experts are armed with a host of other Patterns that can help them in the face of their mismatch. So they often end up swapping out a less-than-ideal Pattern for one that better suits their needs.

So how do you become an experienced Patterns user? I have found that unless people devote significant study to Patterns, they will be in danger of misunderstanding them, overusing them, and overengineering with them.

But is that a reason to avoid them? I think not. I've found them to be so useful on so many projects that I couldn't imagine designing and developing software without them. I believe that a thorough study of Patterns is well worth the effort.

Targets for Your Refactorings

So is XP keeping silent about Patterns because the feeling is that they'll be misused? If that is the case, perhaps the question becomes how can we leverage the wisdom in Patterns, while avoiding the misuse of Patterns within the context of XP development?

Here, I think we must return to *Design Patterns* [Gamma+1995]. In their concluding remarks the authors write:

> *Our Design Patterns capture many of the structures that result from refactoring. Using these Patterns early in the life of a design prevents later refactorings. But even if you don't see how to apply a Pattern until after you've built your system, the Pattern can still show you how to change it. Design Patterns thus provide targets for your refactorings.* [Gamma+1995]

This is the idea we need: targets for your refactorings. This is the bridge between refactoring and Patterns. It perfectly describes my own evolution in using Patterns: Start simple, think about Patterns but keep them on the back burner, make small refactorings, and move these refactorings toward a Pattern (or Patterns) only when there is a genuine need for them.

This process, which requires discipline and careful judgment, would fit nicely into the XP fold of best practices. And this approach is certainly quite different from not knowing about or ignoring Patterns and relying on refactoring to improve a design incrementally.

The danger of relying exclusively on refactoring is this: Without targets, people may make small design improvements, but their overall design will ultimately suffer because it lacks the order, simplicity, and effectiveness that come from intelligently using Patterns. To quote Kent Beck himself, Patterns generate architectures [Beck+1994].

Choosing When to Use Patterns

But Patterns don't ensure disciplined usage. If we use them too much or too soon in a design, we're back to the overengineering problem. We must therefore answer the question, "When is it safe to introduce Patterns into the life cycle of a design?" Recall the quote from *Design Patterns*: "Using these Patterns early in the life of a design prevents later refactorings."

This is a tricky proposition. If we don't know when to deploy a Pattern, we can easily overengineer early in the design life cycle. Again, it all comes down to matching a project's problems to the correct Patterns.

I must here recount certain experiences I've had developing software for various industries. For one client, my team and I were asked to create software in Java that would be the cool, interactive version of their Web site. The client did not have any Java programmers but nevertheless wanted this software to be written in such a way that they could modify its behavior wherever and whenever they wanted, without having to make programming changes. A tall order!

After some analysis of their needs, we saw that the Command Pattern would play an essential role in the design. We would write command objects and let these commands control the entire behavior of the software. The users would be empowered to parameterize the commands, order them, and choose where and when they would run.

This solution worked perfectly, and the Command Pattern was the key to our success. So here we didn't wait to refactor our way to using the Command Pattern. Instead, we saw a need up front and programmed the software using command from the start.

On another project, a system was required to run both as a stand-alone application *and* on the Web. The Builder Pattern played a huge role in this system. Without it, I shudder to think what sort of bloated design would have been cobbled together. The Builder Pattern simply lives for solving problems like how to run on different platforms or in different environments. It was therefore a good early choice of a Pattern.

At this point, I must make it clear that even though Patterns were introduced early in the design life cycle, they were still implemented in their most primitive forms to start. Only later, when additional functionality was required, were these implementations either altered or upgraded.

An example will make this clear. The software that was controlled exclusively via commands was implemented with multithreaded code. There were times when two threads might be using the same Macro-Command to run a sequence of commands. But we had not originally bothered to make our MacroCommand thread-safe. So when we started to encounter weird bugs because of this, we had to reconsider our implementation. The question was, would it make sense to invest time in making our MacroCommand thread-safe or was there an easier way to solve the problem?

Patterns and Simplicity

It turned out that the easier way to solve the problem, and avoid overengineering, was to simply have two separate instances of MacroCommand each to be used by only one thread. We were able to implement that solution in 30 seconds. Compare that to the time it would have taken to implement a thread-safe MacroCommand.

This example shows how the XP philosophy of keeping things simple has an affect on how Patterns are programmed and used. Without the drive toward simplicity, overengineered solutions, like the thread-safe MacroCommand command, can easily proliferate.

So the relationship between simplicity and Patterns is important. When programmers need to make design decisions, it's important that they try to keep their designs simple, since simple designs are usually far easier to maintain and extend than large, complex designs. We already know that refactoring is meant to keep us on the simple path: It encourages us to take small, simple steps to improve our designs incrementally and to avoid overengineering.

But what about Patterns? Do they help us stay simple? Some would argue that they don't. They think that Patterns, while useful, tend to complicate designs. They see Patterns as causing a proliferation of objects and an overreliance on object composition.

This perspective is really the result of a naïve understanding of how to successfully use Patterns. Once again, experience equips a Patterns user to avoid complicated designs, proliferations of objects, and too much object composition.

Experienced users of Patterns actually make their designs simpler when they use Patterns. Again, an example may make my point clear.

JUnit is the simple, useful, Java testing framework written by Kent Beck and Erich Gamma. It is an excellent piece of software, dense with well-selected and simply implemented Patterns. As an experiment, I recently asked some folks to DeGoF JUnit; that is, to remove the Design Patterns from JUnit to see what it would look like without them. This was a very interesting exercise, because it made the participants think really hard about when it is appropriate to introduce a Pattern into a system. To illustrate a lesson they learned, we will DeGoF a few extensions that were added to JUnit in version 2.1.

JUnit has an abstract class called TestCase, from which all concrete test classes descend. TestCase provides no way to run a test multiple times, nor does it provide a way to run a test within its own thread. Erich and Kent implemented repeatable tests and thread-based tests quite elegantly using the decorator Pattern. But what if a team or a pair of programmers didn't know decorator? Let's see what they might develop and assess how simple it would be.

Here's what TestCase looked like in version 1.0 of the JUnit framework. (Comments and numerous methods have been omitted for brevity.)

```java
public abstract class TestCase implements Test {
private String fName;

    public TestCase(String name) {
        fName= name;
    }

    public void run(TestResult result) {
        result.startTest(this);
        setUp();

        try {
            runTest();
        }
        catch (AssertionFailedError e) {
            result.addFailure(this, e);
        }
        catch (Throwable e) {
            result.addError(this, e);
        }

        tearDown();
        result.endTest(this);
    }

    public TestResult run() {
        TestResult result= defaultResult();
        run(result);
        return result;
    }

    protected void runTest() throws Throwable {
        Method runMethod= null;
        try {
            runMethod= getClass().getMethod(fName, new
                        Class[0]);
        } catch (NoSuchMethodException e) {
            e.fillInStackTrace();
            throw e;
        }

        try {
            runMethod.invoke(this, new Class[0]);
        }
```

```
    catch (InvocationTargetException e) {
            e.fillInStackTrace();
            throw e.getTargetException();
    }
    catch (IllegalAccessException e) {
            e.fillInStackTrace();
            throw e;
    }
}

public int countTestCases() {
    return 1;
}
}
```

The new requirements call for allowing tests to run repeatedly, in their own threads, or both. Inexperienced programmers usually subclass when they get new requirements like this. But here, since they know that some TestCases will need to be able to run repeatedly in a thread or repeatedly run TestCases in separate threads, the programmers know that they need to give this some more thought.

One way to implement this would be just to add all the functionality to the TestCase class itself. Many developers, especially those who don't know Patterns, would do this without worrying about the negative effects of bloating their classes. They have to add functionality, so they'll add it where they can. The following code might be their implementation:

```
public abstract class TestCase implements Test {
    private String fName;
    private int fRepeatTimes;

    public TestCase(String name) {
        this(name, 0);
    }

    public TestCase(String name, int repeatTimes) {
        fName = name;
        fRepeatTimes = repeatTimes;
    }

    public void run(TestResult result) {
        for (int i=0; i < fRepeatTimes; i++) {
            result.startTest(this);
            setUp();
```

```
        try {
            runTest();
        }
        catch (AssertionFailedError e) {
                result.addFailure(this, e);
        }
        catch (Throwable e) {
                result.addError(this, e);
        }

        tearDown();
        result.endTest(this);
        }
    }

    public int countTestCases() {
        return fRepeatTimes;
    }
}
```

Notice how the run(TestResult result) method is a little bigger. They've also added another constructor on TestCase. No big deal so far. And here we could say that if this was all they had to do, using decorator would be overkill.

Now, how about running a TestCase in its own thread? Again, here is another possible implementation:

```
public abstract class TestCase implements Test {
    private String fName;
    private int fRepeatTimes;
    private boolean fThreaded;

    public TestCase(String name) {
        this(name, 0, false);
    }

    public TestCase(String name, int repeatTimes) {
        this(name, repeatTimes, false);
    }

    public TestCase(String name, int repeatTimes, boolean
        threaded) {
        fName = name;
        fRepeatTimes = repeatTimes;
        fThreaded = threaded;
    }
```

```java
public void run(TestResult result) {
    if (fThreaded) {
        final TestResult finalResult= result;
        final Test thisTest = this;
        Thread t= new Thread() {
            public void run() {
                for (int i=0; i < fRepeatTimes; i++) {
                    finalResult.startTest(thisTest);
                    setUp();

                    try {
                        runTest();
                    }
                    catch (AssertionFailedError e) {
                        finalResult.addFailure(thisTest, e);
                    }
                    catch (Throwable e) {
                        finalResult.addError(thisTest, e);
                    }

                    tearDown();
                    finalResult.endTest(thisTest);
                }
            }
        };
        t.start();
        result = finalResult;
    } else {
        for (int i=0; i < fRepeatTimes; i++) {
            result.startTest(this);
            setUp();

            try {
                runTest();
            }
            catch (AssertionFailedError e) {
                result.addFailure(this, e);
            }
            catch (Throwable e) {
                result.addError(this, e);
            }

            tearDown();
            result.endTest(this);
        }
    }
}
```

```
public int countTestCases() {
    return fRepeatTimes;
}
}
```

Hmm, this is starting to look pretty bad. We now have three constructors to support these two new features, and the run(TestResult result) method has mushroomed in size.

Despite all the new code, our programmers have still not met the requirements: They still can't run repeated tests that each execute in their own thread. They'd have to add more code for that. I'll spare you.

Refactoring could help this code a little. But consider for a moment what we'd have if just one more requirement comes in. JUnit 3.1 now supports four different TestCase decorators, which can be easily combined to get the functionality needed. And yet the JUnit implementation is simple—it doesn't create cluttered code. It keeps the TestCase class simple and lightweight by decorating TestCases only when needed, and in whatever order or combinations a user likes.

This is clearly an example of how Patterns help to keep designs simple. It also shows how inexperienced developers can improve their designs by knowing which Patterns to target during refactorings.

Becoming Experienced with Patterns

Using Patterns to develop software is intelligent, but if you lack experience with Patterns, it can also be dangerous. For this reason, I am a great advocate of Pattern study groups. Such groups allow people to become proficient with Patterns at a steady pace with the help of their peers.

Patterns are most useful when people know them and use them in a disciplined way: the XP way. Using Patterns the XP way encourages developers to keep designs simple and to refactor to Patterns solely based on need. It encourages the use of Patterns early in a design when they are critical. It encourages the correct matching of problems with Patterns that help solve them. And finally, it encourages developers to write simple implementations of Patterns, which they may evolve as needed.

Patterns are indeed more useful in the context of XP, and XP development is more likely to succeed when it includes the use of Patterns.

References

[Beck2000] K. Beck. Private communication. January 2000.

[Beck+1994] K. Beck, R. Johnson. "Patterns Generate Architectures." *European Conference on Object-Oriented Programming (ECOOP)*, 1994.

[Fowler+1999] M. Fowler, K. Beck, J. Brant, W. Opdyke, D. Roberts. *Refactoring: Improving the Design of Existing Code*. Addison-Wesley, 1999.

[Gamma+1995] E. Gamma, R. Helm, R. Johnson, J. Vlissides. *Design Patterns: Elements of Reusable Object-Oriented Software*. Addison-Wesley, 1995.

[Jeffries1999] R. Jeffries. "Patterns and Extreme Programming." *Portland Pattern Repository*. December 1999.

[Kerth1999] N. Kerth. Conversation. March 1999.

[Kerievsky1996] J. Kerievsky. "Don't Distinguish Between Classes and Interfaces." *Portland Pattern Repository*. 1996.

Acknowledgments

Many thanks to Kent Beck, Martin Fowler, and Ward Cunningham for kindly reviewing this chapter.

About the Author

Programming professionally since 1987, Joshua Kerievsky is the founder and chief programmer of Industrial Logic, Inc. (http://industrial-logic.com), a company specializing in Patterns and XP. As an XP Coach, mentor, and leader of intensive workshops, Joshua helps organizations learn and use the software industry's very best practices. Joshua can be reached at Joshua@industriallogic.com.

Part 4

Pair Programming, Testing, and Refactoring

Chapter 14

The Costs and Benefits of Pair Programming

—*Alistair Cockburn and Laurie Williams*

Knowledge is commonly socially constructed, through collaborative efforts toward shared objectives or by dialogues and challenges brought about by differences in persons' perspectives.

—[Salomon1993]

Pair or collaborative programming is where two programmers develop software side by side at one computer. Using interviews and controlled experiments, the authors investigated the costs and benefits of pair programming. They found that for a 15 percent increase in program development hours, pair programming improves design quality, reduces defects and field support costs, reduces staffing risk, enhances technical skills, improves team communications, and is considered more enjoyable at statistically significant levels.

Introduction

When pair programming, two programmers work collaboratively on the same algorithm, design, or programming task, sitting side by side at one computer. This practice has been nominated several times in the last decades as an improved way of developing software [Beck2000; Constantine1995]. However, convention speaks against having two people work together to develop code—having "two do the work of one," as some people see it. The argument against pair programming can be summed up as follows:

- Managers view programmers as a scarce resource, and are reluctant to "waste" such by doubling the number of people needed to develop a piece of code.
- Programming has traditionally been taught and practiced as a solitary activity.
- Many experienced programmers are very reluctant to program with another person. Some say their code is personal or that another person would only slow them down. Others say that working with a partner will cause trouble coordinating work times or code versions.

At the same time, pair programming is gaining popularity:

- Several well-respected programmers enjoy working in pairs, making it their preferred programming style [Beck2000; Constantine1995].
- Seasoned pair programmers describe working in pairs as "more than twice as fast" [Beck2000].
- Qualitative evidence suggests the resulting design is better, the code simpler and easier to extend.
- Even relative novices contribute to an expert's programming.

This raises some provocative questions. Is pair programming really more effective than solo programming? What are the economics? What about the people factor—do they gain enjoyment on the job?

Based on recent interest in pair programming, the authors examined interview and experimental data to understand the costs and benefits of practice. This chapter presents the results of that investigation. Previous publications [Williams+2000; Nosek1998] have demonstrated that pair programming is beneficial. The purpose of this chapter is to reexamine these results and to further explain why pair programming is beneficial.

A Project Experience

The following excerpt comes from an experienced programmer describing his organization's first venture into pair programming. It reveals many features of the pair programming experience, as will be discussed in this chapter.

In early December my team began a high-risk activity: it involved touching just about every file, merging the code together, and trying to keep everything working. Furthermore, one tree involved fairly deep rearchitecture. So the merge would be composed of both utter tedium and massive thought effort.

The staff agreed with my points that pair programming:

- *Should significantly reduce the risk of subtle errors that would make debugging excruciating;*
- *Would give us a much broader code review than we'd ever had; and*
- *Would provide an opportunity to communicate knowledge between coders.*

For the first few weeks, things didn't work out as envisioned. Instead of doing side-by-side pair programming, the first few people did what I called "partner programming": they coded individually for awhile, and then reviewed the changes with their partner before checking-in the modifications. They reported that they were catching errors early. This was encouraging, but I was disappointed that they weren't working together consistently.

But about four months into the merge, I began to notice that things were changing. One pair in particular spent their whole day together, doing honest-to-goodness pair programming, and the other two pairs were getting much closer to that ideal. In discussions it was clear that they knew why the change was happening. It simply worked better!

They discovered that it took longer to work independently and then review the changes, since the review process involved teaching your partner everything you had learned in making the changes. And that took almost as long as making the changes to begin with. By working together they could avoid "doing it twice," the coding went faster due to the two-brain effect, and they were much more confident in the correctnes of the results.

When we finally made it to the first checkpoint application, we zoomed through QA with hardly a hitch. Everyone, myself included, was amazed that it didn't take weeks to debug, especially given that one of the trees had recently spent six weeks in QA hell. It was obvious that the pairs had dramatically reduced the defect rate.

As the merge progressed the pairs worked together even more closely.

. . . As each subsystem was complete the pairs would get rearranged based on knowledge of the next task. This slowed things down because the new pairs would have to spend time getting in phase with one another

before working effectively. But by August the pairs were fairly well cemented, to the point where they would routinely speak for each other in our twice-weekly team meetings.

Subsequent releases, both internal and external, went smoothly and we rarely hit massive show-stopper bugs. The continual review caught many serious issues midstream, including some major design problems that hadn't been noticed before.

I wasn't involved in a pair until fairly late in the game. Once my partner and I synchronized our brains, it was a great experience.

He was relatively junior, but he asked the right questions and, by struggling for answers, we usually forced ourselves to discover the best solution to each problem.

. . . The team members decided to do it for themselves. None of my pontification had as much effect as experience.

Investigative Paths

We now explore eight aspects of organizational and software engineering effectiveness. Surprisingly, all aspects support pair programming. These investigative aspects are briefly described in the following terms:

⬦ *Economics.* A recent controlled experiment of advanced undergraduates at the University of Utah [Williams2000] found there to be a 15 percent reduction in defect count with a similar (15 percent) increase in development time with the second person. Industry figures for cost of external testing and field repair predict that the fewer defects more than offset the development time increase.

⬦ *Satisfaction.* People working in pairs have found the experience more enjoyable than working alone.

⬦ *Design quality.* The university study found that the programs produced by the pairs were notably shorter than those delivered by solo developers. Though we must be circumspect with assertions about shorter programs having better designs, interviewed practitioners consistently say the pair-generated designs are better than their solo designs.

⬦ *Continuous reviews.* Pair programming's shoulder-to-shoulder technique serves as a continual design and code review, leading to more efficient defect removal rates.

⬦ *Problem solving.* Interview participants constantly refer to the team's ability to solve "impossible" problems faster.

- *Learning.* Pair programmers repeatedly cite how much they learn from each other.
- *Team building and communication.* Interview participants describe that people learn to discuss and work together. This improves team communication and effectiveness.
- *Staff and project management.* Because multiple people have familiarity with each piece of code, pair programming reduces staff-loss risk.

In this chapter, each of these investigative paths is further discussed, the supporting statistical and interview data is reviewed, and the costs and the benefits are highlighted.

Economics

The affordability of pair programming is a key issue. If it is much more expensive, managers simply will not permit it. Skeptics assume that incorporating pair programming will double code development expenses and critical staffing needs. Along with code development costs, however, other expenses, such as quality assurance and field support costs, must also be considered. IBM reported spending about $250 million repairing and reinstalling fixes to 30,000 customer-reported problems [Humphrey1995]. At $100 to $200 per programmer-hour, this $8,000 per defect justifies 400 to 800 hours of additional development programmer time per defect.

In 1999, Laurie Williams ran a controlled experiment at the University of Utah to investigate the economics of pair programming [Williams2000]. Advanced undergraduates in a software engineering course participated in the experiment. One-third of the class coded class projects by themselves, following the Personal Software Process (PSP) [Humphrey1995] to track and improve their work habits. The rest of the class completed their projects with a collaborative partner following a process similar to the Collaborative Software Process (CSP) [Williams2000]. Students recorded how much time they spent on their assignments via a Web-based data recording and information retrieval system. When the students began working, they initiated a timer in the system. When they completed an activity, they stopped the timer. Their elapsed time was saved in a database for further analysis. The results of how much time the students spent on the assignments are shown in

Figure 14.1. After the initial adjustment period in the first program (the "jelling" assignment, which took approximately 10 hours), the pairs only spent about 15 percent more working hours in total completing their assignments, compared to the individuals and this increase is not statistically significant [Williams2000]. (For example, if one individual spent 10 hours on a program, the pair would work together for $5\frac{3}{4}$ hours or $11\frac{1}{2}$ person hours. Because the pairs work in tandem, their cycle time is 42.5 percent shorter.) This demonstrated that development costs certainly do not double with pair programming.

Collaborative programmers in industry sometimes assert that pair programming is "more than twice as fast" as solo programming. This should be further investigated: Would the collaborating students eventually have realized this same improved productivity level, or do professional programmers anecdotally overestimate their productivity?

Significantly, in the experiment, the final code had about 15 percent fewer defects [Williams2000]. (These results are statistically significant with $p < 0.001$.) Figure 14.2 shows the post-development test cases

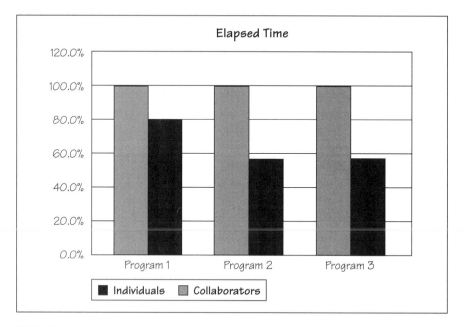

FIGURE 14.1 Programmer time

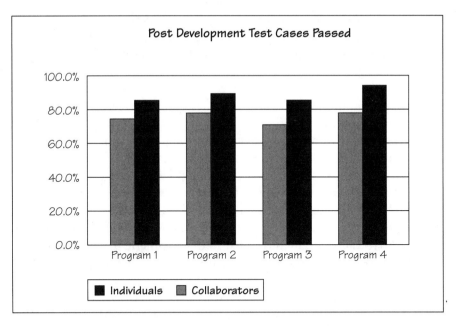

FIGURE 14.2 Code quality

the students passed for each program—essentially the percentage of the instructor's test cases passed.

We feel that the appearance of a 15 percent increase in code development time can be misleading and should be separated out into two components, the elapsed time before the program leaves the hands of the developers and the overall cost of program development. The difference can be significant to the software development organization.

Software that leaves the developers' hands early can help a company capture market share, whether it is defective or not. However, software filled with defects can have very high product lifetime costs once the defect reports are reported from the field. This gives a development company several options. Suppose a company has 10 programmers and needs to develop 10 program features, either in one or several iterations. If it can separate the five most significant features that will bring in revenue right away, it can profit by using pair programming to ship the first five features early and collect revenue on those, while the other five come in 15 percent later. If all 10 features are mandatory and market capture is critical, it can use solo programming on all 10 features and pay for the higher defect rate later, or use pair programming and deliver a higher quality product slightly later. It will be up to the company to choose the optimal strategy for its situation.

Let us briefly explain why we see that 15 percent fewer defects make the pair-programmed software development costs lower. Consider a program of 50,000 lines of code (LOC) developed by a group of individual programmers and by a group of collaborative programmers. At a typical rate of 25 LOC per hour (this was the average productivity rate of 196 engineers who took PSP training [Hayes+1997]), the individuals will develop this code in 2,000 hours. It will take the pairs 15 percent longer, or 2,300 hours. Based on representative statistics [Humphrey1995], programmers inject 100 defects per thousand lines of code, 70 percent of which are typically caught through the development process. The individuals would be expected to have 1,500 defects remaining in their program. Collaborating pairs would have 225 (15 percent) fewer.

In some organizations, the resulting code is passed to an external test or quality assurance department, which finds and fixes many of the remaining defects. Typically, in systems testing it takes between one-half [Humphrey1995] and two [Humphrey1997] work days to correct each defect. At the rate of one work day per defect, the external test team will spend an extra 225 work days correcting the 225 additional defects in individual's code. In this situation, it clearly would be less expensive to have the paired programmers' higher-quality code.

If the program is sent directly to a customer instead of a test department, pair programming is even more favorable. Industry data reports that between 33 and 88 hours are spent on each defect found in the field [Humphrey1995]. Using a fairly conservative factor of 40 hours per defect, if the customer is plagued by these "extra" 225 defects, field support will spend 9,000 hours—30 times more than the collaborators' "extra" time!

Doubtlessly, pair programming can be justified on purely economic grounds. But there are more aspects to consider.

Satisfaction

If pair programming is not satisfying, programmers won't practice it. Many programmers are initially skeptical, even resistant, to programming with a partner. It takes the conditioned solitary programmer out of his or her "comfort zone." One programmer comments:

The adjustment period from solo programming to collaborative programming was like eating a hot pepper. The first time you try it, you might not like it because you are not used to it. However, the more you eat it, the more you like it [from the interview files of L. Williams].

In statistically significant results, pair programming teams who had earlier programmed alone reported that they enjoyed pair programming more and that they were more confident in their programs than when they programmed alone (as the defect rates show they are entitled to be). The graph in Figure 14.3 shows results of anonymous surveys of professional pair programmers (who had typically been pair programming for well over a year) and of student pair programmers (who were relatively new pair programmers) at the University of Utah. Most of the programmers enjoyed programming collaboratively.

A programmer comments:

It is psychologically soothing to be sure that that no major mistakes had been made. . . . I find it reassuring to know that [partner] is constantly reviewing my code while I drive. I can be sure I had done a good job if someone else I trust had been watching and approved [from the interview files of L. Williams].

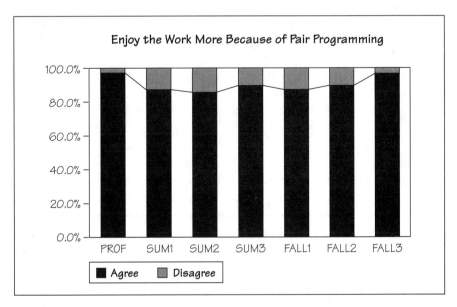

FIGURE 14.3 Pair enjoyment

Another says,

> *It's nice to celebrate with somebody when something works* [from the interview files of L. Williams].

Students Prefer Pair Programming

In the study previously discussed, in each programming assignment cycle, the individual programmers were given one program to complete while the pairs were given two programs to complete. After several programming cycles, one pair complained that this arrangement was unfair. They felt they had to work harder than the individuals during each cycle. The instructor suggested that the students split up and work as solo programmers as part of the "individual" group so they would no longer feel they were being unjustly overworked. Both students rejected this offer almost instantaneously. They did not complain about the "unjustness" of the additional workload again. We feel that this is a strong anecdotal evidence of the satisfaction of pair programming.

Design Quality

In the quantitative study at the University of Utah, the pairs not only completed their programs with superior quality, but they consistently implemented the same functionality as the individuals in fewer lines of code. Details are shown in Figure 14.4. We look at this as a secondary, not primary, indication that the pairs had better designs.

Stronger indicators supporting that pairs produce better designs come from interviews. In 1991, Nick Flor, a masters student of cognitive science, reported on distributed cognition in a collaborative programming pair he studied. Distributed cognition is a field of cognitive science based on the belief that "Anyone who has closely observed the practices of cognition is struck by the fact that the 'mind' rarely works alone. The intelligences revealed through these practices are distributed—across minds, persons, and the symbolic and physical environment" [Salomon1993].

Flor recorded, via video and audiotape, the exchanges of two programmers working together on a software maintenance task. He correlated specific verbal and nonverbal behaviors of the two under study with known distributed cognition theories [Flor+1991], "Searching Through Larger Spaces of Alternatives":

> *A system with multiple actors possesses greater potential for the generation of more diverse plans for at least three reasons: (1) the actors bring different*

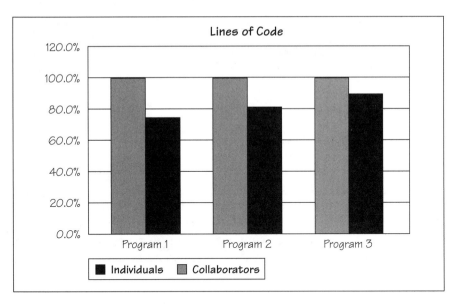

FIGURE 14.4 Lines of code

prior experiences to the task; (2) they may have different access to task relevant information; (3) they stand in different relationships to the problem by virtue of their functional roles. . . . An important consequence of the attempt to share goals and plans is that when they are in conflict, the programmers must overtly negotiate a shared course of action. In doing so, they explore a larger number of alternatives than a single programmer alone might do. This reduces the chances of selecting a bad plan [Flor+1991].

A pair programmer's description matches Flor's:

We often came up with different ideas about how the design should go and the result of arguing over which one was better often led to a truly superior hybrid design.

Finally, there are the comments from a team lead who had never heard of pair programming but settled on a pair structure after observing that one team consistently produced sounder and subtler designs:

As we proceeded with our work, I started to notice that one team consistently produced designs of distinctly better quality than the others. I asked them about this.

They said that they had taken to working together, on both the design and the programming. They found that their designs and programs were better this way. I agreed with them and made it standard for all teams to work in pairs. The design quality is now better [from the interview files of A. Cockburn].

Continuous Reviews

Inspections were introduced more than twenty years ago as a cost-effective means of detecting and removing defects from software. Results [Fagan1976] from empirical studies consistently profess the effectiveness of reviews. Even still, most programmers do not find inspections enjoyable or satisfying. As a result, inspections are often not done if not mandated, and many inspections are held with unprepared inspectors.

Despite a consistent stream of positive findings over 20 years, industry adoption of inspection appears to remain quite low, although no definite data exists. For example, an informal USENET survey we conducted found that 80% of 90 respondents practiced inspection irregularly or not at all [Johnson1998].

The theory about why inspections are effective is based on the prominent knowledge that the earlier a defect is found in a product, the cheaper it is to fix the defect. Many sources [Humphrey1997] state that it is 10 times more expensive to remove a defect for each additional process step.

This exponential cost growth is easy to understand. During an inspection, a programmer might say that the if statement starting on line 450 should also have an else clause. The programmer marks the listing and promptly makes the change at his or her computer. However, if the software is already in the field, a customer makes an irate call to the software shop: "It's Christmas Eve, and all of my cash registers just crashed. I can't sell anything!"

In the first case, the programmer looks directly at the problem that was just identified. In the second case, the field maintenance team must work to translate the symptom (all the cash registers crashed) back to the problem (which exact line(s) of code caused the crash). It is easy to see why the translation of the symptom back to the problem costs exponentially more than direct problem identification. With pair programming, this problem identification occurs on a minute-by-minute basis. These continual reviews not only outperform formal reviews in their defect removal speed, but they also eliminate the programmer's distaste for reviews.

The following, sardonically worded description from a senior (originally skeptical) programmer shows how pairing with even a novice contributed to his programming.

> *I was sitting with one of the least-experienced developers, working on some fairly straightforward task. Frankly, I was thinking to myself that with my great skill in Smalltalk, I would soon be teaching this young programmer how it's really done.*
>
> *We hadn't been programming more than a few minutes when the youngster asked me why I was doing what I was doing. Sure enough, I was off on a bad track. I went another way. Then the whippersnapper reminded me of the correct method name for whatever I was mistyping at the time. Pretty soon, he was suggesting what I should do next, meanwhile calling out my every formatting error and syntax mistake* [Williams+2000].

A final benefit of code reviews is that reviewers learn new coding idioms and language features, as well as more about the system. The continuous reviews of collaborative programming create a unique educational capability, whereby the pairs are endlessly learning from each other.

> *Indeed, review has a unique educational capability: The process of analyzing and critiquing software artifacts produced by others is a potent method for learning about languages, design techniques, application domains, and so forth* [Johnson1998].

In keeping with the known characteristics of code reviews, we find practitioners citing the following:

- ✧ Mistakes are found as they are entered, saving even the cost of compilation and providing the economic benefit of early defect identification and removal.
- ✧ Coding standards are followed more accurately with the peer pressure to do so.
- ✧ Team members learn to talk together and work together.

Problem Solving

There were times we felt that we would have given up except that we "tag teamed." I'd be on the ropes and I'd describe the problem in such a way that he had a valuable insight. Then he'd fight on as long as he could and stop. . . . Then I'd have an insight . . . and so on. I suppose others would call it brainstorming, but it feels different to me [David Wagstaff, software engineer, Salt Lake City].

Pair relaying is our name for the effect Wagstaff describes. Indeed, pairs consistently report that they solve problems faster, and that it is different from improving design quality, or detecting typing errors, or brainstorming. By "problem solving," we refer to when the two are puzzled as to why something doesn't work as expected or simply can't figure out how to go forward.

In interviews and in off-hand remarks, practitioners describe contributing their knowledge to the best of their abilities, in turn. They share their knowledge and energy (and also brainstorming) in turn, chipping steadily away at the problem.

Combining brainstorming and pair relaying is powerful. One seasoned programmer wrote, "I have found that, after working with a partner, if I go back to working alone, it is like part of my mind is gone. I find myself getting confused about things."

Learning

Knowledge is constantly being passed between partners, from tool usage tips (on even just using the mouse), to programming language rules, design and programming idioms, and overall design skill. Learning occurs in a dual-apprenticeship mode. The partners take turns being the teacher and the taught, from moment to moment. Even unspoken skills and habits cross partners.

Line-of-Sight Learning in Apprenticeships

Lave and Wenger [Lave+1991] discuss apprenticeship case studies. These studies range from tailors to flag signalmen in the U.S. Navy to butchers in modern supermarkets. They subtitled the book "Legitimate Peripheral Participation" to highlight three key aspects of apprenticeship: that the novice *actively* participates; that the novice has *legitimate work* to do; and that the novice works on the *periphery*, steadily moving toward some higher rank. The novice's work is initially simple and non-critical. Later work is more critical.

One of the most distinctive characteristics they note of successful apprenticeship environments is that the novice works in a "line of sight" of the expert—that expertise is transmitted, in part, through the ongoing visual (and auditory) field. They describe successful apprenticeship learning in both tailors and Navy signalmen where "line of sight" is available. The beginner explicitly picks up skills from hearing and/or seeing the expert.

The most interesting of the case studies, for this discussion, is that of the butchers in supermarkets, who did not have line-of-sight access to their advanced practitioner. The beginner butchers were given simple cuts to perform but did not have a way to learn how to do more difficult cuts, which were being done by the senior butcher in another room. Lave and Wenger present this as a situation in which apprenticeship learning does not happen.

It should be obvious that most project programming environments match the butcher situation, not the tailor or signalman situation. Indeed, we have found it extremely difficult to set up programming environments in which line-of-sight and line-of-hearing from expert to novice can be accommodated. The novice programmer generally sits in his or her workspace working on simple code; the expert sits in his or her own workspace creating complex code and making architectural decisions. Pair programming makes a better apprenticeship situation.

Expert-In-Earshot

Alistair Cockburn obtained a project management pattern from a set of workshops with 10 senior project managers. The full pattern, listed in the appendix to this chapter, includes examples and caveats. It can be summarized as follows:

> *Use Expert-In-Earshot when novices are not learning good techniques and habits very well, but you don't want to turn the expert into a full-time teacher. Put the expert or leader in the same workspace as the more novice workers, so that the novices can learn by watching and listening, while the expert does his or her usual work. Novices will pick up expertise and (hopefully good) habits from the expert. (Your expert will be disturbed more often, so you will have to set up ways to create personal quiet time.)*

Note the overlap with the apprenticeship studies. It is significant that this pattern wanted to be accepted by the all 10 senior project managers, who would look to apply it within their company.

Pair programming is an example of both Expert-In-Earshot and of legitimate peripheral participation, with line-of-sight/hearing access. We can expect, therefore, that the learning that occurs in pair programming is more significant than merely learning new tool usage or programming language idioms. This expectation matches off-hand reports from practitioners.

Statistical Confirmation

Pair programming was used exclusively in a Web programming class taught by Laurie Williams at the University of Utah. The class consisted of 20 juniors and seniors, familiar with programming, but not with Web programming languages and tools. The students were assigned one partner to work with for the entire semester. The majority of the students had only used WYSIWYG Web page editors prior to taking the class. During the 11-week semester, the students learned advanced HTML, JavaScript, VBScript, Active Server Page Scripting, Microsoft Access/SQL, and some ActiveX commands. In many cases, they had to intertwine statements from all these languages in one program listing.

Unusual for such students, they produced their programs with minimal questions of the teaching staff. The collaborating students were queried about the reasons for their independence in an anonymous survey on the last day of class.

- Seventy-four percent wrote "between my partner and me, we could figure everything out."
- Eighty-four percent of the class agreed with the statement "I learned Active Server Pages faster and better because I was always working with a partner."

We would attribute part of that result to enhanced problem solving in pairs, as described here, and part to enhanced pair learning.

Team Building and Communication

When I arrived, I saw a disheartening sight: Bill didn't have a team; he had a random collection of six bright, talented individuals who didn't work together. They didn't sit near each other. They didn't even like each other. Here is a scene from a weekly staff meeting.

"Let's talk about pair programming." (Benefits of pair programming enumerated.) (Pause.) Therefore, pair programming is mandatory. All production code must be written with a partner present."

An awkward silence descends. Furtive eye glances are exchanged.

"I don't think that's going to work. What if I need to write code and my partner isn't available?"

"Then you find someone else. One of our goals is to spread the knowledge around."

"What if there's no one else around?"

"If I'm available, I'd be glad to work with you. If there really is nobody around, push your keyboard away and wait."

Stunned silence .

Some of the first paired sessions went smoothly. Other sessions were awkward. Communication was serial and parsimonious. I hand-held these guys by becoming a third wheel. I encouraged the developers to think out loud (what Ward Cunningham calls reflective articulation). This did the trick. They actually began to work together, not just take turns coding.

After about a week, I noticed a remarkable phenomenon. The developers were talking to each other. As people. You really would have to have been there at the beginning to appreciate this. Anyway, I noticed them having real conversations. And laughing. They actually began to enjoy and trust each other.

Within several weeks, they became a real team [from the interview files of A. Cockburn].

Peopleware [DeMarco+1977] and *The Psychology of Computer Programming* [Weinberg1998] written 20 and 30 years ago, respectively, still have not been replaced on the topic of teamwork. More recently, Extreme Programming [Beck2000], the Crystal light methodologies [Cockburn2001], and *Adaptive Software Engineering* [Highsmith1999] have strengthened attention given to team building and communication. Cockburn goes further and argues that these are first-order project drivers, not side issues [Cockburn2000].

Pair programming contributes in three ways.

1. People learn to work together, as illustrated in the quote at the beginning of this section. In the University of Utah study, none of the 14 pairs ran into an insurmountable personality clash, which is statistically significant. In industry, off-hand comments indicate personality

clashes occasionally happen, because there is not sufficient pressure or motivation for the people to learn to work together. Interviews with people who have persevered, however, reveal a pattern similar to, but not as extreme as the one in the quote. Often, by having to work together, people learn to work together.

2. Learning to work together means that the people on the team will share both problems and solutions more quickly, and be less likely to have hidden agendas from each other. Teamwork is enhanced.

3. If the pair can work together, they learn ways to communicate more easily and they communicate more often. This raises the communication bandwidth and frequency within the project, increasing overall information flow within the team. Rotating partners increases the overall information flow farther.

All of these are likely to increase team effectiveness, and, indeed, this is what pair programming teams report. We know of no statistical study of these effects.

Staff and Project Management

Project management benefits from improved staff skills and reduced staff risk. The company and the project team both benefit from the increased learning. Over the course of the project, the skills of the team members increase, in programming and in software design.

The risk from losing key programmers is reduced, because there are multiple people familiar with each part of the system. This is referred to as the "truck number" by Jim Coplien of Lucent Technologies: "How many or few people would have to be hit by a truck (or quit) before the project is incapacitated?" The worst answer is "one." Having knowledge dispersed across the team increases the truck number and project safety.

Conclusion

The significant benefits of pair programming are as follows.

- ✦ Many mistakes get caught as they are being typed in rather than in QA testing or in the field (continuous code reviews).
- ✦ The end defect content is statistically lower (continuous code reviews).

- The designs are better and code length shorter (ongoing brainstorming and pair relaying).
- The team solves problems faster (pair relaying).
- The people learn significantly more, about the system and about software development (line-of-sight learning).
- The project ends up with multiple people understanding each piece of the system.
- The people learn to work together and talk more often together, giving better information flow and team dynamics.
- People enjoy their work more.

The development cost for these benefits is not the 100 percent that might be expected but is approximately 15 percent. The extra development cost should be repaid in shorter and less expensive testing, quality assurance, and field support.

References

[Beck2000] K. Beck. *Extreme Programming Explained*. Addison-Wesley, 2000.

[Cockburn1998] A. Cockburn. *Surviving Object-Oriented Projects*. Addison-Wesley, 1998.

[Cockburn2000] A. Cockburn. "Characterizing People as Non-Linear, First-Order Components in Software Development." *International Conference on Software Engineering, 2000* (submitted for consideration). On-line as Humans and Technology Technical Report, TR 99.05, http://members.aol.com/humansandt/papers/nonlinear/nonlinear.htm.

[Cockburn2001] A. Cockburn, *Crystal "Clear": A Human-Powered Software Development Methodology for Small Teams*. On-line draft at http://members.aol.com/humansandt/crystal/clear. 2001.

[Constantine1995] L. L. Constantine. *Constantine on Peopleware*. Yourdon Press, 1995.

[DeMarco+1977] T. DeMarco, T. Lister. *Peopleware*. Dorset House, 1977.

[Fagan1976] M. E. Fagan. "Advances in Software Inspections to Reduce Errors in Program Development." *IBM Systems Journal.* Volume 15, 1976.

[Flor+1991] N. V. Flor, E. L. Hutchins. "Analyzing Distributed Cognition in Software Teams: A Case Study of Team Programming During Perfective Software Maintenance." Presented at *Empirical Studies of Programmers, Fourth Workshop,* 1991.

[Hayes+1997] W. Hayes, J. W. Over. "The Personal Software Process: An Empirical Study of the Impact of PSP on Individual Engineers." *Carnegie Mellon University/Software Engineering Institute-97-TR-001,* December 1997.

[Highsmith1999] J. Highsmith. *Adaptive Software Development.* Dorset House, 1999.

[Humphrey1995] W. S. Humphrey. *A Discipline for Software Engineering.* Addison-Wesley, 1995.

[Humphrey1997] W. S. Humphrey. *Introduction to the Personal Software Process.* Addison-Wesley, 1997.

[Johnson1998] P. M. Johnson. "Reengineering Inspection: The Future of Formal Technical Review." *Communications of the ACM.* Volume 41, 1998.

[Lave1991] J. Lave, E. Wenger. *Situated Learning: Legitimate Peripheral Participation.* Cambridge University Press, 1991.

[Nosek1998] J. T. Nosek. "The Case for Collaborative Programming." *Communications of the ACM,* March 1998.

[Salomon1993] G. Salomon. *Distributed Cognitions: Psychological and Educational Considerations.* Cambridge University Press, 1993.

[Weinberg1998] G. M. Weinberg. *The Psychology of Computer Programming Silver Anniversary Edition.* Dorset House, 1998.

[Williams2000] L. A. Williams. "The Collaborative Software Process." Ph.D. diss. Department of Computer Science, University of Utah. On-line at http://collaboration.csc.ncsu.edu/laurie/Papers/ieeeSoftware.PDF. 2000.

[Williams+2000] L. Williams, R. Kessler, W. Cunningham, R. Jeffries, "Strengthening the Case for Pair Programming." *IEEE Software* July/August 2000. On-line at http://www.cs.utah.edu/~lwilliam/Papers/ieeeSoftware.PDF.

About the Authors

Alistair Cockburn can be reached at Humans and Technology, 7691 Dell Road, Salt Lake City, Utah 84121, 801-947-9277; arc@amc.org. Laurie Williams can be reached at North Carolina State University, Raleigh, NC 27695, 919-513-4151; williams@csc.ncsu.edu.

Appendix

The "Expert-In-Earshot" Project Management Pattern

(Slightly abbreviated from http://members.aol.com/humansandt/papers/expertinearshot.htm.)

Thumbnail	Novices have a hard time developing good habits on their own, so . . . keep an expert within their hearing distance.
Indications	(1) Novices are not learning good techniques and habits very well. (2) Working on the same project, your experts have private offices and your novices use a shared workspace.
Counter Indications	(1) Regulations prevent putting expert and novices in a shared workspace. (2) The expert has poor communication skills or work habits you don't want replicated! (3) The expert spends most of her or his time in activities that would disturb the work of any novices within earshot, such as talking on the phone about other matters.

Forces	(1) You need everyone to get work done, both expert and novices.
	(2) You want the novices to learn, and the expert has good habits worth learning.
	(3) You can afford for the expert to be disturbed a bit more if the novices will learn some good habits.
	But . . .
	(1) You don't want to turn the expert into a full-time teacher.
	(2) People hesitate to disturb the boss or expert with a phone call or a knock on the door.
Do This	Put the expert or leader in the same workspace as the more novice workers, so that the novices can learn by watching and listening, while the expert does his or her usual work.
Resulting Context	(1) Novices will pick up expertise and (hopefully good) habits from the expert.
	(2) Your expert will be disturbed more often, so you or he or she will have to set up ways or conventions to create personal quiet time.
	(3) You and the expert have to watch that the novices do not simply delegate their problems to the expert.
	(4) You will have more people in the room.
Overdose Effect	(1) Too many questions will lower the expert's productivity too much.
	(2) Too many people in the same room will create too many conversations, making it hard to concentrate.
Related Patterns	*Training: Day Care* says, "Your experts are spending all their time mentoring novices, so . . . Put one expert in charge of all the novices; let the others develop the system." [CoSOOP]. This covers the dangers of having the expert try to teach while designing. In *Expert-In-Earshot*, the expert is not responsible for teaching the novices. The situation is only set up so that the novices can see and hear how the expert works, in accordance with the principles. [Cockburn1998]

Pair Programming is a nonconflicting possible partner pattern to *Expert-In-Earshot*. It can be used to bring an expert within earshot of one person (the other person in the pair), or of many people—all the rest of the people in the workspace.

Examples

(1) When Thomas J. Watson, Jr., ex-CEO of IBM, went from being an aviator and playboy to a serious businessman, his father, then CEO of IBM, assigned him to sit at the corner of the senior VP's desk for six months. For those six months, he was to do nothing but watch and listen to how this successful executive ordered his days and handled people. This is an unusual but very clear example of *Expert-In-Earshot*.

(2) A team leader given four junior designers to design a graphics workstation, was also given a private office. After a few weeks, he felt uncomfortable with the distance to his team and moved his desk to the floor with the other designers. Although the distractions were great and his main focus was not teaching the other designers, he was able to discuss with them on a timely and casual basis. They became more capable, eventually reducing the time he had to spend with them and giving them skills for their next project.

(3) The lead programmer worked in a room with six novice programmers. He had two bad habits: He scoffed at the idea of doing design in an orderly way, and instead of talking to the other programmers about how to make a good design or program, he would change their code in the middle of the night. They never knew in the morning if their program was the same as when they left it. After several months, the novices both produced bad designs and refused to design carefully. His heroic attitude had become their ideal. When he left the project, another consultant took his place, also sharing the room. He deliberately discussed designs from his desk, so the others could overhear. After a few months, three of the novices started talking and drawing designs, and soon became skilled in designing as well as programming.

Chapter 15

Unit Testing in a Java Project

—Peter Gassmann

Unit testing is a software development practice that has been around for quite some time. Because it is part of a new development methodology called Extreme Programming (XP), more developers are starting to use it. Unit testing is not testing done by specialized testers; it is part of the daily development routine of a programmer. For a new practice to be accepted by programmers, they must gain something when applying it. This chapter describes the benefits and problems associated with unit testing. It also gives hints and tips on how to write and structure tests. Further it describes the relationship to other XP practices and the advantages of combining unit testing with these practices.

To demonstrate that unit testing is beneficial in real-world projects, there is a short description of the ongoing Java project where the author has had most of the experiences described in the chapter, along with a few figures about the project.

The chapter is intended to help project managers and developers planning or starting to introduce unit tests in their Java project. The reader does not need to be familiar with JUnit and Extreme Programming, but a basic understanding certainly helps.

Extreme Introduction

Unit testing is a development practice and part of the Extreme Programming (XP) methodology [Beck2000]. But since unit testing does not depend on the other XP practices, it may be used in any software development project. In a project with changing and developing requirements, unit tests help stabilize the system. They also allow change to happen much faster and more aggressively, because any errors introduced with a change are detected immediately. And they help create a very short feedback loop for the developer.

Unit testing is not testing done by specialized testers; it is part of the daily development routine of a programmer. Unit testing means testing a unit of code. A unit of code is generally a class in an object-oriented system. However, it could also be a component or any other piece of related code. A unit test is an automated test, where one or more methods of one or more classes are invoked to create an observable result. Automated means that the results are verified automatically. The tests are usually written in the same computer language as the production code. The test verification is therefore code, which compares actual results to expected results. If a result is unexpected, the test fails. This kind of testing is in contrast to the usual print lines (in Java `System.out.println(…)`) mixed into the production code, where the programmer looks at the output on the command line and tries to figure out whether the code behaves as expected.

This chapter contains first an introduction to JUnit [JUnit1999]. After that, there is a section on how to write unit tests. The next part describes the relationship of unit testing to other XP practices. Then there is a section on the benefits of unit testing, followed by a section on pitfalls and problems. This is followed by a description of the project in which the author has made most of his experiences with unit testing. Finally, there are references to other documents and books, and some sample code.

The Unit Testing Environment

The unit tests are written in Java using JUnit. The tests are usually executed directly in VisualAge. However, they do not depend on VisualAge and may be executed on the target platform as well.

Brief Introduction to JUnit

JUnit is a unit testing framework written in Java. JUnit defines how to structure test cases and provides the tools to run them. A test is usually implemented in a subclass of `junit.framework.TestCase`. A test method is public, starts with the word "test" and takes no parameters; for example, `public void testLoad()`. The basic purpose is to compare results. Successful comparisons return true, and unsuccessful return false. Manual verification of the output of the tests, such as looking at the output of `System.out.println()` statements, is not needed. For example, if a result value is expected to be 5, it could be written as `assertEquals(5, result)`. This assert method compares both parameters on equality. If `result` does not have the value 5 during execution of the test, the comparison will return false, the test method is aborted, and the next test method is executed. The class `TestCase` contains various methods to verify results, such as `assert(boolean)`, `assertEquals(Object, Object)`, and so on. There is a GUI testrunner, `junit.ui.TestRunner`, which executes tests and displays whether the tests were successful or failed. A successful run is displayed in green, an unsuccessful run in red. A successful run means all tests ran as expected, at 100 percent. The execution scheme of a test method in JUnit is typically as follows:

```
loop over all test methods{
    setUp();       // template-method, executed before each
                        test-method
    runTheTest(); // execute the test-method, starting with
                        "test"
    tearDown();    // template-method, guaranteed to run after
                        each test-method
}
```

A test class may contain a `setUp` and a `tearDown` method, plus any number of test methods. If a test fails, the execution of the current test method is aborted immediately, but `tearDown` will be executed in any case. A test method typically tests one or more methods of a class of the production code. For a more thorough introduction, see the documentation that comes with JUnit.

Organization of the tests

In this chapter a distinction is made between production code and test code. Production code is the code that implements the functionality of the product. Test code is the code written for the unit tests, including the test bed. A test bed or test fixture is code that helps prepare a test, for example, by providing test data or by initializing a class in a way that it can be tested.

The test classes, which usually extend `junit.framework.TestCase`, plus some helper classes, are placed in test packages. This makes it easy to distinguish production code and test code. Each production package has one corresponding test package. For example, the package `com.fja.move.model` has the test package `com.fja.move.model.test`. An advantage of having separate test packages is a clear separation between production code and test code. By placing the test classes in a separate package, the package-visibility feature of the Java language cannot be used. The advantage is that the class is used in the test as if by an ordinary user of that class. It is impossible to fool ourselves by writing tests that use package-visible features, which an external user of the class could not. The disadvantage is that a larger test bed might be needed if we are to test the class, because package-visible features cannot be accessed. However, the inability to test a class without using private, protected, or package visible features is usually a sign that there is something wrong with the design of the class anyway.

Each test package contains an AllTests class. The AllTests class simply calls all other test classes in the same package. By running AllTests, all test methods in all test classes in the package are executed.

In one test package there is the AllAllTests class. This class in turn executes all AllTests classes in all test packages. The AllAllTests class runs the system test. When we integrate code, all tests executed by AllAllTests must run at 100 percent. In the project described in this chapter, AllAllTests takes around 10 minutes to run in VisualAge on a developer machine. AllAllTests is run about two to four times per day by each developer.

Tool Support

There are a few developer tasks that should be automated. JUnit already provides the framework to verify test results automatically. The following tasks may be automated as well:

⬥ Generating the test class stub. The test class stub should contain a main method that starts the JUnit-GUI. This makes it easy to start a test by simply selecting the test class in the integrated development environment (IDE), such as VisualAge, and run it.

⬥ Generating the AllTests class for a test package

Because VisualAge for Java was used in the project, the development and integration of tools to automate these tasks was straightforward and paid off many times. Sample code of a test class and an AllTests class appear at the end of this chapter.

Writing Unit Tests

Introducing Unit Tests in a Project

Having decided to introduce unit tests in a project, the project manager should ensure that developers understand the benefits of writing unit tests. Some developers have a hard time understanding and accepting unit tests, and they will be reluctant to start writing their own tests. Pair programming certainly helps introduce unit tests. The project manager should also insist that the unit tests be written parallel with or even before the production code. Writing unit tests afterward is a lot harder, and there is less obvious motivation for it.

What to Test

As a principle, the public methods of a class should be tested. It is not necessary to write tests for trivial things, such as simple get and set methods. It also usually does not pay to write tests for all the permutations and combinations that may possibly occur. Tests should be written for the cases that seem to be critical or important. Selecting which tests to write involves betting on the highest risk, on the possibility that something will fail. Failure may occur initially because some coding was forgotten, or later when something needs to be changed or enhanced, possibly by a different developer. Writing a test guarantees that if a developer changes the code in an unanticipated way, the error will be detected immediately when the tests are run. In addition, confidence in the code is enhanced if all tests are still running after a day of coding.

How to Test

Each test should be independent of other tests. This reduces the complexity of the tests, and it avoids false alarms because of unexpected side effects. Particularly with JUnit, test cases should not be expected to run in a certain order.

One test method tests one or more methods of the production code. Ideally a test method tests only one method of the production code. These tests are easiest to understand. But this is quite often not possible, because it is necessary to prepare test data or to test the effect of calling different methods in a certain combination.

A test must verify the results automatically, instead of relying on manual verification of System.out.println() statements. This allows any developer to run all tests, without having to know exactly what is being tested. The thumbs-up sign (the green light) is sufficient. The developer needs to look deeper into the problem only when a test fails.

Tests should be written for the normal cases including the boundaries plus the error cases. The assert methods in junit.framework.TestCase should be used to verify the results. To test that an exception is thrown when expected, the test could be as follows:

```
public void testSaveModel(){
    // prepare ...
    // save declares to throw an exception, so we have to
       catch it.
    try{
        model.save(); // it is expected that save will work
    } catch(ModelException e){
        // the exception is caught here to provide a good
           error message.
        // as an alternative, the exception could be added as
        // a throws clause to the method declaration and
        // would be caught by the Testrunner (part of JUnit).
        fail("unexpected exception in save:"+e);
        // failaborts the test
    }
    // test something else
    // rollback declares to throw an exception, so we have to
       catch it
    try{
        // it is expected that rollback will throw an
           exception
        model.rollback();
        // getting here means the test failed
        fail("modelexception in rollback expected");
    } catch(ModelException e){
        // since this exception was expected, it may be
           ignored
    }
    // ...
}
```

If a method is used in a test that declares to throw an exception, it is good practice to use a try catch in the test code, and to add fail() in the catch clause, in the preceding example as shown. This illustrates the expected use of the method, plus it allows the developer to add an explanation message in `fail()`, which in turn helps locate a failure inside a test method.

Usually errors can be simulated by providing illegal arguments to the component under test. If the expected exception is thrown, the test is successful. Some error conditions, such as IO errors or network errors, are practically impossible to simulate. One solution is to change the working code temporarily to verify whether the test really would react correctly. For example, if the test should fail when an `IOException` is thrown, a `throw new IOException()` should be inserted at the appropriate place in the production code. The test should then be run to see whether the `IOException` is reported as an error. The `throw new IOException()` may then be removed from the production code. Another solution is to write a test bed, such as code to simulate data and events for the test, that can be configured to simulate the problem. For example, when the model layer is tested, it might be possible to plug in code that simulates a database in memory and that can simulate certain error conditions. However, writing such simulation components might be quite expensive. Sometimes more test code is written than the production code!

When to Write Tests

The developer should write the unit tests while developing the production code. Ideally, he or she writes the tests before writing the production code. Other developers write additional tests later. For example, writing tests may help the developer understand how a class or a component can be used. Instead of being discarded afterward, tests can be kept in the test suite.

When a bug has been reported, it is advisable to write a unit test that exposes the bug. Following that the bug can be fixed. This way a lot is learned about the code, which helps the developer fix the bug and enhances the test suite.

Writing a test before the production code may sound like nonsense, but here are some reasons why it is profitable to do so:

⋄ It takes more energy to write a test if the developer believes the code is already working; it takes less energy to write it before.

⋄ Coding is really finished when all tests are green. This is vital, because it helps focus on the really important issues!

- Writing code to make a test run is definitely more fun than writing a test for code that already runs.
- In writing a test, a developer is actually creating a micro design, determining how a class should be named, how a method should be named, what the method parameters are, where responsibility should be placed, and so on. Creating such a micro design helps the developer think more from a caller perspective and less from an implementor perspective. This leads to a more flexible, usable, and cleaner design.
- Writing tests after the production code sometimes leads to situations where the code is untestable, or a very complicated test bed. In the first release of the project mentioned in this chapter, the developers quite often used static references to singletons to obtain, for example, a centrally loaded resource bundle. But to test such a class requires that the singleton class be initialized before testing begins, which might not always be possible. For example if the initialization is coded in a way that requires user interaction, such as entering a password, unit tests cannot use this part of the code.

When and How Often to Run Tests

Tests should be run in the following situations:

- Before and after refactoring a piece of code
- Before starting to implement new functionality in the system, to make sure all tests run. If the tests do not run at 100 percent before starting, it will be unclear whether the additional code made another test (unexpectedly) fail or the failure lay in the original code.
- During integration, to make sure only code with 100 percent working tests is integrated
- Each time a morale boost is needed

The tests should be run at least twice in a row without closing the JUnit window to make sure there are no side effects. (See the section, *Pitfalls and Problems.*)

If running AllAllTests takes longer than a few minutes, developers may be reluctant to run it at all. This will lower the main benefit of the unit tests—immediate feedback. It is worth trying to optimize the test code until it runs in acceptable time. If that is not possible, it is advisable to create AllAllTests for the subsystems developers are typically working on. These subsystem tests might be the AllTests for a test package. The developer can then run AllTests fairly often and run AllAllTests just during integration.

The Code Works, but There Are No Unit Tests

Imagine a situation in which a project team starts development without writing unit tests. At some point the developers decide that they want unit tests for their code, but they do not have the time—a few months—just to write tests. In that case, they should write tests for a component when:

- A component of the system needs to be enhanced
- A bug needs to be fixed
- The developer does not understand what a class or component is doing, and there is no test that explains it clearly enough

In this way a test suite can be built up slowly, until all parts of the system are more or less covered. Depending on the size of the project, it may take months until the tests are satisfactory both in quality and quantity.

Testing GUI Classes

Testing GUI classes with unit tests is very difficult and sometimes even impossible. Instead, factoring all business logic into nonvisual classes that are unit-testable is advisable. The result is that the GUI classes contain only a minimum of untested code. If this is still unsatisfactory, GUI testing tools that allow user actions to record and replay should be considered.

Unit Testing and Other XP Practices

Refactoring

Refactoring [Fowler+1999] without working unit tests is dangerous. How can one know that the system still works after refactoring without tests? As this is impossible, it is much safer to have tests. Tests should be run before starting to refactor, to make sure they are working as expected. The tests should be run again after refactoring.

Refactoring production code and unit tests at the same time should be avoided. It is too much to keep in mind at the same time.

Frequently it happens that the unit tests have to be refactored as, for example, when one discovers that a test setup can be extracted from a test class to be used by other test classes.

Pair Programming

During pair programming unit tests support communication between the two pair programming partners. Instead of discussing the design of a class theoretically, the experienced programmer can explain it to the partner with a unit test. If the idea works, the unit test is already written. If not, the experienced partner can point to the code and explain why it doesn't work, instead of saying "Your idea doesn't work." Pointing to the code focuses on the problem, which lowers the risk of getting into personal or fundamentalist discussions.

Continuous Integration

Unit tests are a key requirement of integration in very short, usually daily, cycles. Integration involves merging the changes made with the code written by the other developers. The unit tests indicate when one is ready to integrate and whether the merge was successful—that is, all tests ran at 100 percent.

Planning Game

When estimating stories and tasks, it is not necessary to estimate writing the tests separately. Writing unit tests is just a part of developing a piece of functionality. As an estimate, a third of the programming time is spent writing unit tests. This time is regained by the reduction of debugging time and the benefits of improved design. Debugging time is reduced drastically because a failed unit test indicates precisely where something went wrong. Experience shows that a lot less time is spent in the debugging with than without unit tests.

Benefits of Writing Unit Tests

Short Feedback Loop

In traditional development, functionality written by a developer is usually tested weeks later by the testing group, if there is one. So much code that could be responsible for the problem has been written by the time the bug is found, that it takes a lot of time and effort for the developers to verify and fix the bug. With unit tests, unanticipated problems are detected as soon as the test suite is run the next time, which is usually only minutes after the change has been coded. The developer will still remember what changes were made since the last time the test suite was run successfully, so one of these changes has to be responsible for the error. This fact is responsible for the dramatic reduction of time spent debugging, compared to a project without unit tests.

Improved Changeability of the System

With unit tests in place, the system can be changed and enhanced much more aggressively than it can without unit testing. There is a lot less need to worry about whether the system will still be working after the change, because the unit tests will either work or highlight the point of failure immediately. The developer is never afraid to change code. He or she can always simply write more unit tests.

Fewer Errors

Unit tests cannot, of course, guarantee an error-free system. After all, the tests might be wrong themselves. But the features that have been tested should work as expected.

Micro Design Improvements

Micro design improvement is one of the most important benefits of using unit tests, besides reducing the number of bugs in the system. The components in a system developed with unit tests are less dependent on each other, and the methods communicate much more error information, for example via exceptions. This is a result of the caller perspective of writing the tests, instead of the implementor perspective usually taken by developers.

Regression Testing

Unit tests help verify that the code does what it is conceived to do anytime, and as often as needed. Because JUnit reports the elapsed time for the tests, it is possible to use that information to detect whether a critical component is getting faster or slower. This does not of course, replace performance testing.

Refactoring Support

Unit tests are a prerequisite for refactoring. If there is need to refactor a part of the system, and if it is feared that something might break, the developer must make sure that the unit tests are running at 100 percent before starting to refactor. If there are no tests, they have to be written first.

Communicating Design/Documenting Code

Unit tests document the micro design of the system by showing how the code is intended to be used and which combinations of input are valid. It furthermore documents which error conditions are reported. When trying to understand a piece of code, developers sometimes would like to step through the code in the debugger to see exactly what happens. But which feature does the developer need to invoke in a larger system so that a certain breakpoint will be reached? It is much easier to just go into the test class for the relevant class, and start stepping through the test cases.

Teaching Junior Programmers

It is advisable to have the experienced programmer write the tests and a junior programmer make them run, that is, implement the production code. This way the design can be influenced by the experienced programmer, while the junior programmer has a chance to learn.

Another way unit tests can be used as a teaching tool is to write a unit test and ask the junior programmer to make the test run—and find and fix any bugs in his or her code. Usually it is quite obvious that the test makes sense, so there is no need to debate. In addition, the junior developer can take pride in getting the unit test to run. The result is that the junior developer will, if necessary, change his or her code to make the test run and will be happy at the end because the test is working.

Installing a Developer Machine

Unit tests can verify whether a developer has everything configured correctly on his or her machine. Usually they cover most of the required components of the system. Therefore if the unit tests work, development may begin.

Boosting Morale

If morale is low, running unit tests can give it a boost. It simply makes people feel good to see the green light appear. When the light is red, it is clear what has to be done next, because there is nothing more important than fixing the production code until the tests run again at 100 percent.

Pitfalls and Problems

Caches

Sometimes it is necessary to test classes that contain some sort of caching functionality, in Java often implemented with static variables or as singletons. The cache might have to be released at the beginning of the test, for example in the setUp method, to make sure there are no side effects. On the other hand, if there is a need to test the caching functionality, this has to be done with great care.

Quite often caching functionality can be found in frameworks.

Out-of-Sync AllTests

Each time a new test class is created in a package, it is essential to update the AllTests class for the package. Otherwise it will be testing only part of the package and not the complete one. JUnit displays the total number of tests. There should be another way to find out how many tests the package contains, so the total number can be verified. In the project mentioned previously, again a VisualAge tool has been implemented that counts the number of test methods in the project or in a package. This number can then be compared to the total displayed by JUnit when AllAllTests are run.

Database Access

It must be kept in mind that there might be data in the database that could make a database access test fail. For example, additional, unexpected hits might occur in a search logic test. One strategy to avoid this problem is using data that does not make sense from a business perspective, the kind of data most probably no one in the team will have in his database, such as nineteenth-century valid-from and valid-to dates or negative numbers for key values.

One general rule is to insert the test data into the database during the test, instead of relying on a particular database content. But care must be taken to delete the data at the end of the test, even if the test fails. This is necessary to avoid side effects when the tests are run the next time. One way to do this is to use the tearDown method for that task by adding all data that needs to be deleted immediately after creating it to a test-class variable, such as a vector. In the `tearDown` method, everything found in the vector is to be deleted, ignoring possible errors. See the sample code at the end of this chapter for an example.

If it is too complicated or time consuming to generate the test data during the test, and if the tests do not change the test data, a database containing the test data could be used. Steps must be taken to ensure that all developers have access to the version of this database corresponding to the integrated code, and that it is clear that the test database is required for the tests.

When testing read-only access to a database, it is not necessary to insert test data for each test method. This also makes the test faster. Instead, the test data for all test methods in the class should be prepared only once, and then all test methods in the class should be run. The class `junit.extensions.TestSetup` might be helpful for this purpose.

Complicated Test Code

The same rules for writing readable and understandable code apply for production code as well as for unit test code. Consider, for example, *extract method* [Fowler+1999] to factor out the test setup code from the actual tests/asserts.

Meaningless, Easy Tests

Of course it is easy to write tests that are green. An empty test method does that. Good tests are hard to write. If there are plans for code reviews in a project, the tests should be reviewed as well, maybe even before the production code. It certainly makes sense to specify what to test together with the specification of the functionality to be implemented.

Problems with People

Probably the most difficult problem is having a developer in the team who refuses to write unit tests. All other developers who write unit tests will feel uncomfortable about touching parts of the system written by this developer. The problem may be solved if all development is done in pairs, so that at least one of the two partners writes unit tests.

Project Description

The project that the author is working on follows to a large degree the XP methodology as described by Beck [Beck2000]. The unit tests are written by the developers, and there is no separate quality assurance group. The tests are developed using JUnit, the unit testing framework for Java, developed by Kent Beck and Erich Gamma [JUnit1999].

The persistency framework used generates classes and interfaces. No tests are written for the generated code, the code is tested indirectly via other classes. Tables 15.1 and 15.2 are snapshots of the system during the second major release.

A few facts to note: About a third of all handwritten code is test code. For every fifth handwritten public method there is one test method. In the model layer, there is about as much test code as handwritten production code, whereas in the GUI layer there is one line of test code on four lines of production code.

Specific Experiences in the Project

Despite the fact that about a third of the code written in the project was test code, the project was always on schedule. The project has already delivered three minor releases to the users. Thanks to the unit tests, remarkably few errors have been found during testing or in production. It was enough to have just a few days of testing before delivering the

TABLE 15.1 Project Features

	Value/Description
Type of system	Insurance-Agent System running on a laptop, usually used off-line. Feature to download and upload data when on-line.
Project duration	3 years, split into 3 major releases
Number of developers	4 + 1 project leader
Development environment	VisualAge for Java 3.0 professional edition; CVS on Linux (central code repository for production code and test code)
Architecture off-line system	Java application, fat client, relational database
Architecture on-line system	Client: Java application, CORBA-client, local relational database Server: Java CORBA-server, relational database on host

TABLE 15.2 Code Metrics

	Total Code	Handwritten Production Code	Generated Production Code	Test Code
NLOC (Noncommented lines of code)	60,183	31,489	13,440	15,254
Classes	666	312	184	170
Total methods	7,620	2,660	3,841	1,119
Test methods	431			431

software, because practically no errors, like `NullPointerExceptions`, slipped past the unit tests.

The project always had to cope with changing requirements. Because of the unit tests, it was always very easy to make changes, since side effects were reported by the unit tests immediately. The developers in the team agreed that, thanks to the tests, making changes to the code was less stressful, and changes could be made much more aggressively.

More than once the project had to incorporate new versions of libraries. This was always very easy because the tests covered practically all usage scenarios of the library. At one time in the project, a switch had to be made to a library from a different vendor, which seemed at first to be a very difficult change. Thanks to the tests, it was done in barely one hour. The tests were also helpful for checking the installation in the target environment, specifically if all libraries were present.

The team had to incorporate unexperienced developers. The unit tests helped the new developers to understand the code, and their existence made it less stressful for the new developers to make changes to the system because they always knew that there was a safety net in place.

And finally, the developers have come to believe that the code is of higher quality, because often (not yet always) the unit tests were written before the production code, and because it was always possible to do refactoring fairly aggressively.

Conclusion

The arguments presented in this chapter should be enough motivation to use unit tests in any project. Unit tests provide not only long-term benefits for the project, but also short-term benefits for the developers. This makes acceptance of this practice a lot easier. The test infection even leads to situations in which developers refuse to work without being allowed to write unit tests.

The experiences in the project described clearly show that the costs of writing the tests is considerably less than what is gained in terms of quality, speed, and changeability, both in the short term and in the long term. It also became clear that unit testing does not or only to a small extent depend on other XP practices. This makes unit testing interesting for non-XP projects as well. It also makes unit testing well suited as the starting practice when XP is adopted.

References

[Beck2000] K. Beck. *Extreme Programming Explained*. Addison-Wesley, 2000.

[Beck+1998] K. Beck, E. Gamma. "Test Infected: Programmers Love Writing Tests." *JavaReport* July 1998.

[Beck+1999] K. Beck, E. Gamma. "JUnit: A Cook's Tour." *JavaReport*. May 1999.

[Fowler+1999] M. Fowler, K. Beck, J. Brant, W. Opdyke, D. Roberts. *Refactoring: Improving the Design of Existing Code*. Addison-Wesley, 1999.

[JUnit1999] K. Beck, E. Gamma. *JUnit*. On-line at http://www.junit.org. 1999.

[Wiki] Anonymous. "UnitTests." *Portland Pattern Repository*. On-line at http://c2.com/cgi/wiki?UnitTests. A Web page about unit testing. 2000.

Acknowledgments

The author would like to thank Claudia Chini, Anna-Maria Münch, and Christian Ulmann for their comments and suggestions for this chapter. He would also like to thank Robert H. Gassmann for helping improve his English skills. Thanks to the anonymous reviewers of the

XP2000 conference for their comments. And finally thanks to Kent Beck for infecting the author with the unit testing virus.

About the Author

Peter Gassmann is working at Sun Microsystems (Switzerland) AG and can be reached at peter.gassmann@acm.org.

Sample Code

A Test Class

```java
package com.fja.move.model.test;
import java.util.Vector;
import com.fja.move.model.PersonModel;

public class PersonModelTest extends junit.framework.TestCase{
    // this vector is used to store models which should be
    // deleted in tearDown
    private Vector modelsToDelete_ = new Vector();

    /**
     * the main-method starts the gui-test-runner, which in
     * turn
     * runs all tests in this class. The test-runner finds all
       tests via reflection, that is why they should
     * start with "test".
     */
    public static void main(){
        String[] myargs = new String[]{PersonModelTest.class.get
                        Name()};
        junit.ui.TestRunner.main(myargs);
    }

    /**
     * A test method starts with "test", accepts no parameters,
     * is public and returns nothing.
     */
```

```java
public void testSaveAndUpdate(){
    PersonModel personModel = new PersonModel();
    // ...
    try{
        personModel.save();
        // if save worked, make sure to delete the model at
        // the end
        modelsToDelete_.addElement(personModel);
    }
    catch(ModelException e){
        // the exception is caught here to provide a good
        // error message.
        // as an alternative, the exception could be added
        // as a throws clause to the method declaration
        // and would be caught
        // by the Testrunner (part of JUnit).
        // fail is a method of TestCase to abort a test
        // with a message.
        fail("unexpected exception in save:"+e);
    }
    // do some more testing ...
    // see the documentation for the various
    // assert...-methods in TestCase
    assert("personModel should not be changed anymore
            after save", personModel.isChanged() == false);
}

/**
 * setUp will be called by the framework before each
 * test-method.
 */
public void setUp(){
    modelsToDelete_ = new Vector();
}

/**
 * tearDown will be called by the framework after each
 * test-method,
 * in any case (even if the test fails).
 */
public void tearDown(){
    TestHelper.deleteModels(modelsToDelete_);
}
}
```

An AllTests Class

```
package com.fja.move.model.test;
import junit.framework.Test;
import junit.framework.TestSuite;

public class AllTests extends junit.framework.TestCase{
    /**
     * the main-method starts the gui-test-runner,
     * which in turn runs all tests in this class.
     * If there is a suite-method, it will be
     * called to start the tests (static approach).
     */
    public static void main{String[] args = new
                            String[]{AllTests.class.getName()};
        junit.ui.TestRunner.main(myargs);
    }

    /**
     * The suite-method is called automatically by the
     * framework.
     */
    public static Test suite() {
        TestSuite suite= new TestSuite();
        // PersonModelTest does not contain a suite-method,
        // the reflection-approach is used.
        suite.addTest(new TestSuite(PersonModelTest.class));
        // ContractModelTest contains a suite-method,
        // the static approach is used.
        suite.addTest(ContractModelTest.suite());
        // add further test classes in the same package ...
        return suite;
    }
}
```

Chapter 16

Retrofitting
Unit Tests with JUnit

—*Kevin Rutherford*

This chapter documents the experiences to date of a small Java development team that adopted a new unit testing regime in the midst of an ongoing, medium-sized project. The team chose to develop the tests using an open-source framework called JUnit.

Introduction

This chapter describes the experiences of a small Java team that attempted to retrofit a new software testing regime during the course of an ongoing development project. The chapter emphasizes the impact of adding new tests to a live software development project and is not intended to provide a detailed description of the JUnit testing framework or its underlying philosophy. The action described took place throughout the last half of 1999 and continues today.

Stingray is a strategic software program designed to produce an integrated end-to-end silicon design environment. It provides a metadata environment that promotes and encourages intellectual property (IP) reuse, in which existing design tools and flows can be executed. Design tools are "encapsulated" by writing wrapper code that bridges the tool's expectations into the metadata environment of Stingray.

The project described in this chapter is Stingray version 1.0, which comprises a Java framework called Corvette, together with an extensible suite of design tool wrappers known as "encapsulations," also written in Java. The Corvette framework provides the runtime environment for design tools and the metadata-based user workspace. The metadata service is provided by a module that implements the standard Java Naming and Directory Interface (JNDI); Corvette is therefore independent of the technology used to store and retrieve IP. Corvette also provides a range of utility classes for use by the encapsulation writer.

Stingray 1.0 is targeted to run on Solaris and HP-UX. The software is being developed under Windows/NT using the JDK version 1.1.8 (JDK2 does not yet exist on HPUX-10). A small portion of the system (less than 100 LOC) is written in C++ and accessed via the Java Native Interface (JNI). The software build environment is based on UNIX-style make, and uses the GNU Cygwin32 UNIX emulation tool kit.

The development team consists of five developers averaging about one year's experience with Java and totaling 45 years software development experience. The author joined the team in August 1999 and was given the task of fixing and completing the JNDI service provider module. The module already contained 40 classes and about 2,000 lines of Java code. Some of it worked as required, some of it was incomplete, and some of it was complete but had bugs in it. There were two test cases, written in JPython, one of which didn't run.

We chose JUnit as our testing framework because the author had used it successfully before, and because the team had previously had little success with ad hoc approaches to unit testing. Our objective was to improve the quality of our software and of our development process.

In round numbers, this story begins with the system comprising about 180 Java classes in 15 packages, with half a dozen ad hoc unit tests written in JPython or embedded in makefiles. At the time of this writing the system comprises around 350 classes in 25 packages, with 85 tester classes implementing 350 test cases.

The JUnit Philosophy

JUnit [Beck+1998; Beck+1999; Fowler+1999] was developed by Kent Beck and Erich Gamma as a Java version of Beck's successful Smalltalk testing framework. These test frameworks form a key part of the Extreme Programming (XP) [Beck2000] approach to software development, which has some implications for how tests are organized.

As seen from the outside, the functionality of a system such as Stingray 1.0 can be broken down into a (probably large) number of user stories (think of function points or, if you're used to use cases, think scenarios). The totality of these stories capture the entire system requirements—including the nonfunctional ones, such as distribution, performance, and resilience (because these all impinge on the user in some way). Therefore it seems reasonable that the primary set of tests for the system should be written in response to these stories. Thus each user story will correspond to one or more system tests. In XP these are (notionally) owned by the user/customer, because they demonstrate that the developers have fulfilled their contract (and that the system does everything requested).

Internally, unseen by the user, programmers will divide the system into a number of modules. Often a module will play a part in supporting more than one story, and conversely most stories will involve the functionality of several modules. (Thus modules and stories form orthogonal dimensions through which the developer and user see the system.) To speed development, each module should be accompanied by a number of tests (called unit tests) that demonstrate that it does the job it was designed to do.

These two testing dimensions are independent. Strictly speaking, only the system tests are required, although the unit tests significantly improve the speed and quality of development and support. In this chapter, we concentrate on our efforts to retrofit a set of unit tests for the Stingray 1.0 system.

With the XP approach, the unit tests are all completely automated. Anyone can run the unit tests for any part of the system, without needing to understand or interpret cryptic messages and log files. If any test fails, the programmer gets simple output of the form:

```
..............F......
22 tests, 1 failure, 0 errors
Failures:
1) ToolProcessTester.test_runDir:
    expected "hello" but was "goodbye"
```

JUnit's central abstraction is the `TestCase` class [Beck+1999], which implements a test interface. Each test case must be implemented by extending this class, which provides a range of methods for making assertions and recording the results. The JUnit framework executes a single `Test`, by calling its `setUp()` method, then running the test, then calling its `tearDown()` method. Thus each test instance creates and destroys its own fixture as required. A `TestSuite` is an alternative implementation of the `Test` interface, and forwards its `setUp()`, `runTest()`, and `tearDown()` methods to the tests it contains. Thus tests can be organized into suites of arbitrary size. In what follows, a "test" is a unit test, unless otherwise stated.

Experiences with JUnit

The first significant step we took was to decide that any tester class we wrote would be a member of the same package as the class under test. This arrangement had the major advantage that the tests could call package-private methods in the tested class, or indeed on any other class in that package. We could therefore, if necessary, provide methods specifically for use by the tests, without those methods becoming visible to our client projects.

We now checked JUnit into our source control system, so that it became an integral part of our build system.

The next task was to provide a simple way for developers to run JUnit on their current package version. Based on early experiments in unit testing the JNDI package, we declared that the tests should be run by invoking

```
java currentPackage.PackageTest
```

Thus we invented a local standard (the first of many!), stating that the complete set of unit tests for all the classes in a package must be in a class called PackageTest, which must have a main() method that invokes JUnit. These main() methods constituted a large number of copies of the same (small) piece of code; more on this later.

Integration with Make

At this point we also wished to add a test target to every existing make-file (one in each package source directory). Later, any new package would also require a makefile with an identical target, and since our makefiles were fairly standardized anyway, we replaced all of the make-files by a single makefile generator called GenMake. GenMake creates a makefile in each Java package directory and includes in it the desired test target. Now the unit tests for any package can be run by typing:

```
mk test
```

and those for all packages below "here" can be run by:

```
mkall test
```

- -

This latter command simply recurses through the directory hierarchy calling `mk test`. It makes no attempt to collect the unit tests it finds into a single suite. This means that the developer has to check many pages of noise for every line of the form

```
..............F......
```

looking for test failures. More on this later.

Growth and Complexity

This simple infrastructure allowed us to begin writing unit tests in earnest. Where sporadic unit tests already existed (usually written in JPython), these were quickly converted into a Java `PackageTest` class. Elsewhere, as developers got used to JUnit, a few additional `PackageTest` classes were written, particularly in parts of the system that were undergoing complex changes.

No specific test-writing activities were scheduled. The major impetus for adding a new unit test was when a bug was discovered in some part of the system that had been thought to be working correctly. Initially these tests were always added to the package's `PackageTest` class, which quickly became unwieldy as a result. After an initial spurt, progress adding new tests slowed, due mostly to the fact that many `PackageTest` classes were now too complex, and therefore too daunting to be easily extended.

Progress was fastest in the JNDI package, because the author had some prior experience working with JUnit. Given the need to document the status of the existing code, we began writing unit tests to check that the JNDI implementation met the assertions in the specification.

Following Fowler [Fowler+1999], we created a `Tester` class for every class in the package's public API, and had the `PackageTest` class group these all together into a JUnit test suite, thus:

```
public final class PackageTest {
  public static Test suite() {
    TestSuite suite = new TestSuite();
    suite.addTest(new TestSuite(
      DistinguishedNameTester.class));
    suite.addTest(new TestSuite(
      ContextTester.class));
    suite.addTest(new TestSuite(
      ContextFactoryTester.class));
    suite.addTest(new TestSuite(
      SymbolicLinkTester.class));
```

```
    //...
    return suite;
  }
}
```

For each public feature in the API we added a corresponding test feature to the Tester class. Thus context.bind() is tested by the new method ContextTester.test_bind(). This general scheme is illustrated in Figure 16.1.

(This technique utilizes a reflection-based feature of the JUnit TestSuite class, which will construct a test case instance whenever it finds a method whose name begins with test in a subclass of Test.)

With only a few days' work we had a comprehensive list of passes and failures, and hence an automatically generated work list for fixing and completing the JNDI package. And as the package later came to be extended, these tests remained, serving as regression tests and providing confidence that the modifications had not broken any existing functionality.

A new practice started to emerge at this point. At the end of a development episode, the developer would run the entire set of unit tests before integrating changes to the master sources. This gave the developers a simple way to check that they hadn't broken any other part of the system, thus boosting confidence and increasing the speed at which they were willing to proceed. However, mkall test can be slow, and the

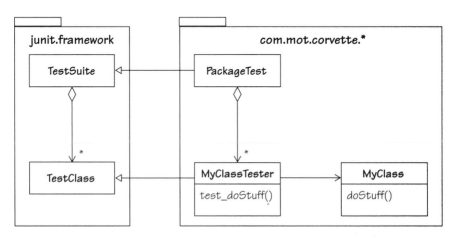

FIGURE 16.1 Organization of tests for MyClass

test reports can get lost in the reams of output generated by make's recursion through the directory tree.

Testing for Portability

Our product is targeted to run on various flavors of UNIX, including Solaris 2.5, 2.6, and 2.7, but our developers all work on Windows/NT. At some point we began receiving bug reports on parts of the system that had tests, and for which the tests all passed. It turned out that certain aspects of the Java `File` class, for instance, behave differently on different platforms and on different filesystem types, so we found we needed to run our tests in the target environments, as well as in the development environment.

We therefore created an hourly batch job that built the entire system from scratch and then ran all the unit tests on the result. If the output contained any test failures these were immediately e-mailed to every member of the development team.

Now, if anyone integrated code that wasn't portable, the batch job discovered this and the problem could be quickly fixed.

Imposing Order

As the number of tests grew, we now started to find that the test classes themselves were becoming a little intrusive: In the source directory for some Java packages it had become difficult to distinguish production code from test code. This was exacerbated in cases where the tests required the development of additional utility classes (e.g., a `TempFile` class that generates random test files and cleans up the filestore afterward).

To help distinguish test code from production code, we took our second significant step: We adopted Fowler's [Fowler+1999] naming convention throughout the system. That is, the unit tests for a class `MyClass` should be in a class called `MyClassTester`. Following the approach used earlier for the JNDI tests, we went around and split up the other `PackageTest` classes into `Tester` classes. The small hit in development time was immediately repaid, as the unit tests were now less daunting again. Test coverage again started to increase steadily.

That helped to some extent, but we had another problem: As we approached the date of our first alpha release, we needed a slick (i.e., automated) way to collect together the production classes into a Jar (a zipped archive containing Java class files), without including any test code in the release. We could now distinguish Tester classes, but was TempFile part of the product or part of the tests?

Here we took our third, and most radical, step: We created two parallel package trees in our source repository, one containing only production code and the other containing only tests and their support classes. Thus a package such as com.mot.stingray now appears as two filestore directories .../packages/com/mot/stingray and .../tests/com/mot/stingray. We then altered our makefile generator so that, in the .../tests package hierarchy, the Java compiler and runtime had both .../tests and .../packages on their classpath (Figure 16.2). Now these tools would see the two package trees as if they were overlaid. The end result is that the tests build with the production code in sight, while the production code cannot see the tests and is not contaminated with test class files. It is now a trivial matter to collect the production code (everything under .../packages) for release, and we have the added bonus that production code cannot accidentally refer to a test class.

Stability

Our development environment now suddenly seemed delightfully uncluttered, and to date we have made no further major changes.

As we continued to develop new tests, we discovered certain test utility classes cropping up time and again. We created a test_support package in the .../tests tree to hold these. This package now also seems

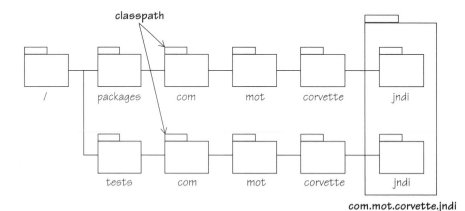

FIGURE 16.2 Overlaid folders create virtual packages

to have become stable, perhaps indicating that our current unit tests span a large proportion of the range of ways to test our product.

One day we found we needed to issue an emergency patch release of one of our libraries. The library contains native C++ code and has a JNI wrapper to make it usable by the Java code in the rest of the system. One of our customers wanted to run on a platform we had never built on or tested on. Once we had access to such a machine, we quickly built the C++ library. Then we ran the unit tests for its Java wrapper—one failed because a compiler option in the makefile was incorrect for that platform. We fixed it and ran the unit tests again, and this time they all passed. Next the unit tests for the whole system—they passed. Finally, we ran the few system tests we currently had, which we knew exercised this library—they all passed. The whole episode had taken only an hour or so, yet we could think of nothing more that might go wrong. We issued the patch library and we have heard of no problems since.

At this point our test coverage seems to have stabilized at around 25 percent (that is, we have a Tester class for one in four of our production classes). This seems low, but in fact each test naturally exercises a class and its close collaborators. We therefore estimate that the code coverage through our unit tests is perhaps as high as 60 percent now.

Table 16.1 charts our progress in developing unit tests for the Corvette system.

The apparent decrease in system size during October—and the corresponding rapid increase in test numbers—reflects the introduction of

TABLE 16.1 Unit Tests for the Corvette System

Date	Product Classes	Tester Classes	Test Cases
1 Sep 1999	260	6	6
1 Oct 1999	312	6	6
1 Nov 1999	289	42	149
1 Dec 1999	297	57	221
1 Jan 2000	319	50	372
1 Feb 2000	325	52	285
1 Mar 2000	337	69	360
1 Apr 2000	344	85	428

the `Tester` naming convention and the conversion of other existing tests to JUnit. Since then, progress has been relatively steady, with the number of tests always rising faster than the size of the product.

Plus Points

This section describes some of the positive benefits of the approach we took to retrofitting unit tests in the Stingray development. Note that many of the benefits we discovered also reflect advantages claimed for XP [Beck2000].

The unit tests serve as excellent documentation. A complete set of tests for a class is often a very good starting point for someone looking at that class for the first time and attempting to discover what it does. And because we know that the tests all compile and all pass, the reader can have more confidence in them than in source code comments, say, which may not have been maintained.

Well-named test cases can also communicate the design intent of a class. For example, we eventually learned that a test case called `test_export()` could be replaced by smaller test cases called `test_export_0files()`, `test_export_1file()`, and `test_export_nfiles()`, giving a clearer picture of the algorithm's scope and boundary conditions.

Separating the production source from that of the tests proved extremely worthwhile and greatly simplified a number of processes that had become intricate or cumbersome.

The introduction of simple naming conventions for test classes and methods has gone some way toward generating "egoless" test source, thus making it easier for all team members to contribute to most parts of the system. The naming conventions have also made possible the generation of metrics showing our progress with testing, since it is now quite easy to count classes whose names end in "Tester" or methods whose names begin with "test."

Development tasks are generally finished more quickly in parts of the system that have comprehensive tests. The tests tell developers when they are done. This is especially true when they add new tests at the same time they add new functionality.

In those areas of the system in which large numbers of tests have been added, architectural change now seems less daunting—the tests give a full and precise report of one's progress. For instance, in the JNDI subsystem we were able to replace a single large class with six smaller classes implementing the Composite pattern [Gamma+1995] surprisingly easily. After each refactoring step we ran the tests, and those that failed quickly told us where we had made an invalid assumption. The entire process took only a couple of hours—and we knew we were done because the tests all passed!

With our hourly batch test run, we often know immediately when a bug has been introduced into the product. As soon as the e-mailed failure report goes out, we quickly check any integrations done during the last hour (usually just one), and we know that new code must have introduced a problem. Bugs are thus caught quickly, and the quality of the system remains high. This is only possible due to the fully automated style of testing encouraged by XP and JUnit.

Another positive side effect of this is that we also know at all times that the system has high quality. So if we need to quickly issue a patch version for any reason, we can always do so from the most recent hourly build. Our release turnaround time, and indeed the risk to our customers, is thus greatly reduced.

Writing the first set of tests for an existing class often caused us to improve the design of the class itself. The main reason for this is that the tests often need to access smaller pieces of the class' functionality, so existing methods must often be split into public and private parts (see Fowler's Extract Method refactoring pattern [Fowler+1999]). A side effect of this is that those classes and packages that have been tested heavily are now generally composed of smaller pieces, displaying more flexibility and embedding fewer assumptions about their clients. These parts of our system therefore now tend to be easier to evolve.

Negative Points

This section describes the downside of the approach we took to retrofitting unit tests in the Stingray development.

As with any testing approach, any part of the system that has a low test coverage can lead to a false positive. If I run the entire suite of unit tests at the end of a development episode, the absence of test failures does not imply the absence of bugs—I may have broken a part of the system that isn't well tested. The run of 300 to 400 dots in the test report, with no Fs or Es to indicate problems, encourages me to stop sooner and integrate what I have. Indeed, this is one of our plus points, because usually this does allow development to proceed more quickly.

But occasionally, that untested area of the system is broken, and it may be a long time before we find out.

The existence of a `Tester` class does not imply that a class is fully tested. In fact, before the general adoption of our test-case method naming conventions, a large and complex `PackageTest` class may easily have appeared thorough, while actually testing only a fraction of the necessary conditions. This could also lead to false positives ("that's a big test case, it surely checks everything"), and sometimes actually reduced our willingness to add new tests.

Our recursive make system makes it easy to run the tests for the package one is altering, but somewhat harder (slower) to run the tests for the entire system. Although this is quick and convenient during development, we often succumb to the temptation to test only one package and then integrate, thinking that our changes will probably have no side effects elsewhere. This is frequently an invalid assumption, with the result that the system temporarily degrades while the updates are fixed.

Every so often an e-mail arrives from the hourly batch test run, indicating that something in the system is now failing on the target platform. Every member of the team now takes a couple of minutes out to look at the log and check their recent changes. Thus one person's error disturbs everyone else in the team.

Adding new tests to an old class can be a slow and painful business. This is particularly true when the class to be tested is badly organized, or when it doesn't define a clear abstraction, so that its responsibilities leak out into its clients and suppliers. Such classes deter the would-be tester. It is usually far simpler just to add the required functionality to the class and leave it untested than it is to bite the bullet and develop the necessary tests, knowing that the class and some of its collaborators must be refactored in the process. This is probably the main reason we have `Tester` classes for only one in four of our production classes.

Old habits die hard. Although all our old unit tests were ported to JUnit, many of them still used ad hoc reporting mechanisms or required user interaction when they failed. Tests like this are a natural consequence of the process of gradually retrofitting new technology and have now all but disappeared. But during the transition period, their presence helped keep parts of the system a little more mysterious than necessary.

Unit tests for the GUI, and for the shell scripts that launch our system, are hard to write—so we don't have any. (Although there exist counterparts of JUnit for most popular programming languages, Bourne shell is not among them.) We have had bugs in both of these areas recently, which went undetected for some time due to the absence of unit tests.

One or two packages of tests came to rely heavily on large and complex test fixtures. For ease of development, these had often been simply extracted lock, stock, and barrel from system tests of the previous version of the product. These test fixtures were therefore often monolithic and contained much more data or structure than was required for a unit test. When the time came to alter the test fixture for a new unit test, the fixture's enormous weight and complexity often made this a daunting task. The new test would not be written, usually meaning that new functionality was added to the system with no accompanying unit tests. Ultimately, one team member took a week out of normal development to slim down these fixtures and refactor the tests to be more lightweight.

Future Plans

This section describes some of the activities we plan to undertake in order to address the negative points.

We need to develop tests for the more difficult parts of the system, especially the GUI. GUIs are notoriously hard to unit test, because of the difficulty of simulating external events. However, users of Java Swing are now starting to evolve JUnit-based testing techniques that largely remove this difficulty [Wake2000]. We plan to adopt this approach to test the Corvette GUIs soon.

We need to reduce the frequency at which the unit tests for a single package are taken to be an adequate measure of the quality of the whole system. One way to do this would be to remove our ability to run the tests in this way and to provide only a single test suite covering all of the production code; such a suite could even be assembled on the fly. We have a simple script that can do this and it currently takes less than a minute to run, but some further work is required before running the unit tests for the entire system is quick and simple.

Although our hourly batch test runs can disturb the entire team, we can't do without them because our product must port to numerous platforms. However, we do need to find a way to include a fast test run into the integration process, so that new code is rejected if it fails on any of our target platforms. We are actively looking for a way to perform a complete build and test in under 10 minutes, and to automatically include that in our source code integration process. (The testing here would include both the unit tests and our growing suite of system tests, which have been developed separately.)

Some team members are beginning to use unit tests in the debugging process. When a reported bug has been analyzed and the cause determined, it is almost always possible to write a new unit test that currently fails, but which would pass if the bug were fixed. Adding this test serves to guide the developer fixing the bug and will prevent us from accidentally reintroducing the bug in the future. As the system evolves from alpha development to supported product, this should become a reflex part of our process.

As the system grows, the tests must continue to grow with it. We are past the early adopter stage with our unit tests now, and yet a number of classes in the system remain stubbornly untestable. One radical approach to both of these problems is that proposed in XP: Whenever new functionality is to be added anywhere, the unit tests are developed *first*. Designing the tests equates to designing the interface and semantics of the new feature [Beck+1998; Wake2000]. And when the tests all pass, development is done. Such an approach promises to improve development quality and speed, while simultaneously offering the benefits we found from more testable (and hence adaptable) production classes. This seems to be an avenue worth pursuing.

Flushed with our success using JUnit, we intend to offer encapsulation developers a simple and rich test framework, to encourage them to write unit tests. The framework would consist of JUnit, together with a package of test utility classes, probably based on those we have developed for testing the main system.

Conclusion

We took an ongoing, medium-sized Java development project and gradually added a unit testing regime. The tests were developed over time, with little impact on development timescales, using an open-source Java framework called JUnit. Current test coverage is sufficient to have greatly improved our confidence in the software's quality.

The pain of moulding ourselves into new habits and new conventions seems to have paid off handsomely. Development speed is now improved in certain areas, as is the adaptability of much of the software. The JUnit approach to unit testing also seems to have speeded up some of our processes, including time to release.

We hope that the lessons we learned along the way will help others get to this point a little more quickly and painlessly.

References

[Beck2000] K. Beck. *Extreme Programming Explained*. Addison-Wesley, 2000.

[Beck+1998] K. Beck, E. Gamma. "Test Infected." *Java Report*. July 1998.

[Beck+1999] K. Beck, E. Gamma. "JUnit—A Cook's Tour." *Java Report*. May 1999.

[Fowler+1999] M. Fowler, K. Beck, J. Brant, W. Opdyke, D. Roberts. *Refactoring: Improving the Design of Existing Code*. Addison-Wesley, 1999.

[Gamma+1995] E. Gamma, R. Helm, R. Johnson, J. Vlissides. *Design Patterns: Elements of Reusable Software*. Addison-Wesley 1995.

[Wake2000] W. Wake, *Using JUnit to Unit-Test GUIs*. Availble at http://users.vnet.net/wwake/xp/xp0001/index.shtml.

About the Author

Kevin Rutherford can be reached at Motorola, located at the Sherwood House, Gadbrook Park, Northwich, UK CW9 7TN, or by e-mail at Kevin.Rutherford@motorola.com.

Chapter 17

Endo-Testing: Unit Testing with Mock Objects

—*Tim Mackinnon, Steve Freeman, and Philip Craig*

Unit testing is a fundamental practice in Extreme Programming, but most nontrivial code is difficult to test in isolation. It is hard to avoid writing test suites that are complex, incomplete, and difficult to maintain and interpret. Using Mock Objects for unit testing improves both domain code and test suites. They allow unit tests to be written for everything, simplify test structure, and avoid polluting domain code with testing infrastructure.

Introduction

"Once," said the Mock Turtle at last, with a deep sigh, *"I was a real turtle."*
—Alice In Wonderland, *Lewis Carroll*

Unit testing is a fundamental practice in Extreme Programming [Beck2000], but most nontrivial code is difficult to test in isolation. You need to make sure that you test one feature at a time, and you want to be notified as soon as any problem occurs. Normal unit testing is hard because you are trying to test the code from outside.

We propose a technique called *Mock Objects* in which we replace domain code with dummy implementations that both emulate real functionality and enforce assertions about the behavior of our code.

These Mock Objects are passed to the target domain code, which they test from inside, hence the term *endo-testing*. Unlike conventional testing techniques, however, in endo-testing assertions are not left in production code but gathered together in unit tests.

Writing Mock Objects is similar to writing code stubs, with two interesting differences: We test at a finer level of granularity than is usual, and we use our tests to drive the development of our production code.

Our experience is that developing unit tests with Mock Objects leads to stronger tests and to better structure of both domain and test code. Unit tests written with Mock Objects have a regular format that gives the development team a common vocabulary. We believe that code should be written to make it easy to test, and have found that using Mock Objects is a good way to achieve this. We have also found that refactoring Mock Objects drives down the cost of writing stub code.

In this chapter, we first describe how Mock Objects are used for unit testing. Then we describe the benefits and costs of using Mock Objects when writing unit tests and code. Finally we describe a brief pattern for using Mock Objects. For those who would like to explore the topic further, we have posted sample code at http://www.mockobjects.com.

Unit Testing with Mock Objects

An essential aspect of unit testing is to test one feature at time; you need to know exactly what you are testing and where any problems are. Test code should communicate its intent as simply and clearly as possible. This can be difficult if a test has to set up domain state or the domain code causes side effects. Worse, the domain code might not even expose the features to allow you to set the state necessary for a test.

For example, the authors have written tools to extend the development environment in IBM's VisualAge for Java, one of which generates template classes. This tool should not write a new template class if one already exists in the environment. A naïve unit test for this requirement would create a known class, attempt to generate a template class with the same name, and then check that the known class has not changed. In VisualAge this raises incidental issues such as whether the known class has been set up properly, ensuring that the user has the right permissions, and cleaning up after the test should it fail—none of which are relevant to the test.

We can avoid these problems by providing our own implementation, which simulates those parts of VisualAge that we need to run our test. We refer to these implementations as Mock Objects. Our Mock Objects can be initialized with state relevant to the test and can validate the inputs they have received from our unit test. In the following example, JUnitCreatorModel is an object that generates test classes in the Visual-Age workspace, and myMockPackage and myMockWorkspace are Mock Object implementations of interfaces provided with VisualAge:

```
public void testCreationWithExistingClass() {
    myMockPackage.addContainedType(
        new MockType(EXISTING_CLASS_NAME));
    myMockWorkspace.addPackage(mockPackage);

    JUnitCreatorModel creatorModel =
        new JunitCreatorModel(myMockWorkspace, PACKAGE_NAME);

    try {
        creatorModel.createTestCase(EXISTING_CLASS_NAME);
        fail("Should fail for existing type");
    } catch (ClassExistsException ex) {
        assertEquals(EXISTING_CLASS_NAME, ex.getClassName());
    }
    myMockWorkspace.verify();
}
```

There are two important points to note here. First, this test does not test VisualAge, it only tests one piece of code that we have written or, with test-driven programming, are about to write. The full behavior is exercised during functional testing. Second, we are not trying to rewrite VisualAge, only to reproduce those responses that we need for a particular test. Most of the methods of a mock implementation do nothing or just store values in local collections. For example, the implementation of the class MockPackage might include

```
public class MockPackage implements Package {
  private Vector myContainedTypes = new Vector();
  ...

  public void addContainedType(Type type) {
    myContainedTypes.add(type);
  }
}
```

A Mock Object is a substitute implementation to emulate or instrument other domain code. It should be simpler than the real code, not duplicate its implementation, and allow you to set up private state to aid in testing. The emphasis in mock implementations is on absolute simplicity, rather than completeness. For example, a mock collection class might always return the same results from an index method, regardless of the actual parameters. We have found that a warning sign of a Mock Object becoming too complex is that it starts calling other Mock Objects—which might mean that the unit test is not sufficiently local. When Mock Objects are used, only the unit test and the target domain code are real.

Not Just Stubs

As a technique, Mock Objects is very close to Server Stubs [Binder2000]. Binder's main concerns about using Server Stubs are that stubs can be too hard to write, that the cost of developing and maintaining stubs can be too high, that dependencies between stubs can be cyclic, and that switching between stub and production code can be risky.

The most important differences between our use of stubs and Binder's is the extent to which we believe that the development of domain code can be driven from the tests and that individual classes can be tested in isolation. As one of our reviewers wrote, "Prior to XP, a tester suggesting [some refactoring of the code for testing] would have been laughed at."

Furthermore, fine-grained unit tests combined with refactored Mock Object code drive down the cost of writing stubs and help ensure that domain components can be tested independently. Mock Objects that become too complex to manage suggest that their domain clients are candidates for refactoring, and we avoid chaining Mock Objects. Finally, our coding style of passing stub objects as parameters, rather than relinking the domain code, clarifies the scope of unit testing and reduces the risk of mistakes during a build.

Why Use Mock Objects?

Localizing Unit Tests

Deferring Infrastructure Choices

An important aspect of Extreme Programming is not to commit to infrastructure before you have to. For example, we might wish to write functionality without committing to a particular database. Until a choice is made, we can write a set of mock classes that provide the minimum behavior that we would expect from our database. This means that we can continue writing the tests for our application code without waiting for a working database. The mock code also gives us an initial definition of the functionality we will require from the database.

For example, we might have a method on a class Employee that updates names and details automically:

```
public void updateNameAndDetails(Connection connection,
                    Statement nameStatement,
                    Statement detailsStatement) throws
                    SQLException {
  try {
    nameStatement.executeUpdate(createUpdateNameSql());
    detailsStatement.executeUpdate(createUpdateDetailsSql());
    connection.commit();
  } catch (SQLException ex) {
    connection.rollback();
  }

}
```

With conventional testing, we would have to set up and connect to a real database, but with Mock Objects we can implement our test as shown here:

```
public void testUpdateEmployee() throws SQLException {
  MockStatement nameStatement = new MockStatement();
  MockStatement detailsStatement = new MockStatement();
  MockConnection connection = new MockConnection();

  nameStatement.setExpectedUpdate(NAME_SQL);
  detailsStatement.setExpectedUpdate(DETAILS_SQL);
  connection.setExpectedCommitCalls(1);

  myEmployee.updateNameAndDetails(connection, nameStatement,
                    detailsStatement);

  connection.verify();
  nameStatement.verify();
  detailsStatement.verify();
}
```

This technique is very easy to implement in modern development environments, especially given industry standard interfaces such as JDBC.

Coping with Scale

Unit tests, as distinct from functional tests, should exercise a single piece of functionality. A unit test that depends on complex system state can be difficult to set up, especially as the rest of the system develops. Mock Objects avoid such problems by providing a lightweight emulation of the required system state. Furthermore, the setup of complex state is localized to one Mock Object instead of scattered throughout many unit tests.

One of the authors of this chapter worked on a project tool that released code from VisualAge to another source control system. As the tool grew, it became increasingly hard to unit test because the cost of resetting the environment rose dramatically. The project tool was later refactored to use mock implementations of both VisualAge and the source control system. The result was both easier to test and better structured.

No Stone Unturned

Some unit tests need to test conditions that are very difficult to reproduce. For example, to test server failures we can write a Mock Object that implements the local proxy for the server. Each unit test can then configure the proxy to fail with an expected problem and the developers can write client code to make the test pass. An example of this is:

```
public void testFileSystemFailure() {
    myMockServer.setFailure(FILE_SYSTEM_FAILURE);

    myApplication.connectTo(myMockServer);
    try {
        myApplication.doSomething();
        fail("Application server should have failed");
    } catch (ServerFailedException e) {
        assert(true);
    }

    myMockServer.verify();
}
```

With this approach, the mock server runs locally and fails in a controlled manner. The test has no dependencies on components outside the development system and is insulated from other possible real world failures. This style of test is repeated for other types of failure, and the entire test suite documents the possible server failures that our client code can handle.

In the case of an expensive widget, we define similar unit tests. We can configure the mock widget with the desired state and check that it has been used correctly. For example, a unit test that checks that the widget is polled exactly once when a registration key is sent would be:

```
public void testPollCount() {
    myMockWidget.setResponseCode(DEVICE_READY);
    myMockWidget.setExpectedPollCount(1);

    myApplication.sendRegistrationKey(myMockWidget);

    myMockWidget.verify();
}
```

The mock widget lets us run tests on development machines with no actual widget installed. We can also instrument the mock widget to verify that it was called correctly, which might not even be possible with the real widget.

Better Tests

Failures Fail Fast

Domain objects often fail some time after an error occurs, which is one reason that debugging can be so difficult. With tests that query the state of a domain object, all the assertions are made together after the domain code has executed. This makes it difficult to isolate the exact point at which a failure occurred. One of the authors of this chapter experienced such problems during the development of a financial pricing library. The unit tests compared sets of results after each calculation had finished. Each failure required considerable tracing to isolate its cause, and it was difficult to test for intermediate values without breaking encapsulation.

On the other hand, a mock implementation can test assertions each time it interacts with domain code, and so is more likely to fail at the right time and generate a useful message. This makes it easy to trace the specific cause of the failure, especially as the failure message can also describe the difference between the expected and actual values.

For example, in the widget code, the mock widget knows that it should only be polled once and can fail as soon as a second poll occurs:

```
class MockWidget implements Widget {
    ...
    public ResponseCode getDeviceStatus() {
```

```
      myPollCount++;
      if (myPollCount > myExpectedPollCount) {
        fail("Polled too many times", myExpectedPollCount,
             myPollCount);
      }
      return myResponseCode;
    }
  }
```

Refactored Assertions

Without Mock Objects, each unit test tends to have its own set of assertions about the domain code. These may be refactored into shared methods within a unit test, but the developer has to remember to apply them to new tests. Such assertions are built into Mock Objects and so are applied by default whenever the object is used. As the suite of unit tests grows, a Mock Object will be used throughout the system and its assertions applied to new code. Similarly, as the developers discover new assertions that need to be made, these can be added once in a Mock Object where they will automatically apply to all existing tests.

During development, the authors have come across situations where assertions in their Mock Objects have failed unexpectedly. Usually this is a timely warning about a constraint that the programmers have forgotten, but sometimes this is because the failing constraints are not always relevant. These cases suggest candidates for refactoring of either the domain code or Mock Objects, and help push the developers toward a better understanding of the system.

Effects on Coding Style

We have found that developing with Mock Objects has had beneficial effects on the coding style of our teams.

First, in languages with controlled scope such as Java, detailed unit testing can be difficult without either breaking the scope by giving the test code access to class or package features, or by moving the unit tests to domain packages. Stroustrup introduced the friend function into C++ to solve just this problem [Stroustrup1994]. Whatever the solution, such code contradicts the intention of the design. Developing with Mock Objects reduces the need to expose the structure of domain code so that a test knows more about the behavior and less about the structure of tested code.

Second, singleton objects are increasingly recognized as a doubtful practice [C2Wiki]. Unit testing in the presence of singletons can be difficult because of the state that must be managed between tests. Furthermore, the singleton objects might not have methods to allow a unit test to set up the state it needs or query the results afterward. Developing with Mock Objects encourages a coding style in which objects are passed into the code that needs them. This makes substitution possible and reduces the risk of unexpected side effects.

Third, developing with Mock Objects teases out different aspects of functionality into smaller, more specialized classes, which are easier to understand and modify. In practice, this means pushing behavior toward visitor-like objects [Gamma+1995] that are passed around; we call these Smart Handlers. For example, rather than having code that queries attributes from an object and prints each one to a writer, a first step would be to pass a writer to the object, which then prints out its attributes. This preserves the encapsulation of the object.

Thus, the code changes from:

```
public void printPersonReport(Person person, PrintWriter
writer) {
    writer.println(person.getName());
    writer.println(person.getAge());
    writer.println(person.getTelephone());
}
```

to:

```
public void printPersonReport(Person person, PrintWriter
writer) {
    person.printDetails(writer);
}

public class Person {
    public void printDetails(PrintWriter writer) {
        writer.println(myName);
        writer.println(myAge);
        writer.println(myTelephone);
    }
    ...
}
```

which can be tested with:

```
void testPersonHandler() {
    myMockPrintWriter.setExpectedOutputPattern(
        ".*" + NAME + ".*" + AGE + ".*" + TELEPHONE + ".*");
```

```
    myPerson.setName(NAME);
    myPerson.setAge(AGE);
    myPerson.setTelephone(TELEPHONE);

    myPerson.printDetails(myMockPrintWriter);

    myMockPrintWriter.verify();
}
```

This test is verifying two things at once: that `Person` is managing its details correctly *and* that these details are being rendered correctly. As this code becomes more complex it becomes difficult to test cleanly because the generic `println` method used in `printDetails` loses information about our understanding of the domain.

Instead, we can write a handler object to reify this dialogue between a writer and a `Person`. `Person` would then have a method to pass its internal contents to a handler:

```
public void handleDetails(PersonHandler handler) {
    handler.name(myName);
    handler.age(myAge);
    handler.telephone(myTelephone);
}
```

This separates the input and output aspects of rendering a `Person` on a writer, and we can now test each aspect independently. The unit test for the handler inputs would then be:

```
void testPersonHandling() {
    myMockHandler.setExpectedName(NAME);
    myMockHandler.setExpectedAge(AGE);
    myMockHandler.setExpectedTelephone(TELEPHONE);

    myPerson.handleDetails(myMockHandler);

    myMockHandler.verify();
}
```

followed by a separate unit test to check that the domain code for `PersonPrintHandler`, a printing implementation of `PersonHandler`, outputs itself correctly:

```
void testPersonPrintHandler() {
    myMockPrintWriter.setExpectedOutputPattern(
        ".*" + NAME + ".*" + AGE + ".*" + TELEPHONE + ".*");
```

```
        myPrintHandler.name(NAME);
        myPrintHandler.age(AGE);
        myPrintHandler.telephone(TELEPHONE);

        myPrintHandler.writeTo(myMockPrintWriter);

        myMockPrintWriter.verify();
    }
```

Factoring out these two aspects makes it much easier to test and implement new features, such as renderings to XML or encrypted mail.

These three effects mean that code developed with Mock Objects tends to conform to the Law of Demeter [Lieberherr+1989], as an emergent property. The unit tests push us toward writing domain code that refers only to local objects and parameters, without an explicit policy to do so.

Interface Discovery

When writing code that depends on other related objects, we have found that developing with Mock Objects is a good technique for discovering the interface to those other objects. For each new feature, we write a unit test that uses Mock Objects to simulate the behavior that our target object needs from its environment; each Mock Object is a hypothesis of what the real code will eventually do. As the cluster of a domain object and its Mock Objects stabilizes, we can extract their interactions to define new interfaces that the system must implement. An interface will consist of those methods of a Mock Object that are not involved with setting or checking expectations. In statically typed languages, one then replaces the references to the Mock Object in the domain code with the new interface.

For example, the Person class in the last example would initially use a MockPersonHandler to get its unit tests running:

```
public class Person {
    public void handleDetails(MockPersonHandler handler) {
        handler.name(myName);
        handler.age(myAge);
        handler.telephone(myTelephone);
    }
    ...
}
```

When the tests all run, we can extract the following interface:

```
public interface PersonHandler {
    void name(String name);
    void age(int age);
    void telephone(String telephone);
    void writeTo(PrintWriter writer);
}
```

We would then return to the `Person` class and adjust any method signatures to use the new interface:

```
public void handleDetails(PersonHandler handler) { ... }
```

This approach ensures that the interface will be the minimum that the domain code needs, following the Extreme Programming principle of not adding features beyond our current understanding.

Limitations of Mock Objects

As with any unit testing, there is always a risk that a Mock Object might contain errors, for example returning values in degrees rather than radians. Similarly, unit testing will not catch failures that arise from interactions between components. For example, the individual calculations for a complex mathematical formula might be within valid tolerances, and so pass their unit tests, but the cumulative errors might be unacceptable. This is why functional tests are still necessary, even with good unit tests. Extreme Programming reduces, but does not eliminate, such risks with practices such as pair programming and continuous integration. Mock Objects reduce this risk further by the simplicity of their implementations.

In some cases it can be hard to create Mock Objects to represent types in a complex external library. The most difficult aspect is usually the discovery of values and structures for parameters that are passed into the domain code. In an event-based system, the object that represents an event might be the root of a graph of objects, all of which need mocking up for the domain code to work. This process can be costly and sometimes must be weighed against the benefit of having the unit tests. However, when only a small part of a library needs to be stubbed out, Mock Objects is a useful technique for doing so.

One important point that we have learned from trying to retrofit Mock Objects is that, in statically typed languages, libraries should define their APIs in terms of interfaces rather than classes so that clients of the library can use such techniques. We have used Mock Objects in the context of several application server environments and have sometimes found that the use of Java visibility modifiers, without corresponding public interfaces, makes unit testing more difficult to set up, although not impossible. For example, we were able to extend VisualAge because the tool API was written in terms of interfaces, whereas the standard java URL class is final with no corresponding interface, making it impossible to substitute.

A Pattern for Unit Testing

As we worked with Mock Objects, we found that our unit tests developed a common format:

- ✧ Create instances of Mock Objects
- ✧ Set state in the Mock Objects
- ✧ Set expectations in the Mock Objects
- ✧ Invoke domain code with Mock Objects as parameters
- ✧ Verify consistency in the Mock Objects

With this style, the test makes clear what the domain code is expecting from its environment, in effect documenting its preconditions, postconditions, and intended use. All these aspects are defined in executable test code, next to the domain code to which they refer. We sometimes find that arguing over which objects to verify gives us better insight into a test and, hence, the domain.

In our experience, this style makes it easy for new readers to understand the unit tests as it reduces the amount of context they have to remember. We have also found that it is useful for demonstrating to new programmers how to write effective unit tests. For example, we have been using pair programming as an interview technique and have found that candidates have been able to make valid contributions to production code within an afternoon.

We use this pattern so often that we have refactored common assertions into a set of expectation classes [Mackinnon2000], which makes it possible to write many types of Mock Object quickly. Currently we have refactored this code into the classes ExpectationCounter, ExpectationList and `ExpectationSet`. For example, the `ExpectationList` class has the following interface:

```
public class ExpectationList implements Verifiable {
    public ExpectationList(String failureMessage);
    public void addExpected(Object expectedItem);
    public void addActual(Object actualItem);
    public void verify() throws AssertionFailedException;
}
```

where the verify method asserts that matching actual and expected items were inserted in the same order during the test. A Mock Object that cares about sequence would either extend or delegate to an `ExpectationList`.

Conclusion

We and our colleagues have used Mock Objects on several projects, such as Web servers, desktop applications, and IDE extensions. We have mocked up standard libraries and parts of several application servers, and developed a significant project using Mock Objects throughout. Our experience is that using Mock Objects is an invaluable technique for developing unit tests. It encourages better structured tests and reduces the cost of writing stub code, with a common format for unit tests that is easy to learn and understand. It also simplifies debugging by providing tests that detect the exact point of failure at the time a problem occurs. Sometimes, using Mock Objects is the only way to unit test domain code that depends on state that is difficult or impossible to reproduce. Even more important, testing with Mock Objects improves domain code by preserving encapsulation, reducing global dependencies, and clarifying the interactions between classes. We have been pleased to notice that colleagues who have also adopted this approach have observed the same qualities in their tests and domain code.

References

[Beck2000] K. Beck. *Extreme Programming Explained*. Addison-Wesley, 2000.

[Binder2000] R. V. Binder. *Testing Object-Oriented Systems: Models, Patterns, and Tools*. Addison-Wesley, 2000.

[C2Wiki] Various Authors. *Singletons Are Evil*. On-line at http://
c2.com/cgi/wiki?SingletonsAreEvil.

[Gamma+1995] R. Gamma, R. Helm, R. Johnson, J. Vlissides. *Design
Patterns: Elements of Reusable Object-Oriented Software*. Addison-
Wesley, 1995.

[Lieberherr+1989] K. J. Lieberherr, I. M. Holland. "Assuring Good
Style for Object-Oriented Programs." *IEEE Software*. Volume 6,
Number 5, September 1989.

[Mackinnon2000] T. Mackinnon. *JUnitCreator*. On-line at http://
www.xpdeveloper.com/cgi-bin/wiki.cgi?JunitCreator.

[Stroustrup1994] B. Stroustrup. *The Design and Evolution of C++*.
Addison-Wesley, 1994.

Acknowledgments

We would like to thank the reviewers and the following colleagues for
their contributions to this chapter: Tom Ayerst, Oliver Bye, Richard Kar-
cich, Matthew Cooke, Sven Howarth, Tung Mac, Peter Marks, Ivan
Moore, John Nolan, Keith Ray, Paul Simmons, and J. D. Weatherspoon.

About the Authors

Tim Mackinnon can be reached at tim.mackinnon@pobox.com, Steve
Freeman at steve@m3p.co.uk, and Philip Craig at philip@pobox.com.

Chapter 18

Refactoring and Re-Reasoning

—*Neelam Soundarajan*

A key feature of the refactoring method is that after each refactoring step we test the modified software to ensure that the software continues to work as it did before the refactoring. This chapter proposes a complementary approach: Following each refactoring step, we re-reason about the behavior of the modified software to ensure that it continues to behave correctly. We consider a number of refactorings and investigate exactly what needs to be done following the particular refactoring. We conclude that re-reasoning after a refactoring step indeed helps in ensuring the correctness of the refactoring.

Introduction

An important component of XP [Beck2000] is refactoring. Refactoring [Beck1997; Fowler+1999; Opdyke1992] allows us to revise the structure or the design of an existing piece of software so that it becomes easier to add (or to modify) functionality. It is important to be able to revise the software's design in this manner because otherwise only additions or modifications that are in some sense consistent with the original design can be made. But of course it is essential that refactoring not introduce bugs into the software; it is for this reason that individual refactoring steps should be small and each should be checked. Fowler in his landmark book on refactoring says: "The rhythm of refactoring [is] test, small change, test, small change, test [Fowler+1999]." The purpose of each test is to ensure that the small change carried out in the immediately preceding refactoring step preserves the behavior of the software being refactored.

This chapter proposes a complementary rhythm to refactoring: reason, small change, re-reason, small change, re-reason. By "re-reason" we mean reason about the refactored code to show that it behaves as expected. But in order for this to be useful, it is necessary that the effort involved in re-reasoning at each step be relatively small, in some sense proportional to the change that has been made. In this chapter, we consider a number of refactorings and investigate how to re-reason following application of the particular refactoring and how much effort would be involved in doing so.

We classify refactorings into two groups, *syntactic* and *semantic*. A syntactic refactoring step, as the name suggests, is a change in some essentially syntactic aspect of the piece of software. An important point to note about such refactorings is that essentially all of the needed work can be carried out by Refactoring Browsers [Brant+1999] and if this is done, there is no need to carry out a test following the refactoring because the browser would have made sure that all the necessary changes have been properly carried out. And, as we will see, such browsers can also mechanize the tasks associated with re-reasoning following a syntactic refactoring step. On the other hand, semantic refactorings modify, in some essential way, the logic of the software and how it functions. Hence browsers will not be able to make the needed changes; rather, the designer will have to do so. And following such a refactoring, the designer will have to test/re-reason to ensure that the refactoring has been done correctly.

The chapter is organized as follows: In the first section we make more precise the distinction between syntactic and semantic refactorings using simple examples. In the next section we briefly summarize the fairly standard approach we use to reasoning about classes. The following section is the main part of the chapter; here we consider a number of refactorings and for each analyze how to re-reason about the software following an application of this refactoring step. It is worth noting that the details of this task, in general, depend very much on the details of the particular refactoring. This should not be surprising; it is similar to having different reasoning rules for different types of statements such as assignments or conditionals or loops. We conclude the chapter by reiterating the importance of re-reasoning in conjunction with testing in order to ensure that refactored programs behave correctly. In the last section we also consider how re-reasoning following refactoring fits in with other aspects of XP.

Syntactic and Semantic Refactorings

Consider the refactoring called *inline-method* [Fowler1999]. In an application of this refactoring, we replace each call to a method $m()$ by its body. The reason for doing this is that the method's body is just as easy to understand as its name, so there is nothing to be gained by having the extra indirection.

Let $m()$ be a member of a class C. There are some requirements that must be satisfied in order for us to apply inline method. First, $m()$ should not be polymorphic; otherwise, it may well be overridden in subclasses of C, and these subclasses will not be able to do so if we inline calls to $m()$ (and remove the method from C). Second, all the calls to $m()$ should be from other methods of C, or each caller of $m()$ should have access to each of the member variables of C that the body of $m()$ accesses.

Clearly, a designer applying this refactoring could easily overlook the second requirement, especially if there are numerous calls to $m()$ (or even the first requirement if there is a deep inheritance hierarchy below C). But a Refactoring Browser [Brant+1999] can check both of these conditions and, assuming the conditions are met, replace each call by the method body. This is the essence of a syntactic refactoring. No analysis based on the behavior of the method(s) is needed. Only syntactic checks are necessary and the actual refactoring is itself a purely syntactic activity.

Next, consider *substitute-algorithm* refactoring. The purpose of this refactoring is to replace an algorithm with a better one, hopefully one that is easier to understand. The main question in performing this refactoring is whether the new algorithm exhibits the same behavior as the algorithm it is replacing. What we mean by "behavior" is functional behavior, specified as usual, using pre- and postconditions; for some types of systems, for example hard real-time systems, equivalence of functional behavior may not be sufficient, but we will ignore such systems in this chapter. In general, equivalence of behavior cannot be checked syntactically. This is the essence of a semantic refactoring: Showing its correctness involves semantic analysis. Since such analysis cannot be mechanized, semantic refactorings cannot be validated by Refactoring Browsers (or other syntactic tools). Instead, we need to use appropriate tests for the purpose; or, following the rhythm being proposed in this chapter, we need to re-reason about the behavior of the refactored software to ensure that its behavior is equivalent to that of the original software. This is not to suggest that there are no syntactic components to semantic refactorings. In the case of the substitute algorithm, a requirement that the new algorithm not refer to, or at least not assign to, any variables that the algorithm being replaced does not refer to[1] is clearly a syntactic condition. The point is that in addition to such syntactically checkable requirements, semantic refactorings have one or more requirements that can only be checked by semantic analysis.

Suppose we have a method $m()$ with a large body[2] and we wish to apply substitute algorithm to replace a segment S of this body with another version S'. In order to ensure the correctness of this refactoring, we only have to reason about the behavior of the segment S'; the reasoning about the rest of the body of $m()$ can remain unchanged. In other words, the reasoning effort following this refactoring step will, in some sense, be proportional to the size of the refactoring. This is important; much of the power of refactoring arises from the smallness of the individual refactoring steps, and the reasoning effort required to validate these refactorings should be proportionately small. For example, following an application of substitute algorithm, if we had to reason about not just S' but the entire body of $m()$, including the portion that is unchanged, software engineers are unlikely to invest in such reasoning effort. Fortunately, for all reasonable refactorings, including all refactorings in the catalog in [Fowler1999], several of which we will consider later, the required reasoning effort is indeed proportional to the change being made in the refactoring.

Reasoning About Classes

We will use a fairly standard approach [Liskov+1994; Martin1995; Meyer1997] to reasoning about classes. Thus the behavior of a method $m()$ of a class CC will be specified in terms of pre- and postconditions. The precondition of $m()$ is an assertion on the state—that is, the values

---

1. This is a reasonable requirement because otherwise there is a good possibility that some other part of the method in question could break as a result.
2. This itself may be an indication that we should try to use the extract method refactoring on $m()$, but we will ignore that for the purposes of this discussion.

of the member variables of *CC*—and the values of any additional parameters to *m()*. The postcondition of *m()* is an assertion on the state at the time that *m()* finishes execution, as well as the values of any result parameters that *m()* returns; in addition, the postcondition assertion may also refer to the state at the time *m()* was called as well as the parameter values received by *m()*; allowing the postcondition to refer to the state at the time of the call, in addition to the state when *m()* finishes, makes it easy to specify many interesting behaviors. As usual, such a specification assures us that if the precondition is satisfied at the time of the call, then the postcondition will be satisfied when the execution of *m()* finishes. In addition to the pre- and postcondition for each method of *CC*, we may also have a class invariant that is satisfied at the start and end of each call to each method.

One important point is worth noting here. Abstraction and encapsulation are, of course, key OO principles; in other words, clients of the class *CC* should be unaware of its internal details, such as the values of its member variables, and should instead view the class in an abstract manner. Correspondingly, in our approach to reasoning about classes, we should use an abstract model of the class, define a mapping from the concrete state of the class—that is, the values of its member variables—to the corresponding abstract state, and specify the pre- and postconditions of the methods in terms of the abstract states. This would encapsulate the concrete state of the class and force the client programmer to work with an abstract model of the class when reasoning about the behavior of his or her code. However, in this chapter, in order to keep the presentation simple we generally ignore abstraction issues and work instead with the concrete state. But it is also worth stressing that the re-reasoning that needs to be performed following certain of the refactorings may in fact directly involve abstraction issues. A simple example is *encapsulate-field* refactoring. The goal of this refactoring is to encapsulate a previously public member variable (we use the terms "field" and "variable" interchangeably) and provide methods that allow controlled access to it. Although within the class the field continues to exist as before and there is no essential difference as far as the concrete state of the class is concerned, from the point of view of the client the picture has changed considerably. Rather than being a field that can be assigned arbitrary values by the client's code, this part of the state can only be manipulated using the newly defined methods. This is best reflected in the re-reasoning by replacing this component with one that more clearly represents the possible behaviors—as allowed for by the newly defined methods.

Let us now consider subclassing and polymorphism. In our reasoning system, we have to account for two important issues that have to do with subclassing and polymorphism. Consider a piece of client code *XX* that has been written to work with an object of type *BB*. The client programmer can reason about the behavior of *XX* using the specification of the class *BB;* suppose the client programmer has, by doing so, established the result *RB* about *XX*. Suppose next that *DD* is a derived class of *BB* and suppose *XX* is applied to an object *KK* that is an instance of *DD;* polymorphism requires (and runtime dispatch will ensure) that during the execution of *XX*, any call to a method defined in the base class *BB* and redefined in the derived class *DD* will be dispatched to the definition in *DD* rather than that in the base class. From the reasoning point of view, the first issue we need to account for is that the result *RB*, which has already been established, must continue to hold since the object *KK*, being an instance of *DD*, is (also) of type *BB*. But *RB* was established by using the specifications of *BB*, and these specifications correspond to the method bodies as defined in *BB* of the invoked methods, whereas the method bodies actually executed as we just noted, given that *KK* is an instance of *DD*, are the ones defined in *DD;* so how can we be sure that *RB* will continue to hold in this situation? This question has received considerable attention in the literature, and the answer is captured in terms of the concept of behavioral subtyping [Liskovt+1994]; behavioral subtyping requires that if a method *m()* is redefined in *DD* then this redefinition be consistent with its specification in the base class *BB*. This may be expressed more precisely as follows: Let *pre.m.b* and *post.m.b* be the pre- and postconditions of *m()* per its specification in the base class *BB*, and *pre.m.d* and *post.m.d* be its pre- and postconditions for its specification in the derived class *DD*. Behavioral subtyping[3] then requires that

$$pre.m.b \Longrightarrow pre.m.d$$
$$post.m.d \Longrightarrow post.m.b$$

---

3. This is a simplified form of behavioral subtyping; for example, it does not account for class invariants, nor does it account for the possibility of the abstract models of *BB* and *DD* being different from each other. For these details, the interested reader is referred to Liskov, Martin, and Meyer [Liskov+1994; Martin1995; Meyer1997].

where "=>" as usual denotes logical implication. If this requirement is satisfied for every method that the code *XX* invokes, we can be sure that *RB* will indeed continue to hold when *XX* is applied to an instance of *DD*. This is because in establishing the result *RB* by appealing to the specification of *BB*, the client programmer must have verified that prior to each call to *m()*, the precondition *pre.m.b* is satisfied; this, by the first implication, ensures that *pre.m.d* is satisfied; this call will be dispatched to the body of *m()* defined in *DD*, hence when the call returns, *post.m.d*, the postcondition for this body will be satisfied; this in turn will ensure, by the second implication, that *post.m.b* will be satisfied. Because, when establishing *RB*, it is only this relation the client programmer could have used concerning this call, we are assured that *RB* will continue to hold.

The second issue we need to address in the reasoning system has to do with the fundamental reason for using subclassing and polymorphism: The class designer has presumably designed the derived class *DD*, in particular the redefined method bodies, to exhibit richer behavior than that of the base class; and the client programmer is applying code *XX*, which was originally designed to be applied to instances of *BB*, to instances of *DD* in order to exploit this richer behavior without having to redesign the code. Correspondingly, our reasoning system must allow us to establish this richer behavior and do so without reanalyzing the code. This issue has received much less attention in the literature than the issue of behavioral subtyping.

We have developed an approach to addressing this issue [Soundarajan+1998; Soundarajan2000]. Briefly, the idea behind our approach is that when reasoning about *XX*, we record all the calls to methods (such as *m()*) that might be redefined in derived classes in a trace of such calls; results such as *RB* are expressed in terms of this trace. Then, when considering the application of *XX* to instances of *DD*, we plug in, to *RB*, via the trace of method calls, the richer behavior of the redefined methods as described by their specifications in *DD* (i.e., *pre.m.d* and *post.m.d*), to arrive at a richer result *RD* that accounts for the richer behavior provided by the class *DD* for its instances. Note in particular that *RD* may well include information about values of new member variables that may have been included in *DD* because the derived class specification of *m()* will provide this information.

In general, a refactoring may have an impact on the pattern of subclassing and/or polymorphism in the system. Following such a refactoring step, we will have to, in the re-reasoning, account for both the behavioral subtyping component and the enriched behavior component of polymorphism.

Re-Reasoning

We consider a number of refactorings in this section. For each we summarize the refactoring and then consider the re-reasoning that needs to be performed following an application of the particular refactoring.

Extract Method

Let CC be a class and $m()$ a method of the class; let $m()$'s body include a fragment of code XX; to apply this refactoring, we extract the code fragment XX, define a new method $n()$ in CC with XX as its body, and in place of the code fragment XX in the body of $m()$, insert a call to the new method $n()$.[4] Some syntactic conditions must be satisfied for this refactoring to be applicable. First, there must not be any name conflicts between the new method and existing methods of CC. Second, the code fragment XX being extracted from $m()$ should not refer to any local variables of $m()$ (because $n()$ will not have access to these variables).[5] These conditions can easily be checked by a Refactoring Browser.

What are the re-reasoning issues here? If $n()$ is declared as a private member of CC, there are none. This is because, in this case, the change affects only $m()$, and as far as this method is concerned, all we have done is to introduce a macro corresponding to the code fragment XX and replaced XX with a call to the macro. Thus the specification of $m()$ will continue to remain valid because the result of executing $m()$ will be exactly the same as it was before the refactoring. And since neither clients nor derived classes of CC can call $n()$, it being private to CC, we do not need to include a specification for it in the specification of CC.

---

4. Fowler [Fowler1+999] catalogs another refactoring, decompose conditional, that is similar to the extract method; the difference is that while the extract method allows us to replace a segment of code with a call to a method that does the same thing, the decompose conditional allows us to replace a complex (conditional) expression with a call to a method that returns a value equal to that of the extracted expression. Most of our discussion applies also to this refactoring, with minor changes to account for the difference between executing code and evaluating expressions.

5. Fowler's extract method [Fowler+1999] is actually a bit more complex than the one described here; for example, the extract method allows references in $n()$ to local variables of $m()$ by passing them in as parameters to $n()$.

But if *n()* is to be a public method, we do have some work to do. We must add to the specification of *CC* an appropriate specification, in the form of a precondition *pre.n* and postcondition *post.n*, for *n()*. This is because, given that *n()* is a public method, any future client code that is written may invoke this method, and to reason about such code, we would need a specification for *n()*. How do we arrive at these assertions? That depends on how well the original method *m()* is documented. If it is fully annotated, (i.e., it includes not just the pre- and postconditions but intermediate assertions at key points in its body including, in particular, immediately before and immediately after the code segment *XX)*, we can simply use these assertions as the pre- and postconditions of *n()*; so no further work is needed in arriving at *n()*'s specification. But if all we have for *m()* is its pre- and postcondition, then we will have to analyze the (original) body of *m()* to arrive at these assertions and use them as the pre- and postconditions of *n()*. The situation is essentially the same if *n()* were protected rather than public since derived classes may invoke *n()*, so it must be provided with a specification.

The extract method is a syntactic refactoring; a browser could extract the pre- and postconditions for *n()* from the annotation of *m()*. Of course, if *m()* is not fully annotated, the browser cannot come up with the required specification; but this is not a feature of the refactoring so much as an omission on the part of the original designer of *m()*.

There is one further point we need to consider. If *n()* can be redefined in derived classes (i.e., it is not flagged as final in Java or is flagged as virtual in *C++*), then any such redefinition can change not only the behavior of *n()* but also that of *m()* (because of the call to *n()* that we have inserted into *m()* during the refactoring). In this case, extract method is similar to the *form-template-method* refactoring, which we consider later, and the re-reasoning issues that are involved in that refactoring will apply also to extract method in this case.

Remove Control Flag

This refactoring allows us to replace a control flag being used to terminate a loop with a break or return. Consider the following example (from Fowler [Fowler+1999]):

```
void checkSecurity(String[] people) {
    boolean found = false;
    for (int i=0; i < people.length; i++) {
        if (!found) {
```

```
            if(people[i].equals("Don")){sendAlert(); found =
                true;}
            if(people[i].equals("John")){sendAlert();found =
                true;}
        }
    }
}
```

found is being used here as the control flag to break out of the loop. Following the refactoring, this becomes

```
void checkSecurity(String[] people) {
    for (int i=0; i < people.length; i++) {
        if (people[i].equals("Don")){sendAlert(); break;}
        if (people[i].equals("John")){sendAlert(); break;}
    } }
```

Because there is no change in the behavior of the method, there will be no changes in its specification either. Nevertheless, we still need to check that the refactored method still meets its original specification. Thus the re-reasoning work is not in coming up with new specifications but in ensuring that the revised code still behaves as expected. Depending on the background and tastes of the individual designer, this may be done formally or informally, or even omitted completely, with the designer relying on the tests to detect any violations. This observation also points to an important relation between reasoning and testing; after all the purpose of the tests is to check that the software is correct, that is, that it satisfies its specifications. So in order to design good tests, we need precise specifications such as we are considering. Once we have the specifications, we can either design suitable tests or use formal verification or use a combination of the two approaches.

Form Template Method

Let *D1, D2* be derived classes of a common base class *CC*. Let *m1()*, *m2()* be methods respectively in *D1, D2* that perform similar steps in the same order; the steps are similar but not identical to each other. This refactoring allows us to extract into *CC* what is common between *m1()*, *m2()*, this being the pattern and order in which the steps are performed, and put this into a template method *m()* in *CC*. *m()* will call methods defined in *D1, D2* corresponding to the individual steps. As usual, the advantage of using polymorphism is not only that the duplication (of the pattern and the order of steps) in *D1, D2* is eliminated, but it also allows for the possibility that if at some future date we wish to define a new class *D3* that needs to have a method with the same pattern but with its own definitions for the details of the individual steps, we can do so by defining *D3* as a derived class of *CC* and defining in *D3* only the methods corresponding to the individual steps.

Let us consider a simple example:

```
class C { protected int i;   … }
class D1 extends C {public void m1(){X2; i = 0; X3;} }
class D2 extends CC {public void m2(){Y2; i = 0; Y3;} }
```

where *X2, X3, Y2, Y3* are some segments of code; *X2* and *Y2* (and similarly *X3, Y3*) are *not* identical to each other. Applying the form template method of refactoring, we would extract the pattern that is common to *m1()*, *m2()* and put it into a method *m()* in *CC*, with *m()* calling methods defined in the derived class(es):

```
class C { protected int i; …
          public void m(){n2(); i = 0; n3();}
          public abstract void n2();
          public abstract void n3(); }
class D1 extends C {
          public void n2(){ X2; }
          public void n3(){ X3; } } }
```

D2 is similar with *Y2, Y3* replacing *X2, X3*.

How do we re-reason following this refactoring? In particular, how do we specify the behavior of the template method *m()*? As we saw earlier, there are two issues we need to address: Our specification must be such that any reasoning that is performed, using this specification, on client code *CC* that is written to invoke *m()* on an object of type *CC*, remains valid if *CC* is applied to an object that is an instance of *D1* or *D2*, or any new derived classes of *CC* that may be defined (or derived classes of *D1* or *D2*); and our specification must allow the client, once he or she knows that the code is being applied to an instance of *D1* (rather than of *D2* or of some other derived class), to arrive at the richer behavior that results from the particular definition of *n2()* and *n3()* in *D1*}. Consider the following postcondition[6] for *m()*:

$$post.m() \equiv (i = 0) \tag{1}$$

---

6. We omit the precondition; it may be something as simple as *true*.

This specification will satisfy our first requirement if the definitions of *n3()* in the derived classes will leave the value 0 in i. How do we impose this condition? By means of the following specification for *n3()* as part of the specification of *CC*:

$$pre.n3() \equiv (i = 0)$$
$$post.n3() \equiv (i = 0) \qquad (2)$$

This says that when *n3()* is invoked *i* will be 0, and that when it finishes, it must leave 0 in *i*. Thus *n3()* is an abstract method in *CC*; nevertheless, we are providing a specification for it. How can an abstract method satisfy this (or any) specification? It cannot; what it means is that when the method is defined in a derived class (or redefined in classes lower in the inheritance hierarchy), the definition must meet the specification in Equation (2); that is, any such definition must be a behavioral subtype of this specification. Given this, any reasoning the client performs concerning the code *CC* by appealing to the specification in Equation (1) will remain valid if *CC* is applied to an object that is an instance of *D1* or *D2* or any other derived class of *CC*.

But the specification in Equation (1) does not address our second issue. For that, as we saw in the last section, we need a richer specification for *m()*, one that will include information about calls to methods such as *n2()*, *n3()* that may be (re)defined in the derived classes:

$$post.m() \equiv [(i = 0) \wedge ((|\tau| = 2 \wedge (\tau[1].m = n2) \wedge (\tau[2].m = n3))] \quad (1')$$

This specifies, as before, that when *m()* finishes, *i* will be 0; and in addition that, during its execution, *m()* will invoke two methods, as indicated by the fact that its trace τ will be of length 2. The method invoked in the first call (as given by the value of $\tau(1).m$) is *n2()*, that in the second call *n3()*. Suppose now that the derived classes *D1*, *D2* each has (integer) member variables *j* and *k*; and that the specifications for *n2()*, *n3()*, in the classes *D1*, *D2* are as follows:

$$post.n2().D1 \equiv (j = 5)$$
$$post.n3().D1 \equiv [(i = \#i) \wedge (j = \#j) \wedge (k = 50)] \qquad (3)$$

$$post.n2().D2 \equiv (j = 10)$$
$$post.n3().D2 \equiv [(i = \#i) \wedge (j = \#j) \wedge (k = 100)] \qquad (4)$$

The # notation in the postconditions refers to the value of the particular variable at the time the method was invoked. Thus Equation (3) tells us that the *n2()* as defined in *D1* sets *j* to 5 and that the *n3()* as defined in *D1* sets *k* to 50, and leaves *i* unchanged (as required by behavioral subtyping, given Equation (2)), and leaves *j* unchanged as well. Equation (4) tells us that the *n2()* of *D2* sets *j* to 10 and the *n3()* of *D2* sets *k* to 100, and leaves *i* unchanged (again as required by behavioral subtyping). If the client knows that his code is being applied to an object that is an instance of *D1*, he can combine Equation (1') with the information provided by Equation (3) about the behavior of *n2()*, *n3()* as defined in *D1* to conclude that a call to *m()* will not only set *i* to 0, but also set *j* to 5 and *k* to 50. Similarly if the client knew that his code was being applied to an instance of *D2*, he can similarly use the information from Equation (4) to conclude that *i, j,* and *k* will be set to 0, 10, and 100, respectively. And the client is able to do this without reanalyzing the code for the template method *m()*, which, of course, is the whole purpose of polymorphism. Admittedly this is a trivial and contrived example but the general method [Soundarajan+2000] applies to more realistic situations.

How much effort is involved in re-reasoning following the application of this refactoring? The most involved component of this effort is in arriving at a characterization of the pattern of calls, recorded in the trace τ, that the template method *m()* makes to the methods to be (re)defined in the derived classes. In our particular example (Equation (1')), this was easy because the pattern was simple. In general the pattern will be more involved and will depend on the values of variables, and so on. Correspondingly, arriving at the trace-based specification will be more difficult but this is a reflection of the complexity of the system. The refactoring will also be difficult in such cases; in particular, we must be careful in constructing the template method so that the correct calls are included, in the correct order, and that the additional statements actually do perform actions that are appropriate for all derived classes.

We conclude this section with a comment about the role Refactoring Browsers can play in the re-reasoning task. Consider again *remove-control-flag*. As we saw earlier, the re-reasoning work needed here was to check that the rewritten method body meets its original specification. Although the browser cannot do this checking, it can identify precisely, and perhaps display in a re-reasoning window exactly what needs to be checked (assuming that the original method was equipped with the appropriate assertions). Thus, browsers can provide considerable help to the designer in applying both syntactic and semantic refactorings.

Conclusion

The importance of refactoring in evolving systems is well recognized. Refactoring allows us to revise the design of the system so it is easier to add or to modify functionality. But it is equally important to ensure that in refactoring, we do not introduce bugs. To help with this, each refactoring step, we believe, should be followed by an appropriate re-reasoning step. In this chapter, we considered a number of refactorings and discussed how the re-reasoning may be carried out following the application of the particular refactoring.

The main contributions of the chapter may be summarized as follows:

◆ Classify refactorings into two groups, syntactic versus semantic refactorings.

◆ Present a case for following each refactoring step with a re-reasoning step.

◆ Consider what impact refactoring has on the standard approach to reasoning about classes and discuss ways to re-reason following several important refactorings.

One important question that we could ask, as indeed a couple of the anonymous referees of the chapter asked, is "What value does the re-reasoning add to what is already provided by testing following refactoring?" There are two answers to this question. First, re-reasoning provides a complementary approach to ensuring that the refactored code behaves as it should; it is not intended to replace testing but rather to supplement testing and to increase our confidence in the refactored code since errors that may be missed by our test suite are likely to be caught by the re-reasoning (and conversely). Second, re-reasoning can actually help in designing the tests; as the work on specification-based testing, see for example [Antoy+2000], shows, tests can be designed based on, indeed even (partly) mechanically generated from, suitable specifications in the form of pre- and postconditions. It also seems likely that tests generated in this manner can easily be used in a framework like JUnit [Beck+1998] since the pre- and postconditions or simple assertions derived from them can be used in the assert statements that appear in such tests. The author plans to investigate this possibility. The idea would be to extend JUnit in such a way that, given a class whose methods are annotated with appropriate pre- and postconditions, the system would automatically or semiautomatically generate a set of test methods to be executed on demand in the standard JUnit-style. And following a refactoring and re-reasoning, the system would generate any needed new tests based on the changes in the specifications arrived at during the re-reasoning. One particular extension to JUnit that would be of particular value would be a mechanism that would automatically save the current state of an object at the start of a method body; this would be very useful because postconditions of even simple methods, as seen in the examples in this chapter, are often expressed as relations between the state of the object at the start of the method and that at the end of the method. Hence if the starting state were automatically saved by JUnit, there would be no need for the individual test methods to worry about this.

Another important concern regarding re-reasoning might be whether re-reasoning is too involved a task to be considered a legitimate component of a light methodology like XP. Implicit in this is the assumption that designing tests is easier than formal reasoning. In general, formal reasoning consists of two distinct components, the first of which is arriving at precise specifications, followed by formal verification that the code meets the specifications. The approach proposed in this chapter focuses entirely on arriving at the precise specifications; formal verification is *not* part of the approach. This is important because it is the formal verification that is by far the more complex of these two activities. Rather than relying on formal verification to check that the code meets the spec, in our approach, as we just noted, we use the specification to help us design the tests and we rely on the execution of the tests to check that the code meets the specification.

Indeed, one could argue that XP developers do exactly this. Recall that XP requires the tests to be written down before the code is designed; but to do this, the designers must clearly be well aware of the specification that they expect their code to meet, and it is this specification that they design the test methods to test. The approach proposed here takes this a bit further and requires the designers to write the specification down precisely and then design appropriate tests (or have them mechanically generated as suggested earlier) rather than design the tests on the basis of an intuitive, gut-level understanding of the specification.

Although writing the specification down precisely is certainly an additional step, it provides numerous advantages. First, in a pair programming setting, it allows the designers to debug each other's understanding of what the component being designed is intended to do. Second, it helps in designing the test methods. Third, it helps other members of the team understand the code better by providing them a more compact description of what the code does. Finally, and this has been the focus of this chapter, during refactoring it helps the designers precisely identify what aspects of the behavior of the code being refactored must be preserved; or, in cases such as the form template method, to arrive at a richer specification that contains information about the pattern of calls made by the (new) template method to the hook methods. For all of these reasons, re-reasoning following refactoring not only helps build robust and reliable systems, but also fits naturally with other aspects of XP.

We conclude with an observation and a proposal: Though most designers find formal verification difficult and of questionable value, formal specifications are important because they precisely capture the intended behavior of the component in question; such specifications, as we noted earlier, can help us design appropriate tests for the component by identifying what to test for. Given this, we propose that descriptions of refactorings should include not only the motivation behind the refactoring, the mechanics of how to do it, and example, as has been the case so far, but also a section on how to re-reason about the software following an application of the particular refactoring.

References

[Antoy2000] S. Antoy, D. Hamlet. "Automatically Checking an Implementation Against Its Formal Specifications." *IEEE Transactions on Software Engineering*. Volume 26, 2000.

[Beck1997] K. Beck. "Make It Run, Make It Right: Design Through Refactoring." *Smalltalk Report*. Volume 6, 1997.

[Beck2000] K. Beck. *Extreme Programming Explained*. Addison-Wesley, 2000.

[Beck+1998] K. Beck, E. Gamma. "Test Infected: Programmers Love Writing Tests." *Java Report*. Volume 3, Number 7, 1998.

[Brant+1999] J. Brant, D. Roberts. *Refactoring Browser.* On-line at http://st-www.cs.uiuc.edu/~brant/RefactoringBrowser.

[Fowler+1999] M. Fowler, K. Beck, J. Brant, W. Opdyke, D. Roberts. *Refactoring: Improving the Design of Existing Code.* Addison-Wesley, 1999.

[Liskov+1994] B. Liskov, J. Wing. "A Behavioral Notion of Subtyping." *ACM TOPLAS.* Volume 16, 1994.

[Martin1995] R. Martin. *Designing Object-Oriented C++ Applications Using the Booch Method.* Prentice Hall, 1995.

[Meyer1997] B. Meyer. *Object-Oriented Software Construction.* Prentice Hall, 1997.

[Opdyke1992] W. F. Opdyke. "Refactoring Object-Oriented Frameworks," Ph.D. diss. University of Illinois at Urbana-Champaign, 1992.

[Soundarajan+1998] N. Soundarajan, S. Fridella. "Reasoning About Polymorphic Behavior." In *Proceedings of TOOLS 26,* E. Singh, Meyer, Riehle, Mitchell, eds., IEEE Computer Society Press, 1998.

[Soundarajan2000] N. Soundarajan, S. Fridella. "Framework-Based Applications: From Incremental Development to Incremental Reasoning." In *Proceedings of the Sixth International Conference on Software Reuse.* W. Frakes, ed., Lecture Notes in Computer Science No. 1844, Springer-Verlag, 2000.

Acknowledgments

The author would like to thank the anonymous referees as well as the XP2000 Program Co-Chairs, Dr. Marchesi and Dr. Succi, for comments on earlier drafts of this chapter, which resulted in considerable improvements in the presentation.

About the Author

Neelam Soundarajan can be reached at the Computer and Information Science Department, Ohio State University, Columbus, OH 43210. His e-mail address is neelam@cis.ohio-state.edu

Part 5

Tools for XP Development

Chapter 19

Developing the Refactoring Browser

—Ralph Johnson

Extreme Programmers currently promote only two kinds of software tools: unit (for unit testing) and the Refactoring Browser. Other tools that they use are so common as not to need promotion. Although many people have been introduced to unit testing by XP, unit testing tools are not new. The only new tools promoted by XP are refactoring tools. The first refactoring tool that was widely used was the Refactoring Browser. This is the story of the Refactoring Browser and how an academic group developed one of the two tools advocated by XP.

Early History

When I first started studying how people developed high-quality software in Smalltalk, I noticed that most of that software had been heavily refactored. In fact, it seemed that all good Smalltalk software had been rewritten many times. I read a lot of code that did not meet the usual standards of the Smalltalk class library and rewrote it to make it better. I tried to make rules describing why I rewrote programs the way I did. This led to a paper with Brian Foote that described what we looked for when we rewrote programs [Johnson+1988]. It discusses getting rid of case statements, renaming methods to increase polymorphism, decomposing methods, and making superclasses abstract. It talks about the

323

need for tools to support rewriting programs but doesn't use the word "refactoring."

Our motivation for refactoring was different than that of XP. XP promotes refactoring to make code simpler and to let developers delay decisions so that they can avoid making unnecessary or wrong decisions [Beck2000]. We were studying refactoring as a way of making reusable software. These motivations are not contradictory; making software simpler makes it easier to understand and hence to reuse. Nevertheless, they are different, and we did not follow many of the tenets of XP other than refactoring and trying to follow coding standards.

Understanding Refactoring

One of the goals of my course on object-oriented programming is to teach people how to write good programs. One tactic of the course is to show examples of good programs and tell students to emulate them. Another tactic is to describe common problems and explain how to fix them. As part of the second tactic, I worked on examples of refactorings and invented names for them. By 1989 I was teaching a short list of refactorings, but it was obvious to me that a lot more work could be done.

Bill Opdyke was the first person to work on refactoring with me full time. He studied how a large C++ system evolved and described its evolution in terms of refactoring. He presented our list of refactorings in a conference paper [Opdyke+1990]. His original goal was to figure out how to make a refactoring tool for C++, but he soon learned that C++ was so complicated that a tool that handled enough of C++ to be useful would be too complex for a single student to implement. So, he settled for prototyping a few refactorings and determining the conditions under which these refactorings were guaranteed not to introduce any bugs. His doctoral dissertation [Opdyke1992] contained a long list of refactorings, a detailed description of how to carry out each one, and when the refactorings were safe.

These refactorings became part of our common vocabulary. We would describe proposed changes to systems as a sequence of refactorings. Not all changes were refactorings, but enough were that we thought a tool for automating refactorings would be worthwhile.

We learned some things about refactoring that transcends tools. For example, refactoring works best when you have a test suite, because running the test suite usually shows when you make an error. Also, refactoring is best done in small steps, so you can make errors one at a time, when they are easy to discover and to fix. XP includes these practices, but this doesn't mean we were practicing XP. We wrote tests after we wrote code and didn't run our tests systematically. About the only extreme practice that we followed was refactoring.

The First Refactoring Tool

Although we had more experience with Smalltalk than with C++, we thought that it would be easier to develop a refactoring tool for C++ because of its static-type system. However, we underestimated the complexity of C++ and the value of Smalltalk's program representation. After prototyping a few refactorings in C++, we decided that it would take 10 person years to build a useful refactoring tool for C++. Smalltalk seemed much easier; because Smalltalk represents programs as objects, it is relatively easy to write a program to modify a Smalltalk program.

Another reason for building our first refactoring tool in Smalltalk was that Smalltalk programmers seemed much more interested in it than C++ programmers were. Bill Opdyke and I gave several talks on refactoring and on our plans to automate some refactorings. The C++ audiences did not think the talks were interesting, but the Smalltalk programmers told us that they couldn't wait until we had developed the tools.

Dan Walkowski built the Smalltalk Refactory for his master's thesis project. It renamed program elements and moved methods up and down the class hierarchy. It reused the VisualWorks parser, the representation of abstract syntax trees, and the database that keeps track of classes and methods. Consequently, it was built with half a year of effort. However, we found it awkward to use because it was a separate tool, not part of the standard tool set. Programmers don't like to jump back and forth between tools. We found that we tended not to use it, because the Smalltalk browser made refactoring nearly as easy.

The Refactoring Browser

To learn how to make better refactoring tools, John Brant used the refactory to refactor HotDraw. He integrated the refactory into the browser and added new refactorings. He decided that if the Refactoring Browser were going to capture the hearts and minds of Smalltalk programmers, it would have to be the best browser in the world, regardess of refactoring support. So he added multiple edit buffers, eliminated a long-standing cause of bugs by updating buffers when they got out of date, improved the way it browsed a class hierarchy, and added little features like the ability to view resources with specialized editors and the ability to create default class comments.

While John Brant was adding refactorings that his projects needed, Don Roberts was working on more theoretical problems. He worked on dynamic program analysis and separated precondition checking from the rest of the refactorings. The two of them worked together to develop the Refactoring Browser.

The structure of the Refactoring Browser developed slowly, driven by the features that were being added. Most of these features were refactorings. The Refactoring Browser was constantly being refactored, and all of the most significant components were created later in the life of the project. They were not all created by refactoring, however.

For example, some of the new refactorings required complex pattern-matching, so John Brant built a pattern-matching engine. Eventually, existing refactorings were rewritten to use it. The pattern-matching engine was used to implement a style checker that could propose possible refactorings. Experts were able to use the pattern-matching engine to look for arbitrary patterns in the code and to rewrite them. The rewrite engine was used by Synchrony Systems as part of their tool for porting applications from one dialect of Smalltalk to another. Thus, a few new features led to an architectural change that made a lot of new features cost effective.

As another example, I had long wanted the Refactoring Browser to be able to undo refactorings. Each refactoring was represented as an object (e.g., the command pattern) but it seemed a lot of work to implement undo for each one. One of the refactorings was making two passes over the system because otherwise it would detect that it was invalid after it had already changed the system. That refactoring was simplified when it was refactored to create change objects instead of making the changes directly. The refactoring would apply the change objects if it didn't detect a problem, but would abort and get rid of them if it did detect a problem. Each change object represented a simple change to the program, such as adding a method or deleting a method. These changes were usually not refactorings, but could be used to express refactorings. Each change object knew how to make the change and how to undo the change. Eventually all the refactorings were rewritten to use change objects, and then it was easy to implement undo for each refactoring. A refactoring just kept track of the changes it had caused, and the refactoring could be undone by undoing its changes.

> *Finally, Kent asked for undo (June 1998).]To impress him with the turnaround time, I refactored the change objects into their current state, created an undo, made all refactorings go through these changes, made the refactoring manager handle these changes, and finally, mailed Kent saying that I had implemented undo. I made sure that the mail was dated the same day as his request* [Brant1999].

For several years, the Refactoring Browser reused the original parser and abstract syntax tree classes of VisualWorks. However, many people asked for the Refactoring Browser to run in VisualAge for Smalltalk. Not only did VisualAge hide the compiler, but we did not want to support two radically different code bases. So we rewrote the parser and abstract syntax tree classes, and used the same code base on both systems. Writing a parser for Smalltalk is easy, but we felt it had to be as fast as the commercial ones, and that was hard. However, this made the Refactoring Browser more portable. We were glad that we had not tried to write a parser in the beginning, however, because that way we avoided a lot of work, and when we finally got around to writing it, we knew just what we needed to write.

In general, we followed the XP rule of doing the simplest thing that could possibly work and we designed by refactoring. Parts of the Refactoring Browser, such as the pattern-matching engine, are complex. However, we never wrote those parts until we needed them. If we had known what we were doing, we would probably have done more up-front design, but we knew that our assumptions were probably wrong so we instead built something simple and started using it.

Finding Customers

University projects often have a hard time finding customers, let alone convincing customers to work closely with them. This is probably why many university projects seem to be about solving problems that are not important. From the beginning, we tried to use our own tools and use the resulting experience to redesign them. We also worked hard to get people to use the Refactoring Browser and to give us feedback on it. As Smalltalk programmers, we are users of the Refactoring Browser, but we often had trouble separating our roles of programmers from our role as customers.

We realized that we needed feedback from customers. We gave the Refactoring Browser away, we gave demonstrations of it at OOPSLA and handed out disks with the source, we taught companies how to use it, and eventually ObjectShare (one of the Smalltalk vendors) included it with their programming environment. John Brant worked with Synchrony Systems to put the pattern-matching engine into their code porting tool, and then he worked with them on a few projects to use it to port systems from one dialect of Smalltalk to another. We set up mailing lists and Web sites for the Refactoring Browser. Many Smalltalk developers are using our browser now, yet we still get few suggestions for improvement. People don't seem to want to give feedback, which is one of the reasons that XP says you must have a customer on site.

XP at Universities

From our experience, XP fits well into a university environment, though some practices fit better than others. Since research projects by definition are experiments and researchers never know what they are doing, it is best to design the simplest thing that could possibly work and to grow the system, refactoring constantly. Continuous integration and collective ownership worked well for us.

The XP approach to testing could work well in a university if people were properly trained. The Refactoring Browser went for years without an automated test suite. In fact, we didn't build a good test suite until after Kent Beck started promoting XP. The Refactoring Browser now has a good test suite, which proved invaluable at Camp Smalltalk when it was ported to five new dialects of Smalltalk. Porting it to a new dialect basically consists of getting the tests to run and then building a GUI for it. Testing is one of the things academics usually ignore. We have been convinced of the importance of testing and try to write tests first, but old habits die hard.

Pair programming is the exception at a university, not the rule. Graduate students tend to program at odd hours of the day and night, and so it is hard for them to pair up. We tend to schedule times to get together, and then to work alone at other times. Many research projects consist of a single person working alone. For the last six or seven years I have been encouraging students taking my courses to work on programming assignments in pairs and have found that this causes very few problems. Pair programmers usually learn more, enjoy the class more, and do better. I am convinced that pair programming is more productive and more pleasurable than solo programming, but it is still hard to make it happen on our research projects.

Part of the reason that pair programming is so hard for us is that all of our developers are part-time. Most of them are not only taking classes but are supported by jobs as teaching assistants, research assistants on other projects, or by outside consulting. If I had a project that had several dedicated research assistants, then I would emphasize pair programming more and would expect it to work. Our experience with pair programming on industrial projects has been positive.

The biggest weakness of most university programming projects is that they have no customer. Even if a project has a customer, the customer is usually not closely connected. This weakens planning. Of all the ways that university projects fail at XP, this is probably the most profound and the hardest to correct.

Conclusion

Although the design of the Refactoring Browser emerged as it was built, it was not by any means an XP project. This was partly because the project started before XP was defined and partly because it was a university project. In general, it is hard to be completely extreme at a university. There is no good reason for academics not to write tests first, but it is harder for us to pair program and to have customers on site.

Even though it is hard to have customers on site, university projects still require feedback and ought to practice incremental development. Feedback is crucial for novice developers or for researchers heading into the unknown. When you have inadequate information, you are likely to make bad decisions, so it is best to postpone any decisions that you can. It is best to design a simple system that can be changed easily, because many of the decisions you make will be wrong. The road from a vision to a working tool is long and takes unexpected turns. You need a lightweight method that lets you quickly change direction. Although it might not be possible to follow every practice of XP at a university, most of the practices are well suited for university research projects.

References

[Beck2000] K. Beck. *Extreme Programming Explained*. Addison-Wesley, 2000.

[Brant1999] J. Brant. On-line at http://wiki.cs.uiuc.edu/Refactoring-Browser/History+of+the+Refactoring+Browser. 1999.

[Johnson+1988] R. E. Johnson, B. Foote. "Designing Reusable Classes." *Journal of Object-Oriented Programming*. Volume 1, Number 2, June/July 1988. On-line at http://www.laputan.org/drc/drc.html

[Opdyke+1990] W. F. Opdyke, R. E. Johnson. "Refactoring: An Aid in Designing Frameworks and Evolving Object-Oriented Systems." In *Proceedings of Symposium on Object-Oriented Programming Emphasizing Applications (SOOPA)*, 1990.

[Opdyke1992] W. F. Opdyke. "Refactoring Object-Oriented Frameworks." Ph.D. diss. University of Illinois. ftp://st.cs.uiuc.edu/pub/papers/refactoring/opdyke-thesis.ps.Z. 1992.

Acknowledgments

Most of the work on the Refactoring Browser has been done by my graduate students. I've been blessed with a great set of graduate students who have taken my ideas and turned them into reality.

For several years we had a grant from UBILAB to work on refactoring. To date they are the only organization that purposefully supported our refactoring work financially. Don Roberts was supported by a fellowship from the John and Fanny Hertz Foundation. Many organizations unknowingly supported our refactoring work by hiring Don and John as consultants.

Many people have helped us by using the Refactoring Browser and suggesting improvements. We especially want to thank Kent Beck for his large number of suggestions and for his enthusiasm in promoting the Refactoring Browser.

About the Author

Ralph Johnson can be reached at the University of Illinois at Urbana-Champaign, Department of Computer Science, 1304 West Springfield Avenue, Urbana, IL 61801; rjohnson@uiuc.edu.

Chapter 20

Team Streams: Extreme Team Support

—*Jim des Rivières, Erich Gamma, Kai-Uwe Mätzel,*
Ivan Moore, André Weinand, and John Wiegand

The code-centric development strategy of Extreme Programming
requires effective team support to coordinate the work on the
shared code base. Many of the requirements of the Extreme Pro-
gramming development processes, such as collective code owner-
ship and continuous change integration, are not particularly
well served by traditional version and configuration manage-
ment systems. We have developed a new paradigm for support-
ing team software development, called team streams, that
provides dynamic and easy-to-use team support. This chapter
describes team streams from the end user's viewpoint and shows
why team streams are eminently suited for Extreme Program-
ming. We start by analyzing the team support requirements for
Extreme Programming. Next we present team streams, followed
by a discussion about how team streams address these require-
ments. The chapter concludes with a report of our experiences
using team streams.

Introduction

Coordinating the work of a team is a typical problem faced by software projects [Babich1986], and Extreme Programming (XP) projects are no different in this regard. In this chapter we introduce team streams as a new paradigm for supporting the development of software in a team. We should admit up front that we didn't develop team streams with XP practices explicitly in mind; indeed, our work on team streams dates back several years, well before the idea of XP had begun to be articulated. Our vision was to support fully parallel development for teams in a straightforward fashion that was easy to learn and to use, incorporating the best practices that we and others [Berczuck1997; Wingerd+1998] had learned for managing software. As XP matured it became clear to us that there were many common threads between XP and our vision of how to develop software in a team. One aspect, support for distributed teams, is particularly important to us because this is the way that we develop software (so do many of our customers); however, this aspect is of less importance to XP.

Team Support for XP

We have found that many XP practices are not supported particularly effectively by traditional version and configuration management (VCM) systems. In this first section, we look at team-related XP practices [Beck2000] and point out how these practices are often at odds with the support offered by traditional VCM systems.

Continuous Integration

Continuous integration of all code ensures that conflicting changes are discovered and resolved promptly. Each build is supplied to all developers, who then continue their work in that context. Frequent integration ensures that the team makes steady progress and counters the natural drift experienced by all software development teams. In traditional software development using traditional VCM systems, builds are typically performed by a central authority (the "buildmeister" or the release engineering team) on a regular schedule, but usually not more frequently than weekly. The weekly build is then distributed to the team members. To increase the frequency of integration, some XP teams have adopted the practice of using a separate computer for performing code integration, rerunning the unit tests, and resolving any conflicts or breakage [SingleReleasePoint]. Switching computers has the positive side effect of clearly separating the coding from the integration work context. However, a single integration machine does not scale up to distributed development. Continuous integration also requires a low overhead integration process. It is not uncommon for developers to integrate their changes into the code base a couple of times per day.

Collective Code Ownership

The XP practice of collective code ownership means that anyone on the team can change any part of the system, and everyone shares ongoing responsibility for the state of the overall system. This ensures that all team members feel empowered to correct or simplify the code as needed. More traditionally, the code base is partitioned and each individual developer is given ongoing (and sole) responsibility for any given module or class. Pessimistic checkin/checkout VCM systems work very well in this world because overlapping changes are relatively rare and each developer generally changes only the code he or she owns. In an XP world, where refactoring is important, there is a much higher likelihood that developers will have overlapping changes and that two developers might change methods in the same class. Changing the same method in different but compatible ways is less common; changing the same method in truly conflicting ways is rare. Consider the case in which one developer changes the implementation of a method and another developer changes the name of the same method in the course of doing a refactoring: The same method is changed in a compatible way.

If files get locked on checkout, one developer could inadvertently impede the progress of other team members who also need to change some of the same files. What XP needs instead is an optimistic concurrency model that avoids locking and does not require the code base to be artificially partitioned. No developer should become a bottleneck for changes.

Conflict Detection and Merging

Following the slogan "Don't coordinate, just do it; integrate frequently" [Jeffries2000] can easily lead to conflicts because it encourages several developers to make simultaneous uncoordinated changes to the code base. These changes can result in both structural and content conflicts. A structural conflict arises when a developer moves a file that was edited by another team member. A content conflict results when two developers change the same file. Both kinds of conflicts need to be detected by the VCM system, which must also provide good support for merging changes.

Atomic Releasing

When a developer has made coordinated changes to several parts of the system, he or she needs to release all the changes that were made as a unit. There must be some way to ensure that changes cannot be lost by one developer inadvertently releasing over the top of the changes made by another developer. When the VCM system cannot ensure atomic releases and surefire conflict detection, the stress level of making a release is increased due to the likelihood of making mistakes. The VCM system must also ensure that other developers cannot end up in an inconsistent state through accidentally picking up only a fraction of the released changes. Pessimistic checkin/checkout-style VCM systems use file locks to serialize changes to a given file and thereby ensure that updates are never lost. (Traditional VCM systems do not provide any support for simultaneously releasing changes across multiple files.) Unfortunately for XP, locks are especially cumbersome when developers need to make sweeping changes as part of a refactoring across the code base.

Tightly Integrated Team Support

Not all XP sessions are successful. When this becomes apparent, the XP developer needs an easy way to start over again. As a consequence, returning to a previous configuration has to be supported well by the tool set used by an XP team. Ideally the ability to version and release code is possible from the coding work context, coupled with the ability to compare and replace code. Most traditional VCM systems are generally separate from, or only loosely coupled with, the tools for developing code. For XP, team support should be tightly integrated into the programming environment. Releasing changes, integrating changes made by others, and discovering and resolving conflicts are all things that should fit naturally into the developer's normal workflow.

Team Streams

Every developer working on a team needs to internalize the model of how members of the team will collaborate. If this model is a simple one, developers will be able to pick it up quickly. And if the tools that developers use day in and day out encourage and reinforce this model directly, collaborating with other team members integrates seamlessly into the normal flow of work.

The team stream model is a novel distillation of well-known practices into a simple form that is easy to learn and that can be embodied directly in an integrated development environment (IDE).

Team streams are a means to synchronize multiple workspaces. A *workspace* is an arbitrary collection of elements arranged into trees. A *team stream* is a kind of shared team workspace. Each individual developer (or XP developer pair) works in his or her own private workspace, which is isolated from those of others. A team stream serves as the primary means for team members to share code and coordinate their work. After a developer has made changes in his or her workspace, the developer catches up with the team stream, tests the changes in the workspace, and finally releases the changes to the team stream. This results in the changes being copied to the shared team workspace, where they are immediately visible to future release and catchup operations involving the team stream.

At any time, a developer can catch up with the team stream. The developer is shown any changes released to the team stream since the developer last caught up or released; the developer accepts these changes, and these are incorporated into his or her workspace, being merged as necessary with any unreleased changes the developer has made locally. Figure 20.1 shows the basic pattern of activity involving a team stream and two developer workspaces. The developer is in complete control of which elements to catch up or release, and when. Concurrency control on the team workspace is optimistic—there are no locks that could create artificial bottlenecks. The system guarantees that a developer cannot inadvertently release over the top of another developer's changes.

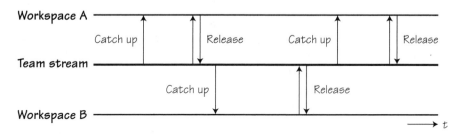

FIGURE 20.1 Interaction between team stream and workspaces

Once a team stream has been created, the developer's cycle is roughly as follows (see Figure 20.2):

1. *Create workspace:* Create a new workspace, connect to a team stream, and catch up.
2. *Edit:* Modify code in workspace and run tests.

3. *Catch up:* Pick up incoming changes and resolve conflicts. Return to Step 2 if incoming changes produce conflicts or invalidate testing.
4. *Release:* Release outgoing changes to team. Return to Step 3 if there are last-minute incoming or conflicting changes.

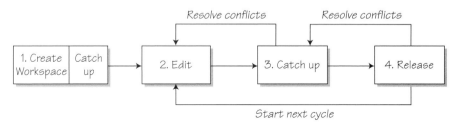

FIGURE 20.2 Development cycle for developer working on a team

Using Team Streams

In this section we describe team streams from the developer's perspective. IBM VisualAge Micro Edition IDE [IBM2000] (which we abbreviate here to VA/ME) is a Java IDE with team support based on the team stream model. As such, VA/ME is an existence proof that the team stream notions can be seamlessly integrated into an IDE. A VA/ME workspace is a collection of projects; these are the top-level elements that can be shared via team streams. Each project consists of a set of Java packages directories containing Java source files, Java binary class files, and arbitrary other resource files.

Connecting to a Team Stream

The developer must first connect his or her workspace to a team stream before he or she can catch up or release to it. Typically this is done just once, when the developer creates a workspace for working in a given project. As the connection is made, the developer catches up with the team stream; if accepted, this brings in any projects present in the team stream but not already in the workspace (see Figure 20.3). The project icon with a double-headed arrow indicates that the project in the workspace is shared with a team stream.

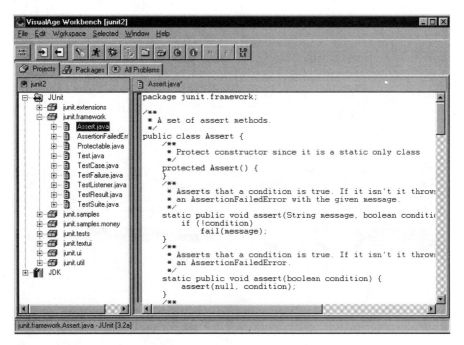

FIGURE 20.3 Workspace `junit2` after initial catch up

Releasing to a Team Stream

Developers do all their work in their own private workspace, where they are isolated from the activities of the other team members. After a developer has made and tested the changes in his or her workspace, the point is reached where the changes are ready to be released to the team stream. As a recommended convention developers first use a catchup operation to check whether the team stream contains any incoming and possibly conflicting changes. If it does, the changes are assimilated and all affected tests are rerun.

The release command brings up a release browser, which presents all the outgoing changes—changes made to elements in the workspace that have not yet been incorporated into that team stream (see Figure 20.4). Outgoing changes are always shown in black and bear an arrow pointing to the left. The team stream is always shown on the left; the workspace, on the right.

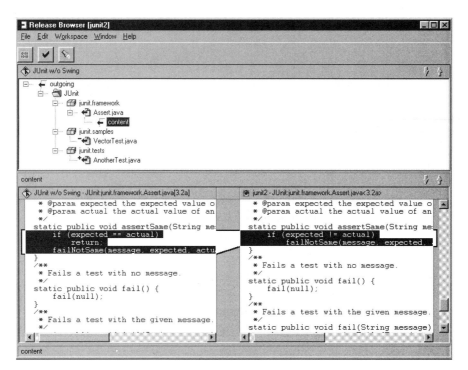

FIGURE 20.4 Release browser highlighting outgoing change

The developer reviews these changes and decides which should be released. The top pane in the release browser shows the changed elements. Below each element, the changed properties are listed. Properties include a project or package comment, version labels, and the contents of a file. Selecting a changed property shows the differences in the merge viewer in the bottom pane.

The merge viewer highlights the line range of a difference. Vertical scrolling of the merge viewer always aligns corresponding lines; if the number of lines in a range differ, the two text panes are scrolled at different speeds, so that the end (or beginning) of the range lines up properly.

Figure 20.4 illustrates a release browser presenting outgoing changes to the `junit.framework` package in the `JUnit` project: the `assertSame` method of the `Assert.java` source file has been edited in the workspace, `AnotherTest.java` has been added to the workspace, and `VectorTest.java` has been deleted from the workspace. The icons of new elements bear a plus symbol; deleted elements a minus symbol.

Throughout the release process, the developer has complete control over which changes get released. The developer is warned if another developer has also released changes to any of the changed elements. The recommended procedure is to abandon the release and to catch up (and rerun the relevant tests) before releasing again.

All changes to the team stream are released in a single atomic operation; there is no chance that another developer will witness a release in progress. However, in the time between when the release browser is opened and the developer decides which elements are to be released, it is possible for another developer to release their changes successfully. The release cannot be allowed to proceed as planned because already released changes may be lost. The developer is informed that the team stream has been modified and told to try again. In our experience, the incidence of release collisions is sufficiently low that additional machinery did not seem warranted.

The team stream paradigm is fully optimistic, and does not require locking (or element ownership) in order to preclude one developer from inadvertently releasing on top of another developer's changes.

Sharing Projects with a Team Stream

Before a newly created project can be released into a team stream, the project's sharing property must first be set (see Figure 20.5). After a project has been associated with a given team stream it is eligible to be released to that team stream.

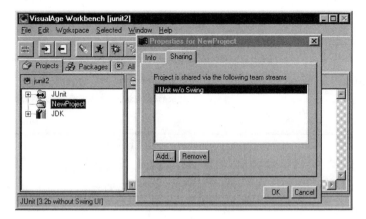

FIGURE 20.5 Sharing NewProject with the JUnit w/o Swing team stream

Catching Up with a Team Stream

While the developer is busy working in his or her private workspace, other developers may have released their changes to the team stream, causing the developer to become out of date with respect to those elements. At any convenient point, the developer can use the catchup command to counter this drift and to reduce the eventual cost of integration. This brings up a catchup browser, which presents all the changes that have been made to the team stream that have yet to be incorporated into the workspace (see Figure 20.6). Incoming changes, tagged with a right-pointing arrow and shown in blue, are ones made to the team stream that do not clash with changes made locally to the workspace. Again, the team stream is always shown on the left; the workspace, always on the right.

Figure 20.6 illustrates a catchup browser presenting incoming changes to the junit.framework package in the JUnit project: The assertSame

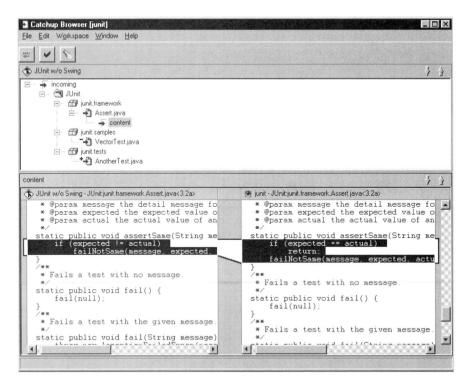

FIGURE 20.6 Catchup browser highlighting incoming change

method in the `Assert.java` file has been edited in the team stream, `AnotherTest.java` has been added to the team stream, and `VectorTest.java` has been deleted from the team stream.

Conflicting changes are ones that overlap with changes made locally to the workspace. Figure 20.7 illustrates a catchup browser presenting a conflicting change to the `Assert.java` file: The developer had added a comment to a line that is also affected by an incoming change. The element icons are tagged with blue incoming and black outgoing arrows, and bear an additional red exclamation point.

A three-way difference browser shows the two states and presents the changes. Controls allow the developer to step through the changes one at a time (up and down buttons) and either accept (check mark button) or reject (cross button) them, or make any adjustments or additional edits required to successfully merge the changes. The status line shows the number of remaining unresolved changes.

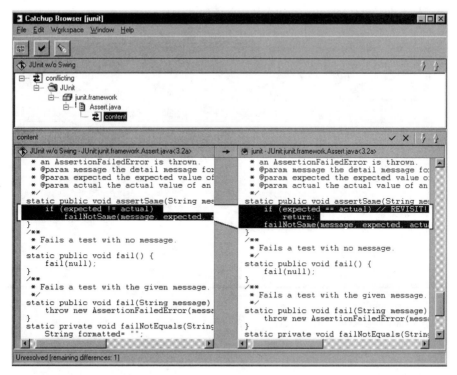

FIGURE 20.7 Catchup browser highlighting a conflicting change

When (and if) all incoming or conflicting changes have been accepted, the developer's workspace is completely caught up with the team stream. Throughout the catchup process, the developer has complete control over what comes into his or her workspace; it is the developer who decides when to catch up and which elements to catch up on.

Advanced Team Stream Features

In addition to the basic facilities described above, team streams also provide some features to make them suitable for more complex environments.

Team Stream Administration

Team streams are created and administered from a special team stream browser (see Figure 20.8).

The bottom pane of Figure 20.8 shows the modification log of the team stream. Each log entry records the author, time of the change, and the detailed structure of what was released.

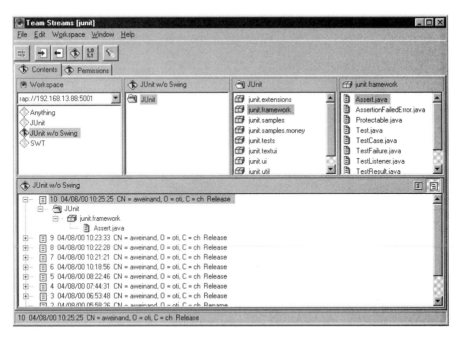

FIGURE 20.8 The team stream browser showing the log of a team stream

Each team stream also has an access control list that controls who can catch up with it, release to it, or administer it. The creator of the team stream is its initial administrator, but this role can be shared or transferred. Administrators manage the team stream's access control list and can freeze the team stream. Freezing a team stream temporarily prevents other developers from releasing to the stream. Administrative and catchup permissions are granted for a team stream as a whole.

Release permission allows one to release changes into the team stream. Release permission can be granted (or denied) selectively to any element and is inherited by subelements. This simple mechanism can be used to establish and enforce various policies, from collective code ownership like in XP to traditional component ownership models.

Connecting a Workspace to Multiple Team Streams

For more advanced usage, a single workspace can be connected to multiple team streams, and a single element can be shared with more than one team stream. Catch up and release apply to a set of team streams; prior to each of these operations, the developer selects the set of team streams involved. A bit later we describe a situation where this capability was put to good use.

Summary

The following list enumerates the team streams' characteristics that make them well suited for XP:

- *Easy to learn and to use:* The notion of a team stream can be fully explained with two concepts: releasing one's changes to the team, and catching up with changes released to the team by other team members.

- *Continuous integration:* Catch up and release are low-overhead operations. Developers do their integration on an ongoing basis. It is straightforward for everyone to work with the current configuration of the team.

- *Collective code ownership:* A team stream can be configured with an unrestricted release policy so that each developer can make and release changes to any part of the code base. Each is responsible for integrating his or her changes into the team stream and for keeping up with changes released by other team members.

- *Fully optimistic concurrency:* Multiple developers can make changes to an element at the same time. The overlap will be discovered automatically at catch up or release time.

- *Conflict detection and merging:* Both catch up and release automatically perform a three-way comparison to detect conflicts and show changes made by the developer in his or her private workspace versus changes made and released to the team stream by other developers. Three-way comparisons are performed for both the entire workspace structure and, if requested by the developer, for the contents of an individual element.

- *Atomic catch up and release:* Both catch up and release are done as atomic transactions. Overlapping changes are automatically detected and presented to the developer for resolution. In the event of almost-simultaneous releases, one release will simply fail. However, no edits are lost; the developer then simply catches up and repeats the release operation.

- *Tightly integrated team support:* VA/ME illustrates one way that team streams can be seamlessly integrated into an IDE.

Comparison with Other VCM Systems

In this section we compare team streams to two of the best-known VCM systems in the XP community: ENVY and CVS.

Comparison with Envy

Team streams are an evolution of the ENVY team programming paradigm that originated with Orwell [Thomas+1988], eventually making its way into the IBM VisualAge for Smalltalk and IBM VisualAge for Java Enterprise Edition products [IBM1994; IBM1998]. We focus on the latter (which we abbreviate here as VA/J) because it is directly comparable to VA/ME.

VA/ME consolidates the following disparate team related features of VA/J.

- *Open project editions:* A team stream takes the place of a VA/J open project edition as the shared entity in the repository around which all team members coordinate their activities. Since team streams are a special kind of entity, with a name and an unlimited life span, we feel this is a more transparent way to present these important entities to the developer than nameless, transient open editions.

✧ *Versioning:* In VA/ME, versioning is orthogonal to releasing to a team stream. Versioning has no impact on other developers; releasing to a team stream is the only way for one developer to affect another. In contrast, versioning a project or package (but not a class) in VA/J affects other team members and, consequently, cannot be done without considering its impact on the team. If a project gets versioned off while a team member with unreleased changes continues to work, the developer discovers (eventually) that he or she has become decoupled from the team and has to seek out (or create) another open edition of the project in which to continue working. In VA/ME, a project can be versioned at any time and, optionally, released to the team stream. Team members continue to catch up and release to the team stream, which is always open for business.

✧ *Releasing:* The release operation in VA/ME is similar to VA/J. One subtle difference is that whereas in VA/J developers release elements (to the containing open edition), in VA/ME they release changes to elements. VA/J only keeps track of which elements are in the workspace and compares them against the repository to determine whether the workspace has unreleased elements. As a consequence of this, VA/J cannot distinguish between a new element that has been released by another developer from an element that has been deleted locally. This is an instance of the classic insert/delete ambiguity faced by synchronizers [Balasubramaniam+1998]. (VA/J avoids this confusion by making the workspace Delete operation immediately release the deletion, a solution which, unfortunately, surprises many teams because it violates workspace isolation.) In VA/ME, developers are always releasing additions, deletions, or changes to elements. VA/ME maintains a hidden third copy of the shared files so that it can compute incoming and outgoing change sets. VA/ME's release is a truly atomic operation even for multiple unrelated elements. VA/J releases multiple elements in rapid succession, with a narrow window of vulnerability between each one.

✧ *Querying unreleased elements:* In VA/J, there is a separate query for finding all unreleased elements—whether incoming, outgoing, or conflicting. In VA/ME, this is built into the catch up and release operations.

✧ *Comparing with released contents:* In VA/J, there is a separate command for comparing an element to its released equivalent. In VA/ME, this function is built into the catch up and release operations.

✧ *Replacing with released contents:* In VA/J, catching up with the team is accomplished with the Replace with Released Contents command. When a developer has no changes to release, he or she can easily catch up with the team by applying this command to the open project editions in the workspace. However, things are more complicated when there are changes in the workspace that the developer does not want to lose but is not in a position to release in their current state. VA/J developers typically reload around the elements they are working on, being careful not to lose any of their changes. In VA/ME, the catchup operation is designed to support this common task directly. VA/ME also supports the Replace with Released Contents command, but its primary use is for discarding temporary changes (e.g., print statements added while debugging).

✧ *Granularity:* In VA/J the finest grained versionable element is the method. In VA/ME it's the Java source or binary class file. This decision was motivated primarily by performance considerations. We are currently investigating ways to compensate for this loss of granularity.

Comparison with CVS

CVS [CVS1998; Fogel2000] is a VCM system that supports a team programming model similar to that of team streams; there are also some notable differences.

✧ *Workspaces:* In CVS, like in VA/ME, each developer has an isolated workspace containing trees of elements. The update and commit operations in CVS are analogous to the catch up and release operations in VA/ME respectively.

✧ *Versioning:* CVS combines version control and team programming support so that the two are inseparable (so does VA/J), with the result that neither feature is quite as simple as it could be if the features were orthogonal. In the team stream model, versioning and team support are orthogonal (in some ways, a bit too orthogonal; the automatic versioning of leaf elements is a commonly requested VA/ME feature).

✧ *Branching:* CVS supports branches directly, whereas team streams do not. In CVS, developers can create their own branches on which to release changes until they are ready to release them to the team. Team streams allow developers to create another team stream for use in the same way but do not provide any way of recording the relationship between team streams; that is, unlike CVS, there is no direct information about which team stream represents a branch of another one.

✧ *Merge ancestors:* CVS normally uses the common ancestor in the version history when performing three-way diffs/merges between branches, leading to well-known difficulties [Fogel2000] with partially merged branches. VA/ME maintains the information about what has been released independent of version history and ensures that outgoing changes can only be released once.

✧ *Merging:* CVS attempts to merge conflicting changes to the same file automatically, provided the line ranges of the changes do not overlap. VA/ME always gets the developer involved to resolve conflicts within a file manually.

✧ *Integration:* CVS has a command line interface and operates on the file system through RCS. CVS has been integrated into several IDEs using tool integration mechanisms provided by the IDE vendors. To our knowledge CVS has not been directly and tightly integrated into an IDE the way team streams have. In VA/ME, all the elements presented in the UI are VCM aware and show version information in place. Developers can do version and release operations from their current working context inside the IDE. They don't have to make a mental switch to the user interface and conventions of an external VCM system.

Our Experience Using Team Streams

As soon as it was possible, we started developing VA/ME with itself. Although our process was not fully compliant with XP, we did use a flexible process that shares many common threads with XP. This section briefly describes our use of team streams and summarizes our experiences to date.

Setup

Five separate teams, located at four different sites (on two continents), actively used VA/ME and its team streams support to develop the VA/ME product. We set up the following structure:

- *Global team stream:* This team stream was used to integrate the work accomplished by the various teams.
- *Main team streams:* Each team maintained its own team stream for coordinating the team's day-to-day activities.
- *Temporary team streams:* Used for ad hoc collaboration inside or between teams.

Process

A team's main team stream represented the overall state of the team's work. The log for one of the main team streams showed 536 release operations occurred over a 12-week period. On average, three developers were actively working in that team, meaning each developer released approximately three times a day. Although our process did not explicitly require developers to release every completed and tested piece of work, the numbers show that the developers were acting in an XP-like mode.

Since we required developers to release code into the team's main team stream only if it was tested, the main team stream always contained a consistent snapshot of the code base under development (limited only by the coverage of our tests).

We decided to designate a separate workspace as the build workspace; only from this workspace would we release anything to the global team stream. The main reasons we did this were as follows:

- We did not want to force anybody to be completely in sync with the team's main team stream at build time, and this would occasionally block a developer from progressing further.
- We wanted to prevent accidental releases to the global team stream.

Our rules were that the build workspace was the only workspace that could be connected to both the team's main team stream and to the global team stream, and in which all projects were shared with both team streams.

At build time the team's main team stream would be frozen, the build workspace would be caught up with the frozen team stream, all tests would be run, and then all changes would be released to the global team stream. As soon as the global team stream contained the successfully integrated work of all teams, the build workspace would be caught up with the global team stream, and all those changes would be released to the team's main team stream. Finally, the main team stream would be unfrozen, and individual developers would catch up with it and begin the cycle again.

Conclusion

For the teams involved in the team stream-based development and build process, the experience had the following interesting characteristics:

⬥ The learning curve for getting new team members on board is quite short. The design of the VA/ME IDE helps orient developers quickly with respect to their teams, and helps them avoid making gaffes that would lose changes.

⬥ There was no perceived difference between intrateam collaboration, interteam collaboration, and the build process. All these tasks are performed with exactly the same means and did not require any special knowledge.

⬥ It was easy to share projects with multiple team streams and thus to split and rejoin code streams. The simplicity of simultaneous sharing also contributes to scalability because it provides a straightforward solution to increase the number of collaborating teams.

⬥ Atomic catch up and release, coupled with three-way comparison among the team stream, the workspace, and the hidden snapshot, boosted our confidence in small-scale integration by removing any worry of accidentally losing changes.

⬥ The time window between conflict resolution on catch up and the subsequent release seemed to be short enough that it could be done without undue fear of colliding with somebody else. Of course, the time window depends on the number of developers directly releasing into the team stream. In our setup, we had a maximum of six developers releasing to any team stream.

References

[Babich1986] W. Babich. *Software Configuration Management: Coordination for Team Productivity.* Addison-Wesley, 1986.

[Balasubramaniam+1998] S. Balasubramaniam, B. C. Pierce. "What Is a File Synchronizer?" In *Proceedings of MobiCom'98*, Dallas, Texas, October 1998.

[Beck2000] K. Beck. *Extreme Programming Explained.* Addison-Wesley, 2000.

[Berczuck1997] S. Berczuk. *Configuration Management Patterns.* On-line at http://www.bell-labs.com/cgi-user/OrgPatterns/ OrgPatterns? ConfigurationManagementPatterns. 1997.

[CVS1998] *CVS—Concurrent Versions System.* Free Software Foundation. On-line at http://www.gnu.org/manual/cvs-1.9. 1998.

[Fogel2000] K. F. Fogel. *Open Source Development with CVS.* CoriolisOpen Press, 2000.

[Jeffries2000] R. Jeffries. *Extreme Programming.* A tutorial at SD2000. On-line at http://www.xprogramming.com/SD2000Tutorial/ index.htm. 2000

[SingleReleasePoint] *Single Release Point.* On-line at http://c2.com/ cgi/wiki?SingleReleasePoint. 2000.

[Thomas+1988] D. A. Thomas, K. Johnson. "Orwell—A Configuration Management System for Team Programming." *OOPSLA 1988 Proceedings.* San Diego, Calif., 1988.

[IBM1994] *IBM VisualAge Smalltalk Enterprise*, Version 5.0. IBM, Inc. On-line at http://www.ibm.com/software/ad/smalltalk/. 1994.

[IBM1998] *IBM VisualAge for Java, Enterprise Edition*, Version 3.0. IBM Inc. On-line at http://www.ibm.com/software/ad/vajava/. 1998.

[IBM2000] *IBM VisualAge Micro Edition*, Version 1.0. IBM Inc. On-line at http://www.ibm.com/software/ad/embedded/. 2000.

[Wingerd+1998] L. Wingerd, C. Seiwald. "High-Level Best Practices in Software Configuration Management." Paper presented at the *Eighth International Workshop on Software Configuration Management,* Brussels, July 1998. On-line at http://www.perforce.com/perforce/bestpractices.html.

About the Authors

Jim des Rivières works at the Ottawa lab of Object Technology International (OTI) and can be reached at jim_des_rivieres@oti.com. Erich Gamma, Kai-Uwe Mätzel, and André Weinand are based at the OTI Zurich lab and can be reached at erich_gamma@oti.com, kai-uwe_maetzel@oti.com, and andre_weinand@oti.com. John Wiegand is located in the OTI Minneapolis lab and can be reached at john_wiegand@oti.com. Ivan Moore, formerly of OTI Ottawa, now works for Connextra in London, England and can be reached at ivan@tadmad.co.uk.

Chapter 21

Support for Distributed Teams in Extreme Programming

—Till Schümmer and Jan Schümmer

The Extreme Programming (XP) methodology relies on collocated collaboration of programming teams. This chapter discusses problems and possible solutions when distributed teams decide to do XP. Communication and awareness support are the keys to the successful distribution of programming teams. The XP methodology is analyzed with respect to these essential issues. We present TUKAN, which is a research prototype of a synchronous distributed team programming environment. In TUKAN, we applied groupware research results to the XP domain and thus provide a scenario, showing how distribution problems can be solved when XP is carried out by distributed teams.

Introduction

The Extreme Programming (XP) methodology [Beck2000] heavily relies on group members being collocated. Rich communications within the team and a high degree of awareness of the actions, which are performed by others, are essential aspects of XP. Unfortunately, collocated collaboration is not possible under certain circumstances:

⬦ Office arrangements simply do not allow the whole team to be situated at one location.

⬦ The team might be too large to fit into one location, and even if this were possible, communication would produce a high level of noise, making concentrated work impossible.

⬦ New models of work, such as telework, explicitly demand distribution.

⬦ In the case of organizations operating at an international level, the team members might be distributed around the world.

The size restriction usually causes traditional XP groups to reduce team size by two to ten programmers. Distribution may be a way to enlarge the size of the team by eliminating noise and space restrictions. Two possible alternatives arise: Either XP is not possible when teams are too large or when teams are not collocated, or teams need technical assistance to tailor an environment comparable to a shared location that supports communication among a large number of people.

Kent Beck [Beck2000] addressed the first alternative; in this chapter we adddress the second. We apply results from the research area of computer-supported cooperative work (CSCW) to the XP methodology. We therefore identify those parts of XP that are particularly difficult in a distributed scenario and then describe how we addressed these problems in the team programming environment. We argue that—with the appropriate technical support at hand—XP might work as well in distributed settings.

The remainder of this chapter is organized as follows. In the next section we point out distribution-critical parts of the XP methodology that demand special attention in the distributed setting. We then describe currently available groupware technology that can be used to support the distribution-critical parts. We present TUKAN, an environment for distributed implementation, which incorporates some of the solutions described in the groupware section and supports the distribution-critical parts of XP. The chapter closes with related work and our conclusions.

Distribution-Critical Parts of XP

The XP method can be summarized as a set of easy-to-understand instructions and rules for all members of the software development team. Looking closer at the practices described for the XP method [Beck2000], we recognize some practices that are related to communication and cooperation, such as pair programming or the planning game, whereas others establish common rules like coding standards or the 40-hour week. We refer to the emphasis on communication-intense practices such as a communication-centered view of XP.

Critical Aspects of the Communication-Centered View on XP

For a distributed setting, the communication-centered view of XP is of special interest. It includes the following practices: the planning game, testing, pair programming, continuous integration, and communication with the external customer.

The Planning Game

In early phases of the project, visions about the system to be built are often quite vague. The planning game establishes rules for a creative communication process between business and development teams that helps clarify the members' visions.

Within the planning game, communication has a well-defined structure. Both partners communicate through story cards, which may be created, modified, reestimated, sorted, or selected. Each of these actions provides information about the project to both customers and developers. Following the rules of the planning game, communication is more effective than it would be in an unstructured way.

The iteration planning game is structured in almost the same way. It is an important tool within the team that is used to coordinate their activities on a fine-grained level.

The cards of the planning game and the iteration planning game reflect the current status of the project. By browsing the cards, team members become aware of:

⬥ Who is responsible for which tasks
⬥ What tasks have to be solved next
⬥ What tasks are already solved

There are two key issues to carrying out the planning game in a distributed setting: The story cards must be remotely accessible, and the partners have to be able to communicate with each other. The planning game, especially the iteration planning game, is more important in the distributed setting than it is when team members are collocated, because more informal methods for coordination work best when team members are fully aware of each other and when there are no obstacles to communication.

Pair Programming

When programming is done in pairs, a large part of the communication occurs as the two people look at the same code at one machine. Comments are expressed through verbal communication. Discussion about the current implementation, possible alternatives, errors, or style violations ensures that the result will be of high quality. Questions can be answered promptly, thus improving the effect of learning.

Apart from the assignment of roles, the communication between the two programmers is not formally structured. The adoption of roles guides the participants during their discussion. The person that uses the keyboard wants to explain his or her intention to the partner. The partner focuses on a strategic discussion and attends to the overall concept. Roles may change about every 15 minutes, in which case it is important to know which role a person currently takes.

The pair's formation changes frequently with every new task. This supports propagation of new concepts within the team, since the concepts are passed on from one partner to another. Possible pair programming partners may be detected easily by looking around in the programming room in the collocated situation where the programmer can easily be aware of how busy other members of the team are at the moment. In the distributed situation, however, the awareness of other team members' activities is lost. This makes the formation of pairs a much harder task.

During a distributed pair programming session, programmers must be able to communicate; they have to see the same part of code not on one shared screen but on their individual screens. At least one of them has to be able to change this code. As both pair members focus on the code they work on and communicate verbally, they must be able to hear but not necessarily to see each other.

Testing

Tests help in understanding the intention of the tested program parts. Tests are an important vehicle for communication, especially when there are assumptions that are not obvious. Tests also provide a communication channel between the persons writing the tests and the users of tests. They can be used to form an opinion on the purpose of the tested artifact within the team.

Tests are implemented and performed by pairs. Failing tests result in a debugging session. This is also performed in pairs. Distributed testing benefits from a good distribution support for pair programming. In addition, support is needed for the distributed execution of tests: Test output must be shared among all members of the testing session. As there are at least two computers involved in the distributed testing, the decision has to be made concerning which machine(s) will be used to execute the test code.

Continuous Integration

Whenever a task card is solved, the solution should be integrated. Integration phases occur several times a day. Because of collective ownership, the changes of one task can have ramifications across the whole system. Other programmers should be informed about the integration to avoid future conflicts. In the current description of XP, there is no explicit rule to ensure this.

During integration, programmers have to know what changes have occurred since they decoupled their work from the common project data. They have to know what artifacts they manipulated and what artifacts were independently manipulated and integrated by other developers. The only way to find out about changes is by browsing through the code. But finding and understanding modified parts of a large software system is a hard task. It is even harder to estimate which changes may affect the part of the system the programmer is currently working on. The environment should thus support the activity of finding and understanding changes, and tell the programmers about the semantic context of the changes. Source code collisions can be shown by a version management system. Semantic collisions may be detected by failing tests.

Communication with the Customer

Communication with external customers is important throughout the project. Most non-XP projects omit this because so much effort is needed to establish communication initially. XP tries to neutralize this with the concept of an on-site customer. But although this solves the problem for the programming team, the customer might prefer a more cost-effective way of optimizing communication with the programming team that makes fewer demands on staff availability.

When XP is distributed, the most important requirement concerning the external customer is keeping communication alive. Additional communication media are thus needed in this setting.

Other Critical Aspects of XP

Besides the practices included in the communication centered view of XP, other aspects will also definitely change when XP is distributed.

Metrics

Metrics are management's tool for communicating the project's state and progress to all team members and as such are critical to the successful distribution of XP.

Distributing metrics via electronic mail might not be a good solution, because e-mail demands explicit action and attention on the recipient's end and thus will be ignored sooner or later. The state chart that is used in the collocated setting is based on a subconscious communication, and for the distributed setting, a similar solution is needed.

Awareness

During their daily work, programmers are aware of the presence and conversation of their collocated colleagues. Thus, they have certain awareness regarding their team members' contribution to the project. They may notice what the tasks of the other programmers are. They may overhear things in conversation that they may find useful in the future. Or a colleague may notice that other programmers are struggling with a problem that he or she solved some days ago and contribute to the solution of the problem.

Reaching this level of awareness is very difficult in a distributed setting. Transmitting everything that's going on at one site to all other sites is not possible since the expressiveness of known communication media is limited. In the collocated setting, filtering of awareness information is done unconsciously by the recipient.

Distribution Problems

Distributed teams are disadvantaged compared to collocated teams in at least in three ways: Communication within the team is hindered, team members are less aware of each other, and common access to physical objects and places (like a printer or the cafeteria) is difficult. CSCW research offers remedies for such communication problems and low awareness. Access to physical objects can be supported as long as there are meaningful electronic representations of these objects (like virtual rooms or electronic blackboards). In the next section we describe the solutions suggested by CSCW research and discuss their applicability to XP.

Groupware

Ellis, Gibbs, and Rein define groupware as "computer-based systems that support groups of people engaged in a common task (or goal) and that provide an interface to a shared environment" [Ellis+1991]. In order to focus on groupware issues relevant to XP, we classify groupware into three categories, which are identified by their main purpose: communication, coordination, and collaboration.

Communication

The most widely used family of groupware applications are e-mail systems or messaging systems such as Netnews. Communication is textual and asynchronous. If the communication has to be highly interactive, synchronous communication tools are needed. These include, in ascending order of expressiveness and bandwidth, text-based chat tools, audioconferencing systems, and videoconferencing systems. For a vivid discussion, as it is needed for pair programming, participants should be connected by an audioconferencing system, because a text-based chat tool hinders communication speed.

Videoconferencing technology may integrate remotely located people into the team even without them being physically present. The team will get a sense of presence of the remotely located person, which is called telepresence [Buxton+1992]. Videoconferences can thus help integrate external customers. After a collocated familiarization phase, implementation teams and the external customer may be distributed again and communicate through a synchronous communication tool.

Coordination

Coordination systems help individuals view, plan, and execute their own actions in relation to their coworkers' actions and to their common goal. Within a coordination system, users must be aware of other users and of their actions. Awareness is a key concept concerning coordination in shared workspaces and is discussed in depth later in this chapter.

Workflow management systems as well as document management systems fall into the category of coordination systems. They coordinate the concurrent access of different users to the documents and inform them of modifications. Such systems apply to XP whenever there are predictable dependencies between tasks. For instance, during testing, a workflow management system can force a debugging session for each test that failed. In creative tasks, however, coordination systems are often too inflexible to be useful.

Distributed version management systems allow concurrent modifications to the sources and assist the users at the point of integration by highlighting conflicts with the work of other users. Some version management systems also provide information about who is currently working on the source code.

Collaboration

Collaboration support combines basic coordination and communication support and adds a shared environment, which serves as the group's focus. All group members can manipulate objects within the shared environment.

Group decision support systems are used for collaborative problem solving. The goal is to increase the quality of a decision or to reduce the time needed for making a decision, or a combination of both. Group decision support systems typically include functionality for problem analysis, for the exchange of arguments, and for voting.

Multiuser editors allow a group of users to jointly edit a common document. Shared whiteboards are the simplest form of the multiuser editor, because their document, a drawing, is rather unstructured. More complex multiuser editors are available to edit, for example, text documents, mind maps, or hypermedia documents. An easy way to implement a multiuser editor is to use an application-sharing system. These systems give a group of users access to an arbitrary application that is running on one participant's machine by distributing the application's visual output. The input control can be passed from participant to participant, but only one user at a time is allowed to control the application (a process called "floor passing"). Physical access to the machine is not necessary in application sharing. Thus application sharing can solve the problem of team members needing access the integration station. If a pair works collocated but has no physical access to the integration station, they can use an X-Window system, as it is implemented in many UNIX environments.

Desktop teleconferencing systems combine the three techniques of multiuser editors, audioconferences, and videoconferences. Microsoft NetMeeting [Microsoft2000] is an instance of this class of application that combines audio- and videoconferences with a shared whiteboard and an application-sharing mechanism.

Awareness

Awareness is an important research topic in the field of groupware. A widespread definition was given by Dourish and Bellotti [Dourish+1992]: "Awareness is an understanding of the activities of others, which provides a context for your own activity. This context is used to ensure that individual contributions are relevant to the group's activity as a whole, and to evaluate actions with respect to group goals and progress." Awareness helps groups reach semantic consistency in their work [Dourish1995]. Often, a computer program cannot solve semantic conflicts caused by activities of users, so it is more appropriate to indicate conflicts and leave the solution to the group members.

Another important subject is workspace awareness [Gutwin+1996a; Haake1999]. Workspace awareness includes knowledge about shared artifacts, coworkers, activities, and extension of the workspace. In addition to awareness of a participant's activities within the workspace, it is often necessary to have awareness of activities in front of the screen. For instance, it may be important to see where another person is looking (gaze awareness [Ishii+1992]) or points (gesture awareness). The latter may be achieved by telepointers that replicate mouse or text cursors of remote users or that are modeled as a graphical object that may be dragged around independently of the mouse cursor [Hayne+1993].

Providing awareness on all aspects of the project may soon result in information overload. Thus only relevant information should be displayed. Several models have been developed to enable computer programs to provide such relevant awareness information. A well-known one is the spatial model, which is used to model interaction in virtual environments [Benford+1993]. Within the spatial model, artifacts are arranged in a three-dimensional space. Users may interact with the artifacts by moving through this space. Other users may always see where their colleagues are within the space, called their presence position.

Rodden enhances this model with the concepts of focus and nimbus [Rodden1996]. His focus-nimbus model consists of objects like artifacts and users, which are distributed in space. Each object has a well-defined distance from all other objects. Around these objects is a focus and a nimbus, which are parts of space. The focus includes all objects that are of interest to the object, whereas the nimbus includes all positions in space where the object might influence other objects. As an example, the focus of a person consists of all people he or she can see, and the nimbus consists of all people who stand next to him or her. In most cases, interest and influence of an object will fade the further a position in space is away from the object's position. With focus, nimbus, and presence position as parameters, a suitable awareness function may be defined whose exact formulation is application dependent [Rodden1996].

TUKAN

TUKAN is a synchronous distributed team programming environment that applies some of the groupware research results described in the previous sections to XP. TUKAN is an enhancement of VisualWorks/ENVY Smalltalk. ENVY provides a shared code repository with a sophisticated distributed version management and simple user management for code ownership. Within ENVY, users can trace changes and load changes made by other users within their workspace. Thus integration may be done in a decentralized way. ENVY provides only simple awareness by indicating when a user's loaded code version is not the released version.

TUKAN adds awareness information, communication channels, and synchronous collaboration mechanisms to ENVY. This functionality was developed on top of the COAST groupware framework, which supports the implementation of highly interactive, synchronous, and distributed applications [Schuckmann+1996; Schuckmann+1999]. Unlike application-sharing systems like NetMeeting, COAST works on shared replicated objects and requires only a low network bandwidth.

The provision of awareness is the essence of the TUKAN concept and is discussed in the next section. Later we focus on the usability of TUKAN's synchronous communication and collaboration support.

Applying Awareness Models to Software Projects

The extended spatial model, as it was described earlier, can be applied to software projects. The artifacts that form the project have to be arranged in space. This can be done automatically by analyzing the artifacts and the relations among them. If a programmer views an artifact, he or she is "standing in front of" the artifact and thus other programmers can sense the programmer at this artifact.

TUKAN uses an extended spatial model with focus and nimbus. When a programmer views a method, his or her focus is on the method. The programmer's presence position is always the same as the position of the focused artifact, which simplifies the calculation of awareness information. Finally, the programmer's nimbus consists of all other software artifacts that are within a specific distance of the method.

To calculate the nimbus, we must define distances between artifacts. TUKAN artifacts are methods, classes, and packages (in ENVY, "applications") of the project. The artifacts are automatically arranged within the artifact space according to their relationships to one another.

Possible relationships are:

◇ *Structure:* A relationship-like inheritance between a class and its superclass or a composition between methods and their class
◇ *Usage:* A relationship between two methods, when within one method the other method is called
◇ *Version:* A relationship between an artifact and a modified version of the artifact

Based on these relationships, a distance function between two artifacts is defined. Artifacts connected by a direct relationship are close to each other, whereas artifacts connected by a path of relationships are farther away. Artifacts without any connection between them are considered to be at an infinite distance away from each other.

All artifacts within the nimbus of an active user are displayed with awareness indicators as shown in Figure 21.1. These indicators reflect two types of information: that there is at least one other user next to this artifact and the distance of the other user's presence position from the artifact.

A color coding is used to impart awareness on the distance to the nearest remote-working user. To avoid information overload when the

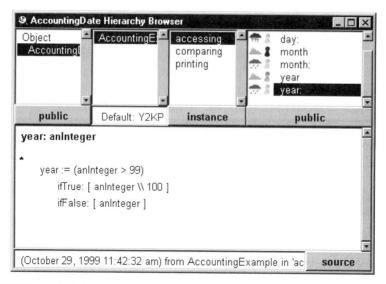

FIGURE 21.1 Collaboration aware hierarchy browser

artifact is part of many remote-working users' nimbus, the browser only shows an indicator for the nearest working user.

If the nearest working user is far away from the artifact, he or she does not influence the awareness information displayed in front of the artifact. If the artifact becomes part of his or her nimbus, a green activity figure is displayed in front of the artifact. The closer the user comes to the displayed artifacts, the more red paint is used to display the awareness indicators.

Figure 21.2 illustrates the awareness icon computation, which was used to calculate the browser visualization of Figure 21.1. The displayed part of an example project consists of one class, AccountingDate with five visible methods (month, year, year:, month:, and day:) and one method <, which is not shown in Figure 21.1. Bidirectional connections in Figure 21.2 represent usage relations with a distance of 1. The method < uses month and year to compare two dates. Unidirectional arrows depict the relationship between the methods and their class. Relations from a method to its class have a distance of 1, whereas the relations of a class to its methods have a distance of 2. (Note that Figure 21.2 shows only relations that are part of the shortest path from month to all other displayed methods.) The same distance measure is

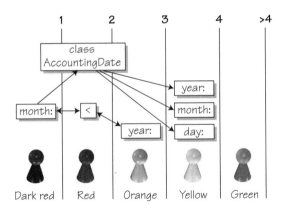

FIGURE 21.2 Spatial model for presence awareness

used to calculate possible configuration conflicts. A configuration conflict exists if one user has changed an artifact and the other users have not yet loaded this artifact.

A weather metaphor is used to symbolize the presence of possible conflict areas. A heavy lightning symbol tells the programmer that this method has been changed. The symbols show better weather for possible conflicts caused by changes on methods that are farther away.

Figure 21.3 shows the relationships used to calculate the conflict icons displayed in Figure 21.1. Arrows have the same semantics as described

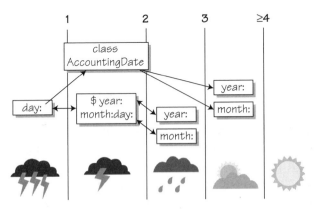

FIGURE 21.3 Spatial model for conflict detection

for Figure 21.2. Because another user created a new edition of the method day:, it is displayed with a heavy lightning symbol. All other displayed methods are related to day:, which causes other bad weather conflict icons to appear in front of their names. Unlike the visualization of nearby working users, TUKAN always displays a conflict icon. If there is no near conflict, a sun is shown to indicate that everything is up to date.

By indicating possible configuration conflicts, TUKAN avoids parallel changes of the same artifact. This realizes the outer limit of continuous integration, as far as the knowledge about other programmers' work is concerned. Changes made by other programmers are not actually reflected in the local programmer's code but in the visualization of the method identifier.

Thus, programmers are allowed to work loosely coupled, able to make local changes while neglecting the relationships to changes made by other programmers. When there are remote changes to an artifact, programmers have the chance to do a local integration of this artifact before applying their own changes.

In a well-structured system, the probability of two changes being made on the same method within a single integration cycle is quite low. Traditional versioning systems can detect conflicting versions of one artifact, but they fail on detecting any change integration problems caused by changes on related artifacts. TUKAN moves one step further by broadening the definition of conflict. From the TUKAN point of view, a conflict may be present whenever two related objects are changed independently.

TUKAN detects configuration conflicts immediately when they are created. There is no need to postpone this detection to an explicit integration session. Thus the continuous integration is done during coding and becomes part of current work.

The information that can be provided through awareness indicators cannot exceed the "something is going on out there" information level. More information would be too much to be displayed as an icon, and if the area were to be extended, the awareness indicators would divert the user's attention from programming. Therefore, TUKAN uses a separate browser to provide additional information about what change caused the conflict or who is currently working nearby. If the work of another user is of interest to a programmer's task, he or she can decide to switch to tighter collaboration and enter a pair programming or integration session using the cooperative class browser.

Cooperative Class Browser

The cooperative class browser enables users at different locations to program in a tightly coupled manner. The lower part of the browser (Figure 21.4) looks almost like a traditional single user browser. It allows the user to select protocols and methods. When a method is selected, its source code is displayed in an editable text field.

Code browsing is done in a tightly coupled mode to ensure that all members of the session see the same method and thus have a common focus (this is called WYSIWIS: What You See Is What I See.).

All users are allowed to edit methods. To provide awareness, cursors of remote users are displayed as telecursors in form of a colored circle. In Figure 21.4 the remote user Till currently edits the comment (he placed his cursor behind the word whol) while the local user Chris has

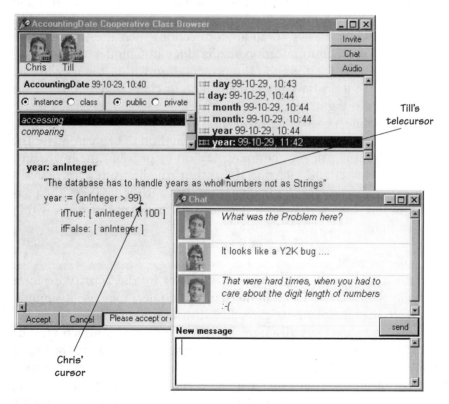

FIGURE 21.4 Cooperative class browser and method chat

placed his cursor behind the boolean expression (`anInteger > 99`), which he is going to change. Telecursors may also be used to point to different parts of the source code. They substitute for the finger that points to a specific portion of code on the screen during a collocated pair-programming session. (This has the positive side effect of no more fingerprints on your monitor. As we mentioned earlier, common access to physical objects is limited in distributed settings.)

Because every user has his or her own keyboard, the strict distinction of roles within a pair programming session is abandoned. Both users may act as writer and programmer. This may lead to fewer strategic discussions. A solution to this problem may be to assign these roles explicitly.

Presence awareness is provided by the user list in the upper part of the browser. All participating users are displayed with their name, picture, and the color of their telecursor.

Programmers can hold conversations via a chat tool or an audio tool. In Figure 21.4, the chat tool shown may be used if bandwidth is low. If bandwidth allows an audio connection, then the use of audio ensures that the communication media does not hinder communication. Indicators at their graphical representation within the user list are displayed when users have opened an audio or chat connection (the little keyboards in Figure 21.4).

If programmers encounter problems that they cannot solve by themselves, they may contact an author of the method. They can invite the author to join the pair programming session by pressing the invite button of the browser and selecting the author's name from a list of available users. After accepting the invitation, the author also sees the pair-programming browser and is a partner with equal permissions within the session.

Activity Explorer

Teams are supported in the planning activity by the activity explorer shown in Figure 21.5. Programmers and customers may use it simultaneously to play the planning game in a distributed setting.

The activity explorer distinguishes three levels of abstraction. The highest level is used to handle story cards. Each story card may be linked to one or more task cards on the second level. Sorting cards by priority is done automatically. Every user may enter a vote for every card, stating how important he or she considers this story or task to be. All votes are counted, and the card with most votes is placed on top of the card list.

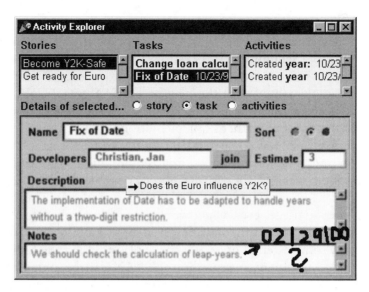

FIGURE 21.5 Activity explorer

If the traditional form interface were to be the only mode of interaction with this electronic representation of cards, they would soon prove to be problematic because they lack the freedom that a piece of paper gives on which you can draw figures or add annotations easily. Therefore, TUKAN provides a second interaction layer that lies on top of the structured layer like a semitransparent pane of glass. On this annotation layer, users may add free annotations in the form of scribbles, graphics, texts, or hyperlinks to other cards. This representation is very close to a printed card that contains all the structured information and on which the programmers do handwritten annotations.

In the activity browser shown in Figure 21.5, the card Fix of Date is currently selected. Two users are editing the annotation layer: The first user annotates the notes field as a reminder that Y2K is a leap year, while the second user has established a hyperlink to the story card Get ready for Euro. At the same time, a third user may change the contents of the structured layer of the card. Maintaining semantic consistency between structured layer and annotation layer is still an open research issue.

At the upper right part of Figure 21.5, the third abstraction level is shown. This level contains information on all programming activities that were fulfilled during implementation of the task.

Current Status

A first implementation of the TUKAN environment was demonstrated at OOPSLA'99 [Schümmer+1999]. It is currently being used for some small projects in order to gain real usage experiences. The largest project we implemented with the help of TUKAN was TUKAN itself. From the moment the awareness mechanisms were stable enough, they were used to assist the further implementation of TUKAN.

The performance was comparable to the ENVY performance, because the groupware functionality does not require high bandwidth. The awareness indicators and the visualization of possible conflicts helped us prevent parallel conflicting changes of the same methods. This was recognized in daily usage, even when we were working collocated. Nevertheless, the final proof can only be given by a large-scale evaluation, including by some external users, which we plan to do in the future.

Up-to-date information regarding TUKAN can be obtained from our group's Web site at http://www.darmstadt.gmd.de/concert.

Related Work

FLECSE [Dewan+1993] is a set of tools to support distributed implementation. It includes shared editors, a shared integration tool based on RCS [Tichy1985], and a shared command line debugger. Within the shared debugger, single lines may be executed cooperatively and the outputs are shared between the participants.

Mercury [Kaiser+1987] allows concurrent manipulation of Modula-2 and Ada programs. It traces dependencies between modules and propagates changes to users of related modules. The Marvel environment [Kaiser+1988] has a more sophisticated relational model and traces dependencies between types and methods. Mercury and Marvel both provide shared feedback to the users. Chime [Dossik+1999] places software artifacts in a three-dimensional environment depending on the relationships between the artifacts. Users may "walk" through this environment to reach the files they want to edit. Other users are displayed within a VR view of the project. Chime provides presence awareness based on the spatial model. Mercury, Chime, and Marvel do not allow tighter coupling of programming or test browsers.

Support for the planning game, as described here, has one major disadvantage to the real world's planning game: There is no means by which to play around with the cards, spread them on a table, or arrange them on a blackboard. Because of limited space on the screen, this cannot be done with ordinary computers. The i-LAND [Streiz+1999] environment addresses this deficit by providing wall-sized interactive displays (DynaWall) and tables with a touch-sensitive display surface (InteracTable). On these devices, information cards (called nodes) can be freely arranged and connections between the cards can be established. Users are allowed to carry the cards with them (for instance from the InteracTable to the DynaWall) by assigning the virtual cards to real-world objects and vice versa.

Comparison

Unlike FLECSE, TUKAN provides awareness of the actions of other users. FLECSE also lacks support for planning and tracking activities, and changes to the project. On the other hand, TUKAN does not yet include a shared debugging module, which is a future research topic.

Mercury and Marvel implement a relation system comparable to TUKAN. Nevertheless, TUKAN works on a finer grained artifact model and can therefore produce more exact awareness information. Because Marvel and Mercury do not include any support for synchronous collaboration, they are not well suited for XP.

Chime provides a good visualization of other users' activities, but again, as is true for Marvel and Mercury, it works on a coarse artifact level.

The i-LAND environment seems to provide appropriate support for the planning game. However, because it is not integrated into the actual programming environment, it is not suited for the rest of XP. Integration with a domain-specific system (e.g., TUKAN) could simulate the physical handling of real cards and at the same time profit from computer automation and distribution. Such an integration is possible (since the i-LAND software uses the same base mechanisms as TUKAN) and is a topic for future work.

Conclusion

We have shown that awareness and communication are key issues with XP in a distributed setting. The TUKAN environment can support distributed XP teams by integrating these key issues into the programming environment. We described a scenario using the TUKAN environment for distributed XP and provided technical means to overcome the distribution problems of XP. The TUKAN system may thus be used to evaluate how real XP projects perform in a distributed setting. Future work will show whether the solutions are appropriate for distributed XP.

TUKAN combines many groupware techniques.

- ✧ TUKAN provides basic communication support (chat and audio).
- ✧ TUKAN is a coordination system that helps to plan and coordinate activities in the planning game.
- ✧ In supporting the planning game, TUKAN is also a group-decision support system.
- ✧ TUKAN includes multiuser editors for code editing and for annotating story cards in the planning game.
- ✧ TUKAN integrates a version management system (ENVY).

References

[Beck2000] K. Beck. *Extreme Programming Explained*. Addison-Wesley, 2000

[Benford+1993] S. BenfordL. Fahlen. "A Partial Model of Interaction in Large Virtual Environments." In *ECSCW'93 Proceedings of the Third European Conference on CSCW*, 1993.

[Buxton1992]W. Buxton. "Telepresence: Integrating Shared Task and Person Spaces." In Baecker, R., ed. Readings in *Groupware and Computer-Supported Cooperative Work*, Morgan Kaufmann Publishers, 1992.

[Dewan+1993] P. Dewan, J. Riedel, J. "Toward Computer Supported Concurrent Software Engineering." *IEEE Computer.* January, 1993.

[Dossik+1999] S. Dossick G. Kaiser G. "Distributed Software Development with CHIME." In *Proceedings of ICSE-99 2nd Workshop on Software Engineering over the Internet,* 1999.

[Dourish1995] P. Dourish. "The Parting of Ways: Divergence, Data Management and Collaborative Work." In *Proceedings of the ECSCW'95,* 1995.

[Dourish+1992] P. Dourish, V. Bellotti. "Awareness and Coordination in Shared Workspaces." *CSCW '92. Conference Proceedings on Computer-Supported Cooperative Work,* 1992.

[Ellis+1991] C. Ellis, S.Gibbs, G. Rein. "Groupware—Some Issues and Experiences." In *Communications of the ACM.* Volume 34, Number 1, 1991.

[Gutwin+1996a] C. Gutwin, M. Roseman. "Workspace Awareness for Groupware." In *Proceedings of the CHI '96 Conference Companion on Human Factors in Computing Systems: Common Ground,* pp. 208–209, 1996.

[Gutwin+1996b] C. Gutwin, M. Roseman, S. Greenberg, S. "A Usability Study of Awareness Widgets in a Shared Workspace Groupware System." In *Proceedings of the ACM 1996 Conference on Computer-Supported Cooperative Work,* 1996.

[Haake1999] J. Haake. "Facilitating Orientation in Shared Hypermedia Workspaces." In *Group'99 Proceedings of the International ACM SIGGROUP Conference on Supporting Group Work,* 1999.

[Hayne+1993] S. Hayne, M. Pendergast, S. Greenberg. "Gesturing Through Cursors: Implementing Multiple Pointers in Group Support Systems." In *Proceedings of the HICSS Hawaii International Conference on System Sciences.* IEEE Press, 1993.

[Ishii+1992] H. Ishii; M. Kobayashi; J. Grudin. "Integration of Interpersonal Space and Shared Workspace: ClearBoard Design and Experiments." *Conference Proceedings on Computer-Supported Cooperative Work,* 1992.

[Kaiser+1988] G. Kaiser, F. Feiler, S. Popovich. "Intelligent Assistance for Software Development and Maintenance." *IEEE Software,* Volume 5, Number 3, 1988.

[Kaiser+1987] G. Kaiser, S. Kaplan, J. Micallef. "Multiuser, Distributed Language-Based Environments." *IEEE Software,* Volume 4, Number 11, 1987.

[Microsoft2000] Microsoft Windows NetMeeting. On-line at http://www.microsoft.com/windows/netmeeting. 2000.

[Rodden1996] T. Rodden. "Populating the Application: A Model of Awareness for Cooperative Applications." In *Proceedings of the ACM 1996 Conference on CSCW'96*, 1996.

[Schuckmann+1996] C. Schuckmann, L. Kirchner, J. Schümmer, J. M. Haake. "Designing Object-Oriented Synchronous Groupware with Coast." In *Proceedings of ACM CSCW'96 Conference on Computer-Supported Cooperative Work*, 1996.

[Schuckmann+1999] C. Schuckmann, J. Schümmer, P. Seitz. "Modeling Collaboration Using Shared Objects." In *Proceedings of the International ACM SIGGROUP Conference on Supporting Group Work*, 1999.

[Schümmer+1999] T. Schümmer, J. Schümmer. "TUKAN: A Team Environment for Software Implementation." In *OOPSLA'99 Companion*. OOPSLA '99, 1999.

[Streiz+1999] N. A. Streitz, J. Geißler, T. Holmer, S. Konomi, C. Müller-Tomfelde, W. Reischl, P. Rexroth, P. Seitz, R. Steinmetz. "i-LAND: An Interactive Landscape for Creativity and Innovation." In *ACM Conference on Human Factors in Computing Systems* (CHI '99), 1999.

[Tichy1985] W. Tichy. "RCS—A System for Version Control." *Software—Practice & Experience*, Volume 15, Number 7, July 1985.

Acknowledgments

The groupware functionality of TUKAN was implemented on the COAST framework for synchronous groupware. We thank our colleagues in the COAST development team. Special thanks are due to Holger Kleinsorgen for his help with the awareness section of this chapter and to Christian Schuckmann for discussions and contributions to the concepts of TUKAN.

About the Authors

Till Schümmer is currently working as a guest researcher at GMD-IPSI (German National Research Center for Information Technology Integrated Publication and Information Systems Institute), Dolivostraße 15,

D-64293 Darmstadt, Germany. He can best be reached by e-mail at Till.Schuemmer@darmstadt.gmd.de.

The author's work is funded by the Deutsche Forschungsgemeinschaft (DFG) in the Ph.D. program "Enabling Technologies for Electronic Commerce" at Darmstadt University of Technology.

Jan Schümmer is working at Intelligent Views GmbH, 64293 Darmstadt, Germany. His e-mail is jan.schuemmer@amc.org.

Chapter 22

Automated Testing for a CORBA-Based Distributed System

—Renato Cerqueira and Roberto Ierusalimschy

In this chapter, we present a test infrastructure used to automate the testing of a CORBA-based distributed system. This infrastructure is based on a flexible programming environment for CORBA systems, called LuaOrb. LuaOrb uses the interpreted language Lua to access and implement CORBA objects, and adopts a dynamic composition approach that, combined to the interactive facilities offered by an interpreted language, makes it a quite suitable platform for test automation.

Introduction

Testing is often a complex task, more so if the tested application is distributed. For instance, the execution of a simple test for a distributed system may require launching many servers and clients in different hosts following a specific order. The high complexity of a test execution may be an obstacle to adopting software development methodologies that apply testing more frequently during the development cycles, such as the Extreme Programming approach [Beck1999; Beck2000].

This chapter describes an infrastructure used to automate the testing of a CORBA-based distributed system. This infrastructure was developed during a project with the Brazilian Navy, when our group developed a distributed sonar simulator that would be integrated with another distributed simulation system developed for training warship commanders. In this development, we used many practices that are common to flexible processes like Extreme Programming: planning game, simple design, testing centered, continuous refactoring, and continuous integration [Beck1999; Beck2000].

The test infrastructure used in this project is based on a scripting tool for CORBA objects called LuaOrb [Ierusalimschy+1998; Cerqueira+1999]. LuaOrb implements a binding between the interpreted language Lua [Ierusalimschy+1996; Figueiredo+1996; Ierusalimschy+1999] and CORBA [OMG1998], and uses the dynamic and reflexive facilities of both systems to support the use of new IDL interfaces and the implementation of CORBA objects at runtime, without the need of precompiled stubs.

The use of interpreted languages like Tcl [Ousterhout1994] to support test automation is a common approach. These languages can take all the effort out of test implementations. Unit tests can be supported by a set of small scripts that validates different aspects of the system components. With high-level abstraction mechanisms and a simple syntax, an interpreted language can also be a powerful tool for an end user—the system customer—to implement functional tests. Features like interactivity and automatic memory management, and no need for recompilations and relinking after each change are very useful for building little test scripts (especially for end-user programming) and allow several design options to be implemented and tested in a short period of time.

Lua fits all those characteristics: It has a very simple syntax and a high-level mechanism for data description. Besides, with LuaOrb, we can use Lua to implement scripts to test either each CORBA object independently or the whole integrated system. By keeping all scripts during the development process, we can easily support automated regression testing [Kernighan+1999] of our system. Besides the scripting tool, the test infrastructure offers some CORBA services to support remote installation of CORBA servers and remote execution of Lua scripts.

Although scripting languages like Lua provide many facilities for testing, the CORBA infrastructure makes testing easier: With the CORBA's reflexive facilities, such as the Dynamic Invocation Interface (DII) and the Interface Repository, test tools can have access to the application components without the previous creation of specific test stubs. Without these reflexive facilities, the test stubs must be generated either with the help of some stub generator, such as SWIG [Beazley1998] and toLua [Celes1998], or manually by the developer. LuaOrb takes advantage of CORBA's reflexive facilities and of the dynamic features of Lua to provide a very flexible programming tool for CORBA systems.

The following sections describe the sonar and the Navy's tactical simulators, the LuaOrb system, and its extensions to support the test infrastructure. The last section is reserved for some final remarks.

The Sonar Simulator

The Distributed Sonar Simulator (DSS), wherein we have applied the distributed test infrastructure, is part of a bigger project to develop a distributed tactical simulator for training warship commanders of the Brazilian Navy. The whole tactical simulator, called SSTT (*Sistema de Simulação Tática e Treinamento*), is responsible for managing and integrating all entities in the simulated environment, such as the vehicles (ships, aircraft, submarines, etc.), their sensors (radars, sonars, GPSs, gyros, links, etc.), and user consoles. Besides these components, which represent real entities, there are also some control components, such as a collision detection module.

Figure 22.1 outlines the SSTT system and shows how the DSS system fits within the structure of a simulated warship. A simulated warship

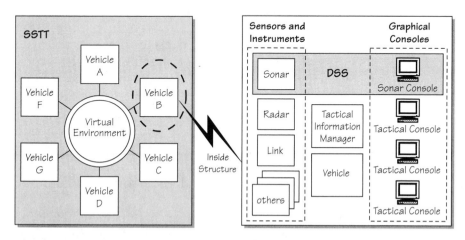

FIGURE 22.1 An outline of the SSTT system

interacts with the virtual environment through its sensors and instruments. Sensors are the only means that a warship has for acquiring information about other vehicles.

Users interact with the system through graphical consoles of the vehicle's navigation instruments and sensors. The navigation instruments allow changes in the vehicle's course and velocity. A sensor display shows the signal generated by a sensor, such as radar or sonar. The tactical information manager component stores all tactical data produced and shared by the warship's tactical consoles (a warship can have more than one tactical console).

The objects that represent vehicles include all information about their relevant mechanical characteristics: position, velocity, course, turn rate, and so on. With these characteristics, the vehicle acts as a deterministic entity, whose position is a function of the time. The SSTT system adopts the dead reckoning approach [IEEE1993; Macedonia+1994]; that is, a sensor object extrapolates the vehicles' positions in function of the time. When the kinetic state of a specific vehicle changes, all sensors must be updated. To perform this update, the observer design pattern [Gamma+1995] is used: A vehicle has a collection with observer objects and, when any change occurs in the vehicle's state, all these objects (listeners) are notified. Figure 22.2 illustrates the pattern behavior. We use this pattern in many other situations that require a notification mechanism.

The DSS system works as another set of components within a simulated warship. The DSS consults its own vehicle to acquire data about its position, velocity, and course, and can also produce information about targets to be shared by the tactical consoles. Because the main goal of the DSS is to provide only the information relevant to tactical procedures, many simplifications could be assumed in its specification. For instance, the detection algorithm and the graphic and sound representations of the sonar contacts could be simplified. Basically, the sonar simulator monitors the simulated vehicles, applies a simplified detection algorithm, and presents in a graphic console the sonar contacts that correspond to the detected targets. The sonar console operator can also create synthetic contacts, classify them, and select some to inform the tactical information manager component.

Due to constraints in the project schedule, both systems, DSS and SSTT, were developed in parallel. Therefore, the two development teams worked together to define the IDL interfaces of all components that are common for both systems:

- ✧ *Target interface:* This interface provides ways to get and set the target attributes, besides offering operations to register listener objects that are interested in changes in the target state. A target can be a vehicle, an offshore petroleum platform, a shoal, a whale, and so on. The sonar simulator, like other simulated entities, uses this interface to monitor the state of all targets.
- ✧ *Vehicle interface:* This interface is a specialization of the target interface that provides additional operations specific for vehicle entities. The sonar simulator uses this interface to interact with its own vehicle.

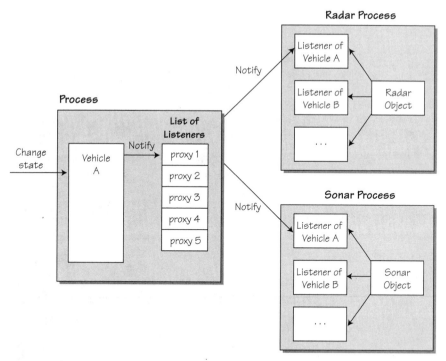

FIGURE 22.2 The basic observer pattern

✧ *Target collection interface:* This interface represents a distributed collection, with operations to insert and remove elements, and iterators for traversing elements. All targets in the simulated environment are registered in a main target collection.

✧ *Tactical information manager interface:* This interface allows operations to update and retrieve tactical information. The console sonar uses this interface to inform the contacts that are selected by its operator.

During the development process, many integration tests were performed and the common IDL interfaces were refined. Figure 22.3 shows a simplified version of the Target and TargetCollection interfaces.

```
struct TargetDescription {
    unsigned long id;
    PlatformDescription platform;
    float x, y, z, vx, vy, vz;
};

interface StateListener {
    void notify(in TargetDescription target);
};

interface Target {
    TargetDescription getDescription();
    void destroy();
    void addStateListener(in StateListener listener);
};

interface Iterator {
    Target first();
    Target next();
    void destroy();
};

interface TargetCollection {
    void insert(in Target obj);
    void remove(in Target obj);
    Iterator createIterator();
};
```

FIGURE 22.3 A simplified version of Target and TargetCollection interfaces

```
module Sonar {
    typedef sequence<TargetDescription> TargetDescrList;

    interface Display {
        void detect( in TargetDescrList targets);
    };

    interface Detector {
        void activate();
        void deactivate();
        void registerDisplay(in Display display);
        void registerTargetCollection(in TargetCollection
                                            collection);
    };
};
```

FIGURE 22.4 The IDL definition for the sonar interfaces

The sonar simulator was designed as a set of distributed CORBA objects, where each object was responsible for one main task. To illustrate how the sonar simulator works, Figure 22.4 presents a simplified version of the actual sonar interfaces (note that the module Sonar refers to some definitions presented in Figure 22.3). The Detector component interacts with the target collection to access the available targets and applies the detection algorithms periodically. After each detection period, this component sends a list of the detected targets' descriptions to the Display component, which is responsible for the graphic and sound presentation.

The LuaOrb System

LuaOrb is a programming tool for CORBA systems that uses the interpreted language Lua [Ierusalimschy+1996; Figueiredo+1996; Ierusalimschy+1999] as its programming language. LuaOrb is based on a language binding that, as usual, defines mappings between Lua and IDL types. However, unlike other bindings, LuaOrb relies on the reflexive facilities of CORBA and the dynamic nature of Lua.

Currently, most CORBA language bindings direct their design to support clients and servers written in a statically compiled language, such as C++, using statically compiled stubs and skeletons. Although

CORBA supports dynamic interfaces, such as the Dynamic Invocation Interface (DII) and the Dynamic Skeleton Interface (DSI), these interfaces are very low level and difficult to use. Static implementations are quite acceptable and even desirable in many cases, but they have shortcomings that can be serious in some contexts, such as rapid prototyping, test stub implementation, scripting for component configuration and testing, and on-the-fly and remote server updates.

A scripting language brings an interesting design alternative to this static nature of CORBA systems: It greatly improves the support for testing, rapid prototyping, and dynamic configuration, because we can load and test new design alternatives for a system in a quick and simple way. For instance, a CORBA object can be tested by a set of scripts, while other services that are not implemented yet, but are required by this object, can be provided by prototypes implemented with the scripting language. Servers implemented with a scripting language can be dynamically modified and extended without compiling or linking phases, and thus, without interrupting their services. With an interpreted language, it is easy to send code across a network, which allows the system to do remote or interactive modifications and extensions to the server.

The main goal of LuaOrb is to offer more suitable support for developing flexible applications, with the dynamic incorporation of CORBA objects. Using the CORBA's features for introspection (Interface Repository) and dynamic construction of method calls (DII), LuaOrb offers a binding wherein scripts can incorporate and make effective use of new object interfaces at runtime. Moreover, as in other bindings, Lua can use external CORBA servers transparently, in the same way it uses internal objects. Using the CORBA's DSI, LuaOrb also supports dynamic implementation of new CORBA object servers.

The OMG recognizes the relevance of scripting languages to manipulate CORBA objects [OMG1996; IBM+1997]. At first sight, it seems that this kind of binding can be one way: The scripting language acts as a client of CORBA objects to coordinate and test them, but it does not need to implement new object servers. However, besides the motivation of rapid prototyping, the binding must work in both directions to support callback objects—such as listeners in JavaBeans [JavaSoft1996]—because those callback objects must be called from the external components. Because the use of callback objects is a pervasive technique in object-oriented programming (for instance, most patterns presented by

Gamma [Gamma+1995] use callback objects), a language without such support would have quite a limited use.

LuaOrb uses proxies for each external CORBA object to be handled by a program, following the design pattern proxy [Gamma+1995]. A *proxy* is an internal object created to represent an external one; its basic functionality is to delegate to the external object it represents any operation performed over itself. To implement this proxy mechanism, LuaOrb uses the reflexive facilities of both CORBA and Lua.

Lua has a mechanism such that operations applied to the proxy, made through the regular language syntax, can be detected and handled by the binding that created the proxy. Moreover, when the binding is evoked, it can access any information concerning the original operation (the "receiver" proxy, the operation name, eventual arguments, etc). As an example, let us use the following IDL interface:

```
interface Calc {
    float add(in float a, in float b);
};
```

Once you have a proxy to a CORBA object with that interface, the method add can be called exactly like any method invocation over native objects. For instance, we can test a Calc object in the following way:

```
assert(calc:add(2,3) == 5)
assert(calc:add(0,3) == 3)
assert(calc:add(2,0) == 2)
assert(calc:add(-2,3) == 1)
...
```

Because LuaOrb redefines the behavior of all proxy tables, this method call generates an event, which calls the corresponding handler (called *tag method* in Lua). This event handler, which is part of the binding, gets the external component that the proxy represents; then it uses introspection to check whether this component has the desired method. The final result is a closure encapsulating the information about the found method. When the closure is called with the given arguments, it executes a sequence of steps. First, for each formal parameter, it checks whether the corresponding Lua argument has a compatible type and converts this value to the corresponding CORBA value. Second, it dynamically builds the method call and performs the call. Finally, it converts back any results (or out parameters), again using the method description and the compatibility rules. (For more details about the binding, see [Ierusalimschy+1998].)

To provide dynamic object implementations with Lua, LuaOrb uses generic adapters. A *generic adapter* is registered in the CORBA Object Adapter as an object servant that provides a specific interface and delegates the real method implementations to an object defined in Lua, in a way similar to proxies: Any operation performed over the adapter is applied over the real implementation. Because these implementations are written in Lua, they can be dynamically created and linked to adapters. The linking between the adapter and the real object uses the same reflexive mechanisms used by our client proxy, but this time these mechanisms are provided by the language interface (the Lua API also allows the dynamic construction of method calls).

As an example of how to implement CORBA servants in Lua, consider the following Lua object that could be used as an implementation of the Calc IDL interface:

```
obj = { add = function(self, a, b)
            return a+b
        end
    }
```

With LuaOrb, a Calc servant can be created as

```
servant = CreateDSIServer("Calc", obj)
```

In this example, the servant object is an instance of a generic adapter that can be exported to some client application. The CreateDSIServer function receives the IDL interface name and the Lua object that should provide the real service implementation.

The key point in this language binding is its dynamic nature. Every step, from type checking to method identification and invocation, is done at runtime. Therefore, a program can incorporate new types and classes without any additional declarations and without stopping for recompilations. The binding also allows some coercions between data types. Therefore, many changes in an IDL interface do not affect its uses in Lua. Examples of such modifications are reordering and removing struct fields, and changing between IDL types that have similar representations in Lua, such as short and long, or array and sequence. This coercion works recursively, so a list of Lua tables can be automatically converted to an array of records, for instance.

To illustrate how we can use LuaOrb to implement simple unit tests, let us consider the IDL definitions in Figure 22.5. We can implement simple scripts to test different aspects of the `Clipping` interface. For instance, a script can create a Lua table that is compatible with a `Region` sequence and use it to test the `setRegion` and `getRegion` operations:

```
region = {{{x = 0.0, y = 0.0}, {x = 1.0, y = 1.0}},
          {{x = -2.0, y = -2.0}, {x = -1.0, y = -1.0}}
         }
clip_obj:setRegion(region)
assert(isEqual(region, clip_obj:getRegion()))
```

Then it can use a set of points to test the operation `isInside`:

```
assert(clip_obj:isInside({x = 0.5, y = 0.5})
assert(clip_obj:isInside({x = -1.5, y = -1.0})
assert(not clip_obj:isInside({x = 5, y = -0.5})
assert(not clip_obj:isInside({x = -0.5, y = -1.0})
```

(A real test script could declare lists of regions and points to be tested, and use a loop to perform all tests.) Readers that are familiar with the binding between CORBA and C++ should consider how many lines are needed to write a client program to do this test in CORBA/C++. A similar script in C++, or even in Java, would be typically three or four times bigger than this (without considering the stub code), besides the complexity that the mapping between CORBA and C++ introduces to memory management.

```
struct Point {
    double x, y;
};
typedef Point Rect[2];
typedef sequence<Rect> Region;

interface Clipping {
    void setRegion(in Region reg);
    Region getRegion();
    boolean isInside(in Point pt);
};
```

FIGURE 22.5 The IDL definition for the `Clipping` service

Because of its dynamic nature, LuaOrb can present a runtime performance penalty, when compared with statically compiled stubs and skeletons. This performance penalty has been greatly reduced with the minimization of the number of queries to the Interface Repository. This has been achieved simply by caching the most recent queries. The current performance penalty, when compared to C++, is about 50 percent, which is quite acceptable for testing.

The Testing Infrastructure

The previous section showed some examples that illustrate how LuaOrb can be used to implement unit test scripts. Another facility that LuaOrb provides for test support is the possibility of implementing, in a simple way, prototypes of components that are required to test another component. For the sonar simulator this feature was very important, because this system required components that would be developed by another group. In the many integration tests that were performed, those prototypes were replaced with the final or intermediate component implementations. Although the interfaces of the shared components evolved during the development process, the prototype components could easily evolve together. Even after the final component implementation had been available, the prototype continued to be used because the final component was typically much more complex than what concerned the sonar simulator. Therefore, we could keep the execution environment of the sonar simulator as simple as possible during its development. Note that, besides the use of an interpreted language, much of this flexibility is a consequence of the strict separation between interfaces and their implementations that CORBA provides.

To make the test automation easier, we extended the test infrastructure with services that support remote installation of CORBA servers and remote execution of Lua scripts. Figure 22.6 shows the IDL interfaces for these services.

❖ The interface Lua::DSIObject allows the remote installation of CORBA servers. This interface encapsulates an object reference (the attribute obj) to a LuaOrb's dynamic server implementation, and offers the operation installOperation to install operation implementations in the dynamic server. This method receives the operation name and its Lua source code.

```
module Lua {
    interface DSIObject {
        readonly attribute Object obj;
        void installOperation(in string op_name,
                              in string lua_code);
    };

    interface Factory {
        DSIObject createInstance(in string interface_name);
    };

    interface Interpreter {
        void doString(in string lua_code);
    };
};
```

FIGURE 22.6 The IDL definition for the test utilities

⬦ The interface `Lua::Factory` is used to create new instances of `Lua::DSIObject`. Note that the method `createInstance` receives the name of the interface that the new dynamic server should use as its own interface (you can find more details about these two interfaces and their usage in [Martins+1999]).

⬦ The interface `Lua::Interpreter` allows developers to send Lua code across a network to be executed in another host process. Note that the Lua code that the remote process executes can change its global Lua environment that is, it can define new functions and variables or change previous definitions.

These services are very useful for scripts that need to manage different hosts to execute their test cases. Moreover, the scripts can be implemented such that we can change the hosts where each component runs without changing the test scripts.

As an example of how we used these services to test the sonar simulator, we use the sonar detector component with the script fragment in Figure 22.7, in accordance with the IDL definitions in Figures 22.3 and 22.4. The sonar display component's prototype is created in the same process that runs the test script (lines 1 through 4). This test stub of the display component receives the list of detected targets and checks

```
1    display = { detect = function(self, targets)
2                    assert(isEqual(targets,expected_targets)
3               end
4            }
5    collection = installService("TargetCollectionService",
                                  host1.factory)
6    runScript("createTargets.lua", host2.interpreter)
7    runScript("detector.lua", host3.interpreter)
8    wait(WAIT_TIME)
9    detector = createproxy{interface="Sonar::Detector",
                             ior=detector_ior}
10   detector:registerTargetCollection(collection)
11   detector:registerDisplay(display)
12   detector:activate()
```

FIGURE 22.7 A simple automated test script

whether this list is equal to the expected result (line 2). A `Lua::Factory` object is used to install the target collection prototype in `host1` (line 5). To simplify the remote installation procedure, we have defined the function `installService`, which receives an implementation identifier and a factory object (`host1.factory`). In the same way, we have defined the function `runScript`, which receives a script name and a `Lua::Interpreter` object, and sends the script to be executed in the specified remote interpreter. This function is used to create the target objects in `host2` (line 6) and to execute the sonar detector component in `host3` (line 7). After we have created all components, we can start to connect them: First, we create a LuaOrb proxy of the detector server (line 9), then we link it to the target collection and the display component prototypes (lines 10 through 11). Finally, we activate the detector component (line 12).

The file `createTargets.lua` and the list `expected_targets` (used in lines 6 and 2, respectively) define a test case. So we can apply this script to different test cases, only changing the file used to create the targets and the list of targets that we expect as result of the detection algorithm.

This test script can use up to four processes to run: one for the sonar detector component, which we are testing, and another three processes for the sonar display component, the target collection service, and the target objects. Note that we can test different configurations for `host1`, `host2`, and `host3` using the same test script.

Conclusion

The infrastructure used to test the sonar simulator system has presented good results: We have automated most of the unit tests, with support from regression testing too. Moreover, we easily implemented integration tests that required us to manage many process in different hosts. We have achieved the same results in other CORBA-based projects, such as a distributed 3D visualization system [Ferreira+1999].

However, we did not achieve the same success when we tried to apply the infrastructure to testing some aspects of the system's graphical user interface (GUI), such as the sonar's graphic and sound presentation. Even test tools such as screen scrapers, which are based on GUI event recording and replaying, did not work, because the GUI layout changed too often. So we performed this kind of functional testing manually. We are planning to improve the test infrastructure to provide better support for GUI testing in another project that we have just started.

In the sonar simulator and other CORBA-based projects [Ferreira+1999; Gomes+1998 Rodriguez+1998], LuaOrb has proved to be a powerful programming tool to support flexible development processes like Extreme Programming. It provides many facilities for testing and rapid implementation. Often, a component prototype implemented with LuaOrb becomes the component's final version, if the performance penalty is not relevant. Otherwise, the component implementation always can be refactored to a more efficient implementation (typically a C/C++ version).

The main ideas of this chapter can be applied to other scripting tools. For instance, we can abstract the CORBA services used in our infrastructure to define design patterns to support test automation of distributed systems. Those patterns could be used with other scripting languages for CORBA or even with other distributed object infrastructures.

References

[Beazley1998] D. Beazley. "SWIG and Automated C/C++ Scripting Extensions." *Dr. Dobb's Journal*. Volume 23, Number 2, 1998.

[Beck1999] K. Beck. "Embracing Change with Extreme Programming." *IEEE Computer*. Volume 32, Number 10, 1999.

[Beck2000] K. Beck. *Extreme Programming Explained*. Addison-Wesley, 2000.

[Celes1998] W. Celes. *toLua—Accessing C/C++ Code from Lua*. On-line at http://www.tecgraf.puc-rio.br/~celes/tolua/tolua.html.

[Cerqueira+1999] R. Cerqueira, C. Cassino, R. Ierusalimschy. "Dynamic Component Gluing Across Different Componentware Systems." In *International Symposium on Distributed Objects and Applications (DOA'99)*, IEEE Press, 1999.

[Ferreira+1999] A. Ferreira, R. Cerqueira, W. Celes, M Gattass. "Multiple Display Viewing Architecture for Virtual Environments Over Heterogeneous Networks." In *XII Simpósio Brasileiro de Computação Gráfica*, IEEE Press, 1999.

[Figueiredo+1996] L. Figueiredo, R. Ierusalimschy, W. Celes. "Lua: An Extensible Embedded Language." *Dr. Dobb's Journal.* Volume 21, Number 12, December 1996.

[Gamma+1995] E. Gamma, R. Helm, R. Johnson, J. Vlissides. *Design Patterns: Elements of Reusable Object-Oriented Software*. Addison-Wesley, 1995.

[Gomes+1998] P. Gomes, B. Feijó, R. Cerqueira, R. Ierusalimschy. "Reactivity and Pro-activeness in Virtual Prototyping." In *2nd International Symposium on Tools and Methods for Concurrent Engineering*, April 1998.

[IBM+1997] IBM Corporation et al. "CORBA Component Imperatives." *OMG TC Document orbos/97-05-25*, Object Management Group. On-line at http://www.omg.org. 1997.

[IEEE1993] Institute of Electrical and Electronics Engineers, International Standard. *Standard for Information Technology, Protocols for Distributed Interactive Simulation*. ANSI/IEEE Std 1278, March 1993.

[Ierusalimschy+1996] R. Ierusalimschy, L. Figueiredo, W. Celes. "Lua—An Extensible Extension Language." *Software: Practice and Experience*. Volume 26, Number 6, 1996.

[Ierusalimschy+1998] R. Ierusalimschy, R. Cerqueira, N. Rodriguez. "Using Reflexivity to Interface with CORBA. In *International Conference on Computer Languages 1998*, IEEE Press, 1998.

[Ierusalimschy+1999] R. Ierusalimschy, L. Figueiredo, W. Celes. *Reference Manual of the Programming Language Lua Version 3.2.* Tecgraf/PUC-Rio, 1999. (ftp://ftp.tecgraf.puc-rio.br/pub/lua/refman.ps.gz.)

[JavaSoft1996] JavaSoft. *JavaBeans, Version 1.00-A.* On-line at http://java.sun.com/beans. December 1996.

[Kernighan+1999] B. Kernighan, R. Pike. *The Practice of Programming.* Addison-Wesley, 1999.

[Macedonia+1994] M. Macedonia, M. Zyda, D. Pratt, P. Barham, S. Zeswitz. "NPSNET: A Network Software Architecture for Large-Scale Virtual Environments." *Presence.* Volume 3, Number 4, 1994.

[Martins+1999] M. Martins, N. Rodriguez, R. Ierusalimschy. "Dynamic Extension of CORBA Servers." In *Euro-Par'99 Parallel Processing*, Springer-Verlag, 1999.

[OMG1996] OMG. "CORBA Scripting Language—Request for Proposal." OMG TC Document orbos/96-06-13, OMG. On-line at http://www.omg.org. 1996.

[OMG1998] OMG. *The Common Object Request Broker Architecture and Specification; Revision 2.3.* On-line at http://www.omg.org. 1998.

[Ousterhout1994] J. Ousterhout. *Tcl and the Tk Toolkit.* Addison-Wesley, 1994.

[Rodriguez+1998] N. Rodriguez, R. Ierusalimschy, R. Cerqueira. "Dynamic Configuration with CORBA Components." *In Fourth International Conference on Configurable Distributed Systems,* IEEE Press, 1998.

Acknowledgments

We would like to thank Tecgraf/PUC-Rio (Computer Graphics Technology Group of PUC-Rio), which hosted the project. This work has been partially supported by CNPq (The Brazilian Research Council) and IPqM (The Brazilian Navy's Research Institute).

About the Authors

Renato Cerqueira can be reached at Tecgraf/PUC-Rio, Brazil; rcerq@tecgraf.puc-rio.br. Roberto Ierusalimschy can be reached at the Computer Science Department, PUC-Rio, Brazil; roberto@inf.puc-rio.br.

Part 6

Practical Experiences

Chapter 23

The VCAPS Project: An Example of Transitioning to XP

—Don Wells and Trish Buckley

This discussion is focused around a large automotive manufacturing company that relies heavily on custom software. We discuss how the Vehicle Cost and Profit System (VCAPS) project evolved into an XP experiment with great success. This success was achieved in spite of the many problems that initially plagued the project. It is a prime example of how XP added flexibility and increased productivity around a system with a tired code base, which had been modified as far as it could go without breaking completely.

A Short History of the Project

Ford Motor Company's Vehicle Cost and Profit System (VCAPS), first launched in 1993, provides a financial analysis tool used to develop material forecasts, determine vehicle line profitability, measure plant performance, and control regulatory requirements (AALA, NAFTA). The customers are provided an income-statement view of data. The major financial elements in the application are revenue, fixed costs, variable costs, and profitability margins. The cost elements represent both material and labor and overhead costs. These financial elements are tracked by vehicle, model, option, vehicle subsystem, and even individual assembly and manufacturing parts—right down to the sand for casting. Various organizational views and markets are also represented.

VCAPS evolved over the years into a highly complex application. Initially, the application was a material, variable cost system for assembly-level bill-of-material. This means no revenue, no fixed costs, no labor and overhead, no manufacturing bill-of-material, and no regulatory application. VCAPS is now very complex because of the number and type of business customers, volumes of data, complexity of data associations, application timing, and an environment of constant change. The data is fed from purchasing, accounting, finance, and manufacturing once per quarter and once again per year. Finance, manufacturing, and regulatory groups do manual inputs and modifications. Regulatory timing is not always in sync with the other business areas, creating the need for additional application cycles. Additional complexity exists in the ability to seek historical revenue or cost differences. Its constant state of change is the result of a steady flow of new functionality necessary to support existing and new business practices, new customers, organizational realignments, and new or revised government regulations.

The early developers of VCAPS were a small group with skills ranging from pure mainframe to one or two who were moderately versed in OO languages such as Smalltalk and GemStone. The project came about as a back-room, low-profile project to introduce a new application concept and technology within Ford. Neither the customers nor IT management were aware of the project in its earliest stages. Later, a working prototype was used to sell the idea and technology to acquire project funding and approval.

Ford had done an excellent job of establishing a reliable infrastructure (people, process, and technology) around its mainframe environment; however, these same standards just did not exist around design, development, testing, releasing, and support in a client/server, OO environment. The technology and skills sets were just too immature within Ford.

The VCAPS project had always been challenged with finding and keeping talented Smalltalk and GemStone developers, training people from different technical skill sets, and establishing a common methodology for developing in this environment. Oftentimes, high-priced Smalltalk consultants were used for short-term quick hits, but with eroding effects on the application. This approach was almost always reactive and provided no contribution toward growing a solid technical team. The fragmented group never developed a solid understanding of the application or technology and was unable to establish practices to remedy the problems. The unmanaged application itself grew to be severely fragmented and unreliable.

In 1997, Don Wells joined the VCAPS team, bringing with him recent XP experience from DaimlerChrylser's payroll project. Don talked with one of the managers, Trish Buckley, about how a project experience could be different from the current VCAPS experience. He discussed how it might be managed, how developers might learn, designs might evolve, code might be tested, productivity and quality might be increased, and morale improved. Don never labeled the ideas he shared as "Extreme Programming." He correctly assessed the merit in slowly revealing pieces of XP in an environment so unfamiliar with these concepts. This enabled the team to slowly develop an appreciation for the meaning and benefits of the XP methodology. He knew, based on his personal experience, that they would take some getting used to by the other developers. Recognizing that XP concepts were critical elements in this kind of development project, he was very anxious to experiment and had resigned himself to the idea that some things would take time to implement.

Trish was encouraged and excited to apply these concepts, which seemed to be obvious improvements and yet were simplistic. She couldn't imagine not attempting to put something in place that would bring short- and long-term value to the development team and its customers. Together, they agreed to define how a project should be run and drew up a list of many ideas. Perhaps the most important was for developers to want to stay on the project and for customers to want to use the system. In the end, both of these lofty goals would be accomplished.

Trish had joined the Manufacturing Finance Systems section in 1995 working on reengineering a mainframe application that provided the assembly bills-of-material into the VCAPS application. She had been closely aligned with the OO development team and was fully aware of the issues and existing experience. In early 1997, Trish was given responsibility for a major integration task within VCAPS. The team she was given consisted of four people—a summer intern with no programming experience, a C developer, a mainframe developer, and Don.

The work that Trish's group was doing was by far the most important in the system since its inception. It would require major changes to the architecture. Why they gave it to a ragtag group like hers is a mystery. Perhaps they expected the group to fail. As the team showed promise of success, they began getting experienced OO people from other managers working with them part time and eventually obtained a full-time staff of Smalltalk developers of six to eleven people. If something important had to get done, Trish's group got the assignment. Eventually her group was given approval to redevelop the VCAPS application.

Even as new life was being brought to VCAPS, it was being considered for replacement by a different system all together—one that would serve a new finance organization along with new business practices. The plan was to deliver a global, VIN-level, analytical, financial data warehouse with Microsoft and relational technology. Knowing this would be years away, and that the new VCAPS application was two weeks from launch, the VCAPS customers wanted to continue to deliver the new VCAPS application. The new application was capable of handling global, VIN-level financial analysis given additional interface feeds. It had a very sound foundation to build on and extend. IT management could not understand this value and years of struggling with the technology led them to abandon it. The new VCAPS application was never launched.

Over the years, the existing VCAPS application required up to 20 people to keep it running in production and deliver enhancements. The changes in application design and code, testing procedures, and releasing techniques brought about by Trish's team has enabled VCAPS to be kept breathing with only a four-person staff. These changes were brought about over an 18-month period.

Statistics from unit and QA test cycles demonstrated significant improvements in the redeveloped VCAPS system. It was one-twentieth (5 percent) the size, infinitely faster (response times went from 15 minutes to coming back immediately), and fully supported by automated tests. The new application provided greater levels of functionality and detail than ever before. It supported reduced business cycle times. The development time to achieve these results had only been six months.

The Good, the Bad, and the Ugly

Among many things that were bad about the VCAPS project were some very good things. VCAPS was built using VisualWorks Smalltalk and GemStone. It was also fortuitous that they began to hire experienced people. Unfortunately this was not enough to make a traditional software development methodology work in this particular environment of constant change and adjustment.

The Smalltalk language and the GemStone OODB made rapid development possible. It was unfortunate that the initial VCAPS prototype had been built with an inexperienced staff and hurried into production. This resulted in a poor foundation on which to extend the application. Although the technology allowed for rapid development it wouldn't be achieved without the introduction of XP. Only then would the team successfully utilize the power of OO technology.

The challenges most difficult to overcome were the changing requirements, sudden about-faces in priorities, lengthy processing times, and poor team morale. Changes were requested for each system processing cycle. Not bug fixes, though those were numerous as well. Rather, the way the system calculated costs usually changed each quarter. Government regulations could also change, though not as frequently. Constantly changing requirements kept us in reaction mode. We never caught up.

It was also not clear what changes should actually be made. We had many customers who often disagreed as to what was most pressing. Customers could agree then change their minds and disagree again. Agreement was often not met until after implementation. The result was a rush on the next change request, again keeping us in reaction mode.

Originally, the business cycle time was 30 days for generating the data and completing its reporting and analysis. Business drivers had progressively pushed cycle times to 15 days and, finally, 10 days. The system took a long time to process and required lengthy manual inputs before producing final outputs. Artificial system constraints limited customers to sequential input entry. A bug could waste precious time by requiring a rerun and causing multiple business areas to recoordinate input entry.

In reactive mode, things just happen. The full development life cycle, including requirements, design, testing, and implementation, were not being effectively addressed by the project and productivity was low. Although Booch diagrams were being used, many were out of date. There was just enough difference to be annoying and deceptive. Most developers were afraid to alter any part of the system they did not personally own. Unexpected side effects would result from a simple change. Copying code from one part of the system to another and then changing it slightly was the only way to reliably modify code. The code base was ugly and getting worse.

There were no testing procedures, not even a manual test script, and no automated testing of any sort. Customers were expected to test new code prior to production release, but had inadequate staffing to do so.

The design was kept in the head of the chief architect and was seldom shared with the developers except when it was misused. The requirements documents contained many errors and were never updated. The documentation and the code never matched up. Coordination among team members was poor and there were no procedures for making a clean launch.

Morale was very low among the project team and its customers. The chief architect displayed great disdain for team members. He was a self-proclaimed expert on the design. He would venture forth and berate the junior programmers as a sort of code review process. And yet he believed he knew more about the domain than the domain experts did. He had lost a sense of what the system architecture actually was. The customers relied on many workarounds just to get the desired calculations. These workarounds resulted in standard procedures for extracting data from the system into Excel spreadsheets and sometimes feeding the information back into the application. The result was a project where no one wanted to be there and it showed—in the code and in the faces of those faced with VCAPS.

One part of Ford management culture is constant movement of Ford resources to new assignments every couple of years. This had a positive and negative impact on the ability to incorporate XP. The negative was that short-timers generally had no real desire to make process changes. The positive was that each time management turned over, a new opportunity for change was presented. If one manger rejected a specific practice the next might not. Trish wanted XP because she wanted to change what had become an undesirable VCAPS way of life. Although she was only one among three managers having direct authority over VCAPS, she was also the newest, the most open to change, and the one whose assignment would have the most significant impact to the application.

Section, department, and executive management had no interest in learning about a new methodology, especially an approach related to an OO technical approach in the minority and on its way out. What value could it possibly have? Speed superceded all else and delivery was what brought rewards. During their short assignments, Ford resources would be measured on whether, not what, they delivered. New ways to build solid foundations for achieving application stability, reliability, and data integrity along with strong teamwork and customer satisfaction were being overlooked.

An environment for XP was found. With barely a methodology intact, change rampant, morale low, and turnover high, customer satisfaction was at an all-time low. The production bugs had become rampant, with severe data integrity, reliability, and stability issues. Unmanaged chaos is what existed. XP is what would work.

VCAPS Reengineering with XP

The Planning Game

Because the most logical way to start was at the beginning, we started with the planning game. It was a total disaster. It was a failure because customers and IT management were unaccustomed to negotiating schedules. IT management preferred to dictate the schedule based on what customers needed and when they needed it. This was done through a high-level planning process that defined delivery dates before much was really known. These early timing estimates were never renegotiated once more details became known, and, worse, they were presented to customer management as intelligent, fact-based planning. The customer's expectations were seldom managed to allow for future schedule or scope adjustments. No matter how much in error, expectations were to somehow make it work. In such a fast-paced and hierarchical environment our customers were typically too busy to "get in the details." Just tell me what I want to hear and don't take too much of my time was the dominant mode of communication. The release plan produced from the planning game was not useful because it didn't show project completion on time and it required interim negotiations, scope trade-offs, and the customer's active, not passive involvement.

Trish decided to swap in Microsoft Project for creating the project schedule. She included tasks and timing that showed completion of the project. The schedule was modified without large meetings that included the entire staff. This type of project schedule delighted other project managers. It was seemingly better in our environment to start with a schedule showing how the project would succeed and to find out later that the schedule has slipped. Reporting a project in trouble was familiar news that was a normal part of project development.

This probably seems like an odd curiosity to most readers. We were expected to deliver late by some experimentally determined percentage of the project's duration. Showing a schedule that accurately predicted the project's completion was unwelcome because this meant we would be way too late when compared against the original customer commitments. Explanations about why our schedule was accurate were ignored. It was humbly accepted that no software project has ever been delivered on time! This was the reputation IT had made for itself and this mindset would not change unless we first proved that we could consistently deliver when we predicted. In the end, we would not have time to provide this proof. The planning game was never reinstated.

CRC Cards

We introduced CRC cards slowly. At first we drew instance diagrams. We found the instance diagrams more concrete and soon replaced the Booch diagrams. The Booch diagrams were much harder to read and hid the real complexity of the application. The existing VCAPS had three duplicated hierarchies of persistent objects. Some of the classes were used in more than one of the hierarchies and had identical fields that might represent different values depending on which tree they resided in. These details were not shown in the Booch diagrams but were easily illustrated with the instance diagrams.

The key idea was to see the system in terms of objects and their relationships instead of as static class hierarchies. The objects had lost much of their potentially dynamic nature because of this static viewpoint. We then began to introduce using the white boards for design work. More interactive than diagrams, they allowed us to begin to talk about eliminating duplications and simplifying our design. As we began to take broader approaches to redesign, we eventually started to use CRC cards to redesign the system. It was not until after we started using the cards that we realized two things. First, our system did not need to be as complex as the code base would indicate. Second, it was possible to represent our system architecture using a simple metaphor, one that everyone could understand.

It is difficult to explain the difference clearly in our discussions with CRC cards. The CRC cards allowed the design discussions to be shorter. They took on a dynamic feel that became reflected in our code base. We eliminated many persistent structures that existed in the legacy design, in favor of temporary objects created only as needed and then destroyed. We actually found a way to shrink our database to one-twentieth (5 percent) of its original size.

Our team used CRC cards differently than what has been documented in the literature [Bellin1997; Wilkinson1995]. CRC cards are just cards—3 × 5, 5 × 8, whatever you find to be a good size. You don't need special cards with graphics printed on them. Most of our cards remained blank. Different colors were found to be useful. If the representation of a card changed, it was easily replaced or eliminated.

The idea was that a card could be a physical representation of an object. We found the importance of CRC cards was their ability to activate the right hemisphere of the brain [Edwards1989]. The right hemisphere is responsible for spatial relationships, color, imagination, and Gestalt or systemic thinking [Buzan1991]. Stimulating the right hemisphere enabled us to think about our problem in terms of objects and relationships. It helped us achieve a big-picture point of view. Design approaches with the left hemisphere usually result in procedural solutions that use little bits and pieces of code. All these pieces of code are difficult to associate and remember. CRC cards allowed us to design at a level higher than individual methods or functions, which are more appropriate for code design.

We used cards to represent instances of classes instead of classes as usual. We sometimes would write the class name of the instance on the card—usually just the first time we introduced it—then leave the rest of the cards blank. Off to the side we might assemble a little class hierarchy so everyone could see it, but usually not. We liked to use four colors of cards, one for each major object type in our system. Related objects used the same color. If we needed more than four colors, we would consider whether all those objects were needed. We then picked up cards and moved them about to demonstrate how they would naturally communicate with each other.

We ran a simulation of the system using the cards. This technique brought our focus to the right level of design—not detailed like individual methods and not so abstract as class hierarchies. The structure or pattern of objects on the table as the simulation proceeded was surprisingly easy to recall later when code was created. Many elements of the object's structure were graphically represented. An object that was composed of other objects had those objects tucked under it slightly to form a little group. In order to represent objects passing objects, we took a card and moved it from on top of one object to on top of another. We represented a collection of objects by grabbing a little stack of cards and laying them on the table.

We used Kent Beck's rule of cards, which states that only two people could stand and move cards around at a time. Everyone can talk, of course, but in order to move the cards someone would convince one of the two currently standing people to sit down. This kept our CRC sessions well in hand. Once we had the card culture established, the rule was rarely broken and didn't even need to be enforced.

CRC cards continued to be effective as the group size increased. They were an excellent communication and learning tool. CRC cards were used to present the application design to IT and customer management. It was easy to explain while methodically rolling out each key piece of the design on the table until the system was fully simulated. When new team members joined the group, the cards were again a quick, easy study. CRC cards were an important part of the work done by the team.

Testing Framework

We created our own unit-testing framework for automated unit tests. We started out small, creating just a few unit and functional tests. Although these few tests only covered a small portion of the system, they began to reduce problem reports of the type "message not understood." This specific type of problem was more common than would be considered normal in a Smalltalk application.

Initially, Don was to spend his time learning the code base. He asked about loading up Kent's public domain unit-test code and learned of concerns about Kent suing. Over the weekend Don wrote a unit-testing framework, and on Monday morning he stamped it "Copyright Ford Motor Company" and put it into the source code repository. A tool was now immediately available to other developers to help gain support for the concept.

Although he was later assigned to mentor other programmers, Don's experience with the planning game told him he wasn't ready to introduce another major change. Instead, he just did some small bits of code the way everyone else did to avoid any waves. As he worked with the team, he found opportunities to communicate thoughts, such as "if only we had automated tests this would be easy. I guess we will have to do it the hard way." His strategy was to arouse enough curiosity that others would ask and want to learn a bit about it—small bits at a time.

Don's next assignment was done solo, of course. He was given two weeks to finish. Since he knew what needed to be done, he first spent two weeks creating unit and functional tests for his code and the underlying sample data to support them. Trish gritted her teeth as Don calmly let the deadline come and go. Fortunately, she didn't abandon him. The next week he created the code and was done. Really done! His new VCAPS software was similar to something else in the system that had historically run very long. Based on the similarity it was estimated to run 16 hours, even after optimization. Instead, Don's code ran in one hour with absolutely no bugs! The code went straight into production. Don was now ahead of schedule because there had been time allotted in the schedule for testing, tuning, and debugging. The code didn't need any of that and everyone was happy.

Because existing VCAPS had a very high bug count, adding unit tests was going to help. The new functional tests could now be applied to other sections of existing code. The biggest problem in applying the testing concept had been the creation of sample test data. What Don had done was to deliver a flexible testing framework and test data. This was critical to achieving successful functional testing.

To move the concept a step further, Don wrote a suite of unit tests for another developer. He handed them over and the very next time she had to change her code she was "test infected." She started writing lots of tests. From her example creating tests became the norm within our group. At about 40 percent functional test coverage, we had dropped the bug count in existing VCAPS by about half.

The path was paved for other team members to learn and begin to expand the test coverage. By the time the team started to redevelop VCAPS, unit tests had become an integral part of how the team worked. The new application had complete test coverage.

Coding Standards

Another problem was the highly variable styles in the existing code base. We introduced a coding standard but initially found it went largely unused. Don carried Kent's book (the best practices book) everywhere he went. When the opportunity arose to help solve someone else's coding problems, he pointed to the answer in Kent's book. Soon, everyone had Kent's book and a coding standard was established.

Pair Programming and Mentoring

The first attempt at pair programming was to pair Don and Trish. Don had Smalltalk experience and Trish had domain experience. The combination was dynamic. We had a fabulous time and it became clear to Trish that a project could be fun. We had also used this time to begin creating unit tests. Some were too simple and should not have been created, but the point was to have that experience. Pairing with the project manager soon came to an end as upper management told Trish "no more development." Ford managers who stayed too active in "technical details" were looked upon as not doing their jobs as managers. Still, the experience was beneficial in that it made Trish understand pair programming. She was firmly hooked on XP and would support pairing other team members.

Dropping pair programming from above onto people who do not want to can be dangerous, and you can get a very negative reaction. The first week or so people will go slower, not faster. It takes a while for people to get used to how it works. It takes even longer for the impact of higher quality and easier to maintain code to be noticed. People will go to great lengths to avoid pair programming when placed in this situation too early, too often.

On any given project there will be a few people who absolutely refuse to pair, a majority who are skeptical that it will be of any value, and a few who are actually interested in trying it. The latter group of people is all you need. Get them working together. Unless something goes terribly wrong they will like it. Now just as Tom Sawyer got the other kids to paint his fence, other programmers will become curious about those pairs having so much fun and getting so much done at the same time. They will want to try pair programming also. Let it spread naturally.

Pair programming caught on slowly at VCAPS. We eventually found two key factors for success—teaching techniques and level of experience. There was resistance across the team from both the experienced and inexperienced developers. We discovered that when learning to pair both people should be of equal experience level. This made a significant difference in productivity and morale. A teacher-student relationship is not an effective pair relationship. When teaching a junior programmer how to pair you must not overwhelm the student with good advice. Work at the same level and pace as the beginner. Let the beginner make mistakes and instead concentrate on the pair relationship. Work together to solve problems instead of jumping directly to the solution.

We found it is best to learn how to pair program with someone who already knows how. Pair programming is not a technical skill. It is a social skill like trying to learn to dance from a book. In the absence of someone who already knows how, you should pair people of near equal experience together. An experienced person and a newbie will usually set up a teacher-student relationship instead of a pair relationship because that is what they already know how to do. Cut them off at the pass by pairing two people at close to equal status. As soon as your people learn to pair program effectively, the issue of status goes away. Everyone will understand that working together produces better results. Everyone will value everyone's contributions. At that point a teacher-student subrelationship can be established without upsetting the primary pair relationship.

We also found some benefit to matching everyone with everyone else. Inexperienced pairs worked well because two inexperienced developers could solve problems while learning from one another in a "safe" setting. They were less likely to feel intimidated and demoralized. Small successes increased confidence levels and improved learning and productivity. The experienced developers were also more challenged by each another. Too much time in unlike pairs resulted in both the experienced and inexperienced people getting burned out, bored, and demoralized. The challenge of an equal at least some of the time was necessary. With equal pairs carefully planned early on, later unequal pairs became more effective. The inexperienced developers were no longer demoralized and began to gain confidence. Morale was improving.

We might also work in threes from time to time. The pair would ask a third developer to provide some insight for a short period. In this form the third partner would sit on the desk and in between the primary pair. The third partner was not expected to type just provide general guidance to the pair.

We also changed the mentoring model. The custom had been for the inexperienced developer to come to the "master" and humbly ask for help. The master would then type up his or her own solution as the newbie looked on in awe and eventually walked away feeling frustrated and humiliated. We decided on another simple yet powerful change. Don, the experienced developer and coach, went to the newbie's cube and let the newbie type. He used encouragement, allowed the other person to save face by indirectly calling attention to mistakes, and let them feel as if ideas were theirs. Real learning began. This was magnificent and Trish decided that Don should make rounds to the newbies' cubes at least once a day.

Integration and Releasing

Integration was one of our biggest problems. There were up to 20 developers all pushing code as fast as possible with no coordinated means for testing or releasing. Code was integrated by someone who stayed the entire weekend merging multiple code paths. This rarely produced a code base without production bugs. No tool or process existed to ensure merging had been done correctly, or to detect previously undetected bugs.

Our solution was to set up a dedicated integration station, and begin integrating and releasing continuously within our own group. At this station we ran a combined suite of unit and functional tests. Initially, we needed to include functional tests as a part of our unit test suite because there were not enough tests for adequate coverage. All developers would integrate their own code with the current code base and run the tests we had. Other groups began to release at our station about monthly. To manage the inadequate test coverage, we posted a list of classes that were not under the control of our unit tests—our "rouge class" list. We manually watched out for changes in these classes.

By January of 1998, we had a 30 percent reduction of bugs reported from the previous quarter in existing VCAPS. We still had bugs, of course, but we eliminated many of the types of bugs caused by integration problems as our test coverage increased. Upper management had noticed and made running the test suite a mandatory integration step for all groups releasing code to production.

Success Factors in the Ford Environment

Coaching

It was possible to have a coach part time to introduce XP, who would fade out completely as the team became acquainted with XP. Don had the role of coach at the beginning of the project because he was the only developer knowledgeable about XP. Instead of enforcing rules and regulations, we actively acquainted the developers on our team with an understanding of XP. Each practice was adopted as an informed team decision. By the end of the project many of the developers were more than able to fill the coach position as required. We would often trade "hats," keeping watch over the project and each other, as a team should.

Two things made our coaching approach successful—trading hats and giving accountability in the form of both responsibility and authority in equal measure. Responsibility can only be accepted along with appropriate authority and vice versa. This approach provided built-in checks and balances on the role of coach, keeping any one person from obtaining too much authority. Any developer could accept the authority of the coach position but was expected also to accept responsibility for process improvement. All developers had equal responsibility for delivering code and they learned to expect the authority to make changes in the system design as well. Any developer who accepted responsibility for fixing a bug also expected the authority to make changes in any portion of the code base and to call on other team members for help as needed.

Final authority over all aspects of the project always remained with the project manager; this was fair because Trish had ultimate responsibility for the project as well. Trish was able to remain in control without being too intrusive into the development process. In other words, she was comfortable with allowing her authority to be delegated to her team as needed. Trish made important decisions easily because developers accepted the responsibility of keeping her well informed and gave her the authority to effect change.

Management

One of the biggest differences between our project and the traditional XP project was our management interface. The planning game, which had been a failure early in the project, was not tried again. We were able to find a simple way to control our project that satisfied our needs from an XP perspective and at the same time allowed management greater control over the project, as desired. This was important in our environment.

We decided to have one-week iterations. It was difficult to continue working for longer than that due to the constantly changing direction. After we had settled on one week it seemed helpful in other ways. We could change direction quicker and, with our small team size, we eliminated some of the overhead associated with planning longer iterations.

Prior to the iteration planning meeting Trish would perform her tracker duties of finding out what progress had been made on the current set of user stories. Trish would then work with customers to find out what was the most important functionality of the system. Trish would uncover which stories had the highest customer value to be implemented first. This is normally done at an iteration planning meeting with the customers present; instead, Trish took on the responsibility of working with all the different customers and unscrambling their often conflicting priorities herself.

Trish had responsibility for representing both the customers and management, and she did so very well. The planning meetings with the customers had always ended in arguments and no planning ever occurred. It never happened that Trish was faced with a decision that she was unsure about, though it could have if she hadn't stayed on top of things the way she did. She also applied management goals to our schedule. Customer goals and management goals were not always the same and Trish made sure both were satisfied. She also made sure that we didn't thrash about as customers changed their minds frequently. She was able to smooth out the bumps so that the developers received more permanent goals. We were always making useful and valued progress.

At the beginning of each meeting Trish would collect the user story cards from the pairs that were worked on the previous week. Each pair would note progress and work remaining right on the back of the story card. She would then decide which user stories would be worked on the next week. It became a ritual and somewhat of a jest that Trish would always ask us to do more than we could in a week. We had a simple way of planning the week. Trish would select four user stories that needed to be moved forward that week. We would then, in ritual form, remind Trish that with six people only three stories could be worked on in any given week. She would comply by removing a story from the table. She would then assign pairs to the three cards. Each pair would then take the card and begin the week, story in hand.

It is typical in XP for tasks to be elected by developers and not assigned. Developers would then negotiate with other developers to team up on tasks. We deviated from this practice. What we found was that because Trish would be talking to developers, in her role as tracker she generally knew better than we did ourselves who needed to pair with whom and who needed to set aside an old story and get something new. Trish always listened to our concerns and would always adjust her plans if the developers found a problem with them. She also made sure that if a story would take yet another week, out of the two people on a story one continued with the story. We found this continuity beneficial in our situation.

We also violated standard XP in having people pair for one week at a time. XP generally recommends a few hours at a time instead. We enjoyed the extended pairing, as we were better able to adjust to each other in terms of style and work schedule. We could change partners in the middle of the week even though it was not planned in advance.

A simple system for tracking the project emerged. At the iteration planning meeting each pair would receive a story card for the week. One story card per pair. The pairs would break down the stories into tasks themselves. Often a task supports more than one story. We used our standup meeting to coordinate efforts on a daily basis. The team could talk about which pair would do which task if we found some overlap between stories. This was a change from standard XP, where stories are broken down into tasks at the iteration planning meeting and then tasks signed up for by individual developers and then estimated. Our pairs worked on a story directly one week at a time. It was a simple yet effective method for our small team size of six developers plus Trish.

Management had simple requirements. They wished to see MS project charts of the projects' projected deadlines and workload. Trish took on the task of translating what her own management required her to produce from our user story cards and what had been assigned at the iteration planning meeting each week. We learned that most managers are very familiar with MS project style output and it was easier to communicate using that medium. That is, we found it easier to communicate with higher levels of management if we spoke to them in their own language.

Although we did indeed violate many XP practices in the way we managed the project we remained true to the base XP values. We communicated as well as possible with our management using their own language. We got feedback from both management and customers through Trish who made that her full-time job. We implemented as simple a way to control the project as possible. We remained courageous about developing XP style in the face of management constraints.

Transitioning

We introduced XP one practice at a time. The primary problem in introducing a few XP practices is that the practices support each other. On a project with few or only small problems it may very well be an uphill climb to introduce XP one practice at a time, with management coming to the conclusion that XP is not effective as a methodology. But on our project we had several serious problems. Adding XP practices to solve each problem was easy. If a big problem could be solved with extra effort it was generally worth the investment. Some of the practices that were introduced late in the process were very difficult to get going.

What we noticed was that when we considered our immediate problems and focused our efforts to solve them one at a time we set the stage for greater chances of success. Our efforts always seemed worthwhile and were easily tied to tangible results when we followed this plan. It was always a struggle when we did not. A good example was how the integration station went much better than the planning game or coding standard. The immediate issue for the VCAPS team was integration and testing. Starting with the planning game was difficult for others to value. Another example was pair programming, which is perhaps the best example of this. Although it is a very important support activity within XP, pair programming did not directly translate to a problem in our project. As such it was difficult to get people to invest the effort required to start it.

Automated Testing

One transition that all projects require when becoming extreme is creating automated unit tests and functional tests. It took awhile to collect enough automated tests to have a large impact on the project. The important thing was getting started collecting them right away. Traditionally testing is scheduled as the last two months of a project's duration. This was unsatisfactory for two reasons. First and foremost, it is impossible to create as useful a suite of tests after the fact. Within the XP methodology the system specifications and many design decisions are encoded in the tests instead of a document. The wisdom of this approach is apparent: You can run a specification encoded as automated tests and know instantly whether the system meets your specifications. Second, testing is the second portion of a project thrown out when time gets tight, right after code reviews, of course.

The amount of coverage required to make a significant and noticeable impact was far from full coverage, as might be expected. We found that 40 percent was enough to have a significant impact. Given this amount of coverage, about half the bugs were found before release. Because we covered the newest and most important functionality, our bugs were not show-stoppers, as had been previously seen. This was a much bigger impact than just cutting the number of bugs in half. We were able to stabilize the product by not releasing and rereleasing numerous times a day for several weeks in a row. By reducing the number of emergency releases we had more time to address the critical bugs properly. The impact on the project is much greater than mere statistics can show.

We discovered late in the project that a special-purpose tool to help build and maintain functional test data would have been beneficial. We used the unit-testing framework for both unit tests and functional tests. In order to use the more generic unit-testing framework we had to hand-code large amounts of data as assignment statements. This was a significant barrier to updating the data for functional tests.

Given that we had tight deadlines, we never gave ourselves the time to create some data abstractions. Even small extensions to allow some data abstraction would have been useful to the developers. Extending that over time into a custom-made, domain specific tool that would aid our customers and us in creating functional tests would have been even better. We probably spent more time creating test data the hard way than would have been spent creating a tool. VCAPS is now in the maintenance part of its life cycle, and though the functional tests are still being run they are not updated or expanded because they require someone familiar with the functional test data to update them or add new data and tests.

Team Building

There are many traditional team building exercises. Many are practiced within the Ford Company. The problem that we have found with these is that they are concentrated, may not actually involve the team needing building, and are forgotten afterward. The section manager had team building meetings that included pizza and presentations from various teams within the organization. These were ineffective as well. People dreaded attending, even given the free lunch potential. These groups were also much too large.

What we found to be true is that team building exercises must be held within the team that is being built and they need to be purely social in nature. What we tried was ice cream meetings for immediate team members. We allowed other teams also to have ice cream if they wanted. This worked out very well in that we were able to schedule them every few weeks and achieved a very relaxed environment. We were surprised to find people discussing very high-level thoughts about the system design at these meetings, although we didn't encourage such discussions. We also found greater effort being applied. It is impossible to say for sure that the ice cream had an impact. We believe that these events did have some impact, however small.

Conclusion

It should be noted that technically VCAPS was not in fact an XP project. By the end of the project we were creating small releases often, had a system metaphor, kept our design simple, did plenty of testing, refactored, pair programmed, practiced collective ownership, used continuous integration, kept our work week to 40 hours, and coded to a standard. But we didn't do the planning game and we didn't have a customer on site full time. These two omissions disqualify us as an XP project. But what we did accomplish was to create a project where the customers were happy with our progress and felt that the system was becoming very stable and adaptable, we had management who were delighted with our cost curve, and developers who did not want to leave the project—ever.

Another key ingredient was a project manager who wanted to introduce XP. She was keen to learn the concepts and was open-minded and patient in finding ways to deploy them in the Ford setting. Many of the XP practices went through subtle transitions before being fully implemented. It required an ability to focus on a distant goal to accomplish this, which is generally the domain of the project manager. The VCAPS project integrated the project manager much more tightly than is typical with XP, and we found great benefit in this.

Our success hinged on having Trish as our project manager. She had a respectful way to manage the project and listened to the team. It is clear that none of the other managers would have embraced XP as she did since none of the others did even after we demonstrated the value of XP. On reflection, we decided that egoless leadership is important. An important side effect of XP is the reduction of ego being involved in the process. Egos must be fed at someone's expense. A manager's ego will be fed at the expense of the team. Following Trish's lead the team pulled together very well and didn't have any ego problems.

One of the more important results of the VCAPS project was how we were able to get the team to commit to the XP process. The process was never well understood right out of the box. You need to live with it a while before you know whether it fits. Having a concept described was often not enough to impart understanding. XP was never forced: It was presented to the group and the group decided. Getting team buy-in was a process in itself. We accomplished this with encouragement but imposed no consequences for noncompliance. People migrated to XP naturally.

An interesting outcome was that our customers never believed XP was helping us. Instead they believed the specific composition of the team was responsible for our success and would have succeeded with any methodology. Perhaps this was because they weren't exposed to the process via the planning game. The project was canceled not because we weren't delivering value but because management decided to stop us.

At a critical point in our transition we did decide to throw away the old system and start fresh. Certainly, very few projects will have this luxury. Starting over helped us because we had already mastered many of the XP practices individually when we decided to make the redevelopment of VCAPS an XP project. This helped a great deal when it was time to ask the question "how extreme do we want to be?" We were able to choose to do 9 out of the 12 XP practices. Pair programming was originally not allowed and was added only after a change in personnel.

It took us one full year to make VCAPS a project that people could enjoy. True to our original goals the customers wanted our system and were disappointed with our management when it was canceled. They even tried to come up with their own budget to continue our work. Our developers wanted to be on the project. We all waited months hoping for the customers to call us back to action. We made some mistakes at VCAPS, but we learned even more.

References

[Bellin1997] D. Bellin, S. S. Simone, G. Booch. *The CRC Card Book*. Addison-Wesley, 1997.

[Buzan1991] T. Buzan. *Use Both Sides of Your Brain*. E. P. Dutton, 1991.

[Edwards1989] B. Edwards. *Drawing on the Right Side of the Brain*. Jeremy P. Tarcher, Inc., 1989.

[Wilkinson1995] N. M. Wilkinson. *Using CRC Cards: An Informal Approach to Object-Oriented Development*. Prentice Hall, 1995.

Acknowledgments

We thank the VCAPS team for putting so much effort into the project. Don thanks Kent Beck and the Chrysler Comprehensive Compensation (C3) team for teaching him so much.

About the Authors

Don Wells has over two decades of programming experience. He has built financial applications, military applications, expert systems, cockpit simulators, computer aided engineering (CAE) systems, Web sites, and even published a video game. Don has been on projects ranging in size from 1 to 150 people. He has developed custom software to run on large corporate mainframes, shrink-wrapped software for home computers, and everything in between. He has been experimenting with ad hoc software development methods for many years. In 1996 he worked on the Chrysler Comprehensive Compensation project followed by the VCAPS project where Extreme Programming was successfully applied. Don has adopted Extreme Programming as his software methodology of choice. Don can be reached at Don@extremeprogramming.org

Trish Buckley is the Manager of the Enterprise Portal project for Ford Motor Company, a position she was appointed to in January 2000. In this position, Buckley is responsible for the expansion and support of the Ford Intranet, which currently has 150,000 users and receives 400,000 hits per day. She has responsibility for driving the business-to-employee (B2E) e-business strategy.

Prior to this appointment, Buckley served as Process Leadership Manager, Treasury, a position she held since November 1998. In this position she oversaw the consolidation of Ford Motor and Ford Motor Credit Treasury organizations and the selection of supporting internal and vendor computer applications.

Buckley joined Ford Motor in 1993 as an undergraduate trainee for Finance Systems. She went on to serve in a variety of information technology positions. Some of her accomplishments include the development and roll-out of a Vehicle Cost and Profit system in the United States, the successful global launch of the Distributed Labor and Overhead Reporting system, and general ledger system support for the Mexican Peso Revaluation and Ford's Corporate reorganization.

Buckley was born in Cincinnati, Ohio in November 1964. She has a BS (Honors) in Information Processing and Administrative Management from the University of Cincinnati, Ohio. She also has an MBA from Oakland University, Michigan. She can be reached at trish@extremeprogramming.org.

Chapter 24

Adopting XP

—Peter Sommerlad

This chapter describes our way to become an Extreme Program-ming (XP) team. XP, as promoted by Kent Beck, is a software engineering process and philosophy based on well-known prac-tices. Our setting with a team working on multiple customer projects simultaneously, but using a single code base (our frame-work for Internet application servers), is somehow special, so I wrote down our stories to tell others about our experiences and to open the ground for discussion on the points we haven't achieved yet to our satisfaction. Because we are a small company, the main questions we deal with in this multiproject situation are:

- *"How do you deal with your external customers?"*
- *"How do you make money from applying XP?" and*
- *"How do you prioritize tasks across multiple projects?"*

This chapter presents our approaches to these questions, collects remaining questions arising from them, and briefly shows our vision of an XP-based e-business solution development process. The conclusion section gives some of the human aspects I learned from XP.

Introduction

Currently published XP practices [Beck2000] derive from projects wherein a large organization wanted to create a solution to a tough business problem. An XP team forms around a common system, a shared metaphor, and delivers to a single customer. XP allows the customer to change its mind on the way to a solution and to achieve the most important goals of the system as early as possible.

Our development situation is different from most of Kent Beck's experiences. As sketched in Figure 24.1 we develop solutions for different external customers at the same time. However, our team forms around a common software platform used by all these projects: WebDisplay, an application framework for Internet server solutions. The main question that arises is:

⋄ How we can apply XP practices to our multiproject development team?

There are several forces that make this problem difficult, and up to today we haven't solved them all.

⋄ How do you deal with external customers?
⋄ How do you make money from applying XP?
⋄ How do you prioritize tasks across multiple projects?

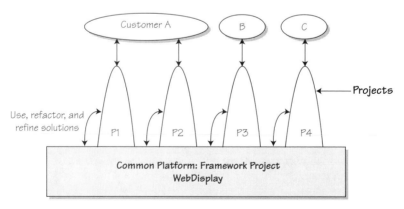

FIGURE 24.1 Our multiproject, multi-customer development scenario with the single code base WebDisplay

This chapter cannot provide all the answers: Many more arose from the partial answers we found for ourselves. This is just a starting point for a discussion of what the future of XP might bring us.

External Customers

Most customers aren't used to a flexible team or vendor that can deal with changing requirements. Customers involved in procurement processes in particular are not ready to deal with XP. Purchasing departments prefer fixed prices and a defined set of deliverables. Fixing a project's deliverables up front is in complete contrast to XP assumptions.

Sometimes existing customers (at least the technical people) were surprised by our ability to react flexibly to changing requirements. However, once accustomed to our flexible reaction, they tended to ask for more and want to pay less for it. The need for refactoring, especially, was something that is very hard to communicate. Refactoring is an investment in the future, very often not understood by customers with usually short-term goals. Which leads us to ask, how do you economically handle the flexibility inherent in XP?

One solution might be to charge by time and material, but this isn't a popular idea with the customer's purchasing department, which might not trust your ability to execute and may not be willing to live with being unable to control project costs. In addition the customer may not be used to paying high rates albeit for very good developers. In such cases we help the customer by providing fixed budgets for a specific time and delivery, according to the customer's requirements. This allows the customer to control the cost and prioritize features. One thing that remains is to explain why we charge for pair programming, writing test cases, and refactoring.

During the next generation of projects we tried using fixed-price solutions with more elaboration of the deliverables up front. However, this worked only partially, because XP's truth of inevitable change caught the customer and us by surprise later.

Once we have a working solution, it is easier for us and the customer to estimate smaller chunks of functionality and charge fixed prices for each of the chunks. Both parties can relax, because on the one hand there are defined deliverables to account for, and on the other hand, there is the flexibility of changing our minds by reprioritizing deliverables or inventing new ones as needed [Fowler+1999].

Dealing with customers is a hard issue. Many questions remain open for the moment, as described in the bullet points throughout this chapter. For example

- How does your customer organize procurement processes to fit the XP process and still maintain control over budget and deliverables?
- How do you, as a development company, educate your customers about the benefits and behavioral rules of XP?
- How do you deal with customers accustomed to "fire-and-forget" orders, that are not used to the XP effort for prioritizing, choosing, and checking deliverables?

Economics of XP

As stated, if you charge your customers for time and material and are not being pressured for early delivery, XP might not be the best way to conduct your software development business. If you are less efficient, you generate higher revenues. In the solution business we are in, efficiency and quality of development does not always pay off.[1]

For example, some of our customers didn't sign a maintenance contract for solutions we build after deployment, because everything ran so smoothly. From an economic viewpoint, we lost money in these projects, because there was no or a late maintenance contract. There were also cases where there was a maintenance contract after deployment, where we made money, because we had very few support requests. In addition, the high quality we achieved allowed us to keep customers and build more solutions for them. Our track record built up, but we may have just been lucky. If you are building solutions in an area where change is inevitable, like e-business, XP's benefits should pay off, at least in theory. We performed well enough to survive in the market, but this is no big deal today. My current belief is that fixed price solutions combined with the ability to adapt to changes throughout the project can be an advantage for us. However, this requires estimates that are rough enough to allow for this change to happen. Many questions remain open for us. I hope to find some answers at XP2000.

- How do you charge for refactoring, test case development, and pair programming? Do you need to tell your customers about these?

---

1. In a product business it might be different, where quality pays off in market reputation and number of customers (at least for a technology believer).

Multiproject Scheduling

During the past few years we were very busy most of the time. Usually there was more customer demand than we were able to deliver. Serving multiple masters (customers) is not an easy task for a team. We try to cope with this situation by taking the team as a whole and scheduling tasks across the team. However, we needed several iterations to get to a solution and there remain open issues.

In the beginning we had individuals or small teams each working separately on a customer project. Some projects even took place at a customer site, so we lacked a common ground for the team. First we introduced a mailing list, where each team member could participate in technical discussions. This was not satisfying, because some team members lacked e-mail access at our customers' sites. A second more major aspect was that each project modified the framework to its needs. We couldn't consciously refactor the solutions to integrate useful stuff back into the common code base. Everyone on the team was unhappy with this situation.

Home Day

We declared one day of the week our "home day." Every development team member was supposed to arrange to stay at our offices that day. We held a meeting that was intended to be short, but that was often extended because of discussions about the framework and our development process. The rest of the day was intentionally arranged around reintegrating solution parts into the framework. From an economic standpoint we lost up to 20 percent of productivity by giving up a whole day of a week, but developers started to collaborate more.

The weekly discussions were the basis for the next improvement. We tried to arrange our projects to be 'solution projects,' where we take responsibility to develop a system on-site at our company and deliver it to the customer. Previously, most of our projects where in a 'body-leasing' style and happened at the customer's site, where we collaborated with other developers. Today, all WebDisplay-based projects are developed at itopia. This doesn't mean we do not talk to customers, but we talk much more among each other. A dartboard at the coffee machine further improved informal communication.

Task Cards

We tried to keep a record of all projects' tasks by keeping them in a database that could be easily accessed. Initially this seemed to work, but after only a few weeks, maintaining this data involved too much overhead and was neglected by the team. We consciously decided to cancel that practice.

The next thing we tried was to write down all the tasks, especially those related to the framework, on index cards. We arranged and prioritized these cards in our weekly meetings. Every developer was to pick a card, perform the task with a pair, and then go on to the next card. This didn't work either. Making the cards was fun, but keeping them continuously prioritized and actively taking a card from the wall didn't happen. One reason for this was that there was no longer any real project responsibility. A typical developer was overwhelmed by the task of prioritizing the cards across all concurrent projects.

Project Leader

This experience led to our next practice. We defined personal responsibilities (project leader) for each of the customer and framework projects. The responsibility of the project leader includes keeping in touch with the customer and representing the customer's stories and priorities for the solution project. All tasks for all ongoing projects were collected in a single table. Developers estimated these tasks and scheduled them. During the planning meeting only the due tasks were looked at. There were two main passes through the list, one for the due tasks, and one per developer to keep track of everyone's workload for the current week. Any adjustments to the list were done immediately as the point arose. This turned out to be too boring and looking at all projects at once involved too much overhead.

Today each project leader is to represent tasks and keep track of them on his or her own. Using a spreadsheet is the recommended way, but some teams stick with a collection of pages on our WikiWikiWeb (a dynamic intranet) instance. Individual project teams now use their own lists to keep track of the project advances, without looking at the other projects. One exception to this rule is the platform project, which gets change requests from the individual project teams and keeps its planning up to date according to all these requests.

Tracking versus Estimating

We found out that keeping track of actual worked hours against estimated hours is too complicated. It is easier to declare a task done than to measure exactly how many minutes every person involved worked on it. Nevertheless, estimation must be based on small enough pieces.

We decided tracking actual hours worked on a task is too fine-grained. Planning fine-grained estimations are okay, but it is too much work to keep track of the details. What is important is making sure all scheduled tasks are done, not how much time each individual task took.

Stories versus Tasks

We tried to keep track of all pending stories the same way. It was too much work to keep everything in sync. Now, each project team selects its own representation of user stories (most of the time on our internal WikiWikiWeb). It is the responsibility of the project leader to include all tasks derived from the project's stories in the project's task list and to update a marker in the story list to show the project's progress.

⬥ How do you keep track, that all tasks related to a story get scheduled?

Goals versus Tasks

Some individual goals cannot be represented easily in the task list. Therefore, we introduced a third representation of weekly goals for each of the team members; these are agreed on in the home-day meeting and are checked for the next week. After a couple of months I feel confident enough to keep this practice as a storyboard for the yearly reviews of the team members.

⬥ Are there really things to do beyond a project's tasks?

Project versus Project

The cross-project scheduling remains difficult. Everyone today is committed to a single project but involved in several,[2] because of pair programming, framework improvements, or just dartboard discussions. The overall team leader acts as a tiebreaker or "customer cooler" in cases where priorities conflict. There is no rule about how these decisions are made; much is decided by gut feeling.

⬥ Is something beyond 'gut feeling' required for cross-project prioritizing?

---

2. Do you know the difference between committed and involved? Consider having ham and eggs for breakfast. The hen was involved in producing your breakfast, the pig was committed.

The biggest question remaining for our growing company is:

◇ How can such an approach scale to more developers, bigger projects, or more simultaneous projects?

Vision

So far, you learned a lot about the things we tried and didn't solve to our complete satisfaction. However, we still believe in the benefits of XP and consider this one of our market advantages.

Quality assurance supported by automatically running test cases is one of the great things we believe in. For our framework we created a thorough set of unit tests. For the servers we build, we've got a stress test tool to ensure they are capable of the load required. For the solutions we deploy, we've got a watchdog program automatically monitoring the system's function and notifying the operating personnel when things go wrong.

Our Process Vision

Our vision of an extreme e-business development process as sketched in Figure 24.2 is to get the round-trip from customer story, through development and integration to a system that operates with all the speed, feed-

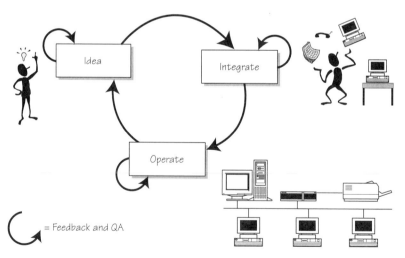

FIGURE 24.2 itopia's extreme e-business development process vision

back and quality assurance XP practices provide. The next big step is to get to a point where our testing support allows direct transformation of customer stories into functional test suites that can run automatically. The mechanics of such support are already given by our other test tools. However, how you can specify such functional tests in a way that they are understandable by the people defining the requirements remains our research topic for the future.

With an increasing number of people working for us we dream of being able to increase the amount of pair programming. Any hints on how to sell this to our customers and to our developers are welcome. At least pair programming allowed our new but experienced developers to become productive with our platform within a month.

Conclusion

XP is not yet so established that you can make an extremely successful IPO based on it. Nevertheless, even in a small company you can apply it to your advantage.

I personally learned that XP does not make team members equal. You have to acknowledge personal preferences and watch for incompatible personalities when suggesting that people should work together.

In a team those members that are able to self-organize their work are those who more easily adopt XP practices. A team member who is not very good at self-organization needs a coach or a leader telling him or her what to do next. Otherwise, consistent performance of the whole team is in danger. Maybe better pair programming will help in this situation. We weren't able to perform in that way yet.

Responsibility needs to be assigned to persons able to take it. Shared code ownership is better than individual code ownership, but this sharing does not scale into the area of project responsibility, especially when there are conflicting goals, as is the case with multiple projects and each goal or project needs a supporter.

Customer education about XP will take some time. The economics of XP will remain an interesting topic, as will be XP-aware procurement processes for our customers.

XP's simple design approach seems to be in contrast with the framework-based approach. We tried to combine both and succeeded so far. However, getting rid of unnecessary flexibility in a framework is much harder than introducing flexibility by refactoring when it is required.

But refactoring of a framework supported with unit tests is a breeze compared to the finger crossing and finger pointing that happened when changing the framework in the past without those tests. I'd never evolve a framework again without unit testing.

References

[Beck2000] K. Beck. *Extreme Programming Explained*. Addison-Wesley, 2000.

[Beck1999] K. Beck. Private communication. 1999.

[Fowler+1999] M. Fowler, K. Beck, J. Brant, W. Opdyke, D. Roberts. *Refactoring: Improving the Design of Existing Code*. Addison-Wesley, 1999.

About the Author

Peter Sommerlad can be reached at itopia—corporate information technology, Technoparkstrasse 1, CH-8005 Zurich, Switzerland; +41-1-355 56 00; peter.sommerlad@itopia.ch.

Chapter 25

Introducing Extreme Programming in a Research and Development Laboratory

—*Karl Boutin*

This chapter presents as a case study the introduction of the Extreme Programming (XP) methodology into a research and development laboratory. Prototypes produced by research and development (R&D) labs often display poor software engineering qualities. The author proposes Extreme Programming as a software development process to solve this problem, and also argues that this approach fits well into the R&D lab's culture. The author's experience with different activities related to XP, such as planning, prototyping, pair programming, refactoring, testing and software releasing, is then presented.

Introduction

Prototypes produced by research and development (R&D) laboratories often display poor software engineering qualities. The development process inherent in such labs can result in an unmanageably complex end product that requires constant modification to compensate for initial design shortcomings.

To address this problem within our own lab, we decided to introduce Extreme Programming (XP) techniques one year ago. XP is a software development methodology that seems highly adapted to the environment and culture of an R&D laboratory. It was our hope that the methodology imposed by Extreme Programming would provide the structure and process necessary to alleviate some of the difficulties we were experiencing with a current project. In addition, we were interested to see whether XP provided a procedural framework that could be applied to future projects.

In this chapter, we would like to present our experience with XP and, in doing so, examine if our initial expectations were satisfied now that we are familiar with the technique. Even though the project to which we applied Extreme Programming is still under construction, we consider that we have accumulated enough experience to present some valid insights and comments.

We begin by describing our organization as well as the project we were undertaking when we introduced XP within our walls. This overview provides some details on the context and culture of our lab, as well as revealing why we were attracted to this new technique of software development. Although we offer a summarized version of our understanding of Extreme Programming, we assume that the reader is already familiar with XP. For the remainder of the chapter, we describe our experience with the methodology—focusing on specific activities and practices that impacted our development effort.

Context

The Laboratory

Our research and development laboratory is part of the Communication Security Establishment (CSE), which is one of Canada's intelligence agencies. The group's mission is to invent new technologies that can be used to help CSE achieve its overall objectives. The job of each member of the unit is to apply its scientific and technical expertise to improving the work of the organization's analysts. The fields of research of our lab cover domains such as pattern recognition, data filtering, and signal enhancement, as well as image, text, and audio processing. The R&D team is composed largely of engineers who can rely on the support of a technologist and a computer scientist. The unit includes seven permanent employees. Within the lab it is common to have temporary personnel—two or three co-op students or contractors—involved in different projects.

The Work

As with most R&D labs, each member of our unit is usually involved in research work as well as development tasks and there is no specific division of labor between the researchers and the developers. The engineers are expected to take charge of the whole process of deploying the innovations born in the lab.

Even though the nature of the work is quite broad, we have observed with experience that a certain work pattern has emerged. The main focus of the members of our lab seems to be aimed at discovering and exploiting the right algorithm or technique. Once the proof of concept stage is reached, there seems to be less interest in constructing a full-fledged application. The culture is such that the efforts placed in initial research work are emphasized, while the construction of a complete product is neglected.

This is not to say that the work performed in our laboratory is exclusively theoretical. In fact, most of the research and development projects tackled by our team involve several hands-on tasks, which generally culminate with the creation of prototypes. A researcher will usually embark on a new project by doing some exploratory work on new ideas that relate to his or her field of research and interest. Our group's most successful path to discovery is to experiment with techniques and innovations in a field and determine how these new approaches could be applied to further CSE's objectives. The results of this kind of R&D process are mostly software programs and modules that serve as proof of concept prototypes.

The Problem

The next step in an R&D endeavor usually involves trying the new prototype on real data. The system is more or less integrated in the operational environment where the engineers can observe its behavior and gather feedback from its eventual end users. This information is used to refine the prototype further by fixing obvious bugs or adding features.

After several iterations of this type, the system is simply left running in the new environment. This is where we believe a problem arises: The system that has been created and field tested by the engineer is still a simple prototype. In operation, it masquerades as an integral software application to the end users and their manager, but fundamentally it remains an experimental system that was designed and constructed as such. At this point, the researcher will often sense pressure to leave the creation in this state and move on to new projects. The manager's argument—which ultimately reflects the customer's view—is that the innovation output of the lab must be optimized. Spending more time on this prototype at this point would probably not add much to its innovation value. This is how prototypes from an R&D laboratory invariably migrate into production.

The Prototype Trap

In our opinion, R&D labs in organizations similar to ours regularly fall into this prototype trap. Systems are hacked together quickly as prototypes, without too much care given to their architecture, design, and implementation, which are essential for the construction of robust information systems. Initially, the system appears appropriate for the job and performs adequately. It must be modified regularly, however, in order to extend a feature or correct a bug. This is when the fundamental flaws of such a prototype become apparent. As time passes the system grows more and more complex until it reaches a state where it becomes impossible to introduce any more modifications. The innovation stops. In a way, the engineers have painted themselves into a corner; they fell into the prototype trap!

Reengineering Task

The Challenge

It had become obvious to the lab's team that enormous amounts of time and effort were wasted on the maintenance of our prototypes. We had to find a better way to conduct our innovation business and develop a new approach for building and deploying systems. The engineers were looking for a process that would guarantee the creation of better systems than those produced by the current prototype mindset.

Our investigations in new software development techniques led us to the domain of object-oriented programming (OOP). This field was mature and, at first glance, its concepts seem to address many issues that we had identified on our defective prototypes. In addition, CSE was in the middle of a business process reengineering effort and OOP was identified as a key technology for the organization's success. The promises, features, and trade-offs of this technique seemed appropriate for the needs of our lab.

The Pilot Project

One of the systems developed by our team was locked deeply in the prototype trap. This system was the fruit of many years of research and development in the fields of speech and signal processing. We had deployed a speech processing system that was running relatively well and was highly appreciated by CSE's analysts. The system was composed of modules, programs, and scripts written in C and Perl, and was performing its back-end speech recognition processing on distributed UNIX platforms. Unfortunately, the prototype had grown in complexity into a set of programs that included more than 11,000 lines of code. Despite the success of the tool among its end users, in the eyes of the engineers who had built it, it remained a nightmare to extend and a monster to maintain.

This prototype would benefit from some reengineering and provide an excellent opportunity to experiment with OOP. Our immediate goal was to fix the current system, but our broader objectives were to initiate the usage of the new technology in our laboratory. We hoped that this pilot project could introduce the team to better software development practices.

Getting Started

Two researchers got involved at the onset of the pilot project. Since none of us had any experience with the technology, early on in the process we hired an experienced consultant specializing in object-oriented analysis and design (OOAD). The original development team was thus composed of an engineer, a computer scientist, and a consultant. During the course of the project, two to three extra members—co-op students—joined the core team in the effort.

Smalltalk was chosen as our primary programming language. This development language was widely used in the rest of our organization, and we hoped we could eventually tap into this community for help and guidance. Since our contractor was highly skilled in Smalltalk and object-oriented techniques, we were expecting to learn a lot of our skills via his mentoring. Other object-oriented programming languages were considered for the project, but we felt that the conventions promoted by Smalltalk would best foster good programming practices.

We embarked on our apprenticeship with books and formal training. There was an initial period of acclimatization with the language and the object-oriented approach, and then the reengineering work began. As the project progressed, we began to integrate the new OOP concepts; we learned about the language style, conventions, and software design patterns. After a while we began to understand how to construct a system the object-oriented way.

Encounter with XP

We became aware of Extreme Programming during our familiarization with Smalltalk and object-oriented programming. No specific methodology had yet been adopted for the development of the project. Still, we were aware that most of the difficulties encountered during previous projects were probably due to a lack of any appropriate software development process.

Though other teams within CSE were applying different methodologies to their projects, most of these approaches seemed too elaborate to us. Such techniques were appropriate for the professional software development units in which they were deployed, but for our purposes, the researchers wanted a simple and lightweight methodology. The lab's team was willing to move toward a software development process, but the techniques would still need to provide some flexibility and allow the freedom we were used to working in.

In light of these requirements, the approach proposed by XP seemed very appropriate and corresponded to customs already found in a laboratory environment. Ideas such as experimenting with the many solutions of a problem, verifying all assumptions with scientific testing, communicating effectively with your peers, and refining methods or processes after a discovery, are all practices commonly performed by researchers.

Thus we decided to implement XP into our pilot project. Our contractor had some knowledge of the methodology and was in fact teaching us some of the best practices of this approach. However, we still needed to investigate further; with the help of the Internet and a seminar at Smalltalk Solutions 99 we gathered useful information. The experiment began without any specific edict to follow. The formalism that has emerged recently was not available at the beginning of our exercise. We had to build a set of guidelines inspired by all of the information gathered on the subject via the Internet, seminars, books, and discussions.

The guidelines followed for this project are summarized in the following paragraphs. A reader familiar with Extreme Programming will recognize some of the key elements of the methodology but may also notice that some elements are missing. These omissions are intentional, because we are simply trying to present a picture of our understanding of XP at the onset of the project. These views have evolved with time but this original draft constitutes the foundation on which our case study is based.

1. *Analysis:* In Extreme Programming, the analysis process starts when the developers sit down with the customers and listen to their requirements. Their goal is to make sense of what is said and to come up with a set of scenarios, or use cases, that the system should be able to execute. Those use cases are written down on simple index cards that constitute the requirements analysis documents of the system.

2. *Design:* The design step of the project is also quite straightforward. All of the members of the development team move to the white board and begin drawing. No need to be too cautious here, whatever is designed will do for now—it is going to change anyway! The time spent during this stage should be limited. The developers can then move in pairs to their workstations and begin to code. At the end of the day what is required from this team is code, not documents.

3. *Testing:* In order to know whether the design being implemented is really going to work, the developers must construct test cases. These tests should be automated because a lot of them will be constructed and each and every one of them must pass. After any addition, removal, or modification of the code, all of the tests must complete successfully.

4. *Refactoring:* As the system's development progresses, the code will need to be modified regularly. Changes will be made to the names and locations of methods, classes, and variables. The relationship of the classes, and objects within the system will also change. These refactorings will correct the code and improve the original design.

5. *Integration:* The components of the new system should be integrated into the operational environment as soon as possible. Experience has shown that the big bugs or the flaws of a system often show up at integration. If such imperfections are exposed early via rapid customer feedback, they can be fixed right away.

This outlines our initial perspective of Extreme Programming. It gives a fairly accurate, though simplified, idea of the guidelines we followed while trying to implement the methodology into our lab.

Our Experience

The pilot project on which this case study is based is not yet completed. One could argue that we therefore could not provide a report that would be as exhaustive as a post mortem analysis. However, we believe that reflecting on the methodology while we are still involved in the project provides a stimulating perspective that could benefit the reader.

Our initial assumption about the XP methodology was that it would appeal to the members of our lab because it is a lightweight process and the values and practices it elicits are in tune with the normal activities of a researcher. This is not to imply that we imagined that the introduction of this software development process would be trivial. We were concerned that the discipline required by XP would be alien to the working habits of researchers who were used to functioning in an environment free of any methodology. In addition, Kent Beck's [Beck2000] handbook was not available at the time and we were uncertain of the steps required to introduce this methodology in the laboratory.

Thus this software development process was implemented to the best of our knowledge, with efforts concentrated on the introduction of the principal practices of the methodology. The following sections present our experience with Extreme Programming to date. The successes and difficulties we faced during the introduction of the methodology are highlighted. We expose the good, the bad, and the ugly aspects of our approach in the hope of providing the reader with some valuable insight.

Planning

The project management practices of XP are the aspects of the methodology that were the most difficult to implement. We had some basic understanding of practices such as the planning game, small releases, and continuous integration, but we did not realize the importance of the interrelations of these practices. In XP, the control of the project relies heavily on the balance of responsibility between customers and developers. Yet from the start, a real customer was not on the development team. We broke the rule of having an on-site customer involved in the development effort and neglected the listening value of XP.

Some analysts had already worked with the original prototype and had provided some valuable feedback on their experience. Their input was considered sufficient, and we believed that the design of the new system could begin based on their findings alone. Because there was no real customer in the development team, we could not really play the planning game. Some rough scenarios were drafted but, with little customer input, the requirements were defined almost unilaterally by the researchers. Once again, both business and technical decisions were made by the technical team alone.

One principle explanation for this oversight has to do with the fundamental character of an R&D laboratory. In such a lab, the systems being developed are usually proposed by the researchers themselves. These tools are the offspring of some earlier discoveries made in-house, and the potential user of these innovations is often not even aware of their development. In such a case, identifying your potential customer is not a trivial task. In practice the researcher approaches the customer with an idea that he or she proposes to implement. With such a scenario the initial requirements originate from the developer, not the customer.

Even in a case where the user is identified from the onset, engineers are often tempted to wait until the system is sufficiently fleshed out before involving a user. The researcher thinks that clients, facing a completely new service that they have never been exposed to before, could not provide much help at this stage. Such an attitude is obviously a mistake from the perspective of Extreme Programming. The isolation that the researchers foster around their development work may be to blame for the ivory tower image that R&D labs often project.

In our case the first draft of the system is now in place so the researchers should no longer be reticent to integrate the end users within the team. In the future, we will encourage every member of our lab to reveal even immature prototypes to the outside world as soon as possible and hence foster input from potential clients. When conducting projects where obvious end users of a system can be identified, we will make sure that they are present at the onset of the development project, ensuring that the management responsibilities are properly balanced. However, we believe that in the work of an R&D engineer there will be times when an idea is still in its infancy and no precise use has yet been identified. In such a case, the researcher must be allowed to play the role of the customer for a while. But this is a dangerous game. It is essential that this game be played only for a short time while a real customer is aggressively sought. Then, for the remainder of the project, the planning game should become the sport of choice.

Prototyping

The Extreme Programming solutions for managing risk were quite adequate for our project. The principle of relying on simple design is very valuable when a developer is tackling a high-risk R&D endeavor such as ours. Early in the pilot project we had some doubts about the capacity of the Smalltalk language to provide the speed required for a speech processing system. The XP methodology suggests beginning development by addressing such issues immediately. In order to ensure that the performance requirements could be met, we experimented with some rudimentary constructs of the core functionality of the system. Once this initial implementation was available, we were able to determine whether performance limits were really an issue. After some accurate measurements of the performance factors, we concluded that most of our original conjecture was wrong.

In our experience, R&D engineers—especially those involved in the field of digital signal processing—tend to be too concerned with system performance. The spike solutions practice was appreciated by our team and helped build confidence in the system developed.

In some cases the spike solutions demonstrated the existence of potential flaws in the proposed approach. Fortunately, simple design helped clearly expose any defects present—most were located at the architectural level. The developers enjoyed making these discoveries early on in the project. They were then able to reorient the design without any fear of jeopardizing the development process.

Pair Programming

The practice of pair programming seemed peculiar to the developers at first, but they understood the value of this approach and thus acquired the habit of doing it. Later on in the project, however, the practice petered out. We believe that our experience clearly illustrates the benefits of employing the technique and the drawbacks of omitting it.

During the project, most of the interactions with our contractor involved pair programming. The main objective was to establish the initial design of the system but we also expected to use the sessions as good learning opportunities. Even though we had received a fair amount of formal training in Smalltalk and OOAD, the most valuable training occurred during pair programming. Mentoring is recognized as one of the best teaching methods; pair programming provides an ultimate mentoring environment.

After a while, the freshly trained developers in turn became mentors to the new intern students joining the core development team. We observed during some pair programming sessions that, contrary to our assumptions, the transfer of knowledge was not always flowing from the senior member to the junior one. On many occasions, the ideas, questions, or critiques of the rookie had a big impact on the code produced.

We also noticed that the exercise of pair programming fostered rapid and efficient communication between the partners in session and helped expose ideas and concerns quickly. Human speech is a high throughput mode of communication. This means that a lot of information can be traded in the course of a single session: mentoring, coding and naming conventions, patterns, best practices, and so on. This mode of exchange is very similar to how researchers work in their scientific domain. They usually seek peer review when a hypothesis must be challenged. Thus, pair programming can be seen as a natural extension of the way researchers work.

In the course of the project, members had to leave the team for other assignments, so we gradually stopped using pair programming. Even though this practice was successful and appreciated, the small size of the development team made it hard to maintain. When only two members were left on the project, a sense of urgency developed and we began to think that we could get more things done if we split our tasks. It is possible that this happened because the developers were not yet convinced that pair programming was a more efficient mode of coding then the standard practice. One could also argue that there is a minimum size to an XP development team.

After pair programming was stopped, we began to experience a decline in the overall understanding of the system by the remaining members of the development team. The constant information exchange experienced during the earlier coding sessions had guaranteed that every member had a good overview of the project. Without pair programming, this understanding was disintegrating and hindered the task of integrating new components developed individually. The researcher wasted a lot of time trying to understand pieces of code that were written in isolation.

The difficulties we experienced here could happen to many design teams. We believe that the temptation to drop pair programming in order to save time is not unique to our lab. More and more today, organizations find themselves challenged by deadlines and a lack of staff. Proponents of XP should be aware that many developers might feel extreme pressure to abandon pair programming when faced with a lack of resources. Recent studies demonstrate the efficiencies of pair programming, even within the context of limited resources. Although it would intuitively appear that dividing up tasks seems quicker, pair programming does not require much more time in the long run. Future XP coaching should emphasize and promote these studies so that new potential users can avoid being sidetracked as we were.

Refactoring

When we initially heard about the concept of refactoring, we thought that it was simply another form of code cleanup. After some analysis, however, we realized that refactoring conveyed more fundamental implications. The modifications made at this stage go beyond renaming or trivial formatting and may even go as deep as altering the basic architecture of a design. This approach appealed to us because it addressed the modification paralysis problem at the heart of the prototype trap.

The essence of refactoring lies in the challenge of determining exactly which elements need to be changed. This is a hard skill to acquire. Fortunately, the Smalltalk language is rich in knowledge, practices, style, and patterns that are very useful for refactoring. We relied intensively on Smalltalk's conventions to perform this job. Throughout this project we used the Refactoring Browser [Brant+1999]. It has been our tool of choice since the beginning of our training in Smalltalk, and we believe that it improved the way we write code. The browser incorporates some of the best practices of the trade and has helped promote coding conventions. Refactoring can be a dreadful job to perform, requiring a lot of detailed work that the developer would push aside if that were possible. With the Refactoring Browser, changing code is safe and easy. This appeals to the reason, and to the laziness, of the programmer.

When used effectively, refactoring yielded another big advantage to our researchers. Most of the members of the lab are researchers first and software developers second—thus they suffer from analysis paralysis when the design phase of a project begins. Because refactoring is an integral part of the construction process, the burden of design decisions is lifted from the developers' shoulders and they can proceed with any solution that seems appropriate. The design can always be modified again later on. This results in a certain flow in the development process that is the exact opposite of analysis paralysis.

Even though refactoring was beneficial to our project we did experience some lapses and made the mistake of putting off this crucial step to a later date. Instead of using refactoring continuously within tight iteration cycles, we shoved this duty aside like we used to do with code cleaning. We now realize the consequences of this oversight. When refactoring is delayed for too long, the developer loses track of the changes required. The efforts needed to complete the refactoring are doubled because the developers must refamiliarize themselves with the details of the components and their interactions before any changes can be made.

Testing

Of all the practices introduced with Extreme Programming, testing was the most readily accepted by the development team. It is an activity that is promoted in all software development methodologies—though not always to the extent seen here—and was therefore a familiar concept to the developers. Testing also echoes some of the processes of the scientific method, which appealed to our researchers.

Although the team is still adapting to the testing-centered approach of XP, our experience has already taught us some lessons. Testing is a big job; a lot of our efforts for this pilot project were put into this activity. For example, the new system is now composed of roughly 20,000 lines of code. Of these, 12,000 are devoted to testing. In fact, this portion of the system became so elaborate at some point that we had to refactor the test cases themselves. Despite these efforts, it does not appear that constructing test suites has significantly extended the project schedule. We merely traded the time we would have spent debugging and focused it instead on testing.

Despite the fact that our testing is not exhaustive, the advantages of our testing are already becoming apparent. The approach has given us confidence in our design beyond what we had ever sensed in our original prototype. We realize now that testing is a key ingredient for a robust system.

Small Releases

During the release phase of our project, the software releasing guidelines extolled by Extreme Programming were not properly followed. Almost a year passed before the first release of the speech-processing system went into production. Rather than integrating the simplest possible subsystem in small releases early on in the schedule, we proceeded only when a major set of components was available. The construction of all of these objects required more testing and refactoring, which contributed to further delays.

We recognize now that delaying deployment means that less feedback is available for the correct integration of the system. In addition, it is an ineffective way to manage our relations with the customers. The longer it takes to deploy a system, the longer we wait before receiving valuable end-user feedback. If these partners are kept in the dark for too long, we cannot expect overwhelming support from them.

We believe that one reason we did not apply the proposed practice of small releases is that a proven operational system was already running. We were reticent to disturb operations and push our new implementation into production. Our fear was in contradiction with XP's courage value. Hopefully, now that the first release milestone has been reached, we will no longer hesitate to regularly deploy small releases of new components into the running system.

We think that the solution to this reticence to deploy is to begin the releasing process of any new system with the initial proof of concept prototype. This will establish a link with the end user early on in the project and good communication should follow. Once this base system is deployed, the incremental refinement should come naturally for the R&D engineer already skilled at this approach. With the XP methodology well in place, it should be possible to extend the system without any danger of falling into the prototype trap again.

Conclusion

As we have shown, some Extreme Programming activities were relatively easy to implement in our R&D environment. For example, we quickly adapted to, and reaped the benefits of, prototyping, refactoring, and testing.

Other XP practices, however, were harder to introduce smoothly. When the attraction of pair programming diminished as the size of our team shrank, the developers had to be firmly reminded that this technique is efficient and that in the long run its value will outweigh all of the shortcuts tempting them. Similarly, when the fear of the prototype trap held back the quick release of a new system, the researchers had to pause and realized the value of the system at hand. As for planning, our failure to quickly bring an end user on board quickly taught us an important lesson about the pitfalls of unilateral decision making. We learned the hard way that, although some liberties can be taken at the construction of the initial development team, lab members should stick to the rules of the planning game and remember that it takes two to tango!

Despite these initial difficulties, most of the XP practices were eventually implemented and worked for us as expected. The pilot project is not yet completed but we believe we have made the right choice of methodology with XP. We required a software development process that would produce systems of better quality than what our previous approach had provided. The methodology had to be simple and flexible to accommodate the culture of our R&D lab. Our experience with XP and the actual state of the new system developed with it lead us to believe that our requirements were met. From now on we will use XP in our lab and we will promote it throughout our organization.

We suspect that many R&D labs get caught like we did in the prototype trap. Such organizations could benefit from a software development process that fosters quality, extensibility, and maintainability. Extreme Programming is a methodology that meets these goals, and it should appeal to the members of a R&D lab who prefer a lightweight methodology over any conventional approach.

At the heart of XP resides the idea that change is a major part of the software life cycle. Change in itself is a concept fundamental to any researcher on a trek for innovations. Good researchers are agents of change—they crave it! Such innovators should, like we have, enjoy Extreme Programming and wholeheartedly embrace change.

References

[Beck2000] K. Beck. *Extreme Programming Explained*. Addison-Wesley, 2000.

[Brant+1999] J. Brant, D. Roberts. *Refactoring Browser*. On-line at http://st-www.cs.uiuc.edu/~brant/RefactoringBrowser.

Acknowledgments

I would like to thank Carolyn Karpoff for her immense help in revising this chapter. Special thanks to Sébastien Diotte and David Buck for joining me with enthusiasm in this XP adventure. Thanks also to every-one in the B4 unit who made valuable suggestions for improving this chapter.

About the Author

Karl Boutin can be reached at Communications Security Establishment, 719 Heron road, Ottawa, Canada, K1G 3Z4; kboutin@omnisig.com.

Chapter 26

After the Fact: Introducing XP into an Existing C++ Project

—Manfred Lange

This chapter describes the journey we had to take when we introduced XP techniques into an existing project. My intention is to show how XP practices can be successfully integrated in existing software development efforts. In addition, I want to encourage those not already using XP; that it is fun to experiment with it, although it may take some time before you see all its benefits. I present my experiences as a story, the issues that we ran into and how we solved them. In addition, I want to show how we started, where we started, and how the mentioned XP practices could be introduced one after the other.

Of particular interest is the fact that the system we are building consists of a set of components, which we implemented using various programming languages, among them Java and C++. Another interesting issue was that many of the components were multithreaded, and that one of the components encapsulates the database access, so we also have additional complexity with transactions, locking conflicts, and so on. I concentrate on this particular database-access component, because it was the most complex part in the project and the one that caused most of the trouble.

How We Started

In July, the project was in deep trouble. We were making little progress regarding stability. For weeks we had tried to nail down the issues regarding concurrency, transactions, locking conflicts, and so on. We had additional consultants from the database vendor on our team. Still, we did not see any progress.

Then I met Kent Beck, who, after working with me for just a few hours, convinced me that I should give XP a try. Where should we start? Kent's answer to that question was "Start where you have the biggest problems."

Because our biggest problem was the quality, we started with test cases. Not that we had no test cases in place, but they were not sufficient, as it turned out. Moreover, we had not put enough emphasis on the test cases, or at least they did not play the role that XP gives them.

> **Lessons Learned:**
> 1. Start where your biggest problem is.
> 2. If quality is your biggest issue, start with test cases.
> 3. It is never too late to start using XP.

Our biggest problem was quality, so we started writing additional test cases. We used a code coverage tool in order to make sure that we did not miss any of the APIs[1] the component implemented. Just by doing this, we discovered several bugs and we made sure that we would not reintroduce the same bugs into the code again.

> **Lesson Learned:**
> 1. Some tests are better than no tests at all.
> 2. Bad tests are better than no tests.
> 3. Having a set of test cases gives you a systematic approach in ensuring the quality.

---

1. Application Programming Interface (API), I use the term in the sense of a function with a set of typed parameters and a typed return value.

Testing

Having more and better test cases in place improved our software quality. However, we had one particular issue: concurrency. In our database access component we could distinguish two types of concurrency: concurrency caused by multiple threads and concurrency caused by multiple processes accessing the same database.

Note that using XP means that you implement the test cases first. However, it our case our implementation was complete (although buggy) when we started to use test cases to that extent.

Testing Race Conditions

Unit tests only invoked each function with a set of parameter values and checked the result against the expected behavior. This was not sufficient. In a multithreaded environment, as is the case with an underlying database with transactions and locks, I needed multithreaded tests. With a colleague, I sat down and we tried to figure out what the typical use case of the database would be in terms of concurrency. When would we lock an object? What kind of lock conflicts can occur? Does it make sense for a database client to wait for a lock? Are there exclusive locks? What if a thread tries to update many objects within a single transaction? This scenario requires many update locks.

Our approach to this was to use a set of representative test cases. We had one test case where we had many threads accessing the database in read-only mode while a single thread was updating the database. All of the threads were working on the same set of data. The expected outcome was that no exception or error occurred during execution.

Another test involved two threads running simultaneously, both reading and writing to the database. Again, we made sure that both threads were working on the same set of objects in the database. And again, the expected outcome was that no error occurred.

Yet another test included collections and queries, which required many read and update locks within a single transaction. This again increased the number of lock conflicts, resulting in a test of the error handling.

> **Lessons Learned:**
> 1. When adding tests to an existing C++ project, add both the standard, well-known unit tests and concurrency tests.
> 2. There are no guarantees that race conditions tests will cover all imaginable situations. I do not know of any deterministic tests for multiple threads.

Separate Test Interface

Our database access component exposes its interfaces through a component technology.[2] So our first set of test cases consisted of functional tests, which simply did not consider the implementation. Later we discovered that this is not sufficient. We had to add specific test cases for queries and collections. For these test cases we investigated which set of parameters would cause the component to execute certain code in the component. We called these our white-box tests.

Even this was not sufficient. It turned out that, for another category of tests, it was necessary to bypass the official interfaces. We therefore added an interface for testing purposes. This interface is available in special debug builds only. This interface was then used to access test classes for testing internal functionality, such as handling of transactions, distribution of objects in the database, and error handling.

> **Lessons Learned:**
> 1. If you use components, have an additional test interface in place in order to bypass the official, published interface.
> 2. Do not only mechanically test the APIs. In addition, do consider that depending on the set of parameters passed to APIs, different code within the component may be executed.

2. By component technology I mean either CORBA or COM+.

Fully Automated Test Driver

For automatically running test cases, we use a C++ test framework that is easy to use. This test framework is comparable to JUnit. It is now in a state, so we can easily reuse it for all our other C++ projects. In addition, we can integrate it in our build process.

C++ needs to be compiled and linked. This is an issue in refactoring. Interpreted languages have much shorter cycles, which means more cycles per time span. We addressed this problem by two means: First, we bought bigger machines with multiple processors, more memory, and faster I/O subsystems. Second, we checked whether it was possible to reduce the number of dependencies between the source files in our design. For instance, we checked whether all include statements were necessary. One policy here was to move include statements into the implementation files (CPP files).

Another solution was to rethink the class hierarchies and the collaboration of classes in order to reduce the number of dependencies between source files. This also helped make the design much easier to understand, as it led to simpler interfaces of the classes. The efforts resulted in a 50 percent reduction in the compile-link time.

We divided our test cases into two categories: unit tests and long-term stability tests. We executed the first set after each single change. However, because the latter took between 45 and 60 minutes to execute, we only ran them two or three times a day. The long-term stability tests also included the concurrency tests.

Lessons Learned:

1. Do not underestimate the importance and usefulness of a fully automated test driver.

2. If people say they have implemented test cases, do not trust them. Most of the time they implemented test cases *after* they completed their code. XP test cases have two characteristics, which distinguish them from traditional tests: They are implemented up front and they are systematic.

3. Even for compiled languages such as C++, it is possible to achieve short compile-link cycles by reducing dependencies between files and using templates sparingly. This accelerates the integration of XP.

Simulating Error Conditions

A database application, especially if it is multithreaded, raises the issue of how to handle error conditions, such as locking conflicts.

The database system uses a UNIX-like signaling mechanism for indicating error conditions. This means that if a client is interested in such signals, they have to implement a callback function called a signal handler. Then the client registers this callback. Finally, if an error occurs, the server component (in our case the database system) invokes the signal handler. The client is not constrained in what the signal handler should do.[3] In the simplest case the signal handler would do nothing. As an alternative, the signal handler could write to a log file for debugging purposes. Unfortunately, in our case the signal handler was not allowed to throw any exception.

We wrote a class CErrorCheck that automatically detected whether the database runtime library called the signal handler during the execution of a series of database calls. If the database runtime library called the error handler, the destructor of that class would then automatically throw an exception.

In order to test error handling, we added code to the CErrorCheck destructor, so that for debug builds the CErrorCheck destructor occasionally threw an exception although the database system had never called the error handler.

> ### Lessons Learned:
> 1. It is impossible to write a test driver for a multithreaded database component with 100 percent coverage. You can achieve 100 percent code coverage eventually. Nevertheless, you will not be able to achieve 100 percent coverage of all possible execution paths.
> 2. To improve the testing of error handling mechanisms, concentrate all error handling to a single place in your code. Then add a simulator to that place in order to increase the number of (simulated) errors during the execution of your test cases.

---

3. The implementation of the signal handler should not execute any lengthy operations, however.

Simple Design

Some of the issues that we found while adapting XP methods caused us to rethink our design. One thing was the implementation of collections and iterators that we needed for accessing objects in the database. At first, templates seemed the obvious solution, but unfortunately, they turned out to cause code bloat. The resulting binaries were one-third bigger than necessary.

Having solid test cases in place, we had enough courage to change the implementation so that we simply did not use templates any more. Within only a few days, everything was running again without problems. Without the test cases, it would have taken much longer.

> **Lessons Learned:**
> 1. Avoid using templates if possible. Not using templates makes your code easier to read and understand. Use templates only if it is your best alternative.
> 2. Having solid test cases makes it easier to simplify the design. The test cases tell you whether your transformation of the code was valid.

Another area for rethinking the design was the code for synchronizing multiple threads. Fortunately, we already had an implementation where the use of synchronization objects such as critical sections and mutexes was already concentrated in a few locations. We reworked this so that locks were automatically released independent of how a function was left, either through a return statement or an exception thrown.[4]

> **Lessons Learned:**
> 1. Simplify your design one step at a time. After each step, your perspective will be different and you will discover new and interesting points in your code that deserve refactoring or a redesign.
> 2. Try to locate the code for a specific feature at one single place, such as the code for transaction handling, for distributing objects in the database, or for managing queries.

---

4. A pattern named "Scoped Locking" can be found at http://www.cs.wustl.edu/~schmidt/patterns/patterns.html.

Refactoring

Refactoring is one of the XP practices [Beck2000]. Using it with C++ is hard. Nevertheless, in some cases, you will choose C++ as the best alternative for implementing a component. In this section, I explain a few refactoring techniques for C++.

Martin Fowler describes many methods [Fowler+1999],[5] so I do not duplicate them here. On the other hand, I found some techniques that Martin either did not describe at all or described but not with a focus on C++.

Replace Template Member Function with Base Class Member Function

Motivation

When you implement in C++, templates can be a powerful means for abstraction. Typical uses are collections and iterators. In some cases, however, the use of templates leads to code bloat. This is especially true if a template class consists of many functions and/or the template takes part in nesting.

In some cases, member functions of a class template do not use the template parameter. In this case, introduce a nonparameterized base class and move the function to that base class.[6]

Mechanics

1. Introduce a new nonparameterized class.
2. Make the new class a base class of the template class.
3. Move the member function from the template class to the new base class.
4. Compile and test.

Example

Using my database access component example, I had a class that implemented queries on the database. I found a convenient way to implement them as a template:

---

5. Note especially the sidebar "Refactoring C++ Programs," by Bill Opdyke in [Fowler+1999].
6. This is a special case of "Pull Up Method."

```
template<class T> class Query {
public:
    // other stuff left out
    int AddPredicate(string aPredicate);
private:
    std::list<string> m_predicates;
};
```

Actually, the predicate collection is the same, independent of the type for which you are actually querying. Instantiating the query class template leads to an instantiation of AddPredicate() for each type.

I introduced a new base class, QueryBase and moved the function up the hierarchy into that class.

```
class QueryBase {
public:
    // other stuff left out
    int AddPredicate(string aPredicate);
private:
    std::list<string> m_predicates;
};

template<class T> class Query : public QueryBase {
    // other stuff left out.
};
```

With this implementation the functionality is the same, but I had only one instantiation of the function AddPredicate().

Replace Macros with Template Functions

Using C++ precompiler macros can lead to code bloat and bad readability. To reduce the code bloat, to increase readability, and to make debugging easier, replace macros with template functions.

Motivation

The C++ precompiler provides macros. You can use macros to implement functions that you need frequently within the program, such as deleting an object and setting the pointer pointing to that object to null. However, there are three major drawbacks to this approach: First, the use of the macro is not type safe; second, debugging a macro can be very annoying; and third it results in code bloat.

Mechanics

Replace the macro with a template function.

Example

Deleting an object from the heap is a frequent task in C++ programs. For additional safety I always check the pointer for null-ness; if it is not null I delete the object and I set the pointer to null, so that I do not use the pointer again. The simplest approach is this:

```
if( NULL != pObject ) {
    delete pObject;
    pObject = NULL;
}
```

Because this is a frequent task, my first solution to make life easier was this:

```
#define CLEANUP(pointer) \
if( NULL != pointer ) { \
    delete pointer; \
    pointer = NULL; \
}
```

With this in place I could write:

```
CLEANUP(pObject);
```

This already reduced typing, but it still was not what I wanted. Here is a better approach:

```
template<class T> void CLEANUP(void*& pointer) {
    if( NULL != pointer ) {
        delete pointer;
        pointer = NULL;
    }
}
```

This approach allows you also to set breakpoints and to step through the code. In addition, as I pass the pointer by reference I work on the original memory, so assigning null means I do not assign null to a copy but to the real pointer. An improvement would be to make the template function in line, which eliminates the overhead for calling the function and returning the function.[7]

---

7. For further details see also Scott Meyers [Meyers1992].

Pair Programming

Some people do not like pair programming. Their first thought is that pair programming reduces productivity. No, it does not. However, we found some other issues that are interesting to note.

Social Issues

Pair programming means that two people must communicate, and sometimes misunderstand each other. My opinion is that developing software is a social activity. In order to create a great product the people involved should not only know each other's names, but also their strengths and weaknesses, not only their technical skills but also regarding personal and interpersonal skills. This helps in various ways: If you know the strengths of other people, it is easier for you to pick the best partner for the development task at hand.

One particular issue I encountered was that I faced a lot of criticism regarding the underlying database. For the first time, we were using an object-oriented database. In addition, I underestimated the effort needed to integrate the product into our software. The combination of the instability and the delay led to the criticism. My critics attributed the problems mainly to the database technology and the database product.

We had a phase when we had all known bugs fixed and still the software did not run stably. Then—in a joint effort of the best engineers on our team—we found out that the cause for the instability was a compiler bug.

Since then the criticism has stopped. When we joined our forces, I learned about the the compiler bug, and my colleagues gained a better understanding of the database access component.

Lessons Learned:

1. Working in pairs helps the first person learn about the experiences the second person has made in other areas. The second person learns about the software module on which the first person is working. Both gain insight and eventually understand the complexity of the module.

2. Pair programming is not only ongoing code review but also involves social aspects. People learn about the feelings and thinking of others.

Differences in Skill Levels

Another issue might be the difference in skill level between engineers. A less-experienced engineer may fear working with a more experienced engineer. We have an engineer on our team who is an excellent C++ programmer. Another engineer was afraid that he would slow the C++ genius. You should not overlook this issue.

> Lesson Learned:
>
> 1. Do not force people to pair program if they do not feel like it. Instead, figure out which engineers would make a good pair and take into account the fear that might be the result of different skill levels.

Conclusion

This chapter just tells half the story. We are just beginning to adopt XP methods. I think the best way is to start with just a few practices and prove that they work. If you can prove it, you will convince the other members of your team.

XP is not a silver bullet and refactoring C++ code is not an easy task. However, with good tools, it becomes a little easier and after a while it pays off. It took us several months, but in the meantime I do not hesitate to rewrite code that is at the core of the database access component. I am convinced that we have good test cases in place, which help us reduce the impact of any changes we might want to apply.

Introducing XP practices helped us gain the software quality we needed to finalize our product. Now a patent is pending for the product and deployment is ongoing: We plan to have more than 1,000 installations worldwide. I attribute this success to the introduction of XP practices.

Acknowledgments

I would like to thank Kent Beck for spending his time at EuroPLoP 1999 and in Zurich with me. He showed me the principles of XP.

References

[Beck2000] K. Beck. *Extreme Programming Explained*. Addison-Wesley, 2000.

[Fowler+1999] M. Fowler, K. Beck, J. Brant, W. Opdyke, D. Roberts. *Refactoring: Improving the Design of Existing Code*. Addison-Wesley, 1999.

[Meyers1992] S. Meyers. *Effective C++: 50 Specific Ways to Improve Your Programs and Designs*. Addison-Wesley, 1992.

About the Author

Manfred Lange is a member of the R&D Staff at Hewlett-Packard GmbH, Network Support Lab, and can be reached at Herrenberger Strasse 130, 71034 Boeblingen, Germany; Manfred_Lange@hp.com or Manfred_Lange@acm.org.

Chapter 27

The XP of TAO: Extreme Programming of Large, Open-Source Frameworks

—Michael Kircher and David L. Levine

Everything is in transition, change is the only constant.
—Prof. Val Samonis, University of Toronto

The Adaptive Communication Environment (ACE) and The ACE ORB (TAO) are cutting-edge, real-time software products that by nature support and grow from change. Therefore, Extreme Programming (XP) would seem to be appropriate for these projects. In fact, their developers have been following many XP practices all along. We describe these practices here and identify some that we do not follow rigorously.

However, three characteristics of ACE and TAO contraindicate the application of XP. These products are (1) large, (2) open-source, and (3) development frameworks, that is, not end-user applications. We explore the impediments to XP for such projects and how we have, or would like to, overcome them. In particular, we introduce remote pair programming as a potential augmentation to traditional pair programming.

This work was funded in part by Boeing, NSF grant NCR-9628218, DARPA contract 9701516, Motorola, Nortel, SAIC, Siemens, and Sprint.

Introduction

Many successful large-scale software projects rely on the open-source model [OReilly1998]. The long lifetime and widespread usage of open-source products leads to incremental feature introduction, rapid development cycles, and, above all, change. The most notable feature of open-source projects is a potentially large and fluid development team.

Extreme Programming (XP) is a natural development approach for open-source products in many respects, because it encourages change and supports rapid evolution. However, the large, distributed, and variously committed open-source development team does not effectively support pair programming. In practice, we have found that XP can be successfully applied to a long-term, open-source development project.

This chapter contributes threefold. First, it documents the development process used in the ACE [Schmidt+1994] and TAO [Schmidt+1998] projects. In particular, it considers the interaction of XP and open-source projects. Second, we attempt to motivate other large, open-source, and/or framework development projects to consider XP. We include some suggestions for development process components. Finally, we discuss the current deficiency we see with XP applied to distributed development: that remote pair programming is necessary for large and/or open-source development projects.

The next section of this chapter documents our development process, and compares and contrasts it with XP. Then we discuss how XP can be successfully applied, in particular, to large and/or open-source projects. We introduce remote pair programming and finally conclude with what we have found to be the keys to successful application of XP.

DOC and XP

The Center for Distributed Object Computing (DOC, or DOC group) at Washington University has long practiced XP. We employed many XP practices before they were identified as such. We discuss how in this section. Our purpose here is not to justify whether or not the DOC group practices XP. Rather, it is to show that our project is different in significant ways from the textbook XP organization. In particular, our development team is large and distributed, because our products are open source. Furthermore, our products are frameworks, and therefore not always simple and minimal. Finally, one of our leading products is standard-based, and therefore constrained in its interface.

How Is DOC Extreme?

The following is a checklist [Cunningham+2000] stated by the "The Three Extremos" [Anonymous1999] in the *Portland Pattern Repository* [Cunningham2000]. We compare our research group against it briefly to demonstrate our adaptation of XP.

❖ *Paradigm: Your project is extreme to the degree you see change as the norm, not the exception, and optimize for change.* Open-source framework development is in constant change; the DOC group would not have succeeded with poor support for change. There are many examples in later sections describing this, for example, how changes in the standard API specification trigger change in our products.

❖ *Values: Your project is extreme to the degree that you honor the four values—communication, simplicity, feedback, and courage—in your actions.* We describe our conformance to this in the next section.

❖ *Power sharing: Your project is extreme to the degree that Business makes business decisions and Development makes technical decisions.* Business decisions are made by the director of the group and his or her research staff; development decisions are made by the domain experts of the core development team. On open-source projects, both the constituency of these domain experts and the development team itself can change often. That is one of the strengths of open-source projects, in that it brings many viewpoints into the development. It is also one of the challenges, because there need to be some constraints on the development process. We address that challenge by retaining source code control in the core development team and a few other select individuals.

❖ *Distributed responsibility and authority: Your project is extreme to the degree that people get to make the commitments for which they will be held accountable.* Masters and Ph.D. thesis work supports this idea. The students get to make their commitments and are responsible for achieving them. Because their thesis work is very often tightly integrated with other work in the team, everybody in the team has an interest in their success. This ensures that everybody is motivated to support them if needed; they do not have to struggle if problems occur. People external to the core team helping with work on the open-source project are responsible for their work, but they cannot be held accountable in the traditional way. The system works slightly differently; the motivation to build proper software or to support the product when bugs occur stems from the public contributors list. Nobody wants his or her name associated with something that does not work or that is of obvious bad quality. Considering all this, it can be stated that our way conforms to the XP way.

⋄ *Optimizing process: Your project is extreme to the degree that you are aware of your software development process, you are aware of when it is working and when it isn't, you are experimenting to fix the parts that aren't working, and you consciously enculturate new team members.* In our group we have a continuous process of improvement. Some of our techniques on process monitoring and insourcing are described in the following sections.

The Four Values

Kent Beck states four values that let you decide if you are doing XP right. We restate them here briefly and describe how we apply them to our development.

The four values of XP are communication, simplicity, feedback, and courage. The DOC group supports the four primary values of XP to various degrees.

Communication is very well supported both internally and externally. Within the group, e-mail and impromptu conversations are the primary modes of communication. There are no scheduled meetings, due to the conflicting schedules of group members and success of the informal mechanisms. Externally, e-mail lists are used to communicate bidirectionally with users and contributors. There are currently four e-mail lists, ace-users, tao-users, ace-bugs, and tao-bugs, and two lists that report changes in ACE and TAO bug report status. The e-mail lists are gatewayed to a newsgroup, comp.soft-sys.ace, for convenient access.

The e-mail lists work very well because they support asynchronous communication, they are persistent, and they are searchable. Asynchronous communication is especially important given the wide geographic distribution of contributors, across time zones. Persistence supports the informal use of the lists as a resource for design and implementation issue discussions. Several commercial sites store the list traffic in searchable form, which helps both new and old users and contributors find discussions of interest.

Simplicity has interesting implications for frameworks. The goal of a framework is to simplify application development. However, the framework itself is typically neither simple nor minimal. Because the cost of framework development effort is amortized over many projects, this trade-off of simplicity for functionality and complexity is often acceptable. We discuss the issue of simplicity for frameworks later in this chapter.

The huge (over 600) user community tests ACE and TAO quality and conformance to standards, such as CORBA, on a very short-term basis. New beta kits are created roughly every other week. This keeps the *feedback* loop very tight. Bugs and nonconformance are reported quickly through the previously mentioned communication media.

This feedback has the desired direct benefit to the code base. It has a further benefit in open-source projects: It links users into the development process. Many contributors to open-source projects started as users who fed back defect reports or enhancement requests. Close contact with, and rapid feedback from, developers encourages users to contribute fixes and enhancements.

The DOC group shows *courage* when developing the ACE and TAO frameworks. Due to the changes coming from customers, performance requirements or standards requirements, such as changes in the CORBA spec, main parts of the ORB architecture have seen huge changes. The core development team did not fear applying these huge changes. Examples of where the team showed courage are:

⬥ Reimplementing the TAO real-time event service
⬥ Restructuring the ORB core [Arulanthu+2000a]
⬥ Adding support for pluggable protocols [ORyan2000]
⬥ Large refactorings on the code generation for implied IDL [Arulanthu+2000b]

A good development process supports courage; you can always easily step back from something that proved not to work. Furthermore, a good development process is well defined and documented yet adaptable. We discuss development process aspects in the following section.

XP for Large Open-Source Projects

Applying XP to Open-Source Projects

Open-source development efforts differ from traditional efforts because the distinction between business and development is blurred. Business may expect ambitious product features and development schedules, whereas development has constraints on resources and/or technology. The group that coordinates development often assumes both roles, especially early in the life of the product. The natural tension between these two roles may not be present. Therefore, formalities such as schedules may not be taken seriously or used at all. In addition, the planning game is often one-sided, because development is not directly bound by a design contract.

XP relies on a tight feedback cycle, as does open-source development, though it can be hard to identify users. Lack of user identification breaks the feedback cycle. An effective remedy is to actively encourage and reward feedback, for example, by public acknowledgment in newsgroups and thanks files.

Open-source projects rely on the contributions of (many) developers. Successful, large, open-source projects require many developers at various levels of effort. Over time, as more and more people contribute, the core development group migrates more toward a traditional business role. It serves as a gatekeeper for the source base, identifies desirable new features, assigns priorities, and schedules. One or more of these activities can be performed by third-party organizations, possibly for profit.

Applying XP to Framework Development

XP prescribes simple designs. In particular, software should have the fewest possible classes and methods. Frameworks must support multiple applications and therefore may not be minimal with respect to any one. Although frameworks may (greatly) simplify application code, frameworks themselves can be very complex, not minimal, internally. Therefore, development of frameworks themselves is atypical for XP.

Nonetheless, XP can be used to great benefit in the building of frameworks. Though XP tries to avoid costs for not yet-needed functionality, the cost and effort of developing and maintaining good frameworks can be quite large and must usually be amortized over many application products.

To place framework development in proper perspective, its immediate purpose must be considered. If a framework is being developed for internal use, simplicity dictates that it only provide the necessary functionality for the immediate target application(s). If additional or modified functionality is required later, the framework can be refactored. If a framework is being developed for external use, then it is an end-user product in its own right. The business demands on the product must drive its evolution, whether the product is a stand-alone application, framework, operating system, or any other software artifact.

How Do Standard APIs Relate to XP?

In this section we discuss how XP can be applied to building software that conforms to standard APIs.

The requirement to conform to a standard API, such as CORBA or POSIX, has a two-fold impact on the developers. On the one hand, developers can profit because they do not have to go through the tough job of domain analysis necessary to come up with the API. On the other hand, it can also limit their freedom in implementing the semantics of standard APIs.

As a result, developers can focus largely on internal design/implementation issues, rather than on doing time-consuming and "mushy" upstream activities, such as trying to figure out what the customer requirements are. In such situations, XP and open-source projects are based on the notion of rapid feedback loops and community development, which are really powerful!

Besides the impact on the effectiveness of the developers, standard APIs also have an impact on the metaphor understood in the team. Standard APIs limit the scope the metaphor can come from. There is less of a need to translate domain concepts into software abstractions, such as metaphors; the domain *is* software abstractions.

XP and Design Patterns

Due to the restriction on where metaphors can come from, we needed to search for a replacement. Ideas, concepts, and solutions needed to be communicated. Because every member in our team is very familiar with design patterns, we used them to communicate our ideas. Design patterns were used to describe the internal mechanisms, the "under-the-hood" of the outside standard API. They are the common language based on a concise and documented vocabulary.

Pattern languages can be an excellent replacement for metaphors. They communicate a global view, as the metaphors are intended to do.

Some of the design patterns used in the architecture of TAO are the Reactor [Schmidt1995], used for event dispatching mechanism; the Acceptor and Connector pattern [Schmidt1997], for abstraction of connection management; and the Service Configurator pattern [Jain+1997] for easy and dynamic reconfiguration. At a higher abstraction level, the Broker design pattern [Buschmann+1996] describes the general interaction between clients and servers with their proxies and stubs in between.

Applying XP in a University Research Group

University research groups usually consist of one or more professors, affiliated staff, doctoral students, masters students, students volunteering on research, and visiting researchers. There is no reason to expect that XP cannot be employed in such environments. However, our experience with XP has revealed some interesting insights.

Because masters or doctoral programs take between two and six years, there is a constant fluctuation of people associated with them. New students need to get insourced all the time. Besides this, there are also shorter cycles, like exchange students or visitors who stay anywhere between 2 and 12 months. Intensive mentoring and support from the whole team help insource new students within a very short time. Every member of the team is always open to questions. Ideas get transported via a common language: design patterns. The first activity of a new member is to study the various design patterns relevant to his or her work. Good source code documentation, external documentation, and research papers about former research projects are necessary to get new members quickly up to speed.

So far we have described the insourcing process within the core development team. In the remainder of this section, we describe the insourcing process of the developers external to the core team.

People external to the core development team are usually either employees of companies or research staff and students of other universities working with the open-source products. Most of them start out as simple users but soon report the first bug or enhancement request. After awhile they usually dig deeper and deeper, and get more and more involved. Soon they contribute their first pieces to the open-source product.

A requirement for the success of such distributed development teams is that everybody follow the basic principles of XP.

- *Rapid feedback:* To drive rapid evolution of the system
- *Assume simplicity:* To best allocate programmer resources given the economics of software as options
- *Incremental change:* For overall development efficiency (and sanity)
- *Embracing change:* To preserve options while delivering what is most needed
- *Quality work:* To leverage the natural tendency to take pride in the efforts of an individual and of the team

Besides these, we found some additional principles very useful when communicating with each other.

- *Respect each other:* We found it essential to respect the opinions of others when discussing problems, solutions, designs, and so on. If people would not show respect for each other, some would turn away in distress.
- *Honor the work of others:* When somebody achieved an important milestone, finished a tough job, or just did refactoring to support the next steps in development, others honored the work by letting that person know what a good job he or she did. Such behavior can be a fundamental engine driving people to do a good job the next time as well.

We have seen pair programming in our research group before it was actually made popular by XP. Students discovered pair programming as a fun way to do their research.[1] They want to have as much fun as possible while working, just as they want to create quality work. Solving problems as team of two while having popcorn and cans of soda is just more fun than solving problems alone. Within a short time, students realized that they were faster. Not only that, but they also had fewer

---

1. We have collected some examples in http://cs.wustl.edu/~doc/ACE_wrappers/etc/DOC-way.html

errors in their code and learned from each other. Having snacks during these sessions relaxes and helps developers sustain their enthusiasm for each programming session.

The working environment, the DOC research lab, supports pair programming in an ideal way. At the beginning, this was more of a coincidence than planned beforehand. The room is large enough to accommodate around 10 people and everyone has a reasonably fast machine on his or her desk. Fast compilation machines are centrally available, via remote access. Remote access to compilation machines is very common to our team, due to the many platforms the products have to support. Developers are responsible for unit testing their code on various platforms. Usually these are two or three different platforms, and it is well known which compilers are the most restrictive and/or nonconforming to the programming language (C++, usually) standard.

The Planning Game

The goal of XP planning is to establish a mutually respectful relationship between the customer and the development team. It abstracts two participants, business and development. Applied to the domain of software developed at a university, business means the people funding the work and development is, clearly, the research group itself. Because it is clear that the research group has great interest in getting funding not only for the current projects, but also for future projects the same kind of interests prevail as in every usual software development process. The planning game can be applied the same way to research groups.

Our story cards are stored as Bugzilla [Mozilla1998] entries. The entries can literally be made by anyone with Web access. They might contain customer requests, bug reports, or just ideas for refactorings. Additional information is entered continuously, often to the level of specific tasks necessary to address the request or problem. Every time a change is made to one of the entries an e-mail notification is sent to the involved persons, including the customer if appropriate.

Business (the core DOC group development team) and development (domain experts in the core development team) periodically assign priorities to the entries, thus doing iteration planning. Customers get feedback on the progress of their requests via e-mail notifications of changes to the Bugzilla entries and via issuance (and announcement) of new beta kits.

We found that on-site customers are not strictly needed in our environment. There are three reasons for this:

- *The nature of framework software:* The framework software alone does not provide any value. It needs to be integrated into applications. But this can be done effectively at the customer sites, too, and does not need to be done at the location of the framework development team.
- *Rapid feedback loops:* Rapid feeback makes progress information and results quickly available to customers via mailing the e-mail lists, newsgroup, and beta kits.
- *Close e-mail contact:* E-mail involves the customer directly in discussions about the schedule, supported features, and planned enhancements.

This allows us to profit from customer involvement and immediate feedback without having an on-site customer.

DOC Group Roles

In the DOC group, everybody is a programmer—there is nobody who only does monitoring or supervising. The following list enumerates the rest of the roles and how we fill them.

- *Customer:* The sponsors funding the research work are the customers in our case. They have an interest in getting work done, whereas mostly the scope and time can vary.
- *Tester:* We have a dedicated tester. This is the person who broke the last set of builds before the release of a new beta version. By this rule, everybody—well almost everybody—gets a chance to play the role of a tester. Internally to the group, the tester has a nickname, the Build Czar or Build Master. This comes from the tradition that the one monitoring the automated tests is also responsible for creating the next beta version. Though all team members are responsible for building and testing prior to committing changes, the Build Czar ensures that builds in fact remain clean.
- *Tracker, coach:* The heads of the research group, together with the affiliated staff are the trackers; they watch the schedule and make

sure progress is made to keep customer promises. They also play the role of coaches, making sure the process works as a whole.

- ❖ *Consultant:* Everybody with a great new idea, technique, or technology plays from time to time the role of a consultant by introducing the idea, bringing it to the attention of the group, although the consultant is never named as such.
- ❖ *Big boss:* This role is usually played by the director of our research group. In general, developers make their own decisions. However, when there is uncertainty or lack of agreement, they may request a decision from the big boss.

Code Ownership

In our group we have collective code ownership, as XP does. Generally, everybody fixes anything that does not work or needs to get enhanced. This holds true especially for ACE. Regarding TAO we have some exceptions—here the ownership is more for resource (people) allocation and efficient use of those resources.

In some source code areas only one or two persons make changes. There are two reasons for this. One is that this is their area of research, the other is that it is just more efficient because the person is already familiar with it. Proper documentation can minimize the risk and effort needed when other people are forced to make changes.

Insourcing

In software development some people talk about outsourcing, which is fashionable in big companies nowadays. Kent Beck talks about *insourcing,* the process of getting new people involved in development. For a research group, especially at a university, insourcing is mandatory. Students come, students graduate, there is a continuous fluctuation in the group. There is always somebody new to the group, getting insourced. This process needs to be optimized for a research group to succeed. New members of the group get slowly introduced to the environment; they get their first chances on small work packages, mostly with mentoring from experienced students. Pair programming brings them quickly up to speed. Finally, after some weeks they start programming on the hard stuff, such as the ORB core in the case of TAO, themselves.

Insourcing at the level of open-source development gets even more challenging. It is more rapid and often of shorter term. People sometimes stay only for the term of a product evaluation and/or project. Key prerequisites are proper documentation, including tutorials and source code documentation.

Testing

Developing ACE and TAO, we always have a test handy to verify our actions. In the case of ACE, we have a special use case for the framework in mind, which triggers its extension/refactoring. In the case of TAO, we have test cases telling us when we comply with the CORBA specification.

Our tests use Perl [Wall+1996] scripts. We use Perl because it is available for nearly all platforms that we support. An OS-independent testing tool is essential because there are so many platforms, sometimes with subtle differences. Monitoring the output of a Perl script is not as easy as watching a bar coloring green or red [Gamma+1999], but it is sufficient. We use conventions such as program exit status of 0 for success and 1 for failure to enable automated testing.

Unit tests are written for almost each class in ACE. TAO is completely based on ACE, which assures its high portability. Unit tests in TAO test functionality not already tested in ACE.

Functional tests are provided by the customers and our research group. The customers regularly run their functional tests—in many cases the test is part of their actual application—against the latest beta kit.

Our functional tests demonstrate compliance with the requirements specified by customers. These functional tests are collected in our regression test suite, which gets run periodically, as often as every three hours, and on demand. The suite executes on multiple platforms concurrently, to make sure the developed code is runnable on all platforms. The suite searches output for potential problems and e-mails these to the group.

Refactoring

These days, ACE has pretty much matured; most refactoring is done on TAO. Refactorings are triggered by new versions of the CORBA specification, requests for support of wider areas of the CORBA specification, and performance optimizations—real-time ORBs just cannot be slow.

Focusing on real-time environments, refactorings aim these days at subsetting efforts, meaning things need to get more and more modular. The footprint needs get small enough to fit applications using the

ORB on small devices. One of the most common refactorings is the removal of dependencies to enhance modularity, which helps reduce the footprint. Such refactorings are often not trivial.

Changing interfaces is very problematic for frameworks already in wide usage. Sometimes it might even be reasonable to set up a new framework. Because ACE is in widespread use, major interface changes are unacceptable. However, interface changes are desired to support lighter-weight subsets for embedded systems. Our approach in this instance is to initiate development of a separate product, ACELite, though that is not a commonly applicable solution for framework software.

40-Hour Week

The 40-hour week guideline holds true in every environment, and the DOC group is surely no exception. One thing that might be different is that people tend to be in the lab quite a long time, as many as 60 hours a week, but that does not mean that they are working all these hours. The DOC group lab can be seen not only as a working place, but also as a living place. Students do their homework, e-mail friends, and have discussions, and these are not only about software development.

When people do not follow the guideline and work long hours, perhaps because exams are coming up or a major release is being created, the care and confidence in developing code decreases dramatically. Learning from these experiences, the students gain something for their later working life. It prepares them to be sensitive to working for excessively long periods of time.

XP for Large Projects

XP is intended to be used by small- to medium-sized teams [Beck2000]. However, our experience with ACE and TAO suggests that it could be successfully used on large projects, which we loosely define as involving 20 or more people. In this section, we address the question of whether XP can scale.

Communication is one of the most critical issues for large projects. It is well known [Brooks1995] that communication overhead can dramatically reduce the productivity of a development team. Besides the large size, there is also the distribution aspect of an open-source development team. It is impossible to convene people for meetings. Asynchronous communication media such as e-mail and newsgroups are preferred, because they do not require simultaneous availability. To avoid chaos, some people need to play the role of a moderator; these are mostly the people of the core development team. Timely replies are appreciated by the submitters, and therefore this is an unspoken rule in our communications: Respond as quickly as possible. This encourages further communication and assistance with solving problems or designing enhancements. In addition, due to the asynchrony, question and answer sets might have to bounce multiple times before an issue can be resolved.

Source code control is invaluable for any serious software development project. The DOC group relies on CVS [SourceGear1999], as an example. We find it invaluable for documenting every file change, for maintaining file versions, for concurrent development, and for supporting branches. Another important use of configuration management tools on large projects is bug isolation. Though we have not yet resorted to an automated-defect-isolation approach, such as delta debugging [Zeller1999], we have used simple scripts to isolate specific problems crudely.

Defect tracking is essential for large software development projects. The DOC group uses Bugzilla [Mozilla1998] to track problem reports and enhancement requests. We currently do not require the use of problem reports, for historical reasons (all changes are documented in ChangeLog entries). However, a refined development process might well require a report for every change. Tracking systems support searching and categorization, contributing to a better development process.

The third component of our development process is a clear definition of the process. The core of this process is a set of steps that must (well, should) be followed for every software change. Although this sequence is not necessarily novel, we show it here to provide an indication of the rigor in our process.

1. Make sure every change to ACE and TAO has a bug report. Changes include fixes, enhancements, updates, and so on.
2. Create a bug report.
3. Accept the bug report if you are going to implement the change.
4. Implement the change in your workspace(s).
5. Test the change sufficiently to demonstrate both that it does what is intended and that it doesn't break anything. The test may be as simple as building and running the ACE tests on one platform or as complicated as rebuilding and testing all of ACE and TAO on all platforms that we have.

6. Create an appropriate ChangeLog entry.
7. Commit the change using a `ChangeLogTag` commit message.
8. Respond to the requester of the change, if any. This must be done *after* committing the change.
9. Make sure that the requester is listed in the thanks file.
10. Update the bug report to indicate resolution.
11. Monitor the next round of build or tests for problems with your change.
12. Respond immediately to reports of problems with your changes.

Coding standards are necessary to support rapid familiarization and refactoring [Beck2000]. Above all, standards must emphasize communication. We have found this to be extremely important on large, open-source projects. Consistency between developers is even more important given their sometimes vastly different experience and goals. To encourage new contributors, there must be a low entry barrier to understand existing code. And consistent coding style assists the gatekeepers in evaluating contributed code for inclusion in the product.

A serious software development project must contain a configuration management component. It must provide read and write access to some developers, but read-only access to others. The source database must reside at a well-known location and be accessible via e-mail, the Web, an intranet, and/or other convenient means.

Ideally, the configuration management approach relies on a problem or feature-tracking component to follow up on every change to the product rigorously. To avoid duplication of change documentation, for example, we continue to maintain that in ChangeLogs. Source code control commit messages consist simply of a `ChangeLogTag`, or link to the appropriate ChangeLog entry. We wrote a short Perl script to view the source code control (CVS) commit messages, expanded to include the appropriate ChangeLog entries. In some cases, problem reports contain more detailed or unnecessary information for the ChangeLog. Therefore, ChangeLog entries contain a problem report identifier (Bugzilla Bug ID).

With a large user community, typical for open-source products, structured feedback is essential. When new beta versions are released, users get notified via the aforementioned e-mail lists. Triggered by this, most of them download and build the new version. Integration with their tests and applications then shows whether existing bugs were properly fixed or new bugs were introduced. For several years, we did not impose any structure on the form of bug reports or queries. Necessary information was often missing and therefore required one or more requests for more information from the user. We added a problem report form, which requests data such as host (and target, for embedded systems) platform type, compiler, and phase at which the error occurred. The structured form draws out the necessary information up front. In addition, it is much easier for developers to find what they are looking for rapidly when a bug report is structured.

Problem report forms for XP projects should contain product version identification. As part of the ACE and TAO kitting process, version numbers are automatically inserted into the appropriate forms. This is especially important for XP projects, with their many releases. There is no need to conserve version identifiers; a new one should be assigned to each iteration.[2]

The large user community of an open-source product is invaluable for testing. Bugs are found almost immediately after release. A large, distributed, heterogeneous test organization stresses a system much better than a static regression test suite. Furthermore, the testers often track down and fix the problems, saving both the effort of the core development team and clock time. The user community triggers a continuous introduction of fresh ideas and techniques to the development team. So there is a huge base of coaches, though they coach in a limited way.

Our experience is that XP can scale well. The reliance on metaphor, testing, and self-documenting code contributes to scalability. A streamlined, tool-supported development process is essential to scalability. Even more important are the XP values: communication, simplicity, feedback, and courage—all support the cooperation that is necessary for the success of large development projects.

The one component of strict XP that does not scale is pair programming. We consider a possible augmentation in the following section.

---

2. We use an automated release script to assign a new version identifier, update version information in the product, assign a source control tag, and create the product kit.

Remote Pair Programming

One of the more prominent features of XP is pair programming. Unfortunately, open-source development does not support pair programming for the following reasons:

- *Remote developers:* Many of the participating programmers are physically distributed all over the world. The Internet connects them via e-mail and configuration management.
- *Transient developers:* Often programmers outside the location of the core development team are part of it just for a short time, mostly for the length of a project. The terms during which these transient developers are participating are often too short to profit from pair programming.
- *Developers interested in only a small portion:* Programmers contracted by a company participating in the open-source development can focus only on a small portion of development. They have special constraints regarding the time and effort they can spend developing for everyone. Exchange of information is limited to this part of the solution.

Pair programming profits from the fact that there is not one mind working but two. Two minds develop ideas around the same set of problems, but from a different kind of perspective. Inductive reasoning suggests that more than two minds could be even better. At first one might say yes; remembering Brooks law, one might say usually, maybe, or no. The problem is the communication overhead, which gets bigger and bigger the more people are involved. This is the theory; now come some facts we experienced.

In the following paragraphs, we elaborate why programming environments, such as open-source environments, are successful. Clearly, traditional pair programming does not always work well, as, for example, with distributed development teams. Still, two or more people can successfully work on the same set of problems. The deficiency one notices first is the presumably high overhead in communication. On the one side, from the separation of locations, eye-to-eye communication is just not possible, because of the number of people working on the ideas. It is clear that three people have to communicate more than two. The solution to this is development environments, as for example the design fest theme *Concept*

Development at OOPSLA 99 [OOPSLA1999]. Such environments bring people together from various locations via editors, chat channels, and eventually voice channels to develop concepts, that is, program designs and implementations, as a team. This requires minimal communication overhead. The communication overhead is small due to the asynchrony and common documents. Documents are shared in real time, obviating meetings, that are otherwise necessary for communicating them. People at different locations can work on a problem as if they all were sitting in front of one machine.

Our successful experiences are based on this kind of development, though our environment has not been that complete. Using our configuration management tool and e-mail, we provide almost immediate updates on the common documents, including source code. Developers working together are sometimes only people of the core team, but sometimes also developers from outside, such as people who reported a bug.

Due to asynchrony, of e-mail for example, we experience more decoupling than the traditional pair programming approach. But there are also some limitations to remote pair programming. These are:

✧ *Weaker concentration:* The remote pair programmers are not physically adjacent and therefore likely not as involved in the programming process. If there is sufficient communication delay, pair programming can degrade to code review. Good support can help avoid this degradation to the extent that it can supply the immediate communication offered by pair programming.

✧ *Speed-up:* Pair programming can speed up development, because two people make fewer mistakes and often have a better design in mind than just one. So fewer mistakes reduce the time of debugging. Furthermore, the better design pays off during refactoring, and maintenance in the long term. Can it be shown that open-source development using remote pair programming can further speed up development due to interleaved schedule of the participants working on subsets?

✧ *Learning:* Coaching can be done effectively using pair programming, due to the tight feedback loop between someone new to development in the project and someone experienced. With open-source development, there is naturally no such optimized feedback loop. However, remote pair programming might alleviate this and leverage it to the same position in coaching.

Remote pair programming is a prerequisite to true support of distributed XP. High-speed video, audio, and data transfer, with reasonable but not exceptional quality, seem necessary. We plan to experiment using the TAO AV Streaming Service; its predictability and high performance are ideally suited to the remote pair programming application.

Conclusion

Based on our experiences, we have found XP to be quite suitable for large, open-source framework development projects. We have found that XP can be applied successfully and beneficially to such projects. XP works with projects that can incrementally grow to be large. It works with open-source projects, given their rapid feedback cycles. And it works for framework development, even if the frameworks are not simple.

Successful open-source development with XP is based on:

✧ High-standard coding guidelines combined with a proper gate-keeper process
✧ Tight feedback cycle via active encouragement and reward
✧ Well-maintained user groups with fast responses

Building frameworks with XP, we had good experiences with:

✧ Using design patterns and pattern languages as metaphors
✧ Making the prevalence of standard APIs an advantage, instead of a limitation

University environments additionally need to:

✧ Optimize insourcing
✧ Use pair programming for mentoring
✧ Have collective code ownership

Especially for large projects we found the following two mechanisms valuable:

✧ Asynchronous communication
✧ Easy to follow development process

One practice that we would like to augment is pair programming. Large projects, including ACE and TAO, often involve distributed development. This is especially true with open-source projects, which encourage a very large number of developers. The vast majority of these developers have intimate knowledge of only a small portion of the system and often are directly involved with development for short time periods. Therefore, it is not feasible to practice traditional pair programming. We would also like to explore alternatives, including advocates in the core development team and remote pair programming.

References

[Anonymous1999] Anonymous. "The Three Extremos." *Portland Pattern Repository.* December 8, 1999. On-line at http://www.c2.com/cgi/wiki?TheThreeExtremos.

[Arulanthu+2000a] A. B. Arulanthu, C. O'Ryan, D. C. Schmidt, M. Kircher, J. Parsons. "The Design and Performance of a Scalable ORB Architecture for CORBA Asynchronous Messaging." In *Proceedings of the Middleware 2000 Conference.* ACM/IFIP, April 2000.

[Arulanthu+2000b] A. B. Arulanthu, C. O'Ryan, D. C. Schmidt, M. Kircher. "Applying C++, Patterns, and Components to Develop an IDL Compiler for CORBA AMI Callbacks." *C++ Report.* Volume 12, March 2000.

[Beck2000] K. Beck. *Extreme Programming Explained.* Addison-Wesley, 2000.

[Brooks1995] F. P. Brooks. *The Mythical Man-Month.* Addison-Wesley, 1995.

[Buschmann+1996] F. Buschmann, R. Meunier, H. Rohnert, P. Sommerlad, M. Stal. *Pattern-Oriented Software Architecture: A System of Patterns.* John Wiley & Sons, 1996.

[Cunningham2000] W. Cunningham. "Wiki Web." *Portland Pattern Repository.* July 3, 2000. On-line at http://www.c2.com/cgi/wiki?WelcomeVisitors.

[Cunningham+2000] W. Cunningham, R. Jeffries, M. Fowler, K. Beck. "Are You Doing XP?" *Portland Pattern Repository*. March 28, 2000. On-line at http://www.c2.com/cgi/wiki?AreYouDoingXp.

[Gamma1999] E. Gamma, K. Beck. *JUnit*. On-line at http://www.junit.org. 1999.

[Jain+1997] P. Jain, D. C. Schmidt. "Service Configurator: A Pattern for Dynamic Configuration and Reconfiguration of Communication Services." In *The Third Pattern Languages of Programming Conference, Washington University Technical Report #WUCS-97-07,* February 1997.

[Mozilla1998] The Mozilla Organization. *bugs*. On-line at http://www.mozilla.org/bugs/. 1998.

[OOPSLA1999] OOPSLA 99. *Designfest*. On-line at http://designfest99.instantiated.on.ca. 1999.

[ORyan+2000] C. O'Ryan, F. Kuhns, D. C. Schmidt, O. Othman, and J. Parsons. "The Design and Performance of a Pluggable Protocols Framework for Real-Time Distributed Object Computing Middleware." In *Proceedings of the Middleware 2000 Conference.* ACM/IFIP, April 2000.

[OReilly1998] T. O'Reilly. *The Open-Source Revolution*. Release 1.0. On-line at http://release1.edventure.com/abstracts.cfm?Counter=2095040. November 1998.

[Schmidt+1994] D. C. Schmidt, T. Suda. "An Object-Oriented Framework for Dynamically Configuring Extensible Distributed Communication Systems." *IEE/BCS Distributed Systems Engineering Journal (Special Issue on Configurable Distributed Systems).* Volume 2, December 1994.

[Schmidt1995] D. C. Schmidt. "Reactor: An Object Behavioral Pattern for Concurrent Event Demultiplexing and Event Handler Dispatching." In *Pattern Languages of Program Design*, J. O. Coplien, D. C. Schmidt, eds. Addison-Wesley, 1995.

[Schmidt1997] D. C. Schmidt. "Acceptor and Connector: Design Patterns for Initializing Communication Services," In *Design Pattern*

Languages of Program, R. Martin, F. Buschmann, D. Riehle, eds. Addison-Wesley, 1997.

[Schmidt+1998] D. C. Schmidt, D. L. Levine, S. Mungee. "The Design and Performance of Real-Time Object Request Brokers." *Computer Communications.* Volume 21, April 1998.

[SourceGear1999] SourceGear Corporation. *CVS.* On-line at http://www.sourcegear.com/CVS. 1999.

[Wall+1996] L. Wall, T. Christiansen, R. L. Schwartz. *Programming Perl,* Second edition. O'Reilly, 1996.

[Zeller1999] A. Zeller. "Yesterday, My Program Worked. Today, It Does Not. Why?" In *Software Engineering—ESEC/FSE '99, Lecture Notes in Computer Science.* Volume 1687, Springer-Verlag, September 1999. Also published as *ACM SIGSOFT Software Engineering Notes.* Volume 24, Number 6, November 1999.

Acknowledgments

We would like to thank Frank Buschmann, Lutz Dominick, Jeff Parsons, Christa Schwanninger, and Nanbor Wang for their insightful comments on drafts of this chapter.

About the Authors

Michael Kircher is the Senior Software Engineer at Siemens AG Corporate Technology in Munich, Germany. His main fields of interest include object-oriented distributed and real-time computing, software architectures, design patterns, and Extreme Programming. He can be reached at Michael.Kircher@mchp.siemens.de.

David L. Levine is the Director of Engineering at CombineNet, in Pittsburgh, PA, USA, and former Director of the Distributed Object Computing Group at Washington University in St. Louis, MO, USA. He can be reached at levinedl@acm.org.

Part 7

XP and Beyond

Chapter 28

Learn XP: Host a Boot Camp

—*Christian Wege and Frank Gerhardt*

In the absence of an XP development team some practices of XP are hard to understand. We show how practioners can gain insights into XP in the absence of a real project and the lessons we learned from our approach. This chapter presents the rationale and the contents of an XP workshop and discusses the benefits for the instructors. We found this approach useful for gaining firsthand experience with a simple but working XP process with a medium-sized team.

The Problem

One of the best ways to learn something new is to do it ("Learn by doing"). Now if you want to learn XP you can't just go to your boss and say that you want to set up an XP project. XP is far from being widely accepted in the industry at this time.

On the other hand, if you want to sell an XP project to management you have to know how it works. In this phase, where XP is still in its infancy, there is only a limited amount of empirical material to use to learn from others' experiences, so you have to gain experience first hand.

We faced exactly this problem when we tried to learn XP. Following the principle "do the simplest thing that could possibly work," we tried to find the most readily available and motivated development team available—a group of students.

This chapter outlines our approach to teaching, shows our experiences with a student workshop, summarizes the feedback we got from the participants, and discusses how the workshop helped us understand XP.

Workshop Rationale

Our approach to teaching embodies the four values of XP: communication, simplicity, feedback, and courage [Beck2000]. We discuss the aspects of these values relevant to this workshop in detail.

Communication

If communication is an important value for *doing* XP, then it is even more important for *learning* XP. This observation leads to several insights. Our approach is to organize the course as a compact workshop rather than weekly lecture sessions. This creates a communicative atmosphere for a free exchange of ideas and experiences. That way the course more closely resembles a real XP development process. Also a workshop gives all participants a more active learning experience than other course organizations [Bellin+1997].

Before every major session there should be some time spent supporting communication within the team. Bellin states that "warm-up time is never wasted" [Bellin+1997], but even in a university setting this is hardly ever practiced. Despite our focus on simplicity the students still have to read a lot of information. A visible checklist [Anthony1996] helps a lot. This visual checklist also helps in the regular flash-back session, where the whole group discusses the practices learned in order to prepare for the next steps. This approach is similar to the LDLL pedagogical pattern (lab-discussion-lecture-lab) of the pedagogical patterns project [Manns+1998], which arranges a discussion after every lab so that students can reflect on the lessons learned.

Besides being one aspect of XP, pair programming also has the potential of changing how programming classes are taught in order to benefit the students' learning experience as empirical studies for the collaborative software process (CSP) show [Williams2000a; Williams+2000b]. For the workshop we extend the "pair-pressure" concept to tasks like acceptance test specification, spike solutions, and even teaching (the course is led by two instructors). The primary idea behind changing the pairs often is to support the understanding of collaborative code ownership. Furthermore, changing the pairs supports skill transfer between the students regarding how to use the tools, the platform, and the practices. The less skilled students learn by doing the practices in a team. The skilled students learn how to explain complex concepts and designs.

Simplicity

For a four-day XP workshop, some things had to be left out. It is currently unclear which practices should be used to start XP or which practices should be used to build some kind of lightweight XP process [Diverse1999]. For the practices we propose please refer to the workshop curriculum presented later in this chapter.

In addition to that, teaching the practices in an incremental manner helps students understand the simplified process. Eckstein uses an incremental approach for teaching object-oriented concepts [Eckstein1998], whereas we teach practices. Using simple tools helps keep the learning curve flat. If most of the students are familiar with one specific editor (e.g., Emacs) then use it. A command line compiler may be sufficient (e.g., pure JDK) as well as a simple command line-driven source code management system (like CVS). Try to find the common sense of the students to get them productive as soon as possible.

The project requirements must be simple enough. The students should be able to implement the system within the timeframe of the workshop. Yet the requirements should not be too simple. If the students don't see a challenge in developing the system they will not see the need for working in a team.

Feedback

Regular feedback sessions allow the students to articulate problems after completing a lab session. The instructors have the opportunity to explain areas that were unclear during the lab and prepare the students for more advanced concepts in the next step.

Keeping the cycles short allows the feedback to be effective and gives the instructors the opportunity to adapt the course according to the feedback from the students.

Each lecture introduces new concepts, practices, or tools that are exercised in the subsequent lab. Based on the feedback, the instructors can vary the number of new concepts and the amount of new project requirements. This contrasts to the LDLL pedagogical pattern mentioned earlier, which proposes introducing new concepts in a lab first, supported by well worked-out, step-by-step instructions and then reflecting about the new concepts in the lecture afterward. We use step-by-step instructions giving the students a quick start with the tool environment.

Courage

Perhaps the most challenging issue for the instructors is trying to teach XP without ever having seen it in reality. The instructors try to work through the learning continuum from reading, listening, questions, and answers to a workshop setting as fast as possible [Bellin+1997] with the workshop being the most active form of learning for both the instructors and the students.

Also the selection of the project must be courageous. If the students could develop the project alone on time, they wouldn't see the need for a team process. On the other hand, if the expectations for success were too high, the students wouldn't see that XP really works. Short cycles and regular feedback help minimize this risk.

A challenging schedule puts the students under some pressure. Combined with pair pressure students are motivated at least to some degree [Williams+2000].

Workshop Realization

In July 1999 we held a four-day XP workshop at the University of Tübingen, Germany.

Background of the Students

The 12 students were mainly students of computer science close to graduation. Most of them knew Java and Emacs. Some of the students were at an expert programmer level, whereas others didn't have much practical experience in programming. To help the less-advanced students come up to speed we gave some of them a quick introduction to programming with Java and the tool environment before the actual course started.

Environment

The workshop was run on a pool of Sun workstations. We decided to use Java as the programming language because Java offered us the best chance to find knowledgable students. We thought seriously about using Smalltalk but feared we would not find enough students because the language is hardly known at our university. We used only freely available software.

The whole tool environment was set up up around Emacs. First of all we used the Java Development Environment package for Emacs [JDE] (including an OO browser, a tree view for the package hierarchy, and much more). For version control we used Concurrent Versions System [CVS] and interfaced it with another Emacs package. The JDK version used was 1.2.

The only big drawback of this environment was that we only had a command line debugger available. We used JUnit for implementing unit tests [JUnit].

We used a Wiki to prepare the workshop and to provide information about the tools and links to XP resources [Wiki]. Wiki was also the teams' communication tool for sharing information about the development environment.

Project

Our first approach was to use a toy application, for which we had a detailed object model and which had been developed by one of the instructors some time before the XP workshop. Choosing this project would have made it easier to estimate the amount of work that would be needed for developing the system. In a preplanning session for the workshop the participants complained about using a toy project, so we took a problem from our work for which we wanted to build a prototype anyway.

The application was a typical business application for managing administrative data. The information had to be stored in a central database with fine-grained authorization control. We started talking about a three-tier architecture with a Java client, business logic, and database but had it in mind to change the customer requirements to a thin HMTL client later on to simulate the real-world behavior of customers.

To keep things simple we reduced the problem to a single-user application with a clear architectural layering. We didn't use a database but stored the data through the Java serialization facility.

Curriculum

The main idea behind the curriculum is to iterate between lecture and exercise. The lecture introduces an idea or practice that is executed in the subsequent exercise. The practices are added in a way such that they build on each other. (E.g., first the participants learn how to implement CRC cards, then they learn about coding standards and refactoring before they integrate their code to a common code base.) The curriculum is outlined in Table 28.1.

TABLE 28.1 XP Course Curriculum

Day 1		
Type	**Activity**	**Description**
Exercise	Team-building activity	Serves as the personal introduction of the participants. Make the participants feel like a team (i.e., have everyone introduce him or herself and explain what he or she wants to learn in the workshop.) This includes the instructors as well.
Lecture	Introduction to XP	Give an overview of XP and show the workshop's agenda. Visualize the topics covered in the course (e.g., practices, tools) so that the participants can always see the context of a specific topic.
Lecture	Planning game and presentation of project	Introduce the roles of the customer and developer. We took a problem from our work where we needed a prototype.
Exercise	Planning game	One of the instructors acts as a customer. Find a metaphor, write user stories, estimate developer time, and so on. Assign user stories to pairs.
Lecture	Simple design	Explain how to set up a simple design based on the user stories. "Do the simplest thing that could possibly work."
Exercise	Write CRC cards	Introduce cards. Show a CRC design based on one user story. Each pair designs its user story.
Lecture	Explain development environment	Explain compiler, source code repository, Wiki, Editor, and so on.
Exercise	Quick start	The participants have the chance to get familiar with the environment with prepared examples (HelloWorld, create project in CVS, etc.).

Day 2

Type	Activity	Description
Exercise	Flash-back	Reflect on the previous day and bring the participants together as a team.
Lecture	Coding standards	Stress the importance of coding standards for communication through source code and discuss a simple standard.
Lecture	Unit testing	Explain JUnit and walk through testing a sample of JUnit.
Exercise	Create tests	Create test classes for CRC cards that have to be implemented.
Exercise	Implementation	Implement CRC cards and GUI front ends using the lessons learned up to now.
Lecture	Acceptance tests	Explain tests from the user perspective.
Exercise	Acceptance tests	The participants create acceptance test descriptions based on the planning game and test the integrated application. This is normally done by the users, not the developers.

Day 3

Type	Activity	Description
Exercise	Flash-back, change pairs	Reflect on the previous day. Discuss problems and experiences with the implementation. Discuss the coding standards. Change pairs.
Lecture	Refactoring	Explain refactoring and give some examples. We used Martin Fowler's examples (Fowler+1999).
Exercise	Refactor code	Refactor existing code to meet coding standards.
Lecture	Collective code ownership	Discuss collective code ownership versus explicit responsibilties and the importance of tests for making collective code ownership work.
Lecture	Small releases	Continuous integration makes short release cycles.
Exercise	Integrate code	Integrate the code of the individual teams.

Continued on next page

TABLE 28.1 XP Course Curriculum (*continued*)

	Day 4	
Type	**Activity**	**Description**
Exercise	Flash-back, change pairs	Reflect on the previous day. Discuss problems and experiences with the implementation. Discuss the coding standards. Change pairs.
Exercise	Implementation	Continue implementation from the previous day. This means refactoring existing code and integration with the collective code base.
Lecture	XP explained	Discuss more theory about variables, values, principles, and things that were missing from the workshop compared to a real XP project.
Exercise	Collect experiences	Collect and discuss the experiences of all participants. Find common observations, benefits, and problems.
Exercise	Feedback	Suggestions for the instructors to improve the workshop.
Exercise	Pizza and wine	Free-for-all as a reward for implementing the prototype in record-breaking time.

Results

The Application

The participants created a prototypical application that was operational and fully tested. The front end is cleanly separated from the model classes. Persistence is achieved by using the serialization feature of Java. In a real application this would be replaced by accessing a real database. In the long run the Java front end would be replaced by a thin HTML front end. For the workshop we used no middleware or backend system in order to have a development environment as simple as possible.

The application consists of 35 working classes and 14 test classes with more than 4,000 lines of code.

Experiences

The workshop was successful in terms of our goals and the students' feedback. All of us had our first experiences with XP in a medium-sized team and learned a new way of programming. The workshop demonstrated that the workshop format is appropriate for teaching and understanding XP.

Specifically we found the following.

- The diversity of skills and preferences helped the workshop rather than slowed it down. It is also a typcial situation in real development projects. You need to prepare for this!
- Changing the pairs not only helped communicate the project knowledge but also helped the students learn from each other. We lost our fear of forcing the team members to change pair partners.
- In XP, big systems are built by starting small and growing incrementally. With collective code ownership everyone adds to the existing system. But even for such an incremental process you have to have a core. In our workshop this core was developed by two very skilled students while the others were specifying acceptance tests.
- A simple source control management system enables developers to practice collaborative code ownership—even if they don't have prior experiences with source control management.
- We finished the prototype application despite the fact that some students didn't have too much experience with practical programming. It was a surprise to see how far we could develop the prototype. In the beginning of the workshop many of the participants felt we would never get anything going.
- Using a traditional development methodology the project would probably not have been finished in time.
- The students needed a lot of information in advance to prepare for the workshop. Although we required them to know object-oriented concepts and at least one object-oriented programming language, it took quite some time to set up the tools for everybody and for them to learn how to use them. Next time we would give them reading material beforehand.
- We didn't have a metaphor because we thought it wouldn't add value to the prototype. It would have hindered us in thinking about the problem. In another workshop at the University of Berne with Beck the metaphor was given up after coding had started because it hindered more than it helped.

- The participants would have liked UML diagrams instead of CRC cards because they thought UML would be more expressive.
- As workshop instructors we had the coach and the customer roles at the same time. It was not always easy to make the separation between these two roles visible for the participants. Maybe a real hat would have helped.
- For some participants it was hard to see XP as a discipline.
- We wanted the coding standards to evolve during the development so we didn't present a complete coding style guide. Within the short timeframe of the workshop this probably would have been necessary. However this still leaves the problem of how to make the team accept the standard [Beck2000].

Psychological Aspects

Compared to other workshops at the university, our workshop attracted many students. The participants were very skilled and motivated. About half of them participated in the workshop out of interest rather than needing the workshop's credit points.

In the beginning one pair used a different development environment (Visual J++) than the rest of the group. They intended to check in their code later. It turned out that they held on to their code for a long time. This was very inefficient because it was a huge effort to integrate their code later on. This pair was split and both students were integrated into the team. This observation is a strong indication that XP is a very strict discipline in the sense that all participants have to agree on one common way of working [Beck2000]. This reveals a general problem of XP that all developers have to adapt to the common way. There is not much space for individual preferences that—in our experience—could conflict with some developers' reluctance to adapt to another tool set and process. As a consequence you either have to find a way to integrate those developers into the team or choose the team members appropriately.

Another interesting observation is that you need at least one very skilled student who can push forward the rest of the team (prima donna in wiki-slang). Those students created the inital core system from which the incremental development started and worked on the collective code base to bring it into an operational state. Their code also served as a reference implementation for other developers.

Questions

During the workshop we identified a number of questions we could not resolve. In this respect, as mentioned earlier, the workshop helped us gain a deeper understanding of XP.

- ✧ How can we make the students really share the code and not stick to their own piece of code (without spoiling everybody's mood)?
- ✧ How can we enforce coding the unit tests first, and to prevent untested code from being checked in?
- ✧ Some participants said that we had too many theoretical sessions. How can the theory be explained more compactly and clearly?

Conclusion

We described the rationale behind an XP workshop, described the experiment of doing a workshop, and summed up the results. Specifically we showed that:

- ✧ Hosting an XP boot camp is an excellent way to gain firsthand experiences with an XP development in a medium-sized team.
- ✧ Working in an XP process enabled the students to learn fast and produce excellent results.
- ✧ Instructors of a boot camp like ours need not have practical experience with a real XP development project in advance. Be courageous!

References

[Anthony1996] D. L. G. Anthony. "Patterns for Classroom Education." *Pattern Languages of Program Design 2, Software Patterns Series*, J. M. Vlissides, J. O. Coplien, N. L. Kerth, eds., Addison-Wesley, 1996.

[Beck2000] K. Beck. *Extreme Programming Explained*. Addison-Wesley, 2000.

[Bellin+1997] D. Bellin, S. Simone. *The CRC Card Book*. Addison-Wesley, 1997.

[CVS] Concurrent Versions System. On-line at http://www.cvshome.org.

[Diverse1999] Diverse. *Starting with Extreme Programming*. Discussion about how to start with XP. On-line at http://c2.com/cgi/wiki?StartingWithExtremeProgramming. 1999.

[Eckstein1998] J. Eckstein. Incremental Role Play. Pattern paper for EuroPLoP, 1998.

[Fowler+1999] M. Fowler, K. Beck, J. Brant, W. Opdyke, D. Roberts. *Refactoring: Improving the Design of Existing Code*. Addison-Wesley, 1999.

[JDE] *Java Development Environment for Emacs*. On-line at http://sunsite.auc.dk/jde/.

[JUnit] *JUnit*. Testing Framework for Java. On-line at http://www.junit.org.

[Manns+1998] M. L. Manns, H. Sharp, M. Prieto, P. McLaughlin. "Capturing Successful Practices in OT Education and Training." *JOOP*, March/April 1998.

[Wiki] On-line at http://c2.com/wiki.

[Williams2000a] L. Williams. "The Collaborative Software Process" Ph.D. diss. University of Utah, Salt Lake City, UT, 2000.

[Williams+2000b] L. Williams, R. R. Kessler. "The Effects of 'Pair-Pressure' and 'Pair-Learning' on Software Engineering Education." In *Proceedings of the Conference of Software Engineering, Education, and Training*, 2000.

Acknowledgments

First of all we would like to thank the students who participated in this experiment. Without their interest this experiment wouldn't have been possible. Don Wells gave very valuable input to several versions of this chapter. Thanks to Herbert Klaeren, Wolfgang Rosenstiel, Andreas Speck, and Carsten Schulz-Key for supporting us at the University of Tübingen. Our manager, Wilfried Reimann, gave us time to run this workshop and found a way to sponsor the pizza reward at the end of the workshop.

About the Authors

Christian Wege can be reached at wege@acm.org and Frank Gerhardt can be reached at fg@acm.org.

Chapter 29

Legacy to the Extreme

—Arie van Deursen,
Tobias Kuipers, and Leon Moonen

*We explore the differences between developing a system using
Extreme Programming techniques and maintaining a legacy
system. We investigate whether applying Extreme Programming
techniques to legacy maintenance is useful and feasible.*

Introduction

In this chapter, we explore the relationship between legacy systems and
Extreme Programming. We explain how the use of (reverse engineering) tools can help reduce the cost of change in a legacy setting and
illustrate the use of these tools. Subsequently, we discuss how and
which XP practices can be incorporated into the maintenance of legacy
software systems, and we analyze how and why the positive effects for
regular and legacy XP projects are different. We conclude with an episode in which a pair of XP programmers face the task of changing hostile COBOL code (examples included) and are able to do so thanks to
their tools and bag of XP practices.

One of the key elements of Extreme Programming (XP) is *design for
today*, so that the system is equally prepared to *go any direction tomorrow*.
As Beck argues, one of the reasons XP gets away with this minimalist
approach is because it exploits the advances in software engineering technology, such as relational databases, modular programming, and information hiding, all of which help reduce the cost of changing software

[Beck2000]. The result of this is that the software developer does not need to worry about future changes: The change-cost curve is no longer exponential, but linear. Making changes easily is further supported by XP in various ways:

⬥ Releases are small and frequent, keeping changes small as well.
⬥ The code gets refactored for every release, keeping it concise and adaptable.
⬥ Testing is at the heart of XP, ensuring that refactored code behaves as it should.

The assumption that the system under construction is easily modifiable rules out an overwhelming amount of existing software: the so-called *legacy systems*, which by definition *resist change* [Brodie+1995]. Such systems are written using technology such as COBOL, IMS, or PL/I, which does not permit easy modification. (As an example, we have encountered a 130,000-line COBOL system containing 13,000 GO-TO statements.) Moreover, its internal structure has degraded after repeated maintenance, resulting in systems consisting of duplicated (but slightly modified) code, dead code, support for obsolete features, and so on. The extreme solution that comes to mind is to throw such systems away—unfortunately, it takes time to construct the new system, during which the legacy system will have to be maintained and modified.

Now what if an Extreme Programmer were to maintain such a legacy system? (Which probably means he or she was either forced to do so or seduced by an extreme salary.) Should that programmer drop all XP practices because the legacy system resists change? We try to demonstrate in this chapter why this is not necessary. The programmer could write test cases for the programs to be modified, run the tests before modification, refactor the code after modification, argue for small releases, ask for end-user stories, and so on—practices that are all at the heart of XP.

Tools Make It Possible

Refactoring legacy source code is, in principle, no different from refactoring regular source code. Refactoring is done to improve the code, but improving can mean many things. Modifications can be made to improve adaptability, readability, testability, or efficiency. There are some things particular to refactoring legacy code. In order to make sure that a refactoring does not alter the functionality of the system, unit tests are run before and after the refactoring. In a legacy setting there are no unit tests beforehand, so they need to be written specifically for the refactoring.

Refactoring also requires the developers to have a great deal of detailed knowledge about the system. A good example of this is the modification of the transaction interface as described by Beck [Beck2000]. This knowledge can come from someone who knows the system intimately or can be provided by tools that allow a developer to get to these details quickly and accurately.

Modern development systems in general provide those details. They provide all sorts of development time and runtime information that allows hunches to be verified within seconds. Most legacy maintenance (and development) is done on a mainframe, however, and the mix of JCL, COBOL, and others has to be controlled without advanced development tools. Usually, even basic search tools such as *grep* are not available. The development team manages to get by, only because part of the team has been working on the system for years (ever since that mainframe was carried into the building). New team members are introduced to the system on a need-to-know basis.

More and more often, these systems get *outsourced* (the development team is sold off to another company, and the maintenance of the system is then hired from this new company). After such an outsourcing the original development/maintenance team usually falls apart, knowledge of the system is lost, and it is still running on that same mainframe, without grep.

Consequently, maintenance on these systems will be of the breakdown variety. Only when things get really bad will someone don a survival suit and venture inside the source code of the system, hoping to fix the worst of the problems. This is the state most administrative systems in the world are in [Belady+1976; Brodie+1995].

The Legacy Maintenance Toolbox

We have been developing a tool set over the last few years that integrates a number of results from the areas of reverse engineering and compiler construction. The tool set is called the Legacy Maintenance Toolbox (LMT). It consists of a number of loosely coupled components. One of the components is DocGen [Deursen+1999a], (so called because of its basic ability to generate documentation from the source code). DocGen generates interactive, hyperlinked documentation about legacy systems. The documentation is interactive in that it combines various views of the system and different hierarchies, and combines those with a code browser. (See Figure 29.1 for an example session.) DocGen shows call graphs both for the whole system and per program. It shows database access and can visualize data dependencies between different programs. We try to provide the programmer with as much information as we can possibly get from the source. (One of the problems is that the source may be written in a vendor-specific dialect of a more conventional language, of which no definition is published.)

We augment the basic DocGen code browsing facility with Type-Explorer [Deursen+1999c], a system that infers types for variables in an

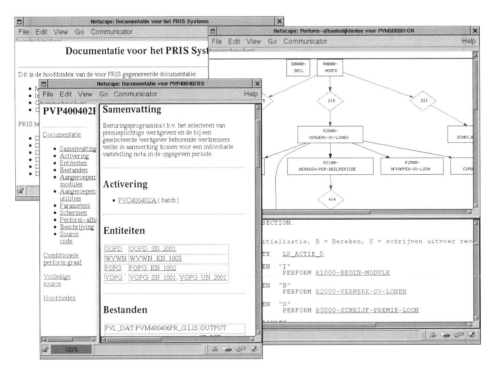

FIGURE 29.1 An example of a DocGen session

untyped language (typically COBOL) and lets the programmer browse the code using those types. TypeExplorer can be used, for instance, to aid in impact-analysis sessions. When the requirements of a financial system change from "make sure all amounts are British pounds" to "make sure all amounts are Euros," this will inevitably have an impact on all data (both variables in the code and data in databases) that are of type "amount." Because TypeExplorer can come up with a list of all variables that are in the same type equivalence class, the programmer only has to identify a single variable that deals with amounts to identify all variables in the same type equivalence class (and therefore also dealing with amounts).

The combination of DocGen and TypeExplorer proves to be a powerful tool for gaining insight into the details of a system. DocGen and TypeExplorer get their information from a repository, which is filled by a combination of parsing (if we have a grammar for the legacy system's language) and lexical analysis. This repository can also be queried directly, using standard SQL queries.

One of the key properties of LMT is that it is open: External tools can be easily integrated. An example tool is CloneDr, from Semantic Designs, which detects (near) clones (or "copy-paste code") in sources and removes them (for instance by replacing them with a single procedure and a number of calls to that procedure) [Baxter+1998]. Code clone removal can be seen as an automated refactoring operation that adheres to the XP principle "say it once and only once." Apart from the obvious benefit of reducing the amount of code to be understood, a less-expected benefit comes from having to give a name to the newly created procedure. This obviously is a human activity and helps focus the thoughts of a maintainer on a particular piece of code, which, since it was duplicated in the original program, must be of some relevance.

Newer (less developed) components of LMT are concept analysis, which aids in the remodularization of legacy systems [Deursen+1999b; Kuipers+2000], and data flow analysis, which aids in tracking data through the system [Moonen1997].

Using LMT, maintenance programmers can learn about the legacy system. They gain confidence about their knowledge by verifying that, for instance, a database table is only written to and never read from, and therefore can be removed. They can see that two variables do not occur in the same type equivalence class, so values of the first variable never get passed to the second, and so on. As they use LMT initially to hunt down specific problems, they automatically increase their knowledge of the system, much like they would have when they were brought in during the development of the system.

More Tools

LMT is the result of research in the area of reverse engineering and program understanding, and builds on related work in those areas (see [Deursen+1999b; Deursen+1999c] for a detailed overview of this related work). Two tools that are similar in nature to LMT are Rigi [Wong+1995] and PBS [Bowman+1999], which also can extract various pieces of data from the sources and which can present them in various ways. Rigi and PBS have been used more for C than for COBOL, which involves significant differences (for example, the lack of types and a parameter mechanism in COBOL, and the data-intensive nature of typical COBOL systems). On the commercial side, related COBOL tools are Viasoft's Existing Systems Workbench, Reasoning's InstantQA tools, and McCabe's testing and understanding tools. These tools tend to be closed, making it not only difficult to integrate them with other tools but also to deal with customer or application-specific issues (think of dialects, coding conventions, I/O utilities, and so on), which occur very frequently in COBOL applications. Outside the COBOL arena are various tools to analyze C, C++, or Java code, such as TakeFive's Sniff+ tools.

Adopting XP Step by Step

Adopting the XP approach in a legacy setting can only mean one thing: Aim at simplicity. How does this affect us when we decide to introduce XP in an existing legacy maintenance project?

First of all, we have to get a picture of the existing code base. This means that we generate on-line, hyperlinked documentation, using the DocGen technology discussed in the previous section. This allows us to browse through the legacy system and to ask queries about the usage of programs, copybooks (the COBOL variant of an included source file), databases, and so on. Moreover, this documentation can be regenerated after any modification, thus ensuring that it is up-to-date and consistent.

Next, we have to get into contact with the end user. We need to collect end-user stories for modification requests. Given the current state of the system, such modification requests are likely to include technical requests as well, such as increasing the stability of the system.

Then we have to divide the modification stories into small iterations. For each modification, we identify the affected code and estimate the effort needed to implement the request. Observe that such an impact analysis can only be done with some understanding of the code, which is provided by the TypeExplorer technology presented in the previous section. As in regular XP, the effort estimates are made by the developers, whereas the prioritization (which story comes first) is done by the end user.

We then start working iteration by iteration. Each iteration goes through a series of steps:

1. We write test cases for the code that is to be affected by the change request and run the tests.

2. We refactor the affected code so that we can work with it, using the reverse engineering tools described earlier. This means removing extreme ugliness, duplicated functionality, unnecessary data, and copy-paste clones, standardizing the layout, and so on. We then rerun the test cases just constructed, in order to make sure that no damage has been done during refactoring.

3. After that, the code is in such a shape that we feel sufficiently confident that we can modify it. If necessary, we adapt the test cases to reflect the modified features, implement the modification request, and rerun the test cases.

4. Finally we refactor again, retest, and regenerate the system documentation.

For XP programmers these steps will sound extremely familiar. So what are the differences between this and regular XP?

First of all, the productivity per iteration is lower than in regular XP. This is because (1) there are no test cases, which will have to be added for each refactoring and modification; (2) the code has not been previously refactored; and (3) the programming technology used is inherently more static than, for example, Smalltalk.

Second, the code base itself is not in its simplest state. This means that program understanding, which constitutes the largest part of actually changing a program, will take much more time. Luckily, XP programmers work in pairs, so that they can help each other in interpreting the code and the results from invoking their tool set. The code not being in its simplest state also means that while studying code (during impact analysis, for example), the pair is likely to identify many potential ways of refactoring, for example when encountering duplicated code.

One might consider doing a one-shot, up-front refactoring of the entire legacy system to avoid such problems. However, successful refactoring is not an automatic process but requires human intervention. Moreover, there are no test cases available a priori. Last but not least, a total refactoring may be unnecessary anyway if parts of the system do not need modification or are likely to be removed (simplicity requires us not to worry about things we are not going to need).

Another observation is that in normal XP the positive effects of refactoring are accumulated, keeping the system flexible at all times. When XP is applied to a legacy system, only the parts of the system that need modification get refactored. The accumulated effect of this is much lower than in regular XP.

A final question to ask is whether the scenario sketched is realistic. If it is so good, why has it not been done before? Reasons may include a lack of awareness of XP opportunities, fear of the overwhelming amount of legacy code leading to paralysis, confusion with the expensive and unrealistic one-shot refactoring approach, or a plain refusal to invest in building test cases or refactoring. The most important reason, however, is that it is only during the last few years that reverse engineering technology has become sufficiently mature to support the XP approach sketched here. Such technology is needed to assist in the understanding needed during planning and modification, and to improve existing code just before and after implementing the modification.

XP on Legacy Code

So how would all of this benefit a bunch of maintenance programmers facing a mountain of COBOL code? We will try to answer that question by describing a concrete, step-by-step maintenance operation. The example is from the invoicing system of a large administrative system (from the banking/insurance world). All code used in this example is real. We have changed it slightly to camouflage actual amounts and account numbers.

But first, some culture. In the Netherlands, bill paying is largely automated: Companies send out standardized, optically readable forms called "accept-giro" (see Figure 29.2 for an example). Normally, all informa-

FIGURE 29.2 An example accept-giro

tion, including the customer's account number, the company's account number, and the amount to be paid, is preprinted on these accept-giros, and all the customer has to do is sign them and send them back to accept the mentioned amount being charged off the account. These forms then are read automatically by a central computer operated by all associated Dutch banks, and the appropriate amount is transfered from one account to the next, even between different banks.

The task at hand for the programmers is that a company has changed banks or account numbers, and all invoices printed from next month should reflect that. That is, all bills should be paid to our new account number.

Once the team understands the task, it starts to work. First it needs to find out what file is being printed on the blank forms. It knows that its system only creates files and that these files are then dumped to a specialized high-volume printer somewhere. After asking around and looking at the print job descriptions, the programmers discover that all data for the invoices is in a file called INVOP01. Because INVOP01 is the end product of this particular task, the team runs the system on its test data and keeps a copy of the resulting INVOP01 file. Now the developers know that when they are finished with the task, the INVOP01 file they generate should be the same as the current INVOP01, apart from the account number. The INVOP01 on the test data can be seen in Figure 29.3.

```
xxxx yyyy
zzzz wwww                         100 00          xxxx yyyy zzzz wwww

100 00


                            TESTNAME T
                            TESTST 12
                            9999 XX TESTCITY


555.12.12                   555.12.12
LARGE                       LARGE CORP.
CORP.                       AMSTERDAM



X                    xxxxyyyyzzzzwwww+        10000x+5551212+37>
```

FIGURE 29.3 An example accept-giro

Because it has the system analysis tools described previously, the team can now check what programs do something with the INVOP01 print file. Figure 29.4 shows all facts that have been derived for INVOP01.

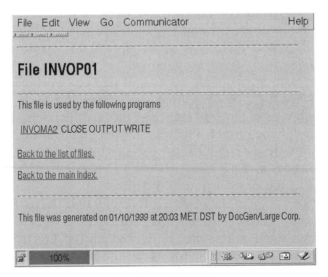

FIGURE 29.4 All facts derived for file INVOP01

```
    05 P009-BEDRAG-CONTR PIC 9.
    05                  PIC X     VALUE "+".
    05                  PIC X(10) VALUE SPACE.
    05 P009-CONSTANTEN.
*      07               PIC 9(8)  VALUE 8765432.
*      07               PIC X     VALUE "+".
*   05                 PIC X(4)  VALUE " 37>".
       07               PIC 9(09) VALUE 5551212.
    05                  PIC X(4)  VALUE "+37>".
```

FIGURE 29.5 Code found by searching for 5551212

It turns out that the only program operating on INVOP01 is
INVOMA2. The information derived from INVOMA2 shows that this
program only uses one input file: INVOI01. Executing the system on the
test data reveals that INVOI01 does not contain account numbers—it
contains the names and addresses of customers. If the account number is
not read from file, and INVOMA2 does not access any databases, then
the account number should be in the code! The team does a search on
the string 5551212 in the code, and they find the code as shown in Figure 29.5. (Note an even older account number commented out in the
three lines starting with an asterisk.) They change the account number to
1212555 (the new account number) and run the system using the test
data. Much to their surprise, the test version of INVOP01 comes out as
shown in Figure 29.6.

```
xxxx yyyy
zzzz wwww                        100 00        xxxx yyyy zzzz wwww

100 00

                       TESTNAME T
                       TESTST 12
                       9999 XX TESTCITY

555.12.12              555.12.12
LARGE                  LARGE CORP.
CORP.                  AMSTERDAM


X                      xxxxyyyyzzzzwwww+        10000x+1212555+37>
```

FIGURE 29.6 Test version of INVOP01 after modification

```
03  P008A.
    05              PIC X(19) VALUE SPACE.
    05              PIC X(09) VALUE "555.12.12".
03  P008B.
    05              PIC X(09) VALUE "555.12.12".
    05              PIC X(07) VALUE SPACE.
    05              PIC X(11)
                    VALUE "LARGE CORP.".
```

FIGURE 29.7 Code found by searching for 555.12.12

The last line of the test file shows the correct account number, together with the +37> that is also visible in the code. This is the part of the form that will be read optically. However, the part of the form that is meant for humans still shows the old account number. The team looks at each other, shakes their heads, and does a search on 555.12.12 in the source code. What shows up is in Figure 29.7.

They change the two account numbers and run the test again. Now everything comes out as expected. They write a to-do item that this part of the code needs urgent refactoring, or maybe they immediately implement a procedure that formats account numbers. They dream of the day the system can be left to die and they can spend their time on an XP reimplementation of the whole system.

Conclusions

In this chapter we have looked at Extreme Programming from the viewpoint of legacy systems. We observed that the programming environment used for regular XP projects provides capabilities not available for most mainframe-based legacy systems. At the same time we described progress in the area of reverse engineering tools that can be used to overcome these limitations. We used these findings to come up with a way to adopt XP practices during legacy system software maintenance.

References

[Baxter+1998] I. D. Baxter, A. Yahin, L. Moura, M. Sant'Anna, L. Bier. "Clone Detection Using Abstract Syntax Trees. In *International Conference on Software Maintenance, ICSM'98*. IEEE Computer Society Press, 1998.

[Beck2000] K. Beck. *Extreme Programming Explained*. Addison-Wesley, 2000.

[Belady+1996] L. A. Belady, M. M. Lehman. "A Model of Large Program Development. *IBM Systems Journal*. Volume 15, Number 3, 1976.

[Bowman+1999] I. T. Bowman, R. C. Holt, N. V. Brewster. "Linux as a Case Study: Its Extracted Software Architecture." In *Twenty-first International Conference on Software Engineering, ICSE-99*. ACM, 1999.

[Brodie+1995] M. L. Brodie, M. Stonebraker. *Migrating Legacy Systems: Gateways, Interfaces and the Incremental Approach*. Morgan Kaufman, 1995.

[Deursen+1999a] A. van Deursen, T. Kuipers. "Building Documentation Generators." In *International Conference on Software Maintenance, ICSM'99*. IEEE Computer Society, 1999.

[Deursen+1999b] A. van Deursen, T. Kuipers. "Identifying Objects Using Cluster and Concept Analysis." In *Twenty-first International Conference on Software Engineering, ICSE-99*. ACM, 1999.

[Deursen+1999c] A. van Deursen, L. Moonen. "Understanding COBOL Systems Using Types." In *Proceedings of Seventh International Workshop on Program Comprehension, IWPC'99*. IEEE Computer Society, 1999.

[Kuipers+2000] T. Kuipers, L. Moonen. "Types and Concept Analysis for Legacy Systems." In *Proceedings of the International Workshop on Programming Comprehension (IWPC 2000)*. IEEE Computer Society, 2000.

[Moonen1997] L. Moonen. "A Generic Architecture for Data Flow Analysis to Support Reverse Engineering." In *Theory and Practice of Algebraic Specifications; ASF+SDF'97. Electronic Workshops in Computing*, A. Sellink, ed. Springer-Verlag, 1997.

[Wong+1995] K. Wong, S. R. Tilley, H. A. Müller, M.-A. D. Storey. "Structural Redocumentation: A Case Study." *IEEE Software*. Volume 12, Number 1, 1995.

About the Authors

Arie van Deursen, Tobias Kuipers and Leon Moonen are co-founders of the Software Improvement Group, an Amsterdam-based company that specializes in helping customers solve their legacy problems. Arie van Deursen and Leon Moonen work for CWI, the National Research Institute for Mathematics and Computer Science in the Netherlands. Tobias Kuipers is employed by the Software Improvement Group. The authors can be reached via e-mail at arie@cwi.nl, tobias@acm.org and leon@cwi.nl and via postal mail at CWI, P.O. Box 94079, 1090 GB Amsterdam, The Netherlands. They maintain Web presence at http://www.cwi.nl/~arie/, http://www.software-improvers.com/, and http://www.cwi.nl/~leon/.

Chapter 30

The Design Is in the Code: Enhanced Reuse Techniques in C++

—*Andrei Alexandrescu*

Extreme Programming emphasizes the coding activity in all its aspects. It would be useful, then, if new coding techniques could render the code higher level, more compact, more reusable, and easier to change. This chapter describes policy classes in C++, a new approach that combines generic programming and object-oriented techniques. The goal is to make it easier to express and convey design entities directly in code. Using policy classes, library writers can make it possible to achieve the "write once and only once" goal by providing high-level, powerful, extensible libraries. Leveraging design patterns [Gamma+1995] and language-specific idioms as recipes for successful solutions, generic libraries using policy classes truly democratize good designs. The example used throughout this chapter is defining a truly generic, flexible, portable smart pointer—a popular C++ idiom and an incarnation of the Proxy design pattern [Gamma+1995].

Introduction

Extreme Programming puts a significant emphasis on coding. XP includes pair programming and continuous refactoring as essential components of the development process. In old fashioned processes, design modifications are the exception; in XP, change (refactoring) is the rule. New code structures, then, should make it easy for the programmer to introduce significant changes to a design. These coding structures should be high level, concise, expressive, easy to understand, and easy to change.

Traditionally, coding is seen as the process that takes a design to its ultimate detail. For this reason, sometimes the ideas underlying a piece of code, like a design pattern [Gamma+1995], get lost in the avalanche of details, context-related idiosyncrasies, and tweaks that the code has to provide to ensure proper functionality. There is an explanation for each line of code, but as a whole, the code blurs the design. Usually, developers help themselves with comments: "This class implements an observer for objects of type `Widget`, which generate synchronous events of type `WidgetChanged`" or "Class `App` is a singleton that supports multi-threaded access." Short of analyzing the code of `App`, there is no simple way to figure out whether `App` is a multithreaded singleton or not, and, for that matter, whether it is correctly and efficiently implemented. Seasoned designers know what a multithreaded singleton is; the problem is that this information resides in a chunk of code that must be dug out, instead of in a clear, declarative statement. Also consider the innumerable ways in which the singleton object can be initialized. Moreover, specialized techniques and recipes, like making a singleton thread-safe [Schmidt+1998] have limited portability. All these issues effectively limit one's ability to define a truly portable library that provides typical pattern implementations, thus missing an important reuse opportunity.

Switching between two well-known variants of a design pattern is a nontrivial process, because pattern variants don't map to code in a straightforward manner. For instance, changing the identifier type in a parameterized factory method [Gamma+1995] incurs cascading changes to the code and the data structures in the implementation space. This means that changes that are very simple and natural at the design level become unacceptably clumsy at the coding level. Design and code evolve separately, and since the code dictates the actual behavior, usually the design is doomed to obsolescence. Hence the ironic adage, "The code is the design."

Certain generic programming techniques, presented here and treated at length in Czarnecki [Alexandrescu2001; Czarnecki+2000], render coding with design patterns and advanced C++ idioms simpler and change more affordable. They make it possible to express some common design patterns and idioms in as little as a couple of clear declarative statements. If the default behavior is not satisfactory, a programmer doesn't have to restart from scratch but can override the defaults to support an open-bounded range of behaviors.

These techniques map design much more directly to code, transforming the adage into the more desirable "The design is *in* the code."

The Multiplicity of Design

Much of the difficulty in implementing a software system lies in choosing among various competing solutions for each architectural issue, at all levels. The solutions are similar in the sense that they all ultimately solve (or promise to solve) the problem at hand. Yet they sport different costs and trade-offs, and have distinct sets of advantages and disadvantages. In turn, each solution might have a large number of variants, and this multiplicity manifests itself at all levels of a design problem, from highest to lowest.

Design patterns come with a systematic way of discovering and documenting sound design solutions. Idioms do practically the same in the narrower context of a specific programming language. However, programmers, although they might use these higher-level structures, must implement them in most cases starting from first principles.

This problem exists because of the combinatorial nature of design. A design is a deliberate choice of a set of trade-offs, out of a combinatorial space. For instance, a singleton object can be single-threaded or multithreaded; allocated statically, on the free store, or in some implementation-specific memory space; and constructed with various numbers and types of parameters. All these features can be combined freely. In the presence of such open-ended options, it is hard to provide a library singleton that's not too rigid. A flexible implementation should leave the user full freedom to tweak any of its aspects, in addition to providing a good set of defaults.

For implementing design structures and for working with design patterns, a library should help in the following ways:

⋄ Cope with the combinatorial nature of design with a reasonably small code base
⋄ Allow the user to combine trade-offs and design decisions in any ways that make sense

- ✧ Validate the chosen set of trade-offs at compile time
- ✧ Make the resulting code reasonably efficient
- ✧ Do not incur a penalty in space or runtime for options that are not used
- ✧ Make the resulting implementation small, terse, and easy to explain to peers
- ✧ Make it easy to change the design options after the fact

No built-in feature or idiom of traditional procedural, functional, or object-oriented programming supports these requirements.

Procedural programming combines behaviors by using pointers to functions. Functional programming uses function objects. Object-oriented programs use inheritance and containment in various forms.

Each of these forms of coping with combinatorial behaviors has its own advantages and disadvantages. They all share the disadvantage of postponing to runtime things that should be performed at compile time. Most design decisions—like the threading model of a class—are immutable at runtime. Unnecessary dynamism wastes essential checking and optimization opportunities.

Generic programming techniques, implemented herein with C++ templates, can provide combinatorial behaviors with a linear amount of code. The mixing and matching is checked at compile time. In addition, possible behaviors are open-ended, thus reducing the need to start a design implementation from scratch whenever a special circumstance occurs.

Template Parameters as Design Constraints

Originally, parameterized types were introduced in C++ to allow creation of generic type-safe containers. Needs such as creating fixed generic arrays led to the addition of nontype (integral and address) template parameters. Over time, to accommodate more and more powerful generic programming idioms, the template engine of the compiler evolved into an intricate pattern-matching engine, combined with the integral arithmetic calculator that was already available.

Templates work at a metalinguistic level; they form a little metalanguage on top of the rest of C++. Template code can be seen as guidelines to the compiler to generate actual code. The generated code is in non-templated C++. This viewpoint leads to the idea that templates can be used to help various tasks that belong to the realm of compile time, like design itself.

The elements controlling code generation are template parameters. Each template parameter is one degree of freedom on which generated code can vary. By fixing one of those parameters, you fix a dimension of variability, while the others can still control code generation on other dimensions. A description of this fertile view of templates can be found in Coplien [Coplien1999].

Link this concept with perusing a design pattern that offers many design choices. Combined, the choices lead to a plethora of variants, making traditional reusable design impractical, complicated, and hard to optimize. However, if design choices are mapped to the template parameters of a template class, we can achieve combinatorial effect with a linear amount of well-chosen primitives. The compiler generates and combines the appropriate primitives as requested at template instantiation time and ignores the unused ones. The following C++ idiom helps build flexible libraries of typical design implementations.

Policy Classes

Policy classes are implementations of elemental design choices. They are not intended for stand-alone use; instead, they are inherited from, or contained within, other classes. A policy class defines a C++-specific interface. The interface consists of inner type definitions, member functions, and possibly member data definitions. In this respect, policy classes resemble traits classes [Alexandreseu2000]. Unlike most traits classes, policy classes can be either templated or not templated. They also are typically more behavior-rich than traits classes.

A policy class not only defines an interface; it also implements that interface. This sets an important distinction between policy classes and interfaces, without putting them in competition. Interfaces are a communication device; policy classes are an implementation device. In particular, a policy class can implement an interface. For example, each of the following three policy classes implements a locking policy that corresponds to a specific threading model. Each locking policy class defines an inner type called Lock. The policy states that for the duration of a Lock object, operations on its host policy object are guaranteed to be atomic. This defines a simple, yet lucrative, threading model.

```
template <class T>
class SingleThreaded
{
public:
    class Lock
    {
    public:
        Lock(SingleThreaded&) {}
    };
};


template <class T>
class ClassLevelLockable
{
public:
    class Lock
    {
    public:
        Lock(ClassLevelLockable&) { mutex_.Acquire(); }
        ~Lock() { mutex_.Release(); }
    };
private:
    static Mutex mutex_;
};


template <class T>
class ObjectLevelLockable
{
public:
    class Lock
    {
    public:
        Lock(ObjectLevelLockable& obj) : m_(obj.mutex_)
        { m_.Acquire(); }
        ~Lock() { m_.Release(); }
    private:
        Mutex& m_;
    };
private:
    Mutex mutex_;
    friend class Lock;
};
```

The three policy classes defined here provide different threading models under the same interface. A class that wants to take advantage of locking inherits one of the policies. The actual policy class chosen depends on what kind of locking is needed, as shown:

```
template <class Pointee>
class SmartPtr : public ClassLevelLockable<SmartPtr>
{
    ...
    SmartPtr& operator=(const SmartPtr& other)
    {
        Lock guard(other);
        ... perform operation ...
    }
private:
    Pointee* pointee_;
};
```

The question arises then, regarding what advantage ClassLevelLockable gives us. For one thing, the parameter passed to Lock's constructor is unused, and SmartPtr could have used a static Mutex directly—a standard, easy-to-understand locking strategy. However, if SmartPtr used a locking strategy directly, changing that strategy would have incurred changes to several SmartPtr member functions. The quality of locking (for instance, correctly pairing the Acquire/Release calls in the presence of early returns and exceptions) would have depended largely on SmartPtr's implementer. Moreover, to figure out the actual locking strategy used, a reviewer must analyze the SmartPtr implementation.

The approach using a locking policy class has important advantages in flexibility and clarity: The locking strategy of SmartPtr can be figured simply by looking at the SmartPtr base class list. All locking strategies have the same interface, which means that you can later change the locking model only by changing SmartPtr's base class and recompiling SmartPtr. The three locking policies are highly reusable classes that distill the threading aspect in defining a class without interfering with other aspects. Therefore, locking policies can be carefully implemented, documented, and put in a library.

Compilers commonly optimize out unused arguments and empty base classes, leading to a SmartPtr implementation that's as efficient as a handcrafted one. However, in the setting shown previously, the user cannot use a single-threaded `SmartPtr` and a multithreaded one in the same application. If at least one `SmartPtr` is multithreaded, all `SmartPtr` instantiations will pay the locking price. To solve this problem, we must make the locking policy a template parameter of `SmartPtr`.

```
template <class Pointee,
    class LockingPolicy>
class SmartPtr : public LockingPolicy
{
    ...
};
```

The required interface of a locking policy is an inner class `Lock`. The semantics of `Lock` is that it makes operations on an object atomic for the lifetime of a `Lock` object. Any conforming implementation of the locking policy can be plugged in `SmartPtr`.

Policy Classes with Generic Behavior

The threading policy class defined here has semantics independent of the `SmartPtr` or pointee type. In general, however, policy classes have generic behavior. For instance, imagine defining a null checking policy for our `SmartPtr`. Depending on the speed and the safety needed by the application, smart pointers might sport various checking levels. A fast `SmartPtr` might implement no checking at all, whereas in some applications a null check before each dereference is desirable.

A possible interface for a null checking policy class would consist of a unique function, `Check`. Because `Check` might need the type and the value of the pointee object, the null checking policy is a template class (as opposed to a simple class like the threading policy is). The following policy throws a standard error object if the pointer passed to `Check` is null. The text of the exception thrown contains the name of the pointee type, which makes it necessary to know the pointee type (`Pointee`) in `Check`.

```
template <class T>
class FullCheckingPolicy
{
public:
    static void Check(const T* p)
    {
```

```
              if (p) return;
              throw std::runtime_error(
                  std::string("Null pointer of type ") +
                  typeid(T).name() + " detected");
      }
};
```

Generic (templated) policy classes have considerably more flexibility than simple policy classes. In practice, only the simplest policies are non-templated. Most policy classes either are templates or have template member functions.

If a class needs to enforce a policy class to be template, it can do this by requiring a template template parameter:

```
template
<
    class Pointee,
    template <class U> class CheckingPolicy
>
class SmartPtr
{
    ...
};
```

This setting is particularly useful when SmartPtr needs to use the checking policy with two types instead of only with Pointee. Template template parameters also avoid repetition of the Pointee type, as in the slightly uncomfortable SmartPtr<Widget, FullCheckingPolicy<Widget> >.

Combining Multiple Policy Classes

In isolation, policy classes provide the known advantages of a modular design and the potential of increased reuse. However, the true power of policy classes comes from their ability to combine freely. The client of a template class designed around policies can combine policies either by mixing and matching predefined policies, or by adding new ones. By combining several policy classes in a template class with multiple parameters, one achieves combinatorial behaviors with a linear amount of code. In addition to increasing the amount of reuse, this property of policy classes makes them suitable as building blocks in higher-level libraries.

Let's combine a locking policy and a checking policy in the `SmartPtr` class template:

```
template
<
    class Pointee,
    template <class> class LockingPolicy =
        SingleThreaded,
    template <class> class CheckingPolicy =
        FullCheckingPolicy
>
class SmartPtr
    : public LockingPolicy<SmartPtr>
    , public CheckingPolicy<Pointee>
{
    ...
    SmartPtr& operator=(const SmartPtr& other)
    {
        Lock guard1(*this);
        Lock guard2(other);
        ... perform copy operation ...
    }
    Pointee& operator*()
    {
        return *operator->();
    }
    Pointee* operator->()
    {
        CheckingPolicy<Pointee>::Check(pointee_);
        return pointee_;
    }
private:
    Pointee* pointee_;
};
```

The copying operation in `operator=` can—and should—be defined by yet another policy class. As suggested by the preceeding incomplete implementation, in an implementation built around policy classes, the `SmartPtr` template class becomes the syntactic glue that joins several policy classes. Each of these policy classes implements a specific aspect of the smart pointer behavior.

Suppose we define three policies for locking (threading model) and four policies for checking. We already have 12 possible behaviors of `SmartPtr`. These behaviors are selected by the user of `SmartPtr` with a single type definition. For instance, the following type definition defines a pointer to `Widget` objects that support class-level locking semantics and null checking with the `assert` macro (the `AssertChecked` policy class, not shown, is trivial to implement).

```
typedef SmartPtr
<
    Widget,
    ClassLevelLockable,
    AssertChecked
>
WidgetPtr;
```

Because class templates using policies, such as `SmartPtr`, are likely to have many template parameters, almost any reasonable use thereof should be through a type definition. Type definitions are not only a convenience but also an abstraction. In the space of designing with policies, type definitions are the equivalent of function definitions in traditional implementation. A practical consequence of concentrating policy selections in type definitions is that the resulting type definitions provide unique points of maintenance.

As multiple policies are defined and used with a class, the advantages of a policy-based approach becomes increasingly evident and even spectacular. The `SmartPtr` class template described in *Modern C++ Designs* [Alexandrescu2001] uses four policies: one each for storage, ownership, implicit conversion, and checking. Although each policy is easy to implement and needs little code, the policies combine to provide over 300 different behaviors, easily selectable by feeding appropriate template arguments to `SmartPtr`. It is very hard to deal with such a multitude of behaviors with traditional means.

A policy-based class thoroughly documents the syntactic and semantic requirements for each of its policies, so that users can develop and use their own policies, which add to the prebuilt ones. This makes a policy-based approach very flexible and suitable even in the most particular applications.

Because each policy in `SmartPtr` implements a well-defined decision or constraint in the smart pointer design space, `SmartPtr` users deal with high-level concepts such as error-handling strategies or ownership strategies. In contrast, when developing a smart pointer starting from scratch, a programmer has to deal with all smart pointer design issues, plus a plethora of subtle syntactical issues. A handcrafted, more specialized, smart pointer is likely to be more rigid and less resilient to design changes than an instantiation of a policy-based smart pointer.

Policy-based implementations reach many of the goals stated in the introduction to this chapter. Their use fosters a more natural mapping of design choices and constraints to implementation artifacts. Policies cope with the combinatorial nature of design with linear effort in an economic, organized manner. A policy-based class combines little selectable structural and behavioral entities into larger structures.

Conversions Between Policies

An application can use the same policy-based class template (SmartPtr in our example) instantiated with various design decisions. For instance, most smart pointers are checked on each dereference, whereas some performance-critical code might use unchecked smart pointers.

From a compiler's perspective, two different instantiations of the same class template are completely different types. However, for the program, certain conversions between smart pointers are sensible. For instance, an unchecked smart pointer should be convertible to a smart pointer with dereference checking. On the other hand, converting a multithreaded smart pointer to a single-threaded one is an error that should be signaled at compile time.

Policy libraries can solve conversions in a simple and elegant way by initializing and assigning objects on a per-policy basis. For example, in addition to the copy constructor, SmartPtr gets added a conversion constructor that accepts a SmartPtr instantiation with different template arguments.

```
// Inside SmartPtr's class definition
template <class P, class L,
    template <class U> class C>
SmartPtr(const SmartPtr<P, L, C>& other)
    : pointee_(other.pointee_)
    , LockingPolicy(other)
    , CheckingPolicy<Pointee>(other)
{
}
```

This code initializes SmartPtr policy by policy, passing other to each policy constructor. One of three things might be true:

◇ The source policy is the same as the target policy. This is the case of a simple copy construction.

◇ The source policy is incompatible with the target policy. In this case, the initialization is a compile-time error.

◇ The source policy is convertible to the target policy. (For example, the source policy is derived from the target policy.) In this case, the initialization is legal.

The third case leaves the policy developer the option of deciding which other policies to consider compatible and which to reject. For example, if `FullCheckingPolicy` has a conversion constructor that accepts a `NonCheckingPolicy`, the `SmartPtr` user will be able to construct a checked pointer from an unchecked one.

Caveat

Designing with policy classes is expressive and productive but inherently compile-time bound. Policy classes should be used for those aspects of a design that are fixed at runtime. Overusing policies might lead to excessive recompilation, code bloating, and rigid architectures. Also, using policies is fun, but decomposing classes and choosing the right interface for each policy is hard. The onus of choosing the most orthogonal policy set falls on the component library developer.

A typical effect of choosing a nonorthogonal decomposition is policies that depend on each other. A `SmartPtr`-related example might be the storage policy that deals with memory allocation and deallocation being tied in unfortunate ways with the array policy, which deals with aspects like `operator[]`. Depending on the array policy, the storage policy must issue either a `delete` or a `delete[]` call. Fortunately, library development is usually performed by a minority of experienced designers. From this perspective, policy-based libraries democratize good design practices.

Conclusion

This chapter presents techniques that can help a C++ programmer implement design structures in compact ways. This makes XP practice easier for programmers in the absence of refactoring tools—tools that are notoriously hard to build for C++.

Implementing code based on advanced idioms and design patterns is a tough endeavor when you are starting from first principles. The higher-level design structures do not map to similar code structures naturally, and ultimately the implementation blurs the simplicity and the terseness of the design.

The policy-class C++ idiom fosters defining high-level classes in terms of other classes, each implementing one specific aspect—design choice, constraint—of a design. The high-level class becomes a template class, accepting each of the design constraints as a template parameter. The resulting setting allows library developers to define highly configurable high-level classes without sacrificing performance or flexibility. Well-designed policy-based classes support many different behaviors by combining at compile time a small set of core policies.

References

[Alexandrescu2000] A. Alexandrescu. "Traits: The else-if-then of Types." *C++ Report*. April 2000.

[Alexandrescu2001] A. Alexandrescu. *Modern C++ Design*. Addison-Wesley, 2001.

[Coplien1999] J. O. Coplien. *Multi-Paradigm Design for C++*. Addison-Wesley, 1999.

[Czarnecki+2000] K. Czarnecki, U. Eisenecker. *Generative Programming: Methods, Tools, and Applications*. Addison-Wesley, 2000.

[Gamma+1995] E. Gamma, R. Helm, R. Johnson, J. Vlissides. *Design Patterns: Elements of Reusable Object-Oriented Software*. Addison-Wesley, 1995.

[Schmidt+1998] D. Schmidt, et al. "Double-Checked Locking." In *Pattern Languages of Program Design 3*. Addison-Wesley, 1998.

About the Author

Andrei is a development manager at RealNetworks, Inc. and can be reached at 2601 Elliott Avenue, Suite 1000, Seattle, WA 98199 or by e-mail at aalexand@real.com

Chapter 31

Tracing Development Progress: A Variability Perspective

—Giancarlo Succi, Paolo Predonzani,
and Tullio Vernazza

Software projects need to trace their development progress. This chapter proposes a progress-measurement approach based on the identification and the measurement of variability. The approach is complementary to measurement of functional progress and provides insight into the implications of variability of development effort.

Introduction

Determining the progress of software development at a given time is a fundamental need of project management. Traditionally, this has been done by measuring the implemented functionality versus the total required functionality. We propose a complementary approach based on the explicit identification and measurement of variability. Variability arises from evolution over time and from alternative implementations of a common concept. The fundamentals of the approach are the following:

- ✧ Development is seen as an incremental implementation of variability.
- ✧ Variability is defined in terms of variation points and variants.
- ✧ Planning is done in terms of implemented variants, considering also the sequencing of such implementation.

The rationale for this approach is that variability is a major characteristic of software and a critical factor in software projects. The advantage it offers is better insight into the implications of variability on development and, consequently, better estimation and planning of development effort.

The chapter is structured as follows: The first section presents the background for this proposal; the second section discusses variation points, variants, and how they can be used to trace development progress; then we discuss development planning, with a focus on sequencing the development; and finally we draw conclusions.

Background

The proposed approach derives from the authors' previous work in variability in product lines [Vernazza+2000]. A product line is a group of products that embeds and implements a common strategic idea. Product lines usually deploy products in application domains where technical or market synergies between products can be exploited.

A product line cannot be produced all at once, due to probable limitations on the size of the staff that can be employed. A consequence of this is that the product line development must be spread and planned over a longer period of time. During this time, several variability sources can affect the development. These sources include changes in the client's business process, in the environmental factors (e.g., regulations, laws), or in the technology. Variability can be present at any stage of software development. Choices regarding variability must be traced to their sources throughout the project.

To manage variability effectively, an understanding of it must permeate the whole software development organization. The proposed approach, based on variation points and variants, allows the developers (1) to track the current development progress and (2) to visualize the choices made during the development. It also provides a simple language and a common conceptual framework for addressing such issues.

Tracing Progress Through Variation Points and Variants

Progress can be measured in terms of user stories (or use cases) that have been implemented against the total number of user stories that are expected for the project. Such an approach is widespread and tackles the problem of development progress from a functional perspective.

Our approach tackles the same problem but from a variability perspective. To introduce it, two terms must be understood: variation point and variant. A variation point is a feature that can be implemented in several different ways. A variant is a specific implementation of a variation point. A variation point can be, for instance, the output format of a product; its variants are the possible formats, such as RTF, HTML, or XML. Formally, we represent this situation with a card, as shown in Figure 31.1.

The card represents a piece of our knowledge on the variability in the application domain. It shows what variants are conceivable. With this card, the developer can do the following:

1. Mark those that need to be developed as a consequence of user requirements.
2. Mark those that have actually been developed.

The project's progress is measured as the number of variants of type 1 against the number of variants of type 2.

Generally, the variation points in a real project are many. Multiple cards easily accommodate a high number of variation points, as well as changes in variability. New variants may be discovered or the required variants can change due to changes in the requirements. Also new variation points can be discovered, thus evidencing variability where previously a fixed feature was assumed.

It is important to notice that the proposed approach does not imply that all variants need be implemented. It encourages an early identification of variants but leaves to the developer the choice of which variants to implement and when. The developer, in turn, bases his or her choice

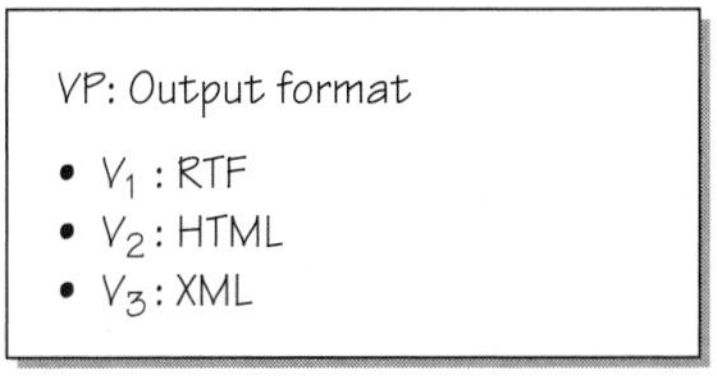

VP: Output format

- V_1 : RTF
- V_2 : HTML
- V_3 : XML

FIGURE 31.1 Variation point with associated variants

on the user's requirements. This is in accordance with Extreme Programming's incremental, iterative approach, which implements only features that are needed at the current development iteration.

Sequencing the Development of Variants

We may think that given a certain number of variants, the effort required to develop them is the same regardless of the order in which they are developed. Actually this is not the case. To understand this we need to study the way variants are implemented more deeply.

Let us suppose that we take an incremental approach and decide, in our example, to develop support for RTF first, then for HTML, and in the end for XML. This order may be dictated by an explicit user requirement or by other environment's constraints (e.g., interface with legacy system). When we start developing the support for RTF we can (1) develop V_1 as a hard-wired solution regardless of the other variation points or (2) develop V_1 as a variation-point-aware solution taking into account that V_2 and V_3 will be needed later. By "VP-aware" we mean that the solution is aware that variability exists and explicitly reserves some code to support it. In the example, the VP-aware solution may consist of a generic module that allows specific modules (for RTF, HTML, XML, etc.) to be plugged in. We can depict the situation as shown in Figure 31.2. At this stage, both solutions offer the same functionality—output in RTF—but clearly the latter requires an extra effort to implement the support for the variation point.

After the implementation of V_1, the implementations of V_2 and V_3 follow. These implementations proceed in different ways according to the chosen initial solution and subsequent development choices. The global picture is shown in Figure 31.3.

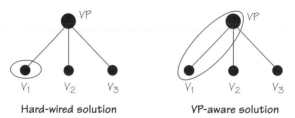

FIGURE 31.2 Hard-wired versus VP-aware solution

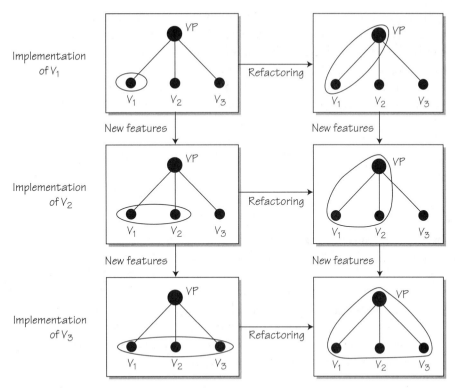

FIGURE 31.3 Evolution of hard-wired and VP-aware solutions

One strategy is to proceed from the initial hard-wired solution through a sequence of other hard-wired solutions (as shown on the left of Figure 31.3). Another strategy is to proceed from the initial VP-aware solution though a sequence of other VP-aware solutions (as shown on the right of Figure 31.3). The latter strategy is supposed to require less effort to implement, because the explicit support for VP allows easier implementation of new variants. The rationale for the difference in effort is that a VP-aware solution only requires implementing and plugging in the new features, whereas the hard-wired solution also requires gluing code due to lack of a common abstraction between the variants.

The two strategies are not totally disjoint. More specifically, it is possible to switch from a hard-wired solution to a VP-aware solution at any point in development. The transition requires, however, a refactoring effort [Fowler+1999].

The need for refactoring arises from the fact that an aggregation of hard-wired solutions becomes, at a certain point, too complex and cumbersome. The decision of the initial solution and, possibly, of refactoring depends on the estimation of the expected benefits and costs.

The proposed approach is not biased toward any of the discussed solutions. Rather, it is meant as a visualization tool to express the knowledge of the variability and to support the planning of variants implementation. The discussed example is a presentation of a simple scenario that demonstrates the possible decisions involved in such planning.

Conclusion

Extreme Programming emphasizes the importance of incremental development. It enforces this by requiring development in small increments, keeping the complexity low and avoiding development of functionality before it is actually needed. In this context, it is important to have an accurate and realistic knowledge of the development progress.

Tracing progress in terms of functionality (user stories and use cases) is widespread. The proposed approach complements this with tracing progress in terms of variability. It allows the following:

- Visualizing the progress in terms of developed variation points and variants
- Accommodating changes in requirements and the incremental discovery on new variation point and variants
- Visualizing the state of refactoring, due to the presence or introduction of variation points
- Planning future development effort

The approach uses terms and visualization techniques that are meaningful and useful for both developers and project managers.

The approach is based on the assumption that variability is a major characteristic of software and a critical factor in software projects. The advantages are the control over variability and the understanding of variability's implications on development effort.

References

[Fowler+1999] M. Fowler, K. Beck, J. Brant, W. Opdyke, D. Roberts. *Refactoring: Improving the Design of Existing Code.* Addison-Wesley, 1999.

[Vernazza+2000] T. Vernazza, S. De Panfilis, P. Predonzani, G. Succi. "Application of Domain Analysis and Engineering to the Domain of Fund Management," In *Proceedings of EASE' 2000,* 2000.

About the Authors

Giancarlo Succi can be reached at the Department of Electrical and Computer Engineering, University of Alberta, Edmonton, Canada; Giancarlo.Succi@ee.ualberta.ca. Paolo Predonzani and Tullio Vernazza can be reached at DIST—Università di Genova, Genova, Italy; {predo, tullio}@dist.unige.it.

Chapter 32

Flexible Manufacturing for Software Agents

—*Luigi Benedicenti, Raman Paranjape, and Kevin Smith*

This chapter describes a lightweight development technique to develop mobile agents. The technique works by delaying the prototypal implementation while maintaining the possibility of executing a design, thus allowing early estimation of software agents. This approach is particularly effective with software agents, because it avoids the pitfalls generally associated with mobile development but is not dependent on the algorithm governing the agent. In particular, our approach avoids implementation glitches, security errors, and all other issues connected with any specific agent execution environment. Moreover, the development model allows a methodical investigation of software agents. The approach described in this chapter is currently employed in evaluating the economic market model for agent interaction. Preliminary results and estimates show a consistent reduction in development time.

Introduction

The development of increasingly better techniques for remote execution of interoperable code and the further refinement of object-oriented concepts have resulted in the deployment of a new type of object: the mobile software agent. Although software agents are still in their infancy, some formal descriptions of them are beginning to appear. In particular, a few standards like CORBA [OMG] and RMI [SUN] have provided the necessary infrastructure for object communication and remote method invocation necessary to set up a distributed environment. On top of them, other protocols and standards like the Mobile Agent System Interoperability Facility [OMG1997] define the interfaces for mobile objects to become active travelers and to be executed on destination machines on which they move.

Due to the novelty of the agent environment and to the intrinsic difficulties in setting up safe and secure distributed networks, mobile agent technology is difficult to realize. Traditional development methods often do not take into account the great flexibility of the agent paradigm, resulting in high single-agent development times, and even higher testing times in a fully distributed environment.

Object-oriented programming can help by means of streamlined classes, but the strength of mobile agents is the diversification of tasks that is difficult to achieve through single-class reuse. Composition of different objects is certainly possible but is arguably the best solution because they do not take into account the fundamental building block of the mobile agent, thus resulting in readability and understandability problems. Multiple inheritance is in general difficult to manage and only a few languages include it in their definition.

We propose a lightweight development method that allows full freedom in developing agents and interaction among them, while maintaining adherence to the current standards. It explicitly encourages agent testing at a specification level so as to promote only promising agents to the implementation stage, thus dramatically reducing the development time.

The method proposed is articulated in three steps: simulation, prototyping, and implementation. Simulation allows initial testing of the agents in a distributed environment to determine an estimate of their performance. Only those agents whose performance is deemed acceptable go to the prototyping step. In this step, agents are implemented and tested in an iterative development process using a self-contained prototype system with default behavior for missing methods. This allows the gradual promotion of the agent from a mere skeleton with limited functionality to a full-fledged component. Because the agent can be run in the prototype system, it can be tested during its development. In the implementation step, the agent is provided with a collating class that implements the prototype interface in a real distributed agent system such as Voyager [Objectspace], Aglets [IBM], or ORBUS [OMG1995].

This development method is particularly useful for the evaluation of open mobile agent systems that interact by means of a model of the economic market [Bredin1999]. In particular, we have emphasized the ease of interaction in the simulator, thus effectively delaying the implementation until the second phase. Thus, each phase is highly targeted and focused, allowing team development with a minimum amount of communication. The complete system is implemented in Java, this being both an advantage to implementation and a limitation to the development scope.

The Development Model

The development model is based on a three-tier architecture (see Figure 32.1). Each tier represents a different level of semantics in the system. At the highest level, developers are concerned with the specifications of the software agent. Then developers design the agent and implement it in a prototypal system, so that the implementation can be built gradually around a predefined skeleton with an implementation-specific "flavor." Finally, developers transfer the fully developed agent into the real agent system of choice, thus being able to refine it

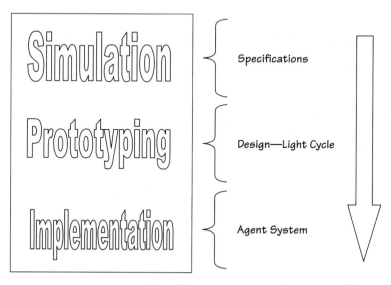

FIGURE 32.1 Three-tier structure

and implement additional security schemes to comply with the details of the specific implementation.

The development of an agent thus follows three phases. However, due to the coherence of the development cycle, it is not necessary to learn three different development methods for each system. Writing agents for the simulation library requires some training on the simulation entry points, but no further training is required to write the agents in the prototype (besides that required to write software agents).

The use of this development model provides the following advantages:

- ✧ *Direct implementation of the specifications:* Programmers can try many different agents in a simulation that does not access the network and runs on a single machine, allowing them to monitor the interaction of hundreds of agents.
- ✧ *Easy agent screening:* The behavior of each single agent can be simulated from its specifications, thus allowing an initial screening of "promising" agents. This makes it possible to concentrate development only on the agents that show positive results in the simulation.
- ✧ *Fast development cycle:* Once the promising agents have been selected, their incremental development is guaranteed by the nature of the prototype.

The following sections describe the model in further detail.

The Simulation

The simulation phase is a crucial point of the development cycle for software agents. The simulator mimics the agent environment and allows multiple agents to work on a single machine without the overload required by a full-fledged agent environment. This supports the possibility of checking the agents' behavior before developing the complete agent. Instead of using a formal mathematical language to define the model, developers use a full programming language to write the agent to be simulated. However, the agent is fully enclosed in an agent template that provides the basic functionality and the means of interaction with the simulator.

The simulation takes care of calculating the lags and overloads for the agent environment. Each agent is then responsible for simulating its behavior. This can be done in two ways. In the preliminary phase, the computation of the interactions does not need to be real. Interactions are computed using a stochastic model, an axiomatic representation of the agent that derives directly from the specifications. For example, the specifications for a commercial agent might say that the agent will have a utility function and it will try to maximize it by interacting with as many other agents as possible. Therefore, this particular agent's operations profile will be more geared toward communications than toward internal computation.

The simulator also requires that an agent have a specific fault function. This function returns a Boolean value. If the value is true, that means that the agent has failed. Because this is just a standard method of a class, it can be customized for specific classes of agents by adding static values, providing full freedom to develop specific failure models. At present the simulator does not include a common package of stochastic objects. This will change in future implementations.

The simulation allows full multitasking. This enables agents to talk to each other in real time and to start as many tasks as possible. Load balancing is not controlled, but there are functions that allow this if necessary. All implementations are in Java. Every agent belongs to the same base class, which is a pure abstract class. This warrants cohesion in the simulation.

The Prototype

Simulated agents still need to be implemented. The implementation of such an agent can be a daunting task. Implementation of an agent depends on the algorithm that the agent uses but is also heavily influenced by the environment in which the agent will run. The prototype system provides two main advantages to the agent development cycle: an incremental development facility and a test facility.

Within the prototype system, the incremental development facility is a collating class for the agent that interfaces the agent to the agent environment. This can be implemented in two ways: either by providing a single interface for the agent that is then translated to the environment, or by providing a class that overloads the classes of the environment and thus acts as an interface. We chose the latter technique, which has the added advantage of allowing the default environment behavior to emerge. The design analysis showed a definite convenience for this.

The incremental development facility provides a number of advantages for developing software agents. First of all, agents can be developed incrementally, since the agent has a default behavior that is defined in the agent base class. This class is different from that of the simulator, because it is really a moniker for the agent environment. However, the moniker augments the functionality with a default implementation that makes it possible to implement agents in subsequent, incremental, steps.

There is no required development cycle because agent development is a single-person task. However, the provision for an iterative development cycle allows complex agents to be developed according to specific functionality, while preserving a generic behavior that warrants thorough testing.

The testing facility allows the developers to test the implementation of an agent in a specific environment. The testing facility is limited because the full agent environment is reproduced in a single machine, but it is still fully functional. This is strictly implementation-dependent and must be programmed for each environment. However, once this infrastructure is in place, it can be used for any number of agents.

Another extremely important advantage is that agent integration has been verified in the preceding step (simulation) and thus the only issues to be considered at this stage are implementation issues.

The actual implementation of the prototype system is still sketchy. We have realized one full prototype that implements only one environment, that is, the Voyager system [Objectspace]. However, the principle is fully expandable to other software systems.

Implementing Prototypal Agents

Given the prototype structure, the implementation of the prototype agent is straightforward. The structure of the implementation is depicted in Figure 32.2. The implementation can theoretically be in any agent system, either proprietary, using for example RMI or some service in JINI/Javaspace [SUN], or standard like JavaBeans, Aglets, Voyager, and Grasshopper.

An important thing to notice is that there still is a class that overloads the agents to ensure a seamless transition from the prototype to the implementation. This class can also be used to further debug the agent or to monitor the final behavior for consistency analysis and pos-

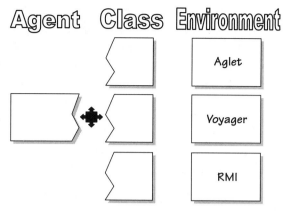

FIGURE 32.2 Agent implementation

sible modification and improvements in the preceding steps. The overloading class can also be removed, thus allowing the implementation to run unconstrained.

Conclusion

This chapter presented a lightweight development technique for software agent development. The architecture is defined through three different levels. The first level consists of a direct translation of the agent's specifications. The execution of the specification is realized through a simulator. The simulator is capable of modeling the network, taking care of delays and failures, and thus makes it possible to inspect an initial set of agents to promote the development of "promising" agents, these being indicated by the results of a predetermined number of simulations.

The second level consists of a prototypal system. Agent development can be undertaken in steps, because the prototype supports agent execution and defaults to a standard behavior in absence of a specialized function upcast in the agent. Agents can be tested in the prototypal system until they are ready to be taken to a full agent environment.

The third level is the complete agent environment. Agents that reach this stage need only the substitution of a class to make them ready for the environment. All levels are tightly integrated by means of a coherent structure that allows seamless development from the specifications to the finished product.

This development technique delays the implementation of the agent, thus allowing the early exploration of many agent behaviors. This provides an initial evaluation of an agent. Although by no means complete, the early evaluation allows the developers to focus development only on those agents satisfying their criteria, while maintaining the possibility to explore innovative agent development.

In the future we wish to refine the system and to use this development platform to explore economic models for agent interaction. In particular, we will expand the number of collating classes to allow the performance assessment of different agent environments.

References

[Bredin+1999] J. Bredin, D. Kotz, D. Rus. "Economic Markets as a Means of Open Mobile-Agent Systems." In *Proceedings of the Workshop "Mobile Agents in the Context of Competition and Cooperation (MAC3)" at Autonomous Agents '99*, May 1999.

[IBM] IBM. On-line at http://www.ibm.com.

[Objectspace] Objectspace. On-line at http://www.objectspace.com.

[OMG] OMG. On-line at http://www.omg.org.

[OMG95] OMG. Common Facilities RFP3, Request for Proposal OMG TC Document 95-11-3. On-line at http://www.omg.org, 1995.

[OMG97] OMG. MASIF Specifications. On-line at http://www.omg.org/cgi-bin/doc?orbos/98-03-09, 1997.

[SUN] SUN Java Language documentation. On-line at http://developer.java.sun.com/developer/infodocs.

Acknowledgments

The authors would like to thank TRLabs for providing the resources to work on this project.

About the Authors

Luig Benedicenti, Raman Paranjape, and Kevin Smith can be reached at the University of Regina, 3737 Wascana Parkway, Regina, SK, Canada S4S 0A2, (306) 585-4701, or by e-mail at {Luigi.Benedicenti, Raman.Paranjape, Kevin.Smith}@uregina.ca.

Chapter 33

How Do Flexible
Processes Relate to
Software Product Lines?

—Jason Yip, Giancarlo Succi, and Eric Liu

Flexible processes and software product lines are two different proposals for improving software development. There is a tendency for software product lines to be associated with building reusable frameworks, which may not fit well with a flexible process. Software product lines are not solely concerned with reusable frameworks and, in fact, many software product line concepts can benefit from a flexible process environment. The two approaches can learn from each other to further improve the effectiveness of a software development effort.

Introduction

Flexible processes and software product lines are two different proposals for improving the productivity and effectiveness of software development.

Flexible processes are value-centric, meaning that the focus is on delivering business value early with evolutionary delivery [Gilb1997] instead of extensive up-front design. Some other defining aspects of flexible processes include reduced artifacts and an emphasis on informal face-to-face communication. Flexible processes promise to improve productivity by reducing overhead.

Software product lines are multiple systems that are developed synergistically in an attempt to exploit scope economies. In other words, software systems are developed in a cooperative way that improves their overall value.Software product lines are a promising approach for the development of software systems because they take advantage of reuse, network economies, and other typical phenomena of the software industry [Succi1999].

There is a tendency for software product lines to be associated mainly with building reusable frameworks [Poulin1997]. Having to develop frameworks based on up-front abstracted analysis is contradictory to flexible process, which would instead focus on evolving systems and avoid a lot of up-front design. A suitable alternative would be to take an evolutionary approach in developing frameworks [Roberts1997]. However, we submit that the entire emphasis on frameworks limits the scope of benefits that software product lines provide.

This chapter attempts to show that software product lines are not solely concerned with generating reusable frameworks and may in some circumstances not be dependent on reuse at all. It explains how other aspects of software product lines can be used to support development in flexible process environment and how flexible processes can support software product lines. Finally, open issues are identified that need to be resolved to effectively combine the benefits of both approaches.

Flexible Processes

Flexible processes share several key features: an acknowledgment that requirements will evolve throughout the entire life of a project, frequent feedback from end users or user representatives, an evolutionary design process, and an emphasis on direct human communication over documentation. Examples of flexible processes include the following:

- *Extreme Programming* [Beck2000]: rapid feedback, assumption of simplicity, incremental change, embracing change, and quality work
- *Crystal Clear methodology* [Cockburn2001]: "deliverables light, communication strong"
- *Evo* [Gilb1997] from which EvoFusion [Cotton1996] and Synchronize and Stabilize [Cusumano+1999] are derived: "The delivery of results to customers and users is planned in approximately 2 percent increments, with the 'most valuable' results earliest, wherever possible."
- *SCRUM* [Beedle+1999]: SCRUM meeting, Sprint, Backlog

Flexible processes take an approach similar to the open source mantra of "release early, release often" [Raymond1999], which leads to an ability to change quickly in response to changing requirements. The use of rapid evolutionary delivery also means that projects may be canceled midstream and still have a product that can be used.

Software Product Lines

As mentioned earlier, there is a general tendency for software product lines to be associated solely with developing reusable frameworks. The Software Engineering Institute uses a definition of software product lines that shows this typical association [Clements1999]: "A software product line is a set of software-intensive systems sharing a common, managed set of features that satisfy the specific needs of a particular market segment or mission." Software product lines thus consist of developing and using a set of common core assets or a framework.

Kent Beck captures the viewpoint of flexible process practitioners on frameworks in this post from the Extreme Programming mailing list [Beck2000b]:

> *Why does everyone think that making money with software is easy when they can barely make money doing something they know how to do? Why do they think they can make generic software when they can barely (or can't) make specific applications?*
>
> *One thing at a time. Make the application. Make it as good as you know how. Refactor like bunnies. Then do another application. Then another. Then you will be in a position to make the framework, but you will be in no better position to make money from the framework. That's a different business. Car companies don't suddenly start selling jewelry.*

Software product lines could be seen as a strategy to be in the "better position to make money from the framework." However, in our view, making money from frameworks is not an exclusive or even key concern of a software product line effort. In contrast with the typical definition, we also consider a set of software products to be a software product line if the products work well together or are otherwise associated through branding, bundling, or other techniques. In other words, software product lines should also be considered from an end-user perspective.

The main justification behind a software product line approach is that the overall value of software products produced cooperatively is greater than producing each product in isolation. The general strategy for this would be to achieve a scope economy by increasing the perceived value of the software as well as sharing costs in marketing, distribution, and development through reuse [Succi1999]. Some key phenomena used to increase perceived value are branding, bundling, and network effects. Branding refers to how users will prefer a product based on past experience with another product having the same brand. Bundling is a way of associating multiple software products by pricing the set to be less than the sum of the cost of each individual product. A product exhibits network effects if there is additional value derived from being able to interact with other users of the product [Liebowitz+1998]. Network effects essentially deal with cross-compatibility and interoperability issues.

Office suites are typical examples of software product lines that take advantage of network effects. The producers always need to ensure that information can be easily exchanged between each of its office applications to maintain the increased overall value of the office suite. Office suites also exploit bundling. A less typical but still valid example of a software product line using network effects would be the standard UNIX tools. Ease of interoperability using the pipes and filters pattern increases the value of all the tools relative to the sum of the value of each tool. A recent example of the importance of branding is shown by the business strategies of Linux distribution firms like Red Hat, which essentially rely entirely on branding because Linux can be obtained for free [Young1999].

Software product lines attempt to increase the value of delivered products by ensuring pricing and features that take advantage of these phenomena. They also attempt to reduce the cost of production, which includes marketing, distribution, and development, through shared costs.

Flexible Processes and Software Product Lines: Mutual Benefits

How Flexible Processes Assist Software Product Lines

One of the key benefits of a flexible process is to deliver and thus expose valuable features early to the customer. This may benefit a product line approach in the sense that earlier exposure will allow quicker establishment of an installed base, with the resulting effect of creating branding and other network effects.

One of the key justifications for using flexible processes is the ability to deal with unpredictable and unstable variation patterns. This type of environment suggests that a software product line approach is not applicable. However, according to Succi [Succi1999], unstable variability in the application domain only means that creating a domain-specific reusable component library is probably not appropriate. The existence of unstable variation patterns thus serves as another reason why a reusable framework should not always be the main emphasis of product line approaches.

How Software Product Lines Assist Flexible Processes

Software product lines may also benefit flexible processes by providing a wider perspective of the kind of requirements that are not always stated. This idea is presented in the following fictional examples.

PRODUCT MANAGER:	You should be able to save the image to a file.
DEVELOPER:	What image format?
PRODUCT MANAGER:	Just a simple text format that can be interpreted by MatLab.
DEVELOPER:	Okay . . . Hold on, do all the user groups use MatLab?
PRODUCT MANAGER:	Mostly . . . but that reminds me, a lot of the users generate these images for publications and apparently most publications don't accept MatLab images. I'll have to check on this. I know we'll need the MatLab format for sure, though.
CUSTOMER:	We only want to be able to get metrics for Eiffel.
DEVELOPER:	Okay. Did you also want other languages?
CUSTOMER:	Not right now but probably later.
DEVELOPER:	We actually have some existing metrics tools for C++ and Java. They both use a common file format and similar user interface. Do you want this Eiffel tool to use the same format and UI?
CUSTOMER:	Sure, that's fine.

These examples emphasize that an awareness of formats can ensure compatibility with services or other products that the current product will interact with. This can obviously be used to push a firm's own products, but even this is valid because it is usually easier to maintain compatibility between products that are developed by the same team. However, this doesn't mean that a customer cannot choose other formats or complementary products. In other words, network effects are not enough to satisfy the customer's needs.

In the case of a product manager who is also the requirements donor, an alternate way of applying software product lines to a flexible process environment would be to isolate any product line considerations as a business concern. This would place software product lines in the scope of product management and marketing and not product development. However, given that most flexible processes emphasize strong interaction with the end users and customers, an awareness of the importance of network effects would still be useful when talking to the customer.

Problems

There is a definite cost to introducing a software product line approach. This is a concern because the additional overhead may add complexity to a flexible process and thus reduce flexibility. There is also the question of whether this will interfere with the delivery of single products.

The simplest response to this problem would be to say that any overhead added would not be added to the development team and would therefore have little impact on product delivery times. Realistically, however, it is likely that product line issues would be brought up during the developmental evolution of the system and wouldn't be isolated from the developers.

A possible solution may be to limit the amount of product line phenomena that are considered. For example, some key candidates from the Sherlock methodology [Predonzani+2000] would be the concepts of user flows and compatibilities.

User flows deal with how users migrate to the current product, whether as new users, from competitors, or from complementary products. This analysis could be used to target the most valuable customer group first, just as feature prioritization targets the most valuable features first. Compatibilities deals with interface management, both with other programs and with people. This will affect discussions on things such as data formats and user interfaces.

There are other parts of the Sherlock methodology, but addressing only user flows and compatibilities would be significant without having to be concerned with larger-scale concepts that tie into framework development.

Conclusion

Software product line approaches are not exclusively concerned with constructing reusable frameworks, and, in fact, reuse should not be considered a requirement for a software product line. A more significant product line concern is whether member products work well together and are otherwise associated to improve the perceived value of all products within the product line. The concepts of branding, modularity, network externalities, minimal marginal costs, and shared organizational costs are still useful when applied to a flexible process environment.

Flexible processes assist software product lines by delivering a usable product earlier, thus allowing faster creation of network effects. Software product lines assist flexible processes by improving the value of the products delivered and providing a wider perspective of customer requirements.

References

[Beck2000a] K. Beck. *Extreme Programming Explained.* Addison-Wesley, 2000.

[Beck2000b] K. Beck. *Re: Scaling/Splitting Teams,* Extreme Programming Mailing List. On-line at http://www.egroups.com/message/extremeprogramming/2110. 2000.

[Beedle+1999] M. Beedle, M. Devos, S. Yonat, K. Schwaber, J. Sutherland. "SCRUM: An Extension Pattern Language for Hyperproductive Software Developmen." In *Pattern Languages of Program Design 4,* Addison-Wesley, 1999. On-line at http://www.jeffsutherland.org/scrum/scrum_plop.pdf.

[Clements+1999] P. Clements, L. Northrop. *A Framework for Software Product Line Practice—Version 2.0.* Carnegie Mellon University, 1999. On-line at http://www.sei.cmu.edu/plp/framework.html.

[Cockburn2001] A. Cockburn, *Crystal "Clear": A Human-Powered Software Development Methodology for Small Teams.* On-line draft at http://members.aol.com/humansandt/crystal/clear. 2001.

[Cotton1996] T. Cotton. "Evolutionary Fusion: A Customer-Oriented Incremental Life Cycle for Fusion." *Hewlett-Packard Journal*, August 1996.

[Cusumano+1999] M. Cusumano, D. Yoffie. "Software Development on Internet Time." *IEEE Computer.* Volume 32, Number 10, 1999.

[Gilb1997] T. Gilb. *Evo: The Evolutionary Project Manager's Handbook,* On-line at http://ourworld.compuserve.com/homepages/ KaiGilb/EvobookRTF.ZIP. 1997.

[Liebowitz+1998] S. Liebowitz, S. Margolis. "Network Externalities (Effects)." *The New Palgrave's Dictionary of Economics and the Law.* MacMillan, 1998.

[Poulin1997] J. Poulin. "Software Architectures, Product Lines, and DSSAs: Choosing the Appropriate Level of Abstraction." In *Proceedings of the Eighth International Workshop on Software Reuse (WISR'97).* On-line at http://www.owego.com/~poulinj/ Papers/WISR97/poulinj.html. 1997.

[Predonzani+2000] P. Predonzani, G. Succi, T. Vernazza. *Strategic Software Production with Domain-Oriented Reuse.* Artech House, 2000.

[Raymond1999] E. Raymond. *The Cathedral and the Bazaar.* On-line at http://www.tuxedo.org/~esr/writings/cathedral-bazaar/. 1999.

[Roberts+1997] D. Roberts, R. Johnson. "Evolving Frameworks: A Pattern Language for Developing Object-Oriented Frameworks." In *Pattern Languages of Program Design 3.* R. Martin, ed., Addison-Wesley, 1997.

[Succi1999] G. Succi. "Software Product Lines—A Succulent Minestrone with Many Flavours." In *Proceedings of the 1999 International Conference on Software Engineering and Knowledge Engineering.* 1999.

[Young1999] R. Young. "Giving It Away: How Red Hat Software Stumbled Across a New Economic Model and Helped Improve an Industry." In *Open Sources: Voices from the Open Source Revolution*. O'Reilly & Associates, 1999. Available at http://www.oreilly.com/catalog/opensources/book/young.html.

About the Authors

Jason Yip and Eric Liu can be reached at ThoughtWorks, Inc. or by e-mail at {eliu, jcyip}@thoughtworks.com. Giancarlo Succi can be reached at the Department of Electrical and Computer Engineering, University of Alberta, Edmonton, AB, Canada, or by e-mail at Giancarlo.Succi@ee.ualberta.ca.

Index